Beginning SOLID Principles and Design Patterns for ASP.NET Developers

Bipin Joshi

Apress®

Beginning SOLID Principles and Design Patterns for ASP.NET Developers

Bipin Joshi
301 Pitruchhaya
Thane, India

ISBN-13 (pbk): 978-1-4842-1847-1   ISBN-13 (electronic): 978-1-4842-1848-8
DOI 10.1007/978-1-4842-1848-8

Library of Congress Control Number: 2016937316

Managing Director: Welmoed Spahr
Lead Editor: James DeWolf
Development Editor: Douglas Pundick
Technical Reviewer: Alex Thissen
Editorial Board: Steve Anglin, Pramila Balen, Louise Corrigan, James DeWolf, Jonathan Gennick,
    Robert Hutchinson, Celestin Suresh John, Michelle Lowman, James Markham, Susan McDermott,
    Matthew Moodie, Jeffrey Pepper, Douglas Pundick, Ben Renow-Clarke, Gwenan Spearing
Coordinating Editor: Melissa Maldonado
Copy Editor: April Rondeau
Compositor: SPi Global
Indexer: SPi Global
Artist: SPi Global

Distributed to the book trade worldwide by Springer Science+Business Media New York, 233 Spring Street, 6th Floor, New York, NY 10013. Phone 1-800-SPRINGER, fax (201) 348-4505, e-mail orders-ny@springer-sbm.com, or visit www.springer.com. Apress Media, LLC is a California LLC and the sole member (owner) is Springer Science + Business Media Finance Inc (SSBM Finance Inc). SSBM Finance Inc is a Delaware corporation.

For information on translations, please e-mail rights@apress.com, or visit www.apress.com.

Apress and friends of ED books may be purchased in bulk for academic, corporate, or promotional use. eBook versions and licenses are also available for most titles. For more information, reference our Special Bulk Sales–eBook Licensing web page at www.apress.com/bulk-sales.

Any source code or other supplementary material referenced by the author in this text is available to readers at www.apress.com. For detailed information about how to locate your book's source code, go to www.apress.com/source-code/.

Printed on acid-free paper

At the holy feet of Lord Shiva.

—Bipin Joshi

Contents at a Glance

About the Author xv

About the Technical Reviewer xvii

Introduction xix

■Chapter 1: Overview of SOLID Principles and Design Patterns 1

■Chapter 2: SOLID Principles.. 45

■Chapter 3: Creational Patterns: Singleton, Factory Method, and Prototype 87

■Chapter 4: Creational Patterns: Abstract Factory and Builder 111

■Chapter 5: Structural Patterns: Adapter, Bridge, Composite, and Decorator 135

■Chapter 6: Structural Patterns: Façade, Flyweight, and Proxy 167

■Chapter 7: Behavioral Patterns: Chain of Responsibility, Command,
Interpreter, and Iterator... 201

■Chapter 8: Behavioral Patterns: Mediator, Memento, and Observer.................. 239

■Chapter 9: Behavioral Patterns: State, Strategy, Template Method,
and Visitor 275

■Chapter 10: Patterns of Enterprise Application Architecture: Repository,
Unit of Work, Lazy Load, and Service Layer.. 309

■Chapter 11: JavaScript Code-Organization Techniques and Patterns 355

■Bibliography 391

Index... 393

Contents

About the Author xv

About the Technical Reviewer xvii

Introduction xix

■Chapter 1: Overview of SOLID Principles and Design Patterns 1

Overview of Object-Oriented Programming 1

    Classes and Objects 2

    Abstraction 2

    Encapsulation 3

    Inheritance.. 6

    Abstract Classes and Interfaces 7

    Polymorphism... 9

Overview of SOLID Principles 14

    Single Responsibility Principle (SRP).. 15

    Open/Closed Principle (OCP)... 15

    Liskov Substitution Principle (LSP).. 15

    Interface Segregation Principle (ISP)... 16

    Dependency Inversion Principle (DIP).. 16

Design Patterns 16

    Gang of Four Design Patterns.. 17

    Categorization of GoF Patterns.. 17

Martin Fowler's Patterns of Enterprise Application Architecture................................ 19

    Categorization of P of EAA.. 20

Design Patterns in JavaScript 20

Applying Design Principles and Patterns 21

You Are Already Using Patterns! A Few Examples 22

Creating an ASP.NET 5 Application Using MVC 6 and Entity Framework 7 23

    Creating a Web Application Using Visual Studio 24

    Configuring Project Dependencies 28

    Configuring Application Settings 29

    Configuring Application Startup 30

    Creating DbContext and Model 33

    Creating the HomeController 34

    Creating the Index and AddContact Views 36

    Creating the ContactDb Database 40

Going Forward: From ASP.NET 5 to ASP.NET Core 1.0 43

Summary 44

■Chapter 2: SOLID Principles 45

Single Responsibility Principle (SRP) 45

Open/Closed Principle (OCP) 54

Liskov Substitution Principle (LSP) 61

Interface Segregation Principle (ISP) 74

Dependency Inversion Principle (DIP) 80

Summary 85

■Chapter 3: Creational Patterns: Singleton, Factory Method, and Prototype 87

Overview of Creational Design Patterns 87

Singleton 88

    Design and Explanation 89

    Example 89

Factory Method 94

    Design and Explanation 94

    Example 95

Prototype 103

   Design and Explanation 103

   Example 104

Summary 109

■Chapter 4: Creational Patterns: Abstract Factory and Builder 111

Abstract Factory 111

   Design and Explanation 111

   Example 112

Storing Factory Settings 122

   Storing Factory Name in the Configuration File 123

   Storing Factory Type Name in the Configuration File 124

Builder 125

   Design and Explanation 125

   Example 126

Summary 134

■Chapter 5: Structural Patterns: Adapter, Bridge, Composite, and Decorator 135

An Overview of Structural Patterns 135

Adapter 136

   Design and Explanation 136

   Example 137

   Object Adapter vs. Class Adapter 143

Bridge 144

   Design and Explanation 145

   Example 146

Composite 152

   Design and Explanation 153

   Example 153

Decorator 159

Design and Explanation 160

Example 161

Summary 166

■Chapter 6: Structural Patterns: Façade, Flyweight, and Proxy 167

Façade 167

Design and Explanation 168

Example 168

Flyweight 177

Design and Explanation 178

Example 179

Proxy 185

Design and Explanation 186

Example 186

Summary 200

■Chapter 7: Behavioral Patterns: Chain of Responsibility, Command, Interpreter, and Iterator 201

Behavioral Patterns 201

Chain of Responsibility 202

Design and Explanation 202

Example 203

Command 212

Design and Explanation 212

Example 213

Interpreter 221

Design and Explanation 221

Example 222

Iterator 229

　Design and Explanation 230

　Example 230

Summary 237

■Chapter 8: Behavioral Patterns: Mediator, Memento, and Observer 239

Mediator 239

　Design and Explanation 240

　Example 241

Memento 253

　Design and Explanation 254

　Example 254

Observer 263

　Design and Explanation 264

　Example 264

Summary 273

■Chapter 9: Behavioral Patterns: State, Strategy, Template Method,
and Visitor 275

State 275

　Design and Explanation 276

　Example 276

Strategy 284

　Design and Explanation 285

　Example 286

Template Method 292

　Design and Explanation 292

　Example 293

Visitor 300

　Design and Explanation 301

　Example 302

Summary 308

■Chapter 10: Patterns of Enterprise Application Architecture: Repository, Unit of Work, Lazy Load, and Service Layer... 309

Overview of P of EAA.. 309

Repository 312

    Design and Explanation..313

    Example..313

Unit of Work.. 322

    Design and Explanation..322

    Example..323

Lazy Load 330

    Design and Explanation..331

    Example..332

Service Layer... 340

    Design and Explanation..340

    Example..341

Injecting Repositories Through Dependency Injection 351

Summary... 353

■Chapter 11: JavaScript Code-Organization Techniques and Patterns 355

Organizing JavaScript Code Using Objects 355

    Object Literals..356

    Function Objects...357

    Immediately Invoked Function Expressions (IIFE) 360

Namespace Pattern... 362

Module Pattern.. 367

Revealing Module Pattern 374

Sandbox Pattern.. 375

Using Design Patterns in JavaScript 379

   Singleton Pattern 379

Façade Pattern 381

Observer Pattern 383

MVC, MVVM, and MVW Patterns 386

Summary 389

■Bibliography 391

Index 393

About the Author

Bipin Joshi is a software consultant, a trainer, an author, and a yogi who writes about seemingly unrelated topics: software development and yoga! He conducts professional training programs to help developers learn ASP.NET and web technologies better and faster. Currently, his focus is ASP.NET, C#, Entity Framework, JavaScript, jQuery, AngularJS, TypeScript, and design and architectural patterns. More details about his training programs are available at `http://www.binaryintellect.com`.

Bipin has been programming since 1995 and has worked with the .NET framework since its inception. He has authored or co-authored more than ten books and numerous articles on .NET technologies. He regularly writes about ASP.NET and other cutting-edge web technologies on his website: `http://www.binaryintellect.net`. Bipin was a Microsoft Most Valuable Professional (MVP) and a Microsoft Certified Trainer (MCT) during 2002–2008.

Having embraced the yoga way of life, he enjoys the intoxicating presence of God and writes about yoga on his website: `http://www.ajapayoga.in`. Bipin has also penned a few books on yoga. He can be reached through his websites.

About the Technical Reviewer

Alex Thissen has been involved in application development since the late 1990s and has worked as a lead developer and architect at both small companies and large enterprises. He has spent a majority of his time teaching other developers the details of the Microsoft development platform and frameworks, and he coaches architects to design and build modern distributed applications. He has received the Microsoft Most Valuable Professional award for Visual Studio and Development Technologies nine times.

Introduction

Software developers want their applications to be flexible, maintainable, and extensible. Writing a codebase that fulfills these expectations is not always an easy task—it requires skills as well as experience. That's where SOLID principles and design patterns can be put to use. If you are an ASP.NET developer looking to learn and apply these principles and patterns to your work, you have picked the right book!

A modern web application is not merely a collection of HTML pages. It involves so many things— HTML, CSS, server-side processing, data access, business logic, client-side and server-side validations, components, Ajax, and more. Obviously, you end up writing good amount of server-side and client-side code. If this code is written adhering to SOLID principles and patterns, future modifications and extensions becomes less painful. To that end, this book discusses the following four important topics:

- SOLID principles of object-oriented design

- Gang of Four (GoF) design patterns

- A few important Patterns of Enterprise Application Architecture (P of EAA)

- Some common JavaScript code-organization techniques and patterns

SOLID is an acronym introduced by Michael Feathers to describe five basic principles of good object-oriented design explained by Robert C. Martin: Single Responsibility, Open/Closed, Liskov Substitution, Interface Segregation, and Dependency Inversion.

Design Patterns are time-proven solutions to commonly occurring software design problems. The most well-known catalog of design patterns comes from Erich Gamma, Richard Helm, Ralph Johnson, and John Vlissides, and the patterns therein are called the Gang of Four (GoF) patterns. This book explains in detail how to apply Creational, Structural, and Behavioral GoF design patterns. Also discussed are a few important Patterns of Enterprise Application Architecture (P of EAA) cataloged by Martin Fowler. Modern web applications use JavaScript to integrate powerful and rich functionality. Hence, a few popular JavaScript code-organization techniques and patterns are also discussed.

What makes this book special is the fact that all the examples presented are developed keeping ASP.NET developers in mind. All the principles and patterns discussed in the book are put to use in ASP.NET web application projects rather than in console or desktop applications. Moreover, an attempt has been made to base these examples on real-world scenarios for better understanding.

Who Is This Book For?

This book is for ASP.NET developers familiar with ASP.NET 5 who want to learn and apply SOLID principles of object-oriented design and design patterns in their existing or new web applications. This book doesn't teach you ASP.NET features as such. I make the following assumptions about you:

- You are an ASP.NET developer and have working experience in web application development.

- You are familiar with ASP.NET 5, MVC 6, and Entity Framework 7.

- You use C# as a server-side programming language while building the web applications.

- You know how to write JavaScript code.

Many examples illustrated throughout this book use Microsoft SQL Server. Thus, familiarity with SQL Server is required. Finally, the book uses Visual Studio 2015 as the development tool. You should know how to work with Visual Studio IDE to perform tasks such as creating projects, writing code, and debugging.

Software Required

In order to work through the examples discussed in this book, you need the following software:

- Visual Studio 2015

- ASP.NET 5 - RC1

- Entity Framework 7 - RC1

- SQL Server 2012 or later with Northwind database

- Any leading web browser

I have used Visual Studio 2015 Professional edition to create all the example projects. However, you can use any edition of Visual Studio 2015. All the data-driven examples were developed using Microsoft SQL Server 2012. I use the Northwind sample database in many examples, and I suggest that you install it at your end. You can download the Northwind database and its script from Microsoft's website. In some examples you will need jQuery and AngularJS. You should consider downloading these from their official websites.

■ **Note**   Although the concepts discussed in this book can be implemented in any flavor of ASP.NET, this book uses cutting-edge technologies—ASP.NET 5 RC1 and EF 7 RC1—for building all the examples. Using these *not yet complete* versions gives you a chance to see what's coming up next. It is exciting and fun to work with such cutting-edge technologies. However, it has its own price—changes are inevitable! As I finish this book, Microsoft has made an announcement that ASP.NET 5 will now be called ASP.NET Core 1.0 and Entity Framework 7 will be named Entity Framework Core 1.0. I have included more information about these changes in Chapter 1. So, make sure to read that information before you begin developing the examples.

Structure of This Book

This book is organized in 11 chapters, as follows:

- Chapter 1 will introduce you to the SOLID principles, GoF design patterns, P of EAA, and JavaScript patterns. It will also walk you through building a simple web application using ASP.NET 5.

- Chapter 2 will give you a detailed understanding of SOLID principles. All five principles of object-oriented design—Single Responsibility, Open/Closed, Liskov Substitution, Interface Segregation, and Dependency Inversion—will be discussed with examples.

- Chapter 3 will dissect three creational design patterns, namely Singleton, Factory Method, and Prototype. Each pattern will be discussed with UML diagrams and a proof of concept example.

- Chapter 4 will cover the remainder of the creational design patterns—Abstract Factory and Builder.

- Chapter 5 will begin discussing the structural design patterns. Four structural patterns—Adapter, Bridge, Composite, and Decorator—will be elaborated with proof of concept examples of each.

- Chapter 6 will cover the remainder of the structural patterns—Façade, Flyweight, and Proxy.

- Chapter 7 will teach the first installment of behavioral design patterns—Chain of Responsibility, Command, Interpreter, and Iterator. As before, each pattern will be discussed with UML diagrams and a proof of concept example.

- Chapter 8 will cover three more behavioral patterns—Mediator, Memento, and Observer.

- Chapter 9 will discuss the remainder of the behavioral patterns: State, Strategy, Template Method, and Visitor.

- Chapter 10 will give you an overview of Patterns of Enterprise Application Architecture and will also cover a few selected patterns that are commonly used in ASP.NET applications. These patterns include Repository, Unit of Work, Lazy Load, and Service Layer.

- Chapter 11 will conclude the book by discussing JavaScript code-organization techniques and patterns. Topics discussed will include JavaScript object literals, function objects, namespaces, Module pattern, Revealing Module pattern, and Sandbox pattern. It will also show, with a few examples, how the GoF patterns can be implemented in JavaScript.

Downloading the Source Code

The complete source code for the book is available for download at the book's companion website. Visit www.apress.com and go to this book's information page. You can then download the source code from the Source Code/Downloads section.

Contacting the Author

You can reach me via my website: http://www.binaryintellect.net. You can also follow me on Facebook, Twitter, and Google+ (visit my website for the links).

CHAPTER 1

■ ■ ■

Overview of SOLID Principles and Design Patterns

Modern programming languages such as C# are object oriented in nature. The C# language allows you to think and program in terms of classes and objects. However, knowing C# language keywords and features is just one part of the story. Equally important is knowing how these features can be put to use in the best possible way so as to result in a better quality code base and ultimately help in building software that is robust, flexible, maintainable, and extensible.

In order to build a better quality code base, developers resort to collective wisdom. This collective wisdom has withstood the test of time and offers proven approaches to solving a software problem instead of your attempting to invent a new solution. This chapter will introduce you to this collective wisdom. Specifically, it will cover the following:

- fundamental concepts of object-oriented programming
- what SOLID principles are and how they help design better object-oriented systems
- Gang of Four (GoF) design patterns and their categorization
- what Patterns of Enterprise Application Architecture (P of EAA) are and their categorization
- how patterns can also be useful in the JavaScript world

This chapter will only touch on the basics of the above topics. The rest of the book will elaborate them in detail. In this chapter I intend to give you a clear picture of the scope of this book so that you have an idea of what's coming up in further chapters.

Overview of Object-Oriented Programming

C# is an object-oriented programming language. As an ASP.NET developer who knows C#, you are probably aware of its features and capabilities. Since this book is about object-oriented design principles and patterns, let's quickly brush up on our knowledge of the fundamental building blocks of object-oriented programming. This section will discuss features of object-oriented programming such as classes, objects,

Electronic supplementary material The online version of this chapter (doi:10.1007/978-1-4842-1848-8_1) contains supplementary material, which is available to authorized users.

© Bipin Joshi 2016
B. Joshi, *Beginning SOLID Principles and Design Patterns for ASP.NET Developers*,
DOI 10.1007/978-1-4842-1848-8_1

abstraction, encapsulation, inheritance, interfaces, and polymorphism. If you are already familiar with these concepts, feel free to skip or skim through this section. If you are unsure about your understanding of these concepts, I suggest that you read this section and make sure that you are comfortable with the material. These features are heavily used in any object-oriented system, and the rest of this book will assume that you understand them. Let's begin!

Classes and Objects

Classes and objects are used everywhere in C# and .NET framework. When you create a console application, its Main() method is housed in a class. When you create an ASP.NET Web Forms application, each web form is nothing but a class. When you create an ASP.NET MVC application, a controller is also a class.

What is a class? Simply put, a class is a blueprint or template for creating a type. A class typically groups data and behavior of a type. For example, fruits, flowers, vehicles, animals, and birds all are classes. Some real-world examples of classes are customers, orders, employees, and so on.

An object is a particular instance of class. For example, orange is an instance of fruit. Or an employee with ID 1234 is an instance of the Employee class. In C# you create classes and objects as shown here:

```
public class Employee
{
    ...
}

Employee obj = new Employee();
```

You use the class keyword to define a class. Although not shown in the previous example, a class usually contains properties, methods, and events. Once created, a class can be instantiated using the new keyword. So, in the earlier code snippet, Employee is a class and obj is an instance of the Employee class.

Abstraction

You just learned what classes and objects are. But who identifies classes, and how? Of course, as a developer you are responsible for identifying and crafting classes. When you read some business requirement that you are supposed to cater to with your application, you need to study the scenario and identify the software requirements. A scenario may involve many pieces of information as well as many ways, from simple to complex, in which that information is used by the underlying business. Based on your understanding of the scenario, you need to decide which pieces of information are essential for your application and which pieces are unnecessary. The pieces that are essential will then be put into one or more classes. This process of filtering the available information and arriving at a subset that is essential for your application is called *abstraction*.

Suppose you are building a business-contact management application. As a part of the development you identified that you will need a Person class in your application. Now, there can be plethora of details available about a person—first name, last name, e-mail, phone number, company name, address, photo, birth date, number and details of his immediate family members as well as relatives, year in which he or she completed secondary school, his or her favorite color, and many more. Given that your application is supposed to deal with business contacts, do you need to capture all the details just mentioned? Obviously not. Your application will need details such as first name, last name, e-mail, phone number, company name, address, photo, and birth date. But other personal details such as number and details of his immediate family members as well as relatives, year in which he or she completed secondary school, and his or her favorite color are irrelevant to your application. Thus, while creating the Person class, you will skip these unwanted pieces of information. The process of abstraction is shown in Figure 1-1.

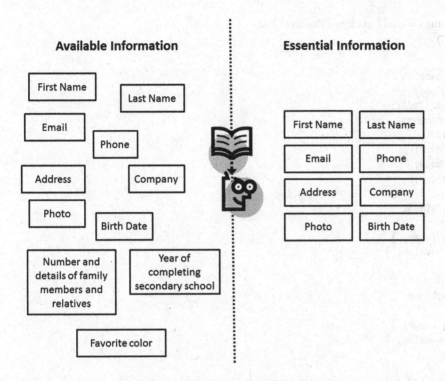

Figure 1-1. *Process of abstraction in object-oriented programming*

To summarize what we just discussed, abstraction is a process of filtering out unwanted pieces of information and picking what is essential for your application based on given requirements or context.

Encapsulation

The process of abstraction helps you clarify which pieces of information are needed by your application. You usually bundle these pieces into one or more classes. Continuing the example we discussed in the preceding section, you will put the essential information about a business contact into a class named Contact. Although you have identified and bundled the required pieces into a class, should other parts of the application be allowed to see and manipulate them directly? Or should there be some prescribed way in which the data can be dealt with? These thoughts comprise a process called *encapsulation*.

Suppose you created a Contact class that bundles the first name, last name, e-mail, phone number, address, company name, photo, and birth date of a person. If you simply bundle these details together without any prescribed way of reading and writing them, the other parts of the application that use the Contact class are free to access them in any way they want. For example, some part of the application may assign a value of 1234 to the email address. Obviously, this is unacceptable. So, you should devise some mechanism such that only a valid e-mail address can be assigned to a contact. Similarly, you may want to reveal the photo of a contact only to some special users of your application (for example, administrators or paid users). Again, you need some prescribed way to handle this type of access. That's where encapsulation comes into the picture. Encapsulation is a process by which you both bundle data and operations (or functions) that work on that data into a class and also establish a prescribed way to read, write, and process the data.

In terms of C#, you encapsulate data using classes, properties, and methods. Listing 1-1 shows what your Contact class that encapsulates the required data might look like.

Listing 1-1. Encapsulating Contact Data into a Contact Class

```
public class Contact
{
    private string fname;
    private string lname;
    private string emailaddr;
    private string phoneno;
    private string addr;
    private string cname;
    private byte[] photo;
    private DateTime dob;

    public string FirstName
    {
        get { return fname; }
        set { fname = value; }
    }

    public string LastName
    {
        get { return lname; }
        set { lname = value; }
    }

    public string EmailAddress
    {
        get { return emailaddr; }
        set
        {
            if(emailaddr.Contains("@") && emailaddr.Contains("."))
            {
                emailaddr = value;
            }
            else
            {
                throw new Exception("Invalid Email address!");
            }
        }
    }

    public string PhoneNo
    {
        get { return phoneno; }
        set { phoneno = value; }
    }
```

```csharp
public string Address
{
    get { return addr; }
    set { addr = value; }
}

public string CompanyName
{
    get { return cname; }
    set { cname = value; }
}

public byte[] Photo
{
    get { return photo; }
    set { photo = value; }
}

public DateTime BirthDate
{
    get { return dob; }
    set
    {
        if ((DateTime.Today.Year - value.Year) > 18)
        {
            dob = value;
        }
        else
        {
            throw new Exception("Invalid birth date. Age must be greater than 18.");
        }
    }
}
```

The Contact class stores contact information in private variables. These variables are hidden from the external world. This way data cannot be tampered with directly from code external to the Contact class. Access to these private variables is granted through public properties. Notice how the EmailAddress and BirthDate properties perform validations on the values being assigned to the respective properties. They reject invalid values by throwing exceptions. Of course, you can write much more sophisticated logic to validate these values, but the point is that you have not only bundled data in a class but also established a prescribed way to access the data. That's what encapsulation is about. Figure 1-2 summarizes our discussion.

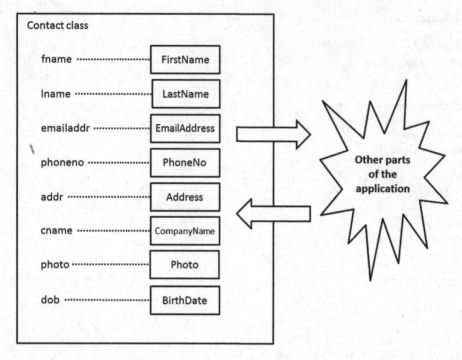

Figure 1-2. *Encapsulating data using class and its properties*

As you can see from Figure 1-2, you have put a "fence" of properties over your data, thus hiding the data from the external world and restricting how the data can be accessed. You can also use methods to encapsulate data in a similar fashion, depending on the requirements.

Inheritance

A real-world application involves many classes. At times these classes share something in common. For example, imagine that our contact manager application needs to take into account different types of contacts, such as business contacts (companies you interact with), professional contacts (individuals such as doctors and tax consultants that provide professional services), personal contacts (school friends, neighbors, people from your social network, and so on. Obviously you need a class to represent each type of contact, say BusinessContact, ProfessionalContact, and PersonalContact. As you might have anticipated, these classes share many common attributes. For example, all of them will have first name, last name, address, e-mail, and phone number. Can you do something to avoid this duplication? That's where inheritance comes into the picture. Inheritance allows you to isolate common pieces of data and operations into a class and then create specialized classes based on that class. The class containing common data and operations is called the *base class*, whereas the specialized classes are called *derived classes*. The derived class and the base class are related to each other through an "is-a" relationship. This means a derived class (say, BusinessContact) *is a* kind of base class (say, Contact). The derived classes can add data and operations that are specific to themselves. They can also redefine the operations defined by the base class. To carry the same example further, you would create a Contact base class and BusinessContact, ProfessionalContact, and PersonalContact derived classes that inherit from the Contact class. Inheritance not only promotes code reuse but also helps you organize code into hierarchical structures. Listing 1-2 shows what these classes look like.

Listing 1-2. Inheriting from a Contact Base Class

```
public class Contact
{
    ...
}

public class BusinessContact:Contact
{
    ...
}

public class ProfessionalContact : Contact
{
    ...
}

public class PersonalContact : Contact
{
    ...
}
```

Abstract Classes and Interfaces

In the preceding section you used inheritance as a means to reusing code. There are times when classes can have a parent-child relationship, but there can't be any possibility of code reuse. Consider that you are building a taxation system that is supposed to calculate taxes based on certain logic. In addition, let's suppose that your application needs to support tax calculation in three countries—say the USA, the UK, and India. Now the taxation rules and logic in a country are usually quite specific to that country, and you may not be able to reuse any of this code. However, the operation—calculating tax—is needed in all of them. In such cases, although you can't reuse any code, you can reuse "contract." In such cases, developers resort to abstract classes or interfaces.

An *abstract class* is a class that cannot be instantiated. It usually contains property and method signatures but no implementation. The derived classes are required to write the implementation of these members by overriding them. So, with an abstract class in place, the preceding example can be represented as shown in Listing 1-3.

Listing 1-3. Using an Abstract Class

```
public abstract class CountryTaxCalculator
{
    public abstract decimal CalculateTaxAmount();
}

public class TaxCalculatorForUS : CountryTaxCalculator
{
    public override decimal CalculateTaxAmount()
    {
        ...
    }
}
```

```
public class TaxCalculatorForUK : CountryTaxCalculator
{
    public override decimal CalculateTaxAmount()
    {
        ...
    }
}

public class TaxCalculatorForIN : CountryTaxCalculator
{
    public override decimal CalculateTaxAmount()
    {
        ...
    }
}
```

C# also allows you to create interfaces that serve a similar purpose. Unlike abstract classes, which can contain code of their own, interfaces simply provide a set of property and method signatures with no implementation code at all. Classes then implement one or more interfaces depending on the requirements. The same example we just discussed can be presented using interfaces, as shown in Listing 1-4.

Listing 1-4. Defining and Implementing an Interface

```
public interface ICountryTaxCalculator
{
    decimal CalculateTaxAmount();
}

public class TaxCalculatorForUS : ICountryTaxCalculator
{
    public decimal CalculateTaxAmount()
    {
        ...
    }
}

public class TaxCalculatorForUK : ICountryTaxCalculator
{
    public decimal CalculateTaxAmount()
    {
        ...
    }
}

public class TaxCalculatorForIN : ICountryTaxCalculator
{
    public decimal CalculateTaxAmount()
    {
        ...
    }
}
```

Throughout this book you will frequently need to create either abstract classes or interfaces as a part of our exploration of SOLID principles and design patterns. So, take a moment and ensure that you are comfortable with inheritance, abstract classes, and interfaces.

■ **Note**   We won't go into the discussion of abstract classes versus interfaces here. It is suffice to say that both allow us to define contracts of properties and methods that are then implemented by other classes. You may read more about abstract classes and interfaces in MSDN documentation.

Polymorphism

Polymorphism means multiple forms of something. Let's say you own a washing machine and a vacuum cleaner. Both are machines and can be started and stopped using their respective switches. However, your order to start and stop a machine is obeyed quite differently by the respective machines. And it also results in different results. A washing machine, when started, is going to wash clothes, whereas a vacuum cleaner is going to clean the floor when started. Thus, the same order—"start"—has two different results based on the machine to which it has been issued. The same can be said about the "stop" instructions.

How does this apply to classes? Imagine the preceding real-world example in terms of classes. The WashingMachine and VacuumCleaner classes bear an "is-a" relationship with the Machine class. The Machine class, the WashingMachine class, and the VacuumCleaner class have a Start() method. But each Start() implementation would be different for obvious reasons. Thus the same method—Start()—has multiple forms. Polymorphism comes in different flavors, such as operator overloading, method overloading, polymorphism via inheritance, and polymorphism via interfaces. Our main interest is in the last two flavors. That's because you will be using these types of polymorphism extensively in the examples presented later in this book. So, let's try to understand them with code examples.

Polymorphic Behavior Through Inheritance

Suppose we are building our contact management application and decide to have four classes named Contact, BusinessContact, ProfessionalContact, and PersonalContact. For the sake of this example, let's assume that you are writing the following code in a Console Application project. The Contact class is the base class for the remaining three classes and is shown here:

```
public class Contact
{
    public string FirstName { get; set; }
    public string LastName { get; set; }
    public string EmailAddress { get; set; }
    public string PhoneNo { get; set; }

    public virtual string GetDetails()
    {
        return FirstName + " " + LastName + " (" + EmailAddress + "," + PhoneNo + ")";
    }
}
```

The Contact class consists of four properties (FirstName, LastName, EmailAddress, PhoneNo) and a method (GetDetails). The properties and the method are quite straightforward. What's worth noting is that GetDetails() is marked as a virtual method. This means you can override it in the derived classes. The GetDetails() method simply returns FirstName, LastName, EmailAddress, and PhoneNo to its caller for formatting.

Next, the BusinessContact class inherits from the Contact class and looks as shown here:

```
public class BusinessContact : Contact
{
    public string CompanyName { get; set; }
    public string Designation { get; set; }

    public override string GetDetails()
    {
        return FirstName + " " + LastName + " (" + Designation + ", " + CompanyName + ")";
    }
}
```

As you can see, the BusinessContact class adds two more properties (CompanyName and Designation). It also overrides the GetDetails() method and redefines it to return FirstName, LastName, Designation, and CompanyName to the caller.

Along similar lines, you will create ProfessionalContact and PersonalContact classes that inherit Contact. These classes are shown here:

```
public class ProfessionalContact : Contact
{
    public string Service { get; set; }
    public string Address { get; set; }
    public string Timing { get; set; }

    public override string GetDetails()
    {
        return FirstName + " " + LastName + " (" + Service + ", " + Timing + ")";
    }
}

public class PersonalContact : Contact
{
    public string Address { get; set; }
    public DateTime BirthDate { get; set; }

    public override string GetDetails()
    {
        return FirstName + " " + LastName + " (" + BirthDate.ToString("dd-MMM-yyyy") + ")";
    }
}
```

Now that you have all four classes ready, let's observe their polymorphic behavior. Add a method to the Program class (the class that houses the Main() method) as shown here:

```
public static void ShowDetails(Contact c)
{
    string details = c.GetDetails();
    Console.WriteLine(details);
    Console.ReadLine();
}
```

The ShowDetails() method accepts a single parameter of the Contact class—the base class of the other classes. Inside, it simply invokes the GetDetails() method and then outputs the details on the console window.

Now, add the following code inside the Main() method:

```
static void Main(string[] args)
{
    BusinessContact c1 = new BusinessContact();
    c1.FirstName = "Nancy";
    c1.LastName = "Davolio";
    c1.EmailAddress = "nancy@localhost";
    c1.PhoneNo = "(206) 555-9857";
    c1.CompanyName = "Northwind Traders Inc.";
    c1.Designation = "Sales Representative";
    ProfessionalContact c2 = new ProfessionalContact();
    c2.FirstName = "Andrew";
    c2.LastName = "Fuller";
    c2.EmailAddress = "andrew@localhost";
    c2.PhoneNo = "(206) 555-9482";
    c2.Service = "Doctor";
    c2.Address = "908 W. Capital Way, Tacoma, USA";
    c2.Timing = "10 AM to 6 PM";
    PersonalContact c3 = new PersonalContact();
    c3.FirstName = "Janet";
    c3.LastName = "Leverling";
    c3.EmailAddress = "janet@localhost";
    c3.PhoneNo = "(206) 555-3412";
    c3.BirthDate = new DateTime(1971, 3, 20);
    ShowDetails(c1);
    ShowDetails(c2);
    ShowDetails(c3);
}
```

The preceding code basically instantiates BusinessContact, ProfessionalContact, and PersonalContact classes. It also sets various properties of these objects. Finally, it calls the static ShowDetails() method by passing the objects just created. Notice that the ShowDetails() method takes a parameter of type Contact, but we are passing objects of type BusinessContact, ProfessionalContact,

11

and PersonalContact, respectively. How is that possible? That's because all these classes are derived from the Contact class. Thus, objects of a derived type can be used where the base type is expected. What is more interesting is that a run of the application will reveal that although ShowDetails() is invoking GetDetails() on a Contact class, it is the GetDetails() method of the individual derived type that gets executed. Figure 1-3 shows a test run of the application.

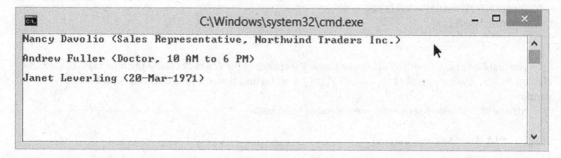

Figure 1-3. *Polymorphic behavior through inheritance*

As you can see, when you pass an object of type BusinessContact, GetDetails() of BusinessContact is getting executed and not GetDetails() of Contact. This is because the base class method is marked as virtual and the derived class overrides it. Similar behavior can be seen from ProfessionalContact and PersonalContact objects. This is polymorphism! The same method, GetDetails(), behaves differently based on the underlying object.

Just for the sake of testing, remove the override keyword from all the GetDetails() methods for the derived classes. Run the application again (see Figure 1-4).

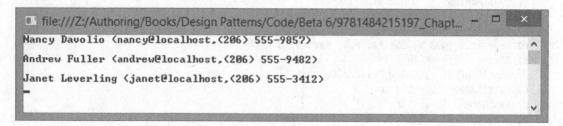

Figure 1-4. *Effect of removing virtual and override keywords*

What happens? All the calls to GetDetails() now execute the base class version of the method and return only FirstName, LastName, EmailAddress, and PhoneNo. No more polymorphic behavior! That's the significance of virtual and override keywords.

Polymorphic Behavior Through Interfaces

Now that you know how to achieve polymorphic behavior through inheritance, let's shift the focus to polymorphic behavior through interfaces. As an example, let's take the same scenario of the tax calculation application that we discussed while learning about interfaces. You can code this example as a Console Application project. Have a look at Listing 1-5.

Listing 1-5. ICountryTaxCalculator Being Implemented in Three Classes

```
public interface ICountryTaxCalculator
{
    decimal CalculateTaxAmount();
}

public class TaxCalculatorForUS : ICountryTaxCalculator
{
    public decimal CalculateTaxAmount()
    {
        return 10000m;
    }
}

public class TaxCalculatorForUK : ICountryTaxCalculator
{
    public decimal CalculateTaxAmount()
    {
        return 20000m;
    }
}

public class TaxCalculatorForIN : ICountryTaxCalculator
{
    public decimal CalculateTaxAmount()
    {
        return 5000m;
    }
}
```

As you can see, the ICountryTaxCalculator interface defines a method—CalculateTaxAmount()— that returns the tax amount as a decimal. ICountryTaxCalculator is implemented by three classes— TaxCalculatorForUS, TaxCalculatorForUK, and TaxCalculatorForIN. Each of these classes implements the CalculateTaxAmount() method and returns some arbitrary test values to the caller.

The Program class has a ShowDetails() method for displaying tax details. ShowDetails() is shown here:

```
public static void ShowDetails(ICountryTaxCalculator t)
{
    decimal tax = t.CalculateTaxAmount();
    Console.WriteLine("Tax Amount : " + tax);
    Console.ReadLine();
}
```

Notice that this time, ShowDetails() accepts a parameter of type ICountryTaxCalculator. Inside, it invokes the CalculateTaxAmount() method and writes the tax amount on the console.

The Main() method of the application is as follows:

```
static void Main(string[] args)
{
    TaxCalculatorForUS t1 = new TaxCalculatorForUS();
    TaxCalculatorForUK t2 = new TaxCalculatorForUK();
    TaxCalculatorForIN t3 = new TaxCalculatorForIN();

    ShowDetails(t1);
    ShowDetails(t2);
    ShowDetails(t3);
}
```

The Main() method creates three objects of types TaxCalculatorForUS, TaxCalculatorForUK, and TaxCalculatorForIN, respectively. ShowDetails() is then called by passing these objects as parameters. So, this time the parameter is an interface type and you are able to pass any object that implements that interface. Figure 1-5 shows a test run of this application.

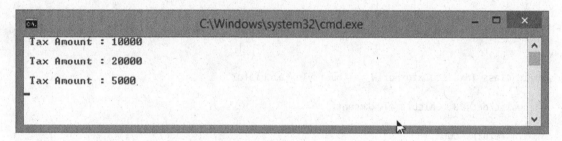

Figure 1-5. *Polymorphic behavior through interfaces*

This same method, CalculateTaxAmount(), behaves differently, returning different tax amounts depending on the underlying object. This is polymorphic behavior through interfaces.

Overview of SOLID Principles

Writing code in C# is relatively easy as compared to other languages available decades ago. C#, being an object-oriented language, uses all the object-oriented features we discussed earlier, such as encapsulation, classes, inheritance, interfaces, and polymorphism. However, these features by themselves don't guarantee that your code is written in the right way. It is not at all uncommon for a beginner to use these features in a wrong or unintended way. For example, by creating a class with a lot of methods and properties that should not have been part of that class at all, or by using inheritance hierarchies in the wrong way. In an object-oriented system, identifying classes and objects and deciding how they interact with each other can become complex depending on the given business problem. Moreover, your design needs to be flexible enough so that future extensions are easy. Wouldn't it be great if you knew of some standards or guidelines that you could keep in mind while writing C# code? That's what SOLID principles are!

In their book *Agile Principles, Patterns, and Practices in C#*, Robert C. Martin and Micah Martin elaborate on five principles of object-oriented software design. These principles are named as follows:

- **Single Responsibility Principle**

- **Open/Closed Principle**

- Liskov Substitution Principle
- Interface Segregation Principle
- Dependency Inversion Principle

Michael Feathers introduced an acronym—SOLID—to help us remember these principles easily. As you can see, the first letter of each of these principles makes the word SOLID, and hence collectively they are referred as SOLID principles.

These principles form the fundamental guidelines for building object-oriented applications. Following these principles while writing C# code will help you to build a robust, extensible, and maintainable code base. Moreover, these principles also form a vocabulary with which to convey the underlying ideas between other team members or as a part of technical documentation.

In the following paragraphs I will give a brief overview of each of these principles. In the next chapter you will learn each of these principles in detail and will also develop a working code sample demonstrating them.

Single Responsibility Principle (SRP)

Single Responsibility Principle (SRP) suggests that a class should have one and only one responsibility. A class is like container. One can add any amount of data, properties, and methods into it. However, if you try to achieve too much through a single class, soon that class will become bulky. Any small change you need will result in your changing this single class. And since you changed the class, you will also need to test it again. If you follow SRP, your classes will become compact and neat—each is responsible for a single problem, task, or concern. This way a change in the system requires a change in the corresponding class, and only that class needs to be tested again. SRP is a way to divide the whole problem into small parts, and each part will be dealt with by a separate class.

■ **Note** You may come across another principle of object-oriented design, Separation of Concerns (SoC), that conveys a similar idea.

Open/Closed Principle (OCP)

Open/Closed Principle (OCP) states that a class should be open for extension and closed for modifications. This means that once you create a class and other parts of the application start using it, you should not change it. Why? Because if you change the class, it is quite possible that your changes may cause the otherwise working system to break. If you require some additional features, you should extend that class rather than modifying it. This way the existing system won't see any impact from the new changes. Also, you need to test only the newly created class.

Liskov Substitution Principle (LSP)

Liskov Substitution Principle (LSP) states that derived classes should be substitutable for their base classes. When you create a class that inherits from some other class, you are free to add new features into the derived class. They may even work without any problem as long as you use the derived class on its own. However, when you resort to polymorphic behavior through inheritance, the derived class, if not following LSP, can pose problems in the system. That's because you are now using it in a place where the base class was expected.

15

Interface Segregation Principle (ISP)

Interface Segregation Principle, or ISP, states that clients of your classes should not be forced to depend on methods they do not use. Think of a class that has ten methods—five are needed by desktop clients and five are needed by mobile clients. Thus, the same interface consisting of ten methods is being used by both desktop and mobile clients. Now, tomorrow if a method required by a desktop client changes, you will need to update both versions of your application, because even the mobile client is dependent on the same interface, even though it is not using the changed method. This is unnecessary, and ISP suggests you avoid such situations. So, as per ISP, you would have to create two separate interfaces—one containing the five methods required by the desktop client and the other consisting of the remaining five required by the mobile client.

Dependency Inversion Principle (DIP)

Dependency Inversion Principle, or DIP, states that high-level concrete classes should not be dependent on other low-level concrete classes. Instead, they should depend on abstract classes or interfaces. This simply means that you should not use concrete low-level classes inside a high-level class, because then the high-level class becomes tightly coupled with those low-level classes. Tomorrow if any of the low-level classes change, the high-level class may break. As per DIP, the high-level classes should depend on abstraction (in the form of abstract classes or interfaces) and so should the low-level classes. The tight coupling is removed by coding both levels of classes against interfaces.

Now that you have some understanding of the SOLID principles, let's move our attention to Gang of Four (GoF) design patterns.

Design Patterns

A software design refers to the plan, blueprint or layout on which the software under consideration is based. As a part of software development you solve some problem or another. From a real-world perspective your solution should solve a business problem. And from the software development perspective, your solution should solve a software problem. What is a software problem? A software problem is basically a task that you wish to accomplish. For example, creating an object and filling it with data from a database is a software problem. There are countless such problems that you will come across. Many times these problems are recurring, and so are their solutions.

Over the years, the software industry has developed a collective wisdom with which to solve such recurring problems. This wisdom guides us in the development of our applications. Design patterns are an important part of this collective wisdom. Simply put, a design pattern is a time-proven solution for a known design problem. Instead of spending your time finding a new solution you can resort to the one that has already been used and tested by thousands of developers worldwide. This way you are sure that your approach is the best possible approach in a given context. It should be noted that design patterns solve known problems. If you come across a totally new problem that has not been dealt with before, chances are that there won't be any design pattern to solve that problem. Luckily, over the years the software industry has gathered a rich set of patterns that cover most of the problems you will face as a software developer.

Just to get a clear picture of what design patterns are, let's look at a real-world analogy. Suppose you wish to go for a trekking expedition to the Himalayas and that you haven't been there before. What would be your first step? Obviously, you would try to decide on a travel and trekking plan. You would consider factors such as type of travel available (train or air travel), possible trek routes you could take, weather conditions possible during your visit, your physical fitness, and so on. As an individual you could find out all these pieces of information and chalk out a plan yourself. However, it is possible that you overlooked some aspect of the travel planning (maybe because you haven't been there before or due to ignorance). Wouldn't it be easy to consult some traveller or trekker who has been there many times? Or to check with a travel company that has rich experience in organizing such an expedition? If you go by the first approach your expedition might end up with some hiccups or even some unpleasant experiences. It would be far wiser to resort to the second approach. That's because an experienced helping hand will be there for you to guide you throughout your expedition.

I think you must now understand the idea behind design patterns. Instead of spending (maybe even wasting) your efforts in finding new solutions to known problems, it would be better to utilize known and proven solutions. In a nutshell, you attempt to reuse solutions rather than rediscovering them. That way your development as well as your testing becomes smooth.

Gang of Four Design Patterns

In their book *Design Patterns: Elements of Reusable Object Oriented Software*, authors Erich Gamma, Richard Helm, Ralph Johnson, and John Vlissides have cataloged a set of design patterns. Today their catalog is considered one of the most popular sources of information about design patterns. Since the catalog was documented by the four authors, the patterns therein are called Gang of Four, or GoF, design patterns. A large part of this book discusses GoF patterns in detail.

The GoF catalog includes 23 design patterns. The authors have placed these 23 patterns into three categories, namely creational patterns, structural patterns, and behavioral patterns. Each pattern is described with many pieces of information. Some of the important pieces are as follows:

- Pattern name and category it belongs to

- Intent or purpose of the pattern

- Motivation behind using that pattern

- Applicability of a pattern

- Structure of a pattern, usually expressed as a UML diagram

- Participants in a design pattern

- Collaborations between the participants

- Consequences of using a design pattern in terms of outcome, benefits, and trade-offs

- Implementation details about a pattern

The next section will discuss the three categories mentioned earlier in more detail. It will also list the 23 patterns in their respective categories.

Categorization of GoF Patterns

The 23 GoF design patterns are organized into the following three categories:
- Creational patterns

- Structural patterns

- Behavioral patterns

Let's examine each of these categories in a bit more detail.

Creational Design Patterns

Creational design patterns deal with how objects are created. Typically you create new object instances using a new keyword in your C# code. However, at times instantiating an object may not be that straightforward. It may involve some logic or conditions. Creational patterns are intended to take away such complexity from your code. There are five design patterns in this category:

- Factory Method
- Abstract Factory
- Builder
- Prototype
- Singleton

■ **Note**   Don't worry about the individual patterns at this stage. The following chapters are going to explain each of them in detail. Here, our focus is on the categorization of the 23 GoF design patterns.

Structural Design Patterns

Structural design patterns deal with the composition of classes and objects. These patterns simplify the structure of a system by identifying the relationships between objects. There are seven design patterns in this category:

- Adapter
- Bridge
- Composite
- Decorator
- Façade
- Flyweight
- Proxy

Behavioral Design Patterns

Behavioral design patterns deal with the interaction and communication between various objects. They attempt to reduce the complexity that may otherwise result when objects communicate with each other. There are eleven design patterns in this category:

- Interpreter
- Template Method
- Chain of Responsibility
- Command

- Iterator
- Mediator
- Memento
- Observer
- State
- Strategy
- Visitor

Martin Fowler's Patterns of Enterprise Application Architecture

In the preceding sections you learned about GoF design patterns. There is another catalog of patterns compiled by Martin Fowler. This catalog is called Patterns of Enterprise Application Architecture (P of EAA). What is the difference between GoF patterns and P of EAA? After all, patterns from both catalogs are used while building software systems. However, as you can probably sense, P of EAA are geared more toward enterprise applications. In simple words, an enterprise application is a software system that is quite big as compared to many other small systems. Such an application is usually complex, highly scalable, and distributed in nature. So, Martin Fowler's catalog is arranged so as to keep in mind such large-scale applications. It is important to remember that there is no yard stick that precisely measures this distinction. As a developer your job is to pick the patterns that are appropriate to solve a given problem. A single application may use a few patterns from the GoF catalog and a few from the P of EAA catalog.

■ **Note**　Throughout this book I will generically call patterns from both catalogs either *patterns* or *design patterns*. If I wish to mention a specific catalog, I will explicitly state *GoF* or *P of EAA* as the case may be.

Martin Fowler has documented P of EAA in his book. Just like GoF patterns, patterns in this catalog are elaborated using many pieces of information. Some of them are as follows:

- Name of a pattern
- Intent and the sketch of a pattern
- Motivation behind using a pattern
- How a pattern works
- When to use a pattern
- Code examples

Fowler's catalog of patterns organizes them into ten categories. These categories will be discussed next.

Categorization of P of EAA

Martin Fowler's book *Patterns of Enterprise Application Architecture* organizes patterns into ten categories. Unlike GoF design patterns (which are organized by their purpose), these patterns are organized by the application layer they belong to. The following list denotes these ten categories:

- Domain-logic patterns
- Data-source architectural patterns
- Object-relational behavioral patterns
- Object-relational structural patterns
- Object-relational metadata-mapping patterns
- Web presentation patterns
- Distribution patterns
- Offline concurrency patterns
- Session-state patterns
- Base patterns

Each of these categories contains many patterns. I am not going to list all those patterns here since we won't be discussing the whole catalog of P of EAA in this book (and also to save us some space and to avoid mentioning an overwhelming number of pattern names at one go). In Chapter 10 you will learn a few important patterns from the catalog of P of EAA. At that time I will also mention the category they belong to and of course their detailed explanation.

■ **Note** Two catalogs—GoF and P of EAA—describe the respective patterns in their own way (see discussion in earlier sections). In this book I am going to use a normalized and simplified style to describe each pattern, including each pattern's name, purpose, explanation (with diagrams wherever necessary), and code example(s). My goal is to simplify the patterns so that you can easily learn and use them in your own ASP.NET applications.

Design Patterns in JavaScript

One of the good features of design patterns is their independence from a particular programming language. Your knowledge about patterns can be easily translated and reused in any programming language or framework. Most of the modern web applications use JavaScript heavily for a variety of purposes. Libraries such as jQuery are quite popular already. Frameworks such as AngularJS are also becoming popular among web developers. Dozens of JavaScript libraries are available to choose from. Upcoming specifications, such as ES6 (ECMA Script 6), are attempting to add many new features (for example, classes) to JavaScript. The point is clear—JavaScript is going to dominate future web development.

The concept of object-oriented (OO) principles and patterns can also be used on the code written in JavaScript. If your JavaScript is merely a handful of mouse-over effects or event handlers, using design patterns will probably be overkill. But as your JavaScript code base grows (think of a Single Page Application, or SPA, that does almost everything on client-side code and talks to the server through Web API and Ajax), applying good OO principles and patterns makes complete sense. You can get the same benefits for your JavaScript code as for your server-side C# code.

In Chapter 11 you will learn how to apply some of the GoF patterns to your JavaScript code. You will also learn some code-organization patterns that are frequently used with JavaScript code—patterns used for neatly organizing your JavaScript code.

■ **Note**   While studying SOLID principles and design patterns you may come across the term *anti-patterns*. Simply put, anti-patterns indicate bad programming practices and designs that exist in the software development industry. In a way, anti-patterns are the opposite of design patterns—design patterns promote good design practices and anti-patterns promote bad design practices. A discussion of anti-patterns is beyond the scope of this book.

Applying Design Principles and Patterns

For beginners, the most challenging aspect of design principles and patterns is how to apply them in an application. Although there is no straightforward technique to do so, I will supply a few tips based on my personal experience with the hope that you too will find them useful.

- Beginners often believe that every application must use design patterns. That's not necessary. Although design patterns are helpful in solving known business problems, one needs to determine whether using them adds undue complexity to the project. For example, if you are writing a simple batch script used only once in a while for something not mission critical, applying design patterns may be overkill.

- You will realize that you may or may not use design patterns in an application, but at a minimum you will use one or more of the SOLID principles. This is because these principles are so foundational to object-oriented design that even a simple set of classes can rely on them during their construction or extension.

- Another mistake beginners might make is to stuff too many patterns into a single application. This not only increases the complexity of the project but may also add errors. Try to develop a habit of identifying patterns that can go into a system. You may find that you end up using some patterns more than others. Some patterns will become your personal favorites. Developing such a habit calls for regular practice, and you have to start somewhere. Based on this practice, you will build experience over a period of time.

- If you consider GoF and P of EAA catalogs together then you end up having a relatively large set of design patterns to learn. Learning them is a gradual and continuous process. I would suggest that you first make yourself comfortable with GoF patterns and then jump to commonly used P of EAA. That's why this book follows the same flow—first SOLID principles, then GoF patterns, then comes P of EAA, and finally the book concludes with JavaScript patterns.

- Another difficulty beginners face is in recollecting patterns while studying project requirements. Again, this requires some practice. What I used to do during my early days as a software developer was to create cheat sheets of design practices and patterns. You can jot them down with the help of figures, labels, and keywords and then have a look at them whenever you get spare time—during a tea break, during lunch break, while travelling, and whenever you can squeeze in some time. This constant reflection on the patterns helps you to keep them fresh in your mind, and your recollection of them will be better.

- Remember that SOLID principles and patterns are not just useful during the initial development of the code base, but are also of great value while extending or maintaining the existing code base.

- Study code written by experts from your organization that makes use of SOLID principles and design patterns. This will help you understand how seasoned developers are applying them, and you will learn the technique in the process.

You Are Already Using Patterns! A Few Examples

By now you must have some idea of what SOLID principles and design patterns are. Believe it or not, you are already using them in some form or another in your ASP.NET applications. Let's see a few examples:

- As an ASP.NET developer, chances are you have already created ASP.NET MVC applications. You are probably aware that MVC itself is a pattern. Using an MVC pattern, you divide the whole functionality of an application into three distinct pieces: models, views, and controllers. Each piece is responsible for a specific job. For example, models represent application data, views are responsible for user interface, and controllers are responsible for the interaction and flow between models and views. In the P of EAA catalog MVC is categorized as a Web Presentation Pattern.

- The System.IO namespace defines several stream classes, such as `BufferedStream` and `GZipStream`. Here, the .NET framework uses the Decorator design pattern outlined in the GoF catalog. The classes, such as the ones mentioned previously, "decorate" the underlying `Stream` object. For example, you can pass any `Stream` instance to a `GZipStream` constructor and then work with that object, which in turn manipulates the `Stream` you passed.

- Have a look at the following line of code:

```
int i = Convert.ToInt32("1234");
```

  The code uses the `ToInt32()` method of the `Convert` class. You passed a string to the `ToInt32()` method. It then created a new integer for you and assigned the newly created integer to `i`. This is the Factory pattern in action. Factory basically creates something for you—a new integer, in this case. Factory pattern and its variants are also outlined in GoF catalog.

- The `foreach` loop of C# that iterates through a collection is an example of the Iterator pattern. Such a loop basically iterates through an `IEnumerable` of a set of objects. The Iterator pattern allows you to sequentially access a collection object. The Iterator design pattern is listed in the GoF catalog.

- The Entity Framework implements the Repository and Unit of Work patterns. The Repository pattern allows you to work with your data as if it were a collection. Methods such as `Add()` and `Remove()` do that for you. The Unit of Work pattern keeps track of your operations (add / modify / delete) during a business transaction. It then plays these operations on the database as a single unit. The `SaveChanges()` method executes these operations in a transaction as a unit of work. Both of these patterns are cataloged in P of EAA.

As you can see, you are already using a few patterns in your applications in an indirect way. Also, notice that the MVC pattern has been applied to the whole application or project. Thus, in a way, it governs the overall architecture of your application. On the other hand, GoF design patterns such as Decorator, Factory, and Iterator are closer to a specific piece of code than to the whole application.

Creating an ASP.NET 5 Application Using MVC 6 and Entity Framework 7

■ **Note** Microsoft recently announced that ASP.NET 5 is now ASP.NET Core 1.0 and Entity Framework 7 is now Entity Framework Core 1.0. However, for the sake of consistency, this book will still reference these technologies as ASP.NET 5, MVC 6, and EF 7. Read the section at the end of this chapter for more details about this change.

The concepts discussed throughout this book are framework and language independent. However, for the sake of uniformity you will use Visual Studio 2015, ASP.NET 5, MVC 6, Entity Framework 7, and C# (any supported Windows OS will do) to develop the examples presented in this book. You can easily port most of the examples to MVC 5.x or even Web Forms applications if required. Using ASP.NET 5, you can build applications targeting .NET Core or .NET Framework. Many examples presented in this book will run on both targets, and some will work only on the .NET Framework.

Although concepts such as models, views, and controllers remain the same in both MVC 5.x and MVC 6, there are differences as to how an application is created and configured. I assume that you are already familiar with the basics of MVC 6 and Entity Framework 7. The following sections are intended only as a quick brush-up of what you already know. Detailed coverage of MVC 6 and Entity Framework 7 is beyond the scope of this book.

■ **Note** You may visit `http://www.asp.net` and `http://docs.asp.net` to read more about ASP.NET 5 and MVC 6.

In the sections that follow you will develop a simple web application that stores contacts to an SQL Server database. Throughout this book I will point you to these sections for information about creating and configuring MVC 6 applications. So, chances are you will revisit these sections again and again.

The application that you will develop in this section is shown in Figure 1-6.

Figure 1-6. Contact management application

The application presents a list of existing contacts in a table and allows you to delete them using the Delete link. The Add New Contact link takes you to another page, where new contact details can be entered. This page is shown in Figure 1-7.

Figure 1-7. *Adding a new contact*

The Add New Contact page accepts four pieces of information—First Name, Last Name, Email, and Phone. All these pieces are mandatory, and basic validation is also wired into the page. Clicking on the Submit button saves the contact in an SQL Server database.

The following sections will guide you in building this example.

Creating a Web Application Using Visual Studio

In this section you will create a new ASP.NET web application that uses MVC 6. Begin by opening Visual Studio and clicking on File ➤ New ➤ Project. Doing so will open the New Project dialog, as shown in Figure 1-8.

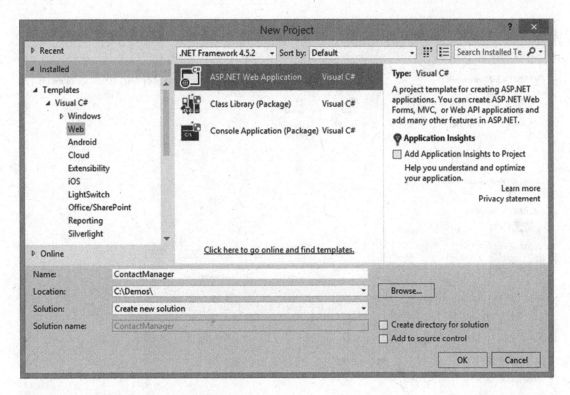

Figure 1-8. *Creating a new web application*

On the left-hand side, expand the Visual C# node and select Web. Then select ASP.NET Web Application in the main area. Specify a folder where the project files are to be stored in the Location textbox. Name the project ContactManager, uncheck the "Create directory for solution" checkbox, and click OK.

■ **Note**   Your project structure might look a bit different if you keep the "Create directory for solution" checkbox checked. These differences don't affect our discussion, but just keep in mind that I have created all the projects needed for this book's examples with this checkbox unchecked.

This will open the project template selection dialog, as shown in Figure 1-9.

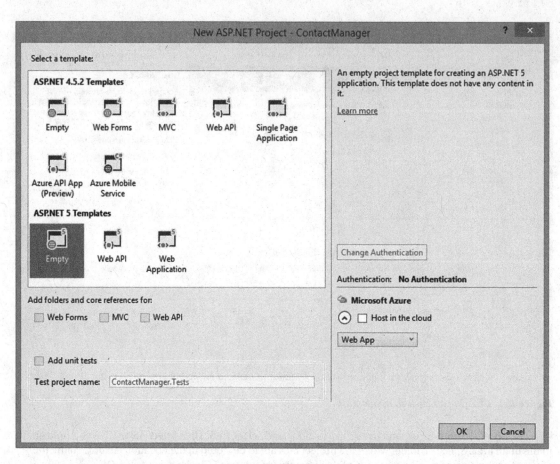

Figure 1-9. *Selecting ASP.NET 5 empty template*

The template selection dialog is divided into two sections: ASP.NET 4.5.2 Templates and ASP.NET 5 Templates. Since you want to create an MVC 6 application, select Empty template under the ASP.NET 5 Templates section. Also, uncheck the "Host in the cloud" checkbox. Now click on the OK button to create a new project.

■ **Note**   You could have also used the Web Application project template. However, it contains many items not needed by this example. Once you know how to create and configure a project using the Empty project template, you can easily use that knowledge to work with the Web Application project template.

Figure 1-10 shows Solution Explorer after the project's creation.

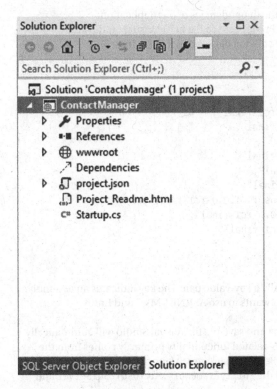

Figure 1-10. *New project structure*

As you can see, the newly created project already contains a few items. Let's list the ones that are of interest, along with their purpose:

- **References:** Lists references of .NET framework assemblies and NuGet packages used by the project

- **wwwroot:** Contains static files such as HTML files, images, CSS files, and JavaScript files

- **Project.json:** Contains a list of .NET framework assemblies, NuGet packages, and project-level configuration stored in JSON format

- **Startup.cs:** Contains startup configuration of an MVC 6 application. This is where you tell the framework what features and services your application needs.

You might have noticed that there are no Models, Views, and Controllers folders. Of course, you will add them whenever your project needs them.

Add a new folder under the project root and name it Core. In all the examples presented in this book, the primary classes related to the example are stored in the Core folder. This way you can easily store and locate them in one place. Similarly, add Controllers and Views folders under the project root to store the respective items.

Configuring Project Dependencies

Now that you have created a new project, let's configure the dependencies of our application. The `Project.json` file is where you do that. So, open the `Project.json` file in the Visual Studio editor.

Then, modify the dependencies section of the `Project.json` file as shown in Listing 1-6.

Listing 1-6. Configuring Project Dependencies

```
"dependencies": {
  "Microsoft.AspNet.IISPlatformHandler": "1.0.0-rc1-final",
  "Microsoft.AspNet.Server.Kestrel": "1.0.0-rc1-final",
  "Microsoft.AspNet.Mvc": "6.0.0-rc1-final",
  "Microsoft.AspNet.Mvc.TagHelpers": "6.0.0-rc1-final",
  "Microsoft.AspNet.StaticFiles": "1.0.0-rc1-final",
  "Microsoft.AspNet.Tooling.Razor": "1.0.0-rc1-final",
  "Microsoft.Extensions.Configuration.Abstractions": "1.0.0-rc1-final",
  "Microsoft.Extensions.Configuration.Json": "1.0.0-rc1-final",
  "EntityFramework.MicrosoftSqlServer": "7.0.0-rc1-final",
  "EntityFramework.Commands": "7.0.0-rc1-final"
}
```

Each entry inside the dependencies section is basically a key-value pair. The key indicates an assembly, and the value indicates its version. Since your application wants to use ASP.NET MVC and Entity Framework 7, you need to specify those dependencies.

When you enter these dependencies in `Project.json` and save the file, Visual Studio will automatically download the required NuGet packages. Note that MVC 6–related functionality primarily comes from the `Microsoft.AspNet.Mvc` and `Microsoft.AspNet.Mvc.TagHelpers` packages. Along the same lines, the Entity Framework 7–related functionality primarily comes from the `EntityFramework.MicrosoftSqlServer` and `EntityFramework.Commands` packages.

Next, modify the commands section of `Project.json` as shown in Listing 1-7.

Listing 1-7. Entity Framework Commands

```
"commands": {
  "web": "Microsoft.AspNet.Server.Kestrel",
  "ef": "EntityFramework.Commands"
}
```

The entry with key `ef` and value of `EntityFramework.Commands` is needed for executing Entity Framework migrations (more on that later).

The frameworks section of `Project.json` allows you to configure the target .NET frameworks (see Listing 1-8).

Listing 1-8. Configuring Target Frameworks

```
"frameworks": {
  "dnx451": { },
  "dnxcore50": { }
}
```

By default, both full .NET framework (`dnx451`) and .NET core (`dnxcore50`) are targeted. If you wish to target a specific framework you can keep just that entry and remove the other one.

Configuring Application Settings

While Project.config specifies the project-level configuration used by the framework and compilation system, you will need a place to store the application configuration. The ASP.NET MVC 6 stores application configuration in JSON files, which are usually named appsettings.json. You can add a configuration file to your project's root folder using the Add New Item dialog (see Figure 1-11).

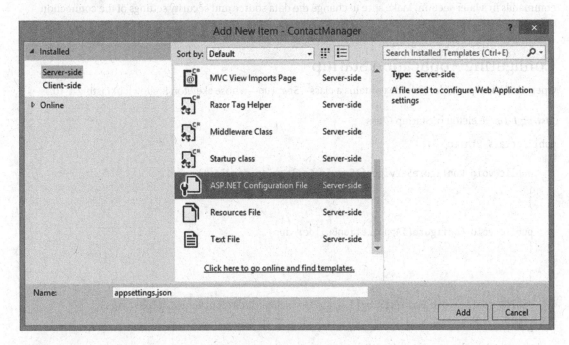

Figure 1-11. *Adding a new ASP.NET configuration file*

appsettings.json contains the configuration settings used by your application code. This could be a database connection string or any such settings.

Open appsettings.json and modify it as shown in Listing 1-9.

Listing 1-9. Storing Application Configuration in appsettings.json

```
{
  "AppSettings": {
    "Title": "My Contact Manager Application"
  },

  "Data": {
    "DefaultConnection": {
      "ConnectionString": "data source=.;initial catalog=ContactDb;integrated security=true;
      MultipleActiveResultSets=true"
    }
  }
}
```

The appsettings.json file contains two sections—AppSettings and Data. The AppSettings section contains a single key—Title—with a value of My Contact Manager Application. You will use this setting to render the page title. You can add more settings as per your needs. Think of it as the <appSettings> section of web.config (although you can name it anything you choose).

The Data section specifies a ConnectionString. The connection string points to the ContactDb database. So far you haven't created this database. You will do that using Entity Framework migration commands in a later section. Make sure to change the data source and security settings of the connection string as per your setup.

Configuring Application Startup

Open the Startup.cs file. This file contains a class—Startup—whose skeleton is shown in Listing 1-10.

Listing 1-10. Skeleton of Startup Class

```
public class Startup
{
    public void ConfigureServices(IServiceCollection services)
    {
    }

    public void Configure(IApplicationBuilder app)
    {
        ...
    }

    public static void Main(string[] args) => WebApplication.Run<Startup>(args);
}
```

The Startup class contains the following items:

- **ConfigureServices:** This method is invoked by the framework. This is where you specify what services your application needs. For example, this application needs MVC and Entity Framework. So, they will be added to the pipeline here.

- **Configure:** This method is called after ConfigureServices and is a place to configure the services. For example, you can configure the routing of MVC here.

- **Main:** This is the entry point for the application.

Let's complete these items one by one and also read the configuration file. Add a constructor to the Startup class and write the code shown in Listing 1-11 inside the newly added constructor.

Listing 1-11. Constructor of Startup Class

```
public Startup(IHostingEnvironment env, IApplicationEnvironment app)
{
    ConfigurationBuilder builder = new ConfigurationBuilder();
    builder.SetBasePath(app.ApplicationBasePath);
    builder.AddJsonFile("appsettings.json");
    IConfigurationRoot config = builder.Build();
}
```

The constructor receives IHostingEnvironment and IApplicationEnvironment objects. These objects can be used to get the filesystem paths and such details about the application. You can also inject them into the controller.

The code instantiates the ConfigurationBuilder class. The SetBasePath() method sets the base path for the configuration files subsequently specified. The ApplicationBasePath property of the IApplicationEnvironment object returns the project root folder's path. The AddJsonFile() method specifies the file that acts as the source of configuration (appsettings.json in this case). Finally, the Build() method loads the configuration into an IConfigurationRoot object. Once loaded, you can use the config object to read the configuration settings.

We also wish to access the configuration settings in our custom classes. There can be various approaches to accomplishing this task, including dependency injection. We won't go into those details here. You will use a simple and typed way to access configuration settings throughout the application.

Right click on the Core folder and select Add ➤ Class from the shortcut menu. Doing so will open an Add New Item dialog, as shown in Figure 1-12.

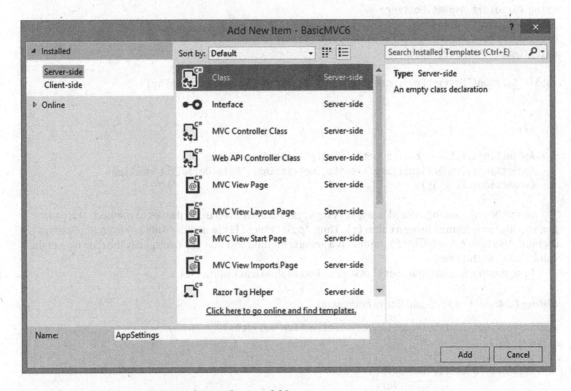

Figure 1-12. *Adding AppSettings class to the Core folder*

Name the class AppSettings and click OK. Then write the code shown in Listing 1-12 in the AppSettings class.

Listing 1-12. AppSettings Class

```
public class AppSettings
{
    public static string Title { get; set; }
    public static string ConnectionString { get; set; }
}
```

This class contains two static properties—Title and ConnectionString. You can load values into these properties as shown in Listing 1-13.

Listing 1-13. Loading AppSettings Properties

```
...
...
using Microsoft.AspNet.Hosting;
using Microsoft.Extensions.Configuration;
using Microsoft.Extensions.PlatformAbstractions;
using ContactManager.Core;

public Startup(IHostingEnvironment env, IApplicationEnvironment appEnv)
{
    ...
    ...

    AppSettings.Title = config.Get<string>("AppSettings:Title");
    AppSettings.ConnectionString = config.Get<string>("Data:DefaultConnection:
    ConnectionString");}
```

Notice how the settings stored in appsettings.json are retrieved using the Get() method. The path to a specific key is formed using a colon (:). Thus, AppSettings:Title means "Title key from AppSettings section." Also notice that the Get() method is a generic method and that you can specify the data type of the value (string, in this case).

Now, modify the ConfigureServices() method as shown in Listing 1-14.

Listing 1-14. Adding MVC and Entity Framework

```
public void ConfigureServices(IServiceCollection services)
{
    services.AddMvc();
    services.AddEntityFramework()
                .AddSqlServer();
}
```

This code adds MVC using the AddMvc() method. The AddEntityFramework() method adds the Entity Framework service. We wish to work with a SQL Server database, and hence the code also calls AddSqlServer() method. Notice how these method calls are chained one after the other.

Finally, configure MVC routing in the Configure() method as shown in Listing 1-15.

Listing 1-15. Configuring MVC Routing

```
public void Configure(IApplicationBuilder app)
{
    app.UseStaticFiles();
    app.UseMvc(routes =>
    {
        routes.MapRoute(
            name: "default",
            template: "{controller=Home}/{action=Index}/{id?}");
    });
}
```

The UseStaticFiles() method enables support for static files such as .html files. The UseMvc() method specifies the route pattern, which includes controller, action, and optional id parameter.

Creating DbContext and Model

In this section you will create an Entity Framework DbContext class needed by your application, as well as the model. Begin by adding a Contact class in the Core folder and write the code shown in Listing 1-16 into it.

Listing 1-16. Contact Class

```
[Table("Contacts")]
public class Contact
{
    [DatabaseGenerated(DatabaseGeneratedOption.Identity)]
    public int Id { get; set; }
    [Required]
    [StringLength(40)]
    public string FirstName { get; set; }
    [Required]
    [StringLength(40)]
    public string LastName { get; set; }
    [Required]
    [StringLength(50)]
    public string Email { get; set; }
    [Required]
    [StringLength(20)]
    public string Phone { get; set; }
}
```

The Contact class contains five properties: Id, FirstName, LastName, Email, and Phone. These properties are decorated with data annotations such as [Table], [DatabaseGenerated], [Required], and [StringLength]. The [Table] attribute maps the Contact class with the Contacts table. The [DatabaseGenerated] attribute marks the Id column as the primary key containing the identity value. When the [Required] attribute is added on top of the properties it indicates that those properties must be assigned some value. The [StringLength] attribute controls the maximum lengths of a property value. Together these data annotations will help during database creation and data validation. Note that these data annotations come from System.ComponentModel.DataAnnotations and System.ComponentModel. DataAnnotations.Schema namespaces.

Then, add an AppDbContext class to the Core folder and write the code shown in Listing 1-17 into it.

Listing 1-17. AppDbContext Class

```
public class AppDbContext:DbContext
{
    public DbSet<Contact> Contacts { get; set; }

    protected override void OnConfiguring(DbContextOptionsBuilder optionsBuilder)
    {
        optionsBuilder.UseSqlServer(AppSettings.ConnectionString);
    }
}
```

The AppDbContext class inherits from the DbContext class (`Microsoft.Data.Entity` namespace) and overrides its OnConfiguring() method. The AppDbContext class has a DbSet—Contacts—that will be used to access contact data.

The OnConfiguring() method invokes the UseSqlServer() method on the optionsBuilder and passes the database connection string to it. This way the DbContext class knows which database to connect to.

Creating the HomeController

To add HomeController to the Controllers folder, right click on the Controllers folder and select the Add ➤ New Item menu option. The Add New Item dialog is shown in Figure 1-13.

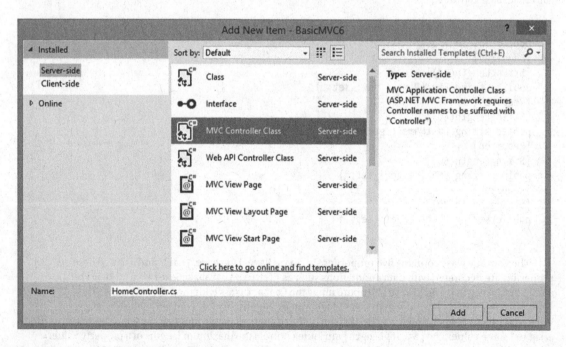

Figure 1-13. *Adding a new Controller class*

You will add four actions to the HomeController. The code for the Index() action is shown in Listing 1-18 into it.

Listing 1-18. Index() action

```
public IActionResult Index()
{
  ViewBag.Title = AppSettings.Title;
  using (AppDbContext db = new AppDbContext())
  {
    var query = from c in db.Contacts
                orderby c.Id ascending
                select c;
    List<Contact> model = query.ToList();
    return View(model);
  }
}
```

The Index() action stores the Title in the ViewBag so that it can be displayed on the view. The code then instantiates AppDbContext (make sure to import the ContactManager.Core namespace) and fetches all the contact data. In order to pass contact data to the Index view, a List of Contact objects is formed and then passed to the View() method.

Next, add two actions that take care of adding a new Contact object. These actions are shown in Listing 1-19.

Listing 1-19. Actions to Add a Contact

```
public IActionResult AddContact()
{
  return View();
}

[HttpPost]
public IActionResult AddContact(Contact obj)
{
  if (ModelState.IsValid)
  {
    using (AppDbContext db = new AppDbContext())
    {
      db.Contacts.Add(obj);
      db.SaveChanges();
      ViewBag.Message = "Contact added successfully!";
    }
  }
  return View(obj);
}
```

The first AddContact() method simply returns the AddContact view to the browser. The second AddContact() is called when the AddContact view submits the form and accepts a Contact parameter. Inside, the code checks the IsValid property on the ModelState to ensure that the Contact object contains valid data as per data annotations.

It then instantiates AppDbContext and adds the contact to the Contacts DbSet using the Add() method. The newly added contact is saved to the database using the SaveChanges() method. A success message is stored in the ViewBag so that the same can be shown to the user.

▪ **Note**   MVC 6 also allows you to inject the DbContext into your controller's constructor. However, for the sake of simplicity and to remain focused on the primary topic of discussion, most of the examples presented in this book don't use dependency injection.

Now, add one more action that takes care of deleting an existing contact. These actions are shown in Listing 1-20.

Listing 1-20. Deleting a contact

```
public IActionResult DeleteContact(int id)
{
  using (AppDbContext db = new AppDbContext())
  {
    var contact = (from c in db.Contacts
                   where c.Id == id
                   select c).SingleOrDefault();
    db.Contacts.Remove(contact);
    db.SaveChanges();
    return RedirectToAction("Index");
  }
}
```

The DeleteContact() action accepts the ID of a contact to be deleted. Inside, it instantiates the AppDbContext and fetches an existing contact by matching the supplied ID. It then removes that contact using the Remove() method. The changes are propagated to the database by calling SaveChanges(). Finally, the control is handed over to the Index action so that the browser reflects the changes.

Creating the Index and AddContact Views

In this section you will complete the application by creating two views, Index and AddContact. First, add a Home subfolder within the Views folder. Then right click on the Views folder and select the Add ➤ New Item menu options to open the Add New Item dialog. Locate the MVC View Imports Page entry and add a view imports file to the Views folder (Figure 1-14).

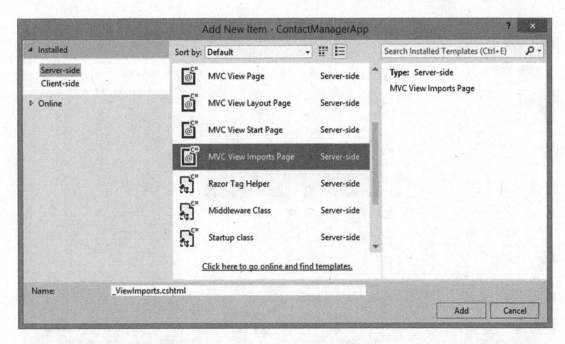

Figure 1-14. *Adding a view imports page*

The View Imports page is used to import namespaces and tag helpers required by all the views. Add the following piece of code to the file:

```
@using ContactManager
@addTagHelper "*, Microsoft.AspNet.Mvc.TagHelpers"
```

Here, you imported the `ContactManager` namespace and also used the `@addTagHelper` directive to indicate that helpers from the `Microsoft.AspNet.Mvc.TagHelpers` assembly should be registered.

To add the required views, right click on the Views ➤ Home folder and select the Add New Item shortcut menu option. Doing so will open the Add New Item dialog, as shown in Figure 1-15.

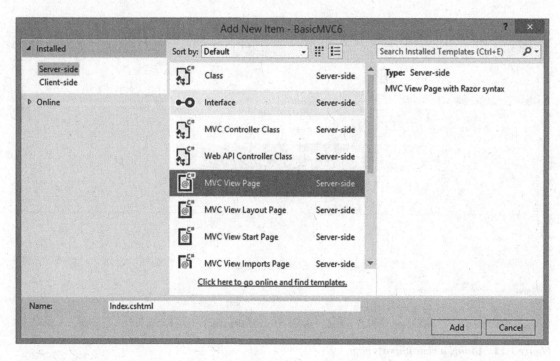

Figure 1-15. *Adding new views*

Select the MVC View Page entry and click on Add. Repeat the same procedure to add the AddContact view. Then write the markup shown in Listing 1-21 inside the Index view.

Listing 1-21. Markup of Index View

```
@model List<ContactManager.Core.Contact>

<html>
<head>
    <title>@ViewBag.Title</title>
</head>
<body>
    <h1>List of Contacts</h1>
    <a asp-action="AddContact" asp-controller="Home">Add New Contact</a>
    <br /><br />
    <table border="1" cellpadding="10">
        @foreach (var item in Model)
        {
            <tr>
                <td>@item.Id</td>
                <td>@item.FirstName</td>
                <td>@item.LastName</td>
                <td><a asp-action="DeleteContact" asp-controller="Home"
                asp-route-id="@item.Id">Delete</a></td>
            </tr>
        }
```

```
    </table>
  </body>
</html>
```

The model for the Index view is set to a list of Contact objects using the @model directive. The Index view displays the ViewBag.Title in the <title> tag.

The anchor tag helper renders a hyperlink that points to the AddContact action of the Home controller. This is done using the asp-controller and asp-action attributes of the anchor tag helper.

Then a table is rendered showing the existing contact details: Id, FirstName, and LastName. This is done using the @foreach Razor code block. Notice how each table row shows a Delete link using the anchor tag helper. The asp-route-id attribute specifies the value that is supplied as the id route parameter (recollect that the DeleteContact() action has an id parameter).

Now open the AddContact.aspx view and write the markup shown in Listing 1-22.

Listing 1-22. Markup of AddContact View

```
@model ContactManager.Core.Contact

<html>
    <head>
        <title>@ViewBag.Title</title>
    </head>
    <body>
        <h1>Add New Contact</h1>
        <a asp-action="Index" asp-controller="Home">Go Back</a>
        <br /><br />
        <form asp-controller="Home" asp-action="AddContact" method="post">
            <table border="1" cellpadding="10">
                <tr>
                    <td><label asp-for="FirstName">First Name :</label></td>
                    <td><input type="text" asp-for="FirstName" /></td>
                </tr>
                <tr>
                    <td><label asp-for="LastName">Last Name :</label></td>
                    <td><input type="text" asp-for="LastName" /></td>
                </tr>
                <tr>
                    <td><label asp-for="Email">Email :</label></td>
                    <td><input type="text" asp-for="Email" /></td>
                </tr>
                <tr>
                    <td><label asp-for="Phone">Phone :</label></td>
                    <td><input type="text" asp-for="Phone" /></td>
                </tr>
                <tr>
                    <td colspan="2">
                        <input type="submit" value="Submit" />
                    </td>
                </tr>
            </table>
        </form>
```

```
<strong>@ViewBag.Message</strong>
<div asp-validation-summary="ValidationSummary.All"></div>

</body>
</html>
```

The model for the AddContact view is set to the Contact class using @model Razor syntax. Then the title of the page is set to the ViewBag.Title value. An anchor tag helper displays a hyperlink pointing to the Index action of the Home controller.

Then a form is rendered using the form tag helper. The asp-controller and asp-action attributes of the form are set to AddContact and Home, respectively. This will submit the form to the AddContact() POST action.

The labels and input fields are displayed using a label tag helper and an input tag helper, respectively. The asp-for attribute of these helpers binds the element to the specified model property. The form has four sets of labels and input fields for FirstName, LastName, Email, and Phone model properties.

A Submit button posts the form to its target action. Recollect that the AddContact() POST action sets a success message in the ViewBag. This message is displayed at the bottom of the page. Finally, a validation summary is displayed in a <div> element using the validation tag helper and its asp-validation-summary attribute.

This completes the application. Before running the application, however, you need to create the ContactDb database.

Creating the ContactDb Database

The application needs to store its data in an SQL Server database. You can create the database either manually or by using Entity Framework migration commands. In this section, you will use Entity Framework migrations to create the database.

■ **Note**   Although this example creates a new SQL Server database, you will also use the Northwind sample database of SQL Server in some examples presented in this book. Make sure that you have it installed in the SQL Server.

To run the Entity Framework migration commands, open the Visual Studio Developer Command Prompt and navigate to the project's root folder. Then issue the following command:

```
> dnvm use default
```

The DNVM is the .NET SDK Manager and provides a set of command-line utilities to update and configure which runtime (DNX) to use.

Then issue the following command to generate Entity Framework migration code:

```
>  dnx ef migrations add MyMigrations
```

The DNX is the .NET Execution Environment and contains the code required to bootstrap and run an application.

The preceding command adds a Migrations folder under your project root and also creates a couple of class files in it. This command reads your appsettings.json file, DbContext class, and Customer entity class and generates some code. The generated class will be named MyMigrations, though you can supply any name of your choice. The code generated by running the preceding command is responsible for creating the ContactDb database and the Contacts table. Figure 1-16 shows the Migrations folder inside Solution Explorer.

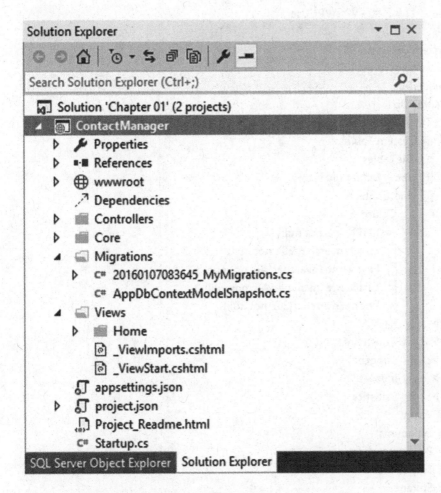

Figure 1-16. *Migrations folder in Solution Explorer*

So far you have added the migration code to your project. However, you haven't applied those migrations as yet. To apply them, issue the following command:

```
> dnx ef database update
```

This command will execute the migration code, and the database will be created for you. Figure 1-17 shows the generated ContactDb database and the Contacts table in SQL Server Object Explorer.

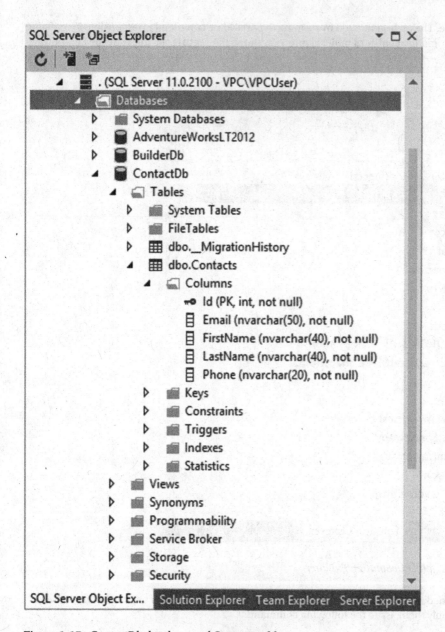

Figure 1-17. ContactDb database and Contacts table

Notice how data annotations such as [Table], [DatabaseGenerated], [Required], and [StringLength] are utilized while creating the Contacts table. The columns are marked as "not null" due to the [Required] attribute, and their lengths are decided by the [StringLength] attribute. The [DatabaseGenerated] attribute makes the Id column the primary key and also marks it as an identity column. Finally, the table name is set to Contacts due to the [Table] attribute.

■ **Note** From the perspective of the examples presented throughout this book, it doesn't matter how you create the database—manually using SQL Server Management Studio or using Entity Framework migration commands. I leave this choice to you. When you see instructions such as "create database for our application," use either of these methods to create the database.

That's it! Your application is complete. Run the application and test whether it works as expected by adding and deleting a few contacts.

Going Forward: From ASP.NET 5 to ASP.NET Core 1.0

This book uses cutting-edge technology—ASP.NET 5 RC1 and EF 7 RC1—to build all the examples. Using these not-yet-complete versions gives you a chance to see what's coming up next. It is exciting and fun to work with such cutting-edge technology. However, it has its own price—changes are inevitable!

As I finish this book, Microsoft has made an announcement that ASP.NET 5 will now be called ASP.NET Core 1.0 and Entity Framework 7 will be named Entity Framework Core 1.0. Based on this announcement and information available as of this writing, I am summarizing the changes below:

- .NET Core 5 will be called .NET Core 1.0

- ASP.NET 5 will be called ASP.NET Core 1.0

- ASP.NET MVC 6 will be termed ASP.NET Core MVC 1.0

- Entity Framework 7 will be named Entity Framework Core 1.0

Luckily, these changes primarily affect the nomenclature of packages, assemblies, and namespaces. These changes don't have much impact on classes, properties, and methods. I expect that a good amount of code discussed throughout this book will remain in a useful form even after these changes come into effect. However, there will be several areas where these changes will be reflected, and thus you will be required to modify the source code.

Although it's too early to give a precise list of all the changes, here are some prominent areas that will need your attention:

- NuGet packages, assemblies, and namespaces with current names of the form Microsoft.AspNet.* will change to Microsoft.AspNetCore.*. You will need to adjust Project.json and the code accordingly.

- NuGet packages, assemblies, and namespaces with current names of the form EntityFramework.* will change to Microsoft.EntityFrameworkCore.*. You will need to adjust Project.json and the code accordingly.

- The version numbers of all the above NuGet packages and assemblies will be reset to 1.0.

- Target framework monikers and versions (dnx451, dnxcore50) will change.

- Tooling and exact commands (dnvm, dnu, and dnx) will change.

I will be updating the source code of the examples discussed throughout this book onto the RC2 of the framework as needed. The updated source code will be made available for download on the Apress website. Of course, you can certainly update the source code yourself if you so wish. In fact, it would be a good opportunity for you to be a frontrunner in knowing these cutting-edge technologies.

Summary

The SOLID principles of object-oriented design is a set of five principles: Single Responsibility Principle (SRP), Open/Closed Principle (OCP), Liskov Substitution Principle (LSP), Interface Segregation Principle (ISP), and Dependency Inversion Principle (DIP). These principles will help you to create object-oriented systems that are robust, extensible, and maintainable.

Design patterns are time-proven solutions to recurring software-design problems. There are two popular catalogs of patterns: Gang of Four (GoF) patterns by Erich Gamma, Richard Helm, Ralph Johnson, and John Vlissides, and P of EAA by Martin Fowler.

Patterns are language independent, and you can apply them to server-side C# code as well as to the client-side JavaScript code. The remainder of this book will discuss SOLID principles, all the GoF patterns, and a few P of EAA, and also shows how JavaScript code can benefit from the use of patterns. To begin with, the next chapter will discuss the SOLID principles of object-oriented design.

CHAPTER 2

■ ■ ■

SOLID Principles

In the previous chapter, you were introduced to the SOLID principles of object-oriented design. This chapter will cover all of them in more detail. Moreover, each principle will be discussed along with a proof of concept example so as to reinforce your understanding. In order to grasp how these principles can help improve class design, the chapter will discuss wrong design first. Then, once you are clear about the problems created by the wrong design, this chapter will present the correct design, which rectifies the shortcomings of the improper design. The explanations will use UML class diagrams to convey the point. Although I won't go into the details of UML, for the sake of clarity I will include the necessary detailing of UML diagrams in the form of notes. To be specific, we will cover the following principles:

- Single Responsibility Principle (SRP)
- Open/Closed Principle (OCP)
- Liskov Substitution Principle (LSP)
- Interface Segregation Principle (ISP)
- Dependency Inversion Principle (DIP)

These principles can be applied to classes belonging to any layer of the application—data access, business logic, or user interface. The point is to arrive at a better class design that contributes to the flexible and maintainable code base.

■ **Note**   As mentioned in Chapter 1, the principles of object-oriented software design discussed in this chapter are elaborated by Robert C. Martin and Micah Martin in their book *Agile Principles, Patterns, and Practices in C#*. The acronym SOLID was introduced by Michael Feathers to help one remember these principles easily.

Single Responsibility Principle (SRP)

Single Responsibility Principle can be stated as follows: **A class should have only a single responsibility**. Any class is intended to do some work. That work can be as simple as holding an application state or as complex as resource-intensive processing. However, if a class is designed to carry multiple responsibilities, it can create problems at a later stage.

Suppose that you are building a web application that deals with customers and orders. As a part of the functionality, you are required to provide search functionality that searches a customer database on certain criteria. Now, let's say you created the CustomerSearch class as shown in Figure 2-1.

© Bipin Joshi 2016

B. Joshi, *Beginning SOLID Principles and Design Patterns for ASP.NET Developers*,
DOI 10.1007/978-1-4842-1848-8_2

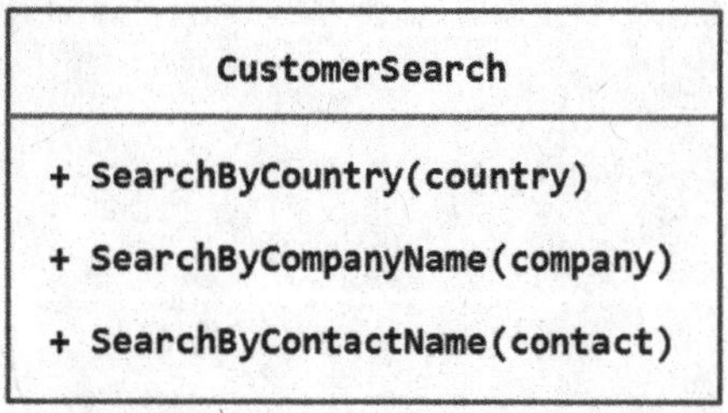

```
+------------------------------------------+
|             CustomerSearch               |
+------------------------------------------+
| + SearchByCountry(country)               |
|                                          |
| + SearchByCompanyName(company)           |
|                                          |
| + SearchByContactName(contact)           |
+------------------------------------------+
```

Figure 2-1. *A class for searching customer data*

As you can see, the CustomerSearch class has three public methods: SearchByCountry(), SearchByCompanyName(), and SearchByContactName(). These three methods search the customer table on the basis of supplied country, company name, and contact person, respectively, and return the search results as a list of Customer objects.

■ **Note** In UML class diagrams, a class is represented by a rectangle with the class name mentioned in the top compartment. Methods are listed inside the rectangle. The + sign indicates that a method is public.

So far, so good. Now, say that one day the need arises to export the search results into the Comma Separated Values (CSV) format so that the end user can download the results and open them in Excel or Notepad for further processing. To deal with this requirement, let's assume that you modified the CustomerSearch class as shown in Figure 2-2.

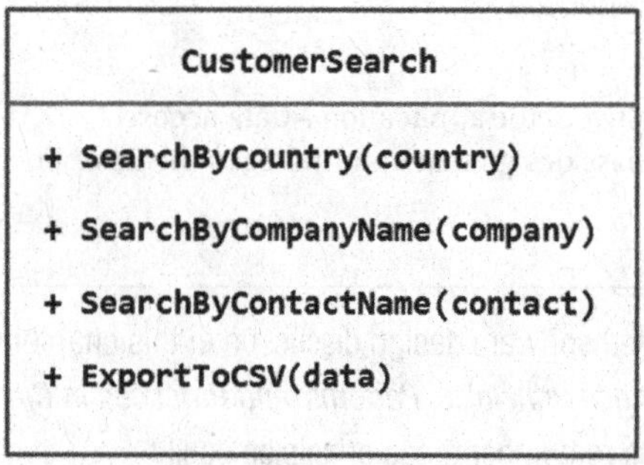

```
+------------------------------------------+
|             CustomerSearch               |
+------------------------------------------+
| + SearchByCountry(country)               |
|                                          |
| + SearchByCompanyName(company)           |
|                                          |
| + SearchByContactName(contact)           |
|                                          |
| + ExportToCSV(data)                      |
+------------------------------------------+
```

Figure 2-2. *Adding a method for exporting customer data*

The CustomerSearch class now has an additional method—ExportToCSV()—that takes the search results as its parameter and then generates the CSV equivalent for the purposes of downloading.

Although this design change sounds quite normal, it has a design flaw. The CustomerSearch class now has two responsibilities. Earlier, the CustomerSearch class was responsible only for searching the customer data; now it is also responsible for exporting the data. Imagine a situation where the need arose to export the data to XML format or PDF format. If that happened, you would need to change the CustomerSearch class again. Although there was no change in the search functionality of the CustomerSearch class (which was the original and primary responsibility of the class), you would need to change it, because the data-export functionality was changed. Any change in the CustomerSearch class would also require testing to ensure that the changes did not affect the rest of the application.

The root issue here is that the `CustomerSearch` class is being assigned multiple responsibilities. There are two possible reasons for changing `CustomerSearch`—change in search functionality and change in the data-export functionality. A change in either of those responsibilities requires a change in the `CustomerSearch` class. This design issue can be corrected if the `CustomerSearch` class is designed adhering to Single Responsibility Principle. Let's see how.

Have a look at Figure 2-3, which shows the modified class design.

Figure 2-3.   Class design after applying SRP

The modified design has two independent classes—`CustomerSearch` and `CustomerDataExporter`. The former class is given the responsibility of searching customer data. The responsibility of exporting search results is handled by the latter class using two methods—`ExportToCSV()` and `ExportToXML()`. This way, `CustomerSearch` and `CustomerDataExporter` each have one and only one responsibility. If in the future you need to export the data into some other format (say, PDF), you would need to modify the `CustomerDataExporter` class only. The `CustomerSearch` class remains unaffected by this change. This also means that only `CustomerDataExporter` requires retesting (since only it got changed). Now the `CustomerSearch` class has one and only one reason to change—change in the searching logic.

Just to make your understanding of SRP clear, let's translate the preceding example into an ASP.NET application. You will use the `Customers` table of the Northwind database as a source of customer data. The main view of the application is shown in Figure 2-4.

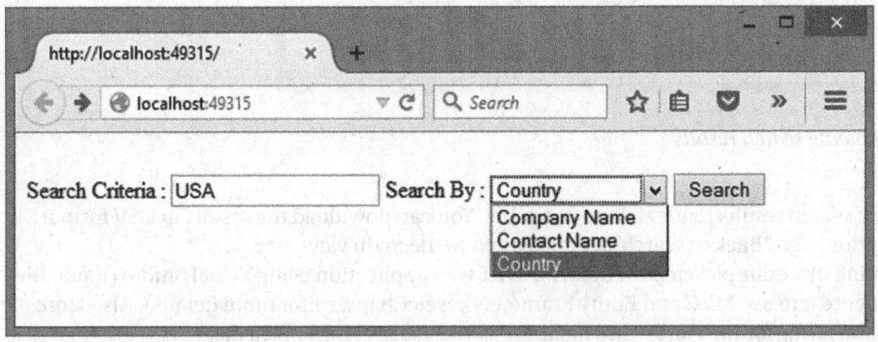

Figure 2-4.   Main view of the customer search application

As you can see, the main view consists of a textbox to specify search criteria, a dropdown list to select the column to search, and a Search button. Upon entering a search criteria and clicking the Search button, results are displayed in another view, as shown in Figure 2-5.

Figure 2-5. *A view showing search results*

The view showing search results renders them in a table. You can download the results in CSV format by clicking the Export button. The "Back to search" link takes you to the main view.

To begin developing this example, create a new ASP.NET web application using Visual Studio (name the project SRP) and configure it to use MVC and Entity Framework (see Chapter 1 for more details). Also store the database connection string for the Northwind database in the appsettings.json file.

Next, add a new class to the Core folder and write the code in it as shown in Listing 2-1.

Listing 2-1. Customer Model Class

```
[Table("Customers")]
public class Customer
{
    public string CustomerID { get; set; }
    public string CompanyName { get; set; }
    public string ContactName { get; set; }
    public string Country { get; set; }
}
```

The Customer class represents a customer from the Customers table and consists of four public properties—CustomerID, CompanyName, ContactName, and Country. Although the Customers table contains several other columns, the preceding code uses just four of them for the sake of simplicity.

Since the application needs to search data from the Northwind database, it needs an entity framework DbContext. So, add a new class in the Core folder and modify it as shown in Listing 2-2.

Listing 2-2. AppDbContext Class

```
public class AppDbContext : DbContext
{
    public DbSet<Customer> Customers { get; set; }

    protected override void OnConfiguring(DbContextOptionsBuilder optionsBuilder)
    {
        optionsBuilder.UseSqlServer(AppSettings.ConnectionString);
    }
}
```

The AppDbContext class inherits from DbContext and contains the Customers DbSet. The overridden OnConfiguring() method sets the SQL Server database to be used by using the UseSqlServer() method.

Next, add the CustomerSearch class in the Core folder and write the code as shown in Listing 2-3.

Listing 2-3. CustomerSearch Class

```
public class CustomerSearch
{
    public static List<Customer> SearchByCountry(string country)
    {
        using (AppDbContext db = new AppDbContext())
        {
            var query = from c in db.Customers
                        where c.Country.Contains(country)
                        orderby c.CustomerID ascending
                        select c;
            return query.ToList();
        }
    }
}
```

```
public static List<Customer> SearchByCompanyName(string company)
{
    using (AppDbContext db = new AppDbContext())
    {
        var query = from c in db.Customers
                    where c.CompanyName.Contains(company)
                    orderby c.CustomerID ascending
                    select c;
        return query.ToList();
    }
}

public static List<Customer> SearchByContactName(string contact)
{
    using (AppDbContext db = new AppDbContext())
    {
        var query = from c in db.Customers
                    where c.ContactName.Contains(contact)
                    orderby c.CustomerID ascending
                    select c;
        return query.ToList();
    }
}
}
```

The CustomerSearch class consists of three static methods—SearchByCountry(), SearchByCompany Name(), and SearchByContactName(). All three methods accept a single parameter (the search word) and return a generic list of Customer objects. These methods basically look for all the Customer entities whose search column (Country, CompanyName, and ContactName, respectively) contains the search keyword (country, company, and contact parameter, respectively).

Now add a CustomerDataExporter class in the Core folder and write the code shown in Listing 2-4 in it.

Listing 2-4. CustomerDataExporter Class

```
public class CustomerDataExporter
{
    public static string ExportToCSV(List<Customer> data)
    {
        StringBuilder sb = new StringBuilder();
        foreach(var item in data)
        {
            sb.AppendFormat("{0},{1},{2},{3}",
                                        item.CustomerID,
                                        item.CompanyName,
                                        item.ContactName,
                                        item.Country);
            sb.AppendLine();
        }
        return sb.ToString();
    }
```

```csharp
public static string ExportToXML(List<Customer> data)
{
    throw new NotImplementedException();
}

public static string ExportToPDF(List<Customer> data)
{
    throw new NotImplementedException();
}
}
```

The CustomerDataExporter class consists of three static methods—ExportToCSV(), ExportToXML(), and ExportToPDF(). Out of these three, only the ExportToCSV() is implemented in the class. The ExportToCSV() method accepts a generic list of Customer objects, Inside, it iterates through the list and generates a CSV using StringBuilder. Finally, the complete CSV string is returned to the caller.

In the beginning of this section, we discussed SRP, and our design of CustomerSearch and CustomerDataExporter adheres to SRP. Note that ExportToXML() and ExportToPDF() can be added to the CustomerDataExporter class at a later stage whenever the need arises.

Now that these two classes are ready, it's time to use them in the controller. Add HomeController to the Controllers folder and write the three actions (and a private helper method), as shown in Listing 2-5.

Listing 2-5. Index(), Search() and Export() Action Methods

```csharp
public IActionResult Index()
{
    return View();
}

public List<Customer> GetData(string criteria, string searchby)
{
    List<Customer> data = null;
    switch (searchby)
    {
        case "companyname":
            data = CustomerSearch.SearchByCompanyName(criteria);
            break;
        case "contactname":
            data = CustomerSearch.SearchByContactName(criteria);
            break;
        case "country":
            data = CustomerSearch.SearchByCountry(criteria);
            break;
    }
    return data;
}

[HttpPost]
```

```
    public IActionResult Search(string criteria,string searchby)
    {

List<Customer> model = GetData(criteria,searchby);
        ViewBag.Criteria = criteria;
        ViewBag.SearchBy = searchby;
        return View(model);
    }


    [HttpPost]
    public FileResult Export(string criteria, string searchby)
    {

List<Customer> data = GetData(criteria, searchby);
        string exportData = CustomerDataExporter. ExportToCSV(data);
        return File(System.Text.ASCIIEncoding.ASCII.GetBytes(exportData),
        "application/Excel");
    }
}
```

The job of the Index() action method is simply to return the Index view.

The GetData() method is a private helper method used by the other two actions. Its main job is to fetch customer data by calling methods on the CustomerSearch class. It accepts search criteria and searchby parameters. Inside, the code checks the searchby value and accordingly the SearchByCompanyName(), SearchByContactName, or SearchByCountry() methods of the CustomerSearch class are called. The GetData() method returns a list of Customer objects to the caller.

The Search() action is responsible for searching the Customers table for a specified criteria. The Index view submits to the Search() method. The criteria and searchby parameters are received from the submitted form through model binding. The model binding allows you to map and bind form field values with action parameters. The GetData() helper method is then called by passing the criteria and searchby parameters. The data returned from GetData() acts as the model for the Search view. Additionally, criteria and searchby values are passed to the view through ViewBag. This is necessary because if the user decides to export the data, your application needs to fetch the data again based on the criteria specified during the search operation.

The Export() action is called by the Export button on the search results page (see Figure 2-5). It takes the same two parameters as Search() does—criteria and searchby. Notice, however, that Export() returns FileResult, because you want the end user to download the CSV data as a file. Inside, the code fetches the required data using the GetData() method. Then this data is supplied to the ExportToCSV() method of the CustomerDataExporter class. The returned CSV string is wrapped inside a FileContentResult object using the File() method of the Controller base class. The first parameter of the File() method accepts the content of the file being returned. This parameter needs to be a byte array. The GetBytes() method converts the CSV string into an equivalent byte array. The second parameter of the File() method indicates the content type of the response. In this case the content type is set as application/Excel so that the end user can directly open the file in Excel if necessary.

This completes the HomeController. Now it's time to create the two views—Index.cshtml and Search.cshtml. Add two views—Index and Search—inside the Views/Home subfolder. The markup of the Index view is shown in Listing 2-6.

Listing 2-6. Markup of Index.cshtml

```html
<html>
    <head>
        <title>Index</title>
    </head>
    <body>
        <br />
        <form asp-controller="Home" asp-action="Search" method="post">
            <label for="criteria">Search Criteria :</label>
            <input name="criteria" />
            <label for="searchby">Search By :</label>
            <select name="searchby">
                <option value="companyname">Company Name</option>
                <option value="contactname">Contact Name</option>
                <option value="country">Country</option>
            </select>
            <input type="submit" value="Search" />
        </form>
    </body>
</html>
```

The Index view uses tag helper of MVC to render a form that submits to the Search() action of the HomeController using POST method. Notice how the asp-controller and asp-action attributes of the form tag helper specify these details. This form houses HTML elements to render a page as shown in Figure 2-4. Notice that the name of the textbox is set to criteria and that of the select element is set to searchby. This is necessary in order for the model binding to work as expected.

The markup of Search.cshtml is shown in Listing 2-7.

Listing 2-7. Markup of Search.cshtml

```html
@model List<SRP.Core.Customer>

<html>
    <head>
        <title>Search</title>
    </head>
    <body>
        <h1>Search Results</h1>
        <form asp-controller="Home" asp-action="Export" method="post">
            <input type="hidden" name="criteria" value="@ViewBag.Criteria" />
            <input type="hidden" name="searchby" value="@ViewBag.SearchBy" />
            <input type="submit" value="Export" />
        </form>
```

```
        <table border="1" cellpadding="5">
            @foreach(var item in Model)
            {
                <tr>
                    <td>@item.CustomerID</td>
                    <td>@item.CompanyName</td>
                    <td>@item.ContactName</td>
                    <td>@item.Country</td>
                </tr>
            }
        </table>
        <br />
        <a asp-controller="Home" asp-action="Index">Back to search</a>
    </body>
</html>
```

The Search view begins by specifying the model of the view to List<SRP.Core.Customer>. The top part of the page has the Export button wrapped inside a <form> element. Notice that this <form> submits to the Export() action of the HomeController. The Search() action passes Criteria and SearchBy properties to this view, and their values are stored in hidden fields. This is necessary, because we need these values to exist inside the Export() action.

The Search view then iterates through the model and renders a table showing CustomerID, CompanyName, ContactName, and Country properties. At the bottom of the view, a hyperlink tag helper is used to render a link pointing back to the Index action.

This completes the application. Run the application through Visual Studio and enter some search criteria into the Index view. When the Search view is displayed in the browser, click on the Export button and see whether a CSV file can be downloaded.

Once you test the application, take a pause and see how you have applied the Single Responsibility Principle to the CustomerSearch and CustomerDataExporter classes. What are the places that will be affected by a future change in the export data format? The primary place affected is the CustomerDataExporter class itself. The second place is the Search view, where you have the Export button. You may need to add a format selection dropdown list to this view (with options such as CSV, XML, and PDF). Accordingly, the Export() action will also need to be changed. In any case, the CustomerSearch class remains unchanged, because data export is not its functionality. The only reason to alter CustomerSearch would be to make a modification to the search functionality. Along the same lines, the only reason to alter CustomerDataExporter would be to change the export data format.

Open/Closed Principle (OCP)

The Open/Closed Principle can be stated as: **A class should be open for extension but closed for modification**.

When you design classes for a moderately complex system, chances are that they will evolve over a time. Usually a small change in the functionality is carried out by modifying the class itself. Although this might work in simple applications, there is always a risk. When you change a class, it's possible that the change may adversely affect some other part of the system. This requires retesting the class. Wouldn't it be nice if we could add functionality without touching the class that has already been tested and is working as expected? That's what OCP is about.

OCP suggests that a class should be open for extensions. This way our need to add extra functionality is catered to. But at the same time, OCP tells us that the class should be closed for any changes. This ensures that the code base (either source code form or compiled form) of the class remains untouched when the new functionality is added to the system. How is this possible? You can accomplish this by abstracting the class design using either inheritance or interfaces. Let's look at this in more detail with an example.

Suppose you are developing a web application that includes an online tax calculator. Users can visit a web page, specify their income and expense details, and calculate the tax payable using some mathematical calculation. Considering this, you created a class—TaxCalculator—as shown in Figure 2-6.

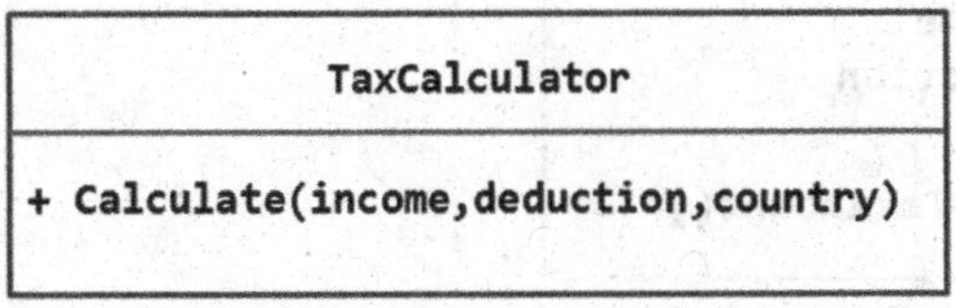

```
┌─────────────────────────────────────────────┐
│                                             │
│         TaxCalculator                       │
│                                             │
├─────────────────────────────────────────────┤
│                                             │
│ + Calculate(income,deduction,country)       │
│                                             │
└─────────────────────────────────────────────┘
```

Figure 2-6. *Class for calculating taxes*

The TaxCalculator class has a single public method, Calculate(), that accepts total income, total deduction, and country of the user. Of course, a real-world tax calculator would do much more, but this simple design is sufficient for our example. The country information is necessary, because tax rules are different across different countries. The pseudo-code of the Calculate() method is shown in Listing 2-8.

Listing 2-8. Pseudo-code of the Calculate() Method

```
public decimal Calculate(decimal income, decimal deduction,string country)
{
    decimal taxAmount = 0;
    decimal taxableIncome = income - deduction;

    switch(country)
    {
        case "India":
            //calculation here
            break;
        case "USA":
            //calculation here
            break;
        case "UK":
            //calculation here
            break;
    }
    return taxAmount;
}
```

The Calculate() method determines the taxable income by subtracting total deduction from total income. A switch statement then checks the country of the user. Depending on the country, tax is calculated and the taxAmount variable is assigned the tax amount (not shown in the code). Although this code looks fine, there is a catch. It considers only three countries at the moment. Imagine a case where the web application becomes popular and users from several countries start using it. When that happens, the TaxCalculator class needs to change to accommodate the new countries and their corresponding taxation rules. Thus, the current design violates OCP.

Now, let's rectify the class design. Have a look at Figure 2-7.

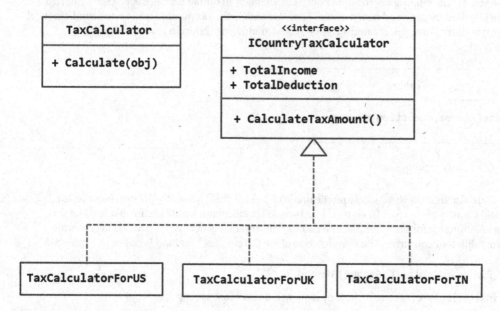

Figure 2-7. *Class design that adheres to OCP*

■ **Note** In Figure 2-7, the first compartment of ICountryTaxCalculator indicates that it's an interface, the second compartment contains a list of properties, and the third compartment contains a method. The classes that implement an interface are shown connected with it using a dotted line with an unfilled arrowhead pointing toward the interface being implemented.

The modified design has an abstraction in the form of the ICountryTaxCalculator interface. This interface contains two properties—TotalIncome and TotalDeduction—and one method—CalculateTaxAmount(). The tax calculation logic is no longer included with the TaxCalculator class. Instead, there are several classes, such as TaxCalculatorForUS, TaxCalculatorForUK, and TaxCalculatorForIN, each implementing ICountryTaxCalculator. This way, tax calculation logic for each country is wrapped in an independent unit. Notice the change to the Calculate() method of TaxCalculator. It now accepts a single parameter, obj, of type ICountryTaxCalculator. The pseudo-code for the modified Calculate() method is shown in Listing 2-9.

Listing 2-9. Modified Calculate() Method

```
public decimal Calculate(ICountryTaxCalculator obj)
{
    decimal taxAmount = 0;
    // some more logic here
    taxAmount = obj.CalculateTaxAmount();
    return taxAmount;
}
```

As you can see, now the `Calculate()` method doesn't check for the country. That's because it receives an object that implements `ICountryTaxCalculator`. So, calling `CalculateTaxAmount()` returns the tax amount no matter which country the user belongs to. Thus, the `TaxCalculator` class now conforms to OCP. If you need to calculate for a country not currently covered, all you need to do is to create another class that implements `ICountryTaxCalculator` and write the tax calculation logic there. `TaxCalculator` is open for extending the functionality (by adding new country-specific classes that implement `ICountryTaxCalculator`), but at the same time, it is closed for modification (you don't need to change its source code).

Now that you know what OCP is, let's translate this example into a project. In this example you will develop a web application as shown in Figure 2-8.

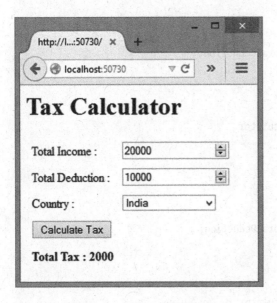

Figure 2-8. *Online tax calculator application*

This application displays two textboxes for entering total income and total deduction, respectively. A dropdown list displays a list of countries. Clicking on the Calculate Tax button does the tax calculation and displays the total tax amount to the user.

To begin developing this example, create a new ASP.NET web application using Visual Studio and configure it to use MVC (see Chapter 1 for more details).

Next, add the `ICountryTaxCalculator` interface to the `Core` folder and write the code shown in Listing 2-10.

Listing 2-10. ICountryTaxCalculator Interface

```
public interface ICountryTaxCalculator
{
    decimal TotalIncome { get; set; }
    decimal TotalDeduction { get; set; }
    decimal CalculateTaxAmount();
}
```

The ICountryTaxCalculator interface has two properties—TotalIncome and TotalDeduction—and a method—CalculateTaxAmount(). ICountryTaxCalculator is implemented by three classes—TaxCalculatorForUS, TaxCalculatorForUK, and TaxCalculatorForIN. Add these three classes to the Core folder. Listing 2-11 shows these classes after ICountryTaxCalculator has been implemented.

Listing 2-11. TaxCalculatorForUS, TaxCalculatorForUK, and TaxCalculatorForIN Classes

```
public class TaxCalculatorForUS: ICountryTaxCalculator
{
    public decimal TotalIncome { get; set; }
    public decimal TotalDeduction { get; set; }

    public decimal CalculateTaxAmount()
    {
        decimal taxableIncome = TotalIncome - TotalDeduction;
        return taxableIncome * 30 / 100;
    }
}

public class TaxCalculatorForUK: ICountryTaxCalculator
{
    public decimal TotalIncome { get; set; }
    public decimal TotalDeduction { get; set; }

    public decimal CalculateTaxAmount()
    {
        decimal taxableIncome = TotalIncome - TotalDeduction;
        return taxableIncome * 35 / 100;
    }
}

public class TaxCalculatorForIN: ICountryTaxCalculator
{
    public decimal TotalIncome { get; set; }
    public decimal TotalDeduction { get; set; }

    public decimal CalculateTaxAmount()
    {
        decimal taxableIncome = TotalIncome - TotalDeduction;
        return taxableIncome * 20 / 100;
    }
}
```

The CalculateTaxAmount() method implemented by these classes finds taxable income by subtracting deductions from the income. This value is treated as a taxable income, and a certain percentage of it (30%, 35%, and 20%, respectively) is returned to the caller as the tax amount.

Now add TaxCalculator class to the Core folder and modify it as shown in Listing 2-12.

Listing 2-12. TaxCalculator Class

```
public class TaxCalculator
{
    public decimal Calculate(ICountryTaxCalculator obj)
    {
        decimal taxAmount = obj.CalculateTaxAmount();
        //do something more if needed
        return taxAmount;
    }
}
```

The Calculate() method accepts an object of a type that implements ICountryTaxCalculator and invokes CalculateTaxAmount() method. The tax amount is then returned to the caller. Although not required in this example, you may do some extra processing in addition to calling CalculateTaxAmount().

Next, add a class to the Models folder and name it IncomeDetails. The IncomeDetails class acts as a view model for the Index view and is shown in Listing 2-13.

Listing 2-13. IncomeDetails Class

```
public class IncomeDetails
{
    public decimal TotalIncome { get; set; }
    public decimal TotalDeduction { get; set; }
    public string Country { get; set; }
}
```

The IncomeDetails class holds total income, total deduction, and country when the user fills in the details on the main page of the application and submits the form.

Now, add the HomeController class to the Controllers folder and modify it to have two actions, as shown in Listing 2-14.

Listing 2-14. Index() Action Methods

```
public IActionResult Index()
{
    return View();
}


[HttpPost]
public IActionResult Index(IncomeDetails obj)
{
    ICountryTaxCalculator t = null;
    switch(obj.Country)
    {
        case "USA":
            t = new TaxCalculatorForUS ();
            break;
        case "UK":
            t = new TaxCalculatorForUK();
            break;
```

```
        case "IN":
            t = new TaxCalculatorForIN ();
            break;
    }
    t.TotalIncome = obj.TotalIncome;
    t.TotalDeduction = obj.TotalDeduction;
    TaxCalculator cal = new TaxCalculator();
    ViewBag.TotalTax = cal.Calculate(t);
    return View("Index", obj);
}
```

The first Index() action deals with GET requests (the initial request to the application), and the second Index() deals with the POST requests as indicated by the [HttpPost] attribute. The second Index() action takes a parameter of the view model type—IncomeDetails. The model-binding framework of MVC will fill in this parameter for you.

Inside, you must check the Country of a user and accordingly instantiate TaxCalculatorForUS, TaxCalculatorForUK, or TaxCalculatorForIN. Notice that variable t is of type ICountryTaxCalculator—the interface type. The TotalIncome and TotalDeduction properties of the ICountryTaxCalculator object are then set to the corresponding properties of the view model. TaxCalculator is then instantiated, and its Calculate() method is called by passing the ICountryTaxCalculator object to it. The tax amount is stored in the ViewBag so that it can be displayed on the Index view.

Now the final piece of the application—the Index view. Add Index.cshtml to the Home subfolder within the Views folder and enter the markup shown in Listing 2-15 into it.

Listing 2-15. Markup of Index.cshtml

```
@model OCP.Models.IncomeDetails

<html>
<head>
    <title></title>
</head>
<body>
    <h1>Tax Calculator</h1>
    <form asp-controller="Home" asp-action="Calculate" method="post">
        <table cellpadding="5">
            <tr>
                <td><label asp-for="TotalIncome">Total Income :</label></td>
                <td><input type="number" asp-for="TotalIncome" /></td>
            </tr>
            <tr>
                <td><label asp-for="TotalDeduction">Total Deduction :</label></td>
                <td><input type="number" asp-for="TotalDeduction" /></td>
            </tr>
            <tr>
                <td><label asp-for="Country">Country :</label></td>
                <td>
                    <select asp-for="Country">
                        <option value="USA">United States</option>
                        <option value="UK">United Kingdom</option>
                        <option value="IN">India</option>
```

```
            </select>
        </td>
    </tr>
    <tr>
        <td colspan="2"><input type="submit" value="Calculate Tax" /></td>
    </tr>
    <tr>
        <td><strong>Total Tax : @ViewBag.TotalTax</strong></td>
    </tr>
</table>
    </form>
</body>
</html>
```

The Index view markup is quite straightforward and uses tag helpers to render a <form> that submits to the Calculate() action of the HomeController. Notice that the two textboxes and the dropdown list are bound to the respective properties of the model using the asp-form attribute. Also notice that at the end of the view, TotalTax is outputted from the ViewBag.

This completes the application. Run the application and test whether it works as expected.

From our previous discussion you know that the TaxCalculator class conforms to OCP. If tax needs to be calculated for additional countries, where would the change be made? First, you would need to create a class for that country and implement ICountryTaxCalculator in it. The CalculateTaxAmount() of the new class will take care of the tax calculation for that country. Second, you need to change the dropdown list on the Index view to include this additional country. Finally, the switch statement of the second Index() method needs to be adjusted to include this country. These changes are quite obvious because they all are related to the additional requirement. Controller and view will change in any case due to the change in the user interface. However, our design ensures that the TaxCalculator class remains unchanged.

■ **Note**   The preceding example uses interfaces to represent the tax calculations. As an exercise, modify the same example to use inheritance; that is, a common base class with abstract members being inherited by TaxCalculatorForUS, TaxCalculatorForUK, and TaxCalculatorForIN classes.

Liskov Substitution Principle (LSP)

Liskov Substitution Principle can be stated as: **A type must be substitutable by its subtypes without altering the correctness of the application.**

In Chapter 1 we discussed polymorphic behavior through inheritance and interfaces. Suppose there is a class named Class1, and two classes—Class2 and Class3—inherit from Class1. Then objects of Class2 and Class3 can be passed wherever Class1 is expected. Just to put this in code, consider this:

```
Class1 obj = null;
obj = new Class2(); //ok
obj = new Class3(); //ok
```

The preceding code fragment declares a variable obj of type Class1. It then assigns an object of type Class2 to obj. This is allowed because Class2 is said to inherit from Class1. If you remove this inheritance link between Class1 and Class2, you will immediately see an error flagged in the Visual Studio code editor. The same can be said about the third line, where obj points to an object of Class3.

The preceding example uses inheritance, but you can demonstrate similar behavior using an interface. For example, let's say there is an interface IInterface that is implemented by classes Class2 and Class3. Then you could have written:

```
IInterface obj = null;
obj = new Class2(); //ok
obj = new Class3(); //ok
```

Now, this polymorphic behavior is part and parcel of C# language features, but it is a developer's responsibility to ensure that such a polymorphic setup doesn't introduce any errors or inaccuracies into the system. Let's try to understand how this can happen with an example.

Let's assume that you are developing a big portal. As a part of the requirements you are expected to provide a good amount of customization to the end users. The customization spans various levels of the system, such as global-level customization, section-level customization, and user-specific customization. Considering this requirement, you arrive at a design as shown in Figure 2-9.

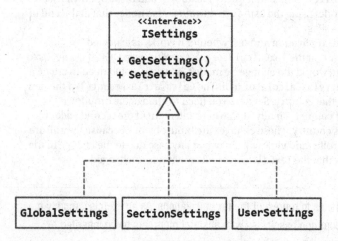

Figure 2-9. *Classes for customizable portal application*

As you can see, there is an interface ISettings that defines two methods, GetSettings() and SetSettings(). These two methods, when implemented, are intended to retrieve customization settings from the database and save them to the database respectively.

The ISettings interface is implemented by three classes—GlobalSettings, SectionSettings, and UserSettings. GlobalSettings are settings that have effects at the whole-application level, such as title, theme, and communication. SectionSettings are applicable to the individual sections of the portal, such as News, Weather, Sports, and so on. These settings could include their appearance and placement on the page. The UserSettings are settings for a specific user, such as e-mail and notification preferences. Further, let's assume that you create a class SettingsHelper that encapsulates the inner workings of setting and getting the settings for all the types of settings. This class is shown in Figure 2-10.

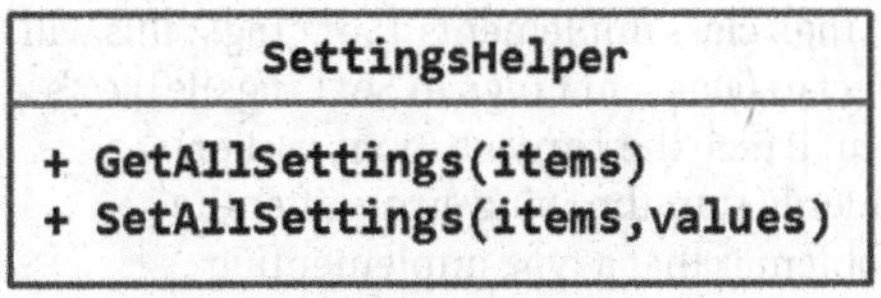

```
       SettingsHelper
+ GetAllSettings(items)
+ SetAllSettings(items,values)
```

Figure 2-10. *SettingsHelper class*

The SettingsHelper class consists of two methods—GetAllSettings() and SetAllSettings(). The GetAllSettings() method accepts a list of objects implementing the ISettings interface. Inside, it iterates through that list and calls GetSettings() on each object in order to retrieve the settings. Finally, it returns all the settings of all the ISettings objects to the caller. Along the same lines, the SetSettings() method accepts a list of ISettings objects and a list of actual settings for each ISettings object passed.

Although we won't go into the exact code of these two methods, it is obvious that both methods will have some sort of loop, such as foreach. With every iteration GetSettings() or SetSettings() will be called on the respective ISettings object. See the following pseudo-code for the sake of clarity:

```
// inside GetAllSettings()
foreach (ISettings item in items)
{
  item.GetSettings();
}

// inside SetAllSettings()
foreach (ISettings item in items)
{
  item.SetSettings(values);
}
```

So far, so good. Everything is working as expected with this design in place. Now suppose that a requirement arises that the application should support guest users. These users are like other registered users with one exception—since they are guest users, they can't save any customization or preferences. They do get some default settings applied to various parts of the application. To incorporate this change, create an additional class—GuestSettings—that implements ISettings. Since GuestSettings is not supposed to save any settings to the database, you won't implement the SetSettings() method. So, the SetSettings() of GuestSettings will look like this:

```
public void SetSettings(Dictionary<string, string> settings)
{
    throw new NotImplementedException();
}
```

Can you sense some problem there? Although the GuestSettings class implements ISettings, this will cause SettingsHelper to break. That's because if you pass an object of GuestSettings to SettingsHelper's SetAllSettings() method, it will attempt to call SetSettings() on it (see the foreach loops earlier) and will generate an exception. So, a working application will suddenly start throwing errors after the introduction of the GuestSettings class. The root cause of the problem is that a type implementing ISettings (GuestSettings in this case) violates LSP by doing something that affects the correctness of the application (throwing an exception in this case).

How do you correct this problem? In this specific example, you can split the ISettings interface into two—IReadableSettings and IWritableSettings—each defining a specific operation. The modified design is shown in Figure 2-11.

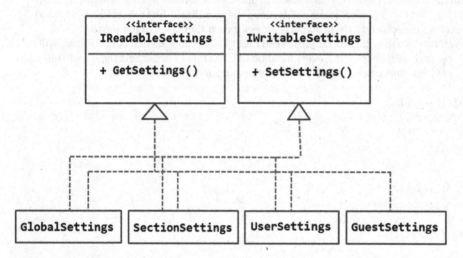

Figure 2-11. *Modified class design*

The methods of ISettings are split into two separate interfaces: IReadableSettings and IWritableSettings. The IReadableSettings interface contains only GetSettings(), whereas IWritableSettings contains SetSettings(). Notice that on the one hand, IReadableSettings is implemented by all the classes—GlobalSettings, SectionSettings, UserSettings, and GuestSettings. On the other hand, IWritableSettings is implemented by only three of them—GlobalSettings, SectionSettings, and UserSettings.

The SettingsHelper class will still contain GetAllSettings() and SetAllSettings(). Earlier, both of these methods were used to accept a list of ISettings objects. Now GetAllSettings() will accept a list of IReadableSettings objects, whereas SetAllSettings() will accept a list of IWritableSettings objects. This design conforms to LSP, because objects are not only substitutable but also work correctly.

To make your understanding clear, let's translate this scenario into an application. In this example you will develop a web application as shown in Figure 2-12.

Figure 2-12. *Displaying all settings*

The main page of the application displays all the default settings for all the four types: GlobalSettings, SectionSettings, UserSettings, and GuestSettings. The button on the top allows you to change the settings. In this example, we won't incorporate any database access to simplify our code. Upon successfully changing the settings, a success page is displayed as shown in Figure 2-13.

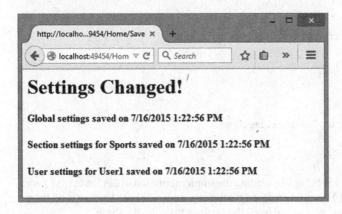

Figure 2-13. *Success message after changing the settings*

To begin developing this example, create a new ASP.NET web application using Visual Studio and configure it to use MVC (see Chapter 1 for more details).

Since LSP is better understood when you are familiar with the inaccuracies introduced by the code, you will first build the erroneous version of the application; then you will correct the application as per the proper design.

Add the ISettings interface to the Core folder and modify it as shown in Listing 2-16.

Listing 2-16. ISettings Interface

```
public interface ISettings
{
    Dictionary<string,string> GetSettings();
    string SetSettings(Dictionary<string,string> settings);
}
```

The GetSettings() method returns settings as a dictionary. The SetSettings() method accepts a dictionary of settings and returns a success message.

Now add four classes: GlobalSettings, SectionSettings, UserSettings, and GuestSettings in the Core folder and implement ISettings in all of them. Since the first three classes are quite similar, we won't discuss them all here. The code in Listing 2-17 shows the GlobalSettings class.

Listing 2-17. GlobalSettings Class

```
public class GlobalSettings :ISettings
{
    public Dictionary<string, string> GetSettings()
    {
        Dictionary<string, string> settings = new Dictionary<string, string>();
        settings.Add("Theme", "Summer");
        return settings;
    }

    public string SetSettings(Dictionary<string, string> settings)
    {
        foreach (var item in settings)
        {
            //save to database
        }
        return "Global settings saved on " + DateTime.Now;
    }
}
```

The GlobalSettings class implements ISettings by writing the implementation of GetSettings() and SetSettings() methods. The GetSettings() method creates a dictionary, adds a Themes key to it, and then returns the dictionary. In a more realistic case, you would fetch the settings from the database.

The SetSettings() method iterates through the dictionary of settings and is supposed to save them to the database. It returns a success message and time stamp to the caller.

You can implement SectionSettings and UserSettings in a similar manner or grab them from the code download of this book. The GuestSettings class is the source of error in this example and is shown in Listing 2-18.

Listing 2-18. GuestSettings Class

```
public class GuestSettings : ISettings
{
    public Dictionary<string, string> GetSettings()
    {
        Dictionary<string, string> settings = new Dictionary<string, string>();
        settings.Add("GuestName", "John");
        return settings;
    }

    public string SetSettings(Dictionary<string, string> settings)
    {
        throw new NotImplementedException();
    }
}
```

The SetSettings() method of GuestSettings is important for our testing. As explained earlier, this method throws a NotImplementedException because guests are not allowed to save customization settings.

Now add a SettingsHelper class to the Core folder and write the code in it, as shown in Listing 2-19.

Listing 2-19. SettingsHelper Class

```
public class SettingsHelper
{
    public static Dictionary<ISettings, Dictionary<string, string>>
GetAllSettings(List<ISettings> items)
    {
        var allSettings = new Dictionary<ISettings, Dictionary<string, string>>();
        foreach (ISettings item in items)
        {
            allSettings.Add(item, item.GetSettings());
        }
        return allSettings;
    }

    public static List<string> SetAllSettings(List<ISettings> items,
    List<Dictionary<string, string>> values)
    {
        List<string> messages = new List<string>();
        for (int i = 0; i < items.Count; i++)
        {
            messages.Add(items[i].SetSettings(values[i]));
        }
        return messages;
    }
}
```

The GetAllSettings() method accepts a list of objects that implement the ISettings interface. Inside, the code iterates through the list and invokes GetSettings() on each ISettings object. The settings returned by GetSettings() are stored in a dictionary. The ISettings object under consideration acts as the key of the dictionary. Once GetSettings() is called on all the objects, the allSettings dictionary is returned to the caller.

The SetAllSettings() method accepts a list of objects implementing ISettings and a list of dictionary objects containing their settings. Inside, the code iterates through the list of ISettings objects and invokes SetSettings() on them one by one. The success message returned after calling SetSettings() is stored in another list, which is returned to the caller once the looping completes.

Next, add HomeController to the Controllers folder and add a constructor to it, as shown in Listing 2-20.

Listing 2-20. Constructor of HomeController

```
public class HomeController : Controller
{
    List<ISettings> settings = new List<ISettings>();

    public HomeController()
    {
        GlobalSettings g = new GlobalSettings();
        SectionSettings s = new SectionSettings("Sports");
        UserSettings u = new UserSettings("User1");
        GuestSettings gu = new GuestSettings();

        settings.Add(g);
        settings.Add(s);
        settings.Add(u);
        settings.Add(gu);
    }
}
```

The code declares a list of ISettings objects (LSP.Core namespace), which is populated in the constructor. Inside the constructor the code creates one instance each of GlobalSettings, SectionSettings, UserSettings, and GuestSettings classes. These instances are added to the settings list for later use.

Now, add the Index() action method to the HomeController as shown in Listing 2-21.

Listing 2-21. Fetching Default Settings

```
public IActionResult Index()
{
    var allSettings = SettingsHelper.GetAllSettings(settings);
    return View(allSettings);
}
```

The code uses SettingsHelper and invokes its GetAllSettings() method by passing the settings list to it. The returned settings are passed as a model to the Index view.

Next, add the Save() method to the HomeController as shown in Listing 2-22.

Listing 2-22. Save() Action Method

```
public IActionResult Save()
{
    List<Dictionary<string, string>> newSettings = new List<Dictionary<string, string>>();

    Dictionary<string, string> app = new Dictionary<string, string>();
    app.Add("Theme", "Winter");

    Dictionary<string, string> sec = new Dictionary<string, string>();
    sec.Add("Title", "Music");

    Dictionary<string, string> usr = new Dictionary<string, string>();
    usr.Add("DisplayName", "Tom");

    Dictionary<string, string> gst = new Dictionary<string, string>();
    gst.Add("GuestName", "Jerry");

    newSettings.Add(app);
    newSettings.Add(sec);
    newSettings.Add(usr);
    newSettings.Add(gst);

    List<string> model = SettingsHelper.SetAllSettings(settings, newSettings);

    return View(model);
}
```

The Index view submits the form to the Save() action method. Inside, the code creates four Dictionary objects and stores some new settings in them. In a more realistic case you would accept these settings from the end user and then fill the Dictionary objects with those user-specified values. Then these dictionaries are added one by one to the newSettings list. Finally, SetAllSettings() method of SettingsHelper is called by passing the list of ISettings objects and newSettings. The success messages returned from SetAllSettings() are sent as a model to the Save view.

Add two views to the Home subfolder in the Views folder—Index.cshtml and Save.cshtml. The markup that goes inside Index.cshtml is shown in Listing 2-23.

Listing 2-23. Markup of Index.cshtml

```
@model Dictionary<LSP.Core.ISettings,Dictionary<string,string>>

...
<body>
    <h1>All Settings</h1>
    <form asp-controller="Home" asp-action="Save" method="post">
        <input type="submit" value="Change Settings" />
    </form>
```

```
<table border="1" cellpadding="10">
    @foreach(var item in Model)
    {
        <tr>
            <td>@item.Key.ToString()</td>
            <td>
                @foreach(var subItem in item.Value)
                {
                    <div>@subItem.Key = @subItem.Value</div>
                }
            </td>
        </tr>
    }
</table>
</body>
```

The Index view receives a dictionary as its model. The keys of this dictionary are the ISettings objects whereas its values are Dictionary objects containing the settings. The Index view consists of a small <form> to house the Change Settings button. This form submits to the Save() action you created earlier. The outer foreach loop iterates through the Model and displays item.Key, while the inner foreach loop iterates through the Value and displays the Key and Value pairs.

The markup of the Save view is shown in Listing 2-24.

Listing 2-24. Markup of Save View

```
@model List<string>

...
<body>
    <h1>Settings Changed!</h1>
    @foreach(var item in Model)
    {
        <h4>@item</h4>
    }
</body>
```

The Save view is quite straightforward. It receives a list of success messages as its model. A foreach loop iterates through the model and displays the messages to the user.

This completes the application. Run the application and check whether the main page resembles Figure 2-12. If you click on the Change Settings button, the application will throw an exception, as shown in Figure 2-14.

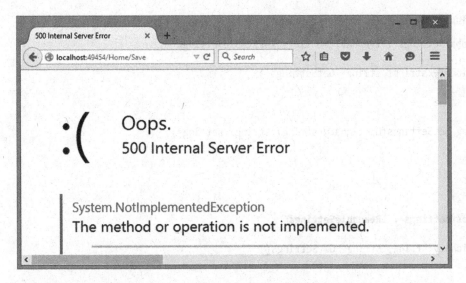

Figure 2-14. *Application throws NotImplementedException*

As expected, the application throws `NotImplementedException` because the `SaveAllSettings()` method of `SettingsHelper` attempts to call `SetSettings()` on a `GuestSettings` object.

This is a violation of LSP. Let's correct the error by implementing the design we discussed earlier. Add two interfaces to the `Core` folder—`IReadableSettings` and `IWritableSettings`. These interfaces are shown in Listing 2-25.

Listing 2-25. IReadableSettings and IWritableSettings Interfaces

```
public interface IReadableSettings
{
    Dictionary<string, string> GetSettings();
}

public interface IWritableSettings
{
    string SetSettings(Dictionary<string, string> settings);
}
```

Now `IReadableSettings` contains only `GetSettings()`, whereas `IWritableSettings` contains only `SetSettings()`. Modify the `GlobalSettings`, `SectionSettings`, and `UserSettings` classes to implement `IReadableSettings` as well as `IWritableSettings`. Also modify the `GuestSettings` class to implement only the `IReadableSettings` interface.

To save some space, all of these classes are not shown here. Listing 2-26 shows the affected parts of the `GlobalSettings` and `GuestSettings` classes.

Listing 2-26. Modified GlobalSettings and GuestSettings

```
public class GlobalSettings : IReadableSettings,IWritableSettings
{
    public Dictionary<string, string> GetSettings()
    {
      ...
    }
    public string SetSettings(Dictionary<string, string> settings)
    {
      ...
    }
}


public class GuestSettings : IReadableSettings
{
    public Dictionary<string, string> GetSettings()
    {
      ...
    }
}
```

Notice the code marked in bold letters and how the interfaces are implemented. Also notice that GuestSettings now has only the GetSettings() method because it implements only IReadableSettings. Now open the SettingsHelper class and modify its methods as shown in Listing 2-27.

Listing 2-27. Modified SettingsHelper

```
public class SettingsHelper
{
    public static Dictionary<IReadableSettings, Dictionary<string, string>> GetAllSettings(L
    ist<IReadableSettings> items)
    {
        var allSettings = new Dictionary<IReadableSettings, Dictionary<string, string>>();
        foreach (IReadableSettings item in items)
        {
            allSettings.Add(item, item.GetSettings());
        }
        return allSettings;
    }

    public static List<string> SetAllSettings(List<IWritableSettings> items,
List<Dictionary<string, string>> values)
    {
        List<string> messages = new List<string>();
        for (int i = 0; i < items.Count; i++)
        {
            messages.Add(items[i].SetSettings(values[i]));
        }
        return messages;
    }
}
```

Note that the GetAllSettings() method uses the IReadableSettings interface instead of ISettings. Similarly, the SetAllSettings() method uses the IWritableSettings interface instead of ISettings. Apart from this change, the other functionality is identical to the previous version.

Next, open the HomeController and modify its constructor, as shown in Listing 2-28.

Listing 2-28. Modified HomeController constructor

```
public class HomeController : Controller
{
    List<IReadableSettings> readableSettings = new List<IReadableSettings>();
    List<IWritableSettings> writableSettings = new List<IWritableSettings>();

    public HomeController()
    {
        GlobalSettings g = new GlobalSettings();

        SectionSettings s = new SectionSettings("Sports");
        UserSettings u = new UserSettings("User1");
        GuestSettings gu = new GuestSettings();

        readableSettings.Add(g);
        readableSettings.Add(s);
        readableSettings.Add(u);
        readableSettings.Add(gu);

        writableSettings.Add(g);
        writableSettings.Add(s);
        writableSettings.Add(u);
    }
```

There are two separate lists—one for IReadableSettings objects and one for IWritableSettings object. The constructor fills four objects in the readableSettings list and fills three objects in the writableSettings list. In this case, the GuestSettings object can't be stored in writableSettings, because it doesn't implement the IWritableSettings interface.

The Index() and Save() methods will also undergo a minor modification. Their modified part is shown in Listing 2-29.

Listing 2-29. Modified Index() and Save() Actions

```
public IActionResult Index()
{
    var allSettings = SettingsHelper.GetAllSettings(readableSettings);
    return View(allSettings);
}

[HttpPost]
public IActionResult Save()
{
    ...
```

```
newSettings.Add(app);
newSettings.Add(sec);
newSettings.Add(usr);

List<string> model = SettingsHelper.SetAllSettings(writableSettings, newSettings);

return View(model);
}
```

Notice the code shown in bold letters. Inside Index(), the code now passes readableSettings to the GetAllSettings() method. Inside Save(), newSettings has only three entries, and SetAllSettings() is now called by passing writableSettings and newSettings.

The final change will be in the Index view—just adjust the model of the view to use IReadableSettings instead of ISettings. This completes the modifications. Run the application and try clicking on the Change Settings button. This time it won't throw any error, and success messages will be displayed as expected.

Interface Segregation Principle (ISP)

In the preceding example covering LSP, your solution was to split one interface into two so that one could choose whichever interface was necessary as per the desired functionality. This solution was actually based on the Interface Segregation Principle. The ISP states the following: **Clients of a class should not be forced to depend on those of its methods that they don't use.**

The client mentioned need not be a separate application or module. It can be any part of the system that is consuming the class under consideration. Although we have seen the problems caused by violating this principle during our previous example, let's review this with another, more specific, example.

Suppose you are developing an e-commerce website that needs to have a shopping cart and associated order-processing mechanism. You devise an interface IOrderProcessor, as shown in Figure 2-15.

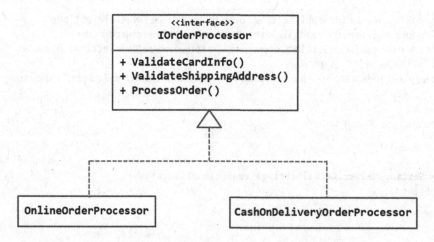

Figure 2-15. *IOrderProcessor violates ISP*

Initially you think that the application will accept only online payments through credit cards. So, you design the IOrderProcessor interface to have three methods. ValidateCardInfo() is intended to validate the credit card information, such as card number and expiration date. The ValidateShippingAddress() method is intended to validate a shipping destination. This might be necessary to ensure that the shipping destination is within the service area of the company. Finally, ProcessOrder() is intended to initiate order processing by placing the order in the system.

The OnlineOrderProcessor class implements IOrderProcessor and implements all the functionality just discussed. Now let's assume that your assumption—that only online credit card–based payments are accepted—is no longer valid. The company decides to accept cash-on-delivery payments in select locations. At first glance, the solution sounds quite straightforward; you can create a CashOnDeliveryProcessor class that implements IOrderProcessor. The cash-on-delivery mode of purchase won't involve any credit card at all, so the ValidateCardInfo() method inside the CashOnDeliveryOrderProcessor class throws a NotImplementedException:

```
public bool ValidateCardInfo(CardInfo obj)
{
    throw new NotImplementedException();
}
```

At this stage your application may work as expected, but a potential problem may arise in the future. Let's assume that for some reason the online credit card–based payment needs extra validation steps. Naturally, IOrderProcessor will be modified to include those extra methods, and OnlineOrderProcessor will implement those additional methods. However, even though CashOnDeliveryOrderProcessor doesn't need any of the additional functionality, you must implement these newly added methods in it (and throw NotImplementedException). In other words, CashOnDeliveryOrderProcessor is forced to change because of the methods it doesn't need. This is in violation of ISP. Also notice that after throwing the NotImplementedException from these methods, the CashOnDeliveryOrderProcessor violates LSP.

The new design (shown in Figure 2-16) splits the required operations into two interfaces— IOrderProcessor and IOnlineOrderProcessor. The IOrderProcessor interface includes only two methods—ValidateShippingAddress() and ProcessOrder(). These two methods are needed by OnlineOrderProcessor as well as CashOnDeliveryOrderProcessor. The ValidateCardInfo() method goes into a separate interface—IOnlineOrderProcessor. The IOnlineOrderProcessor interface is implemented by OnlineOrderProcessor only. Now, any change in the online credit card–based payments is confined to IOnlineOrderProcessor and classes implementing it. CashOnDeliveryOrderProcessor is unaffected by these changes. Thus the new design conforms to ISP.

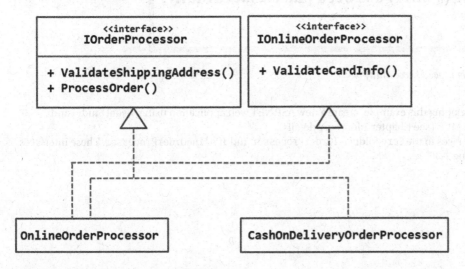

Figure 2-16. *Corrected design of the system*

Now that you understand the ISP, let's translate this example into an ASP.NET application. To demonstrate the functionality of the new design, you will develop an application as shown in Figure 2-17.

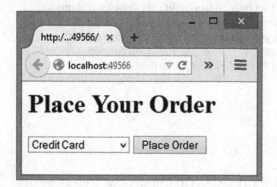

Figure 2-17. *Page to select payment mode and place the order*

You can select a payment from the dropdown list and click on the Place Order button to place the order. The next screen shows a success message, as shown in Figure 2-18.

Figure 2-18. *Order placed successfully*

To begin developing this example, create a new ASP.NET web application using Visual Studio and configure it to use MVC (see Chapter 1 for more details).

Add two interfaces to the Core folder—IOrderProcessor and IOnlineOrderProcessor. These interfaces are shown in Listing 2-30.

Listing 2-30. IOrderProcessor and IOnlineOrderProcessor Interfaces

```
public interface IOrderProcessor
{
    bool ValidateShippingAddress(Address obj);
    void ProcessOrder(Order obj);
}

public interface IOnlineOrderProcessor
{
    bool ValidateCardInfo(CardInfo obj);
}
```

The IOrderProcessor interface contains two methods. The ValidateShippingAddress() method accepts an Address object, and the class implementing this method is supposed to validate the shipping destination. The ProcessOrder() method accepts an Order object. The class implementing this method is supposed to place this order in the system.

The IOnlineOrderProcessor interface contains a single method—ValidateCardInfo()—that accepts a CardInfo object. The class implementing this method is expected to validate this credit card information.

The classes such as Address, CardInfo, and Order are just marker classes in this example. In a more real-world case these classes will actually do some processing. Here we create them just for the sake of testing the application. So, add four empty classes to the Core folder—Customer, Order, Address, and CardInfo. Since these classes don't have any specific code, they are not shown here. You can grab these classes from the code download of this book.

Next, add an OnlineOrderProcessor class and implement both IOrderProcessor and IOnlineOrderProcessor interfaces in it. Listing 2-31 shows the OnlineOrderProcessor class.

Listing 2-31. OnlineOrderProcessor Class

```
public class OnlineOrderProcessor:IOrderProcessor,IOnlineOrderProcessor
{
    public bool ValidateCardInfo(CardInfo obj)
    {
        //validate credit card information
        return true;
    }

    public bool ValidateShippingAddress(Address obj)
    {
        //validate shipping destination
        return true;
    }

    public void ProcessOrder(Order obj)
    {
        //do something with obj
    }
}
```

The OnlineOrderProcessor class is quite straightforward, since it simply implements both the interfaces. The code doesn't contain any real validation or processing. Of course, in a real application you will include those details also.

Along similar lines, add a CashOnDeliveryOrderProcessor class and implement the IOrderProcessor interface in it. This class is shown in Listing 2-32.

Listing 2-32. CashOnDeliveryOrderProcessor Class

```
public class CashOnDeliveryOrderProcessor:IOrderProcessor
{
    public bool ValidateShippingAddress(Address obj)
    {
        //validate shipping destination
        return true;
    }

    public void ProcessOrder(Order obj)
    {
        //do something with obj
    }
}
```

The CashOnDeliveryOrderProcessor class is also quite straightforward and contains implementation of ValidateShippingAddress() and ProcessOrder().

Next, add HomeController to the Controllers folder. In addition to the default Index() action, add one more action, ProcessOrder(), to the controller. Clicking on the Place Order button submits the form to the ProcessOrder() action. The ProcessOrder() method is shown in Listing 2-33.

Listing 2-33. ProcessOrder() Action of HomeController

```
[HttpPost]
public IActionResult ProcessOrder(string paymentmode)
{
    Customer customer = new Customer();
    Address address = new Address();
    CardInfo cardinfo = null;

    Order order = new Order();
    order.OrderID = new Random().Next(1000,9000);
    order.Customer = customer;
    order.ShippingAddress = address;
    order.CardInfo = cardinfo;

    if(paymentmode=="card")
    {
        OnlineOrderProcessor oop = new OnlineOrderProcessor();
        cardinfo = new CardInfo();
        cardinfo.CardNo = "5555555555554444";
        cardinfo.ExpiryMonth = 12;
        cardinfo.ExpiryYear = 2015;
        order.CardInfo = cardinfo;
```

```
        oop.ValidateCardInfo(cardinfo);
        oop.ValidateShippingAddress(address);
        oop.ProcessOrder(order);
    }
    else
    {
        CashOnDeliveryOrderProcessor codop = new CashOnDeliveryOrderProcessor();
        codop.ValidateShippingAddress(address);
        codop.ProcessOrder(order);
    }

    return View("Success",order);
}
```

The ProcessOrder() action receives the paymentmode parameter from the Index view (depending on the option selected in the dropdown list). The code then instantiates Customer, Order, Address, and CardInfo objects (found in the ISP.Core namespace). The code checks the payment mode selected by the end user. If payment mode is "card," an instance of the OnlineOrderProcessor class is created; otherwise, an instance of the CashOnDeliveryOrderProcessor class is created. As you can see, three methods—ValidateCardInfo(), ValidateShippingAddress(), and ProcessOrder()—are called on an OnlineOrderProcessor object, whereas ValidateShippingAddress() and ProcessOrder() methods are called on the CashOnDeliveryOrderProcessor object. Note that a random OrderID is assigned to the order being placed. This is done just for the sake of testing and displaying the success message. Finally, the Success view is rendered by passing an Order object to it as its model.

Next, add two views—Index.cshtml and Success.cshtml—to the Home subfolder in the Views folder. Listing 2-34 shows the markup of the Index view.

Listing 2-34. Markup of the Index View

```html
<html>
<head>
    <title></title>
</head>
<body>
    <h1>Place Your Order</h1>
    <form asp-controller="Home" asp-action="ProcessOrder" method="post">
        <select name="paymentmode">
            <option value="card">Credit Card</option>
            <option value="cod">Cash On Delivery</option>
        </select>
        <input type="submit" value="Place Order" />
    </form>
</body>
</html>
```

The Index view consists of a <form> rendered using tag helpers that submits to the ProcessOrder() action of the HomeController. The form contains a dropdown list with two options—Credit Card and Cash On Delivery. The Place Order button submits the form.

Listing 2-35 shows markup of the Success view.

Listing 2-35. Markup of Success View

```
@model ISP.Core.Order

<html>
<head>
    <title></title>
</head>
<body>
    <h1>Success!</h1>
    <h2>Your order (# @Model.OrderID) has been placed successfully!</h2>
    <a asp-controller="Home" asp-action="Index">Go Back</a>
</body>
</html>
```

The mode for the Success view is the Order class. The Success view displays a success message with an OrderID and also provides a back link so that another order can be placed.

This completes the application. Run the application through Visual Studio and test whether it works as expected.

Dependency Inversion Principle (DIP)

Usually you instantiate dependencies of a class inside that class. In the process, the class becomes tightly coupled with its dependencies. Any change in the dependency may require a change in the class. The root cause of this tight coupling is that the class creates its own dependencies. To loosen this coupling, dependencies can be supplied to a class from the external world. That's where the Dependency Inversion Principle comes into the picture. The DIP can be stated as the following:

A. **High-level classes should not dependent on low-level classes. Both of them should depend on abstractions.**

B. **Abstractions should not depend upon details. Details should depend upon abstractions.**

The Dependency Inversion Principle consists of two parts. The first part talks about the nature of dependency between high-level and low-level classes. Here, a high-level class is a class that does something significant in the application, while a low-level class is a class that does some auxiliary work. Let's take an example. Suppose you are building an authentication and membership system for a web application that needs to manage users. As a part of user management, a way to a change password is required. When a password is changed, a notification is to be sent to the user about the change. In this case the class doing the user management is the high-level class, and the class sending notification is a low-level class.

The first part of DIP says that high-level classes should not depend on low-level classes. Rather, both of them should depend on abstractions. Usually, a high-level class makes use of low-level class by creating one or more instances of it within itself. Consider the classes shown in Figure 2-19.

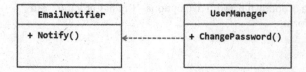

Figure 2-19. *High-level class depends on a low-level class*

■ **Note** In Figure 2-19, a dotted line joining `UserManager` and `EmailNotifier` with an arrow head pointing toward `EmailNotifier` indicates that `UserManager` is dependent on `EmailNotifier`.

As shown in the figure, there is a high-level class, `UserManager`, that contains the `ChangePassword()` method. The `UserManager` class depends on the `EmailNotifier` class for sending email notifications to the user. In this case, `UserManager` creates an instance of `EmailNotifier`, as shown in the following pseudo-code:

```
public void ChangePassword(string username,string oldpwd,string newpwd)
{
    EmailNotifier notifier = new EmailNotifier();
    //change password here
    notifier.Notify("Password was changed on " + DateTime.Now);
}
```

As you can see, the `ChangePassword()` method instantiates `EmailNotifier` and then calls its `Notify()` method to send an email notification. What's the problem in this design? After all, we have been using this style of coding for a long time. The problem here is that `UserManager` has too much dependency on `EmailNotifier`. Every time `EmailNotifier` changes, `UserManager` might need some correction or adjustment. Further, `EmailNotifier` must be made available at the time of writing and testing `UserManager`. So, you are forced to finish writing low-level classes before you code high-level classes. Additionally, future alterations to the notification system may require modifying the `UserManager` class. For example, instead of email notification, you may decide to provide SMS notifications, in which case you must change the code of `UserManager` to replace `EmailNotifier` with the new notification class.

To solve the problem, DIP suggests we depend on abstraction. This abstraction can be in the form of a base class or an interface. Consider Figure 2-20, which shows the modified design.

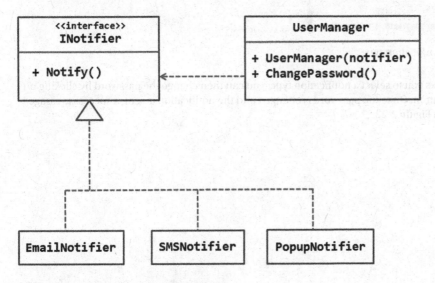

Figure 2-20. *Design conforming to DIP*

The UserManager class no longer uses EmailNotifier directly. Instead, an interface—INotifier—has been introduced. The INotifier interface is implemented by the EmailNotifier class. The constructor of UserManager receives an instance of a class that implements INotifier from the external world. The ChangePassword() method then uses this instance to call the Notify() method. If you decide to switch from EmailNotifier to SMSNotifier or PopupNotifier, this decision won't have any impact on the UserManager class, as you are supplying the dependency from outside. Thus, the direction of dependencies is reversed after applying DIP.

The second part of DIP tells us that abstractions should not depend on details; rather, details should depend on abstractions. This means that you should design the INotifier interface (abstraction) by looking at the needs of the UserManager class. The INotifier interface should not be designed while looking at the needs of EmailNotifier class (details).

Now that you know DIP, let's translate this example into an ASP.NET application. The main view of the application is shown in Figure 2-21.

Figure 2-21. *Selecting notification type*

The main view allows you to select a notification type; you can then change the password by clicking on the Change Password button. Once the password is changed and the notification is sent, a success message is displayed, as shown in Figure 2-22.

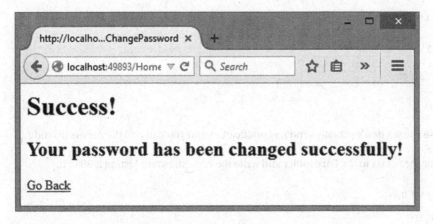

Figure 2-22. *Displaying a success message after changing the password*

To begin developing this example, create a new ASP.NET web application using Visual Studio and configure it to use MVC (see Chapter 1 for more details).

Then add the INotifier interface to the Core folder, as shown in Listing 2-36.

Listing 2-36. INotifer Interface

```
public interface INotifier
{
    void Notify(string message);
}
```

The INotifier interface consists of a single method—Notify()—that accepts a notification message. Then add three classes—EmailNotifier, SMSNotifer, and PopupNotifier—to the Core folder. These classes implement INotifier and are shown in Listing 2-37.

Listing 2-37. Classes Implementing INotifier

```
public class EmailNotifier:INotifier
{
    public void Notify(string message)
    {
        //send notification
    }
}

public class SMSNotifier:INotifier
{
    public void Notify(string message)
    {
        //send notification
    }
}
```

```
public class PopupNotifier:INotifier
{
    public void Notify(string message)
    {
        //send notification
    }
}
```

In our example, these classes don't actually send any notification, but you can add the necessary code in a real system.

Next, add the UserManager class to the Core folder and write the code shown in Listing 2-38 in it.

Listing 2-38. UserManager Class

```
public class UserManager
{

    public INotifier Notifier { get; set; }

    public UserManager(INotifier notifier)
    {
        this.Notifier = notifier;
    }

    public void ChangePassword(string username,string oldpwd,string newpwd)
    {
        //change password here

        //Notify the user
        Notifier.Notify("Password was changed on " + DateTime.Now);
    }
}
```

Notice that the UserManager class defines a public property—Notifier—of type INotifier. It also has a constructor that accepts a parameter of type INotifier. This way, you can either set an INotifier while instantiating UserManager or change it through the Notifier property.

ChangePassword() is supposed to do the job of changing the password and then call the Notify() method with a password-change notification message. As you can see, the UserManager class is totally unaware of the exact INotifier implementation that will send the notification. Thus, a high-level class—UserManager—no longer depends on low-level classes—EmailNotifier, SMSNotifier, and PopupNotifier.

Next, add HomeController to the Controllers folder. In addition to the Index() action, add the ChangePassword() action to the HomeController, as shown in Listing 2-39.

Listing 2-39. ChangePassword() Action

```
[HttpPost]
public IActionResult ChangePassword(string notificationtype)
{
    INotifier notifier = null;

    switch(notificationtype)
    {
        case "email":
            notifier = new EmailNotifier();
            break;
        case "sms":
            notifier = new SMSNotifier();
            break;
        case "popup":
            notifier = new PopupNotifier();
            break;
    }
    UserManager mgr = new UserManager(notifier);
    mgr.ChangePassword("user1", "oldpwd", "newpwd");
    return View("Success");
}
```

The ChangePassword() action checks the value of the notificationtype parameter. This parameter comes from the Index view's dropdown list. Depending on the notification type selected on the Index view, an INotifier implementation (EmailNotifier, SMSNotifier, PopupNotifier) is assigned to the notifier variable.

An instance of UserManager is created by passing this notifier object in the constructor. The code then calls the ChangePassword() method by specifying a test username and password (we didn't use these values in this example). Finally, the Success view is returned to the browser.

This completes the application. Run it through Visual Studio and test whether it works as expected. Take a pause and see how we have reversed the direction of dependencies as suggested by DIP.

Summary

This chapter introduced you to SOLID principles in detail. Moreover, you also developed a proof of concept example for each of these principles. You must have observed that abstraction and polymorphism plays a very important role in SOLID principles, as well as in design patterns in general. You must have noticed that wherever there is a switch statement or a ladder of if-else blocks, such a code is fragile. Such code can break and may need changes whenever system requirements change. Polymorphism helps you to avoid such code. Even if you need to write such code, make a point to keep it outside of your primary system classes. In our examples, such switch- and if-statement-driven code mostly appeared in the controllers but never in the classes that drove the main business logic and processing in the application.

In all the examples developed in this chapter, you used interfaces as a means to abstract the operations. You could have used abstract classes and inheritance in place of interfaces, but a modern trend is to use interfaces over inheritance. Of course, there is no rigid rule that dictates this. As a self-study exercise, try redoing these examples using abstract classes and inheritance.

SOLID principles are the fundamental guidelines of object-oriented design. Keep them fresh in your mind whenever you design any class or module. The next chapter will begin the journey into Gang of Four (GoF) design patterns by discussing a few creational design patterns.

CHAPTER 3

■ ■ ■

Creational Patterns: Singleton, Factory Method, and Prototype

Gang of Four (GoF) patterns are classified into three categories: creational, structural, and behavioral. In this chapter, you will begin by dissecting a few creational patterns. As the name suggests, creational patterns are design patterns that deal with creation of objects, or object instantiation. The C# language uses the new keyword to instantiate an object of a class. Typically, you use the new keyword wherever that object is being utilized. However, this means you must specify a concrete type name at that location. In certain real-world scenarios, as you will learn in this and the next chapter, it becomes necessary to isolate the object instantiation logic and code from the class that utilizes the object. That's where creational patterns come into the picture.

In all there are five creational patterns outlined in the GoF catalog. This chapter will cover three of them, namely singleton, factory method, and prototype. The remaining two, abstract factory and builder, will be covered in the next chapter. Specifically, this chapter will cover the following:

- When to use creational patterns

- Purpose and role of singleton, factory method, and prototype patterns

- UML structure and layout of these three patterns

- A proof of concept example that illustrates the implementation-level details about these patterns

Overview of Creational Design Patterns

Creating objects of a class is a very common requirement in ASP.NET applications. If you are developing a web application that does something useful, chances are you are utilizing objects of the framework defined as well as custom classes. In C# you create an object like this:

```
Customer obj = new Customer();
```

© Bipin Joshi 2016
B. Joshi, *Beginning SOLID Principles and Design Patterns for ASP.NET Developers*,
DOI 10.1007/978-1-4842-1848-8_3

Here, you are creating an instance of a `Customer` class using the new keyword. Most of the time, you write statements like the preceding line inside a method. For example, the following code shows how a method can utilize the new keyword:

```
public class MyClass
{
    Public void DoWork()
    {
        Customer obj = new Customer();
        obj.CustomerID = "ABCD";
        obj.ProcessOrder();
    }
}
```

The code shown consists of a class, `MyClass`, that defines the `DoWork()` method. The `DoWork()` method is assumed to need a `Customer` object for some work, and hence it instantiates `Customer` using the new keyword.

Although this kind of code is very common, there are cases where object instantiation is better removed from the main class (`MyClass`, in this example). Suppose that you are building an ASP.NET application that requires displaying graphical charts to the user. You created a class that does the job of displaying the charts. You also used this class in your ASP.NET application by instantiating it as discussed earlier.

Over a period of time your web application gets split into two versions–free and paid. For the paid version, you decide to provide much richer charts than in the free version. Can you sense the problem? Now you are required to change the code of the ASP.NET application at the point where you instantiate the charting class. This is necessary, because your main code is responsible for creating instances of the charting class. Wouldn't it be great if you could off-load the responsibility of object instantiation to some other class, and simply ask that new class to get you an instance of the desired charting class? In situations like this, creational patterns come to the rescue.

Creational patterns isolate the logic of object instantiation from the main class. The GoF catalog outlines five creational patterns, namely singleton, factory method, prototype, abstract factory, and builder. Although this chapter discusses only the first three, it would be worthwhile to take a quick glance at the purpose of each of these patterns.

- **Singleton:** Ensures that only one instance of a class is created

- **Factory Method:** Creates instance of one of the several classes

- **Prototype:** Creates an instance of a class that is a copy or clone of an existing instance

- **Abstract Factory:** Creates instances of families of related classes

- **Builder:** Separates object construction from its representation

Now that you have some background about creational patterns, let's begin our discussion by dissecting the singleton pattern.

Singleton

Usually, whenever you need an instance of a class, you would use the new keyword and create an instance. That means every new statement would create a fresh instance of a class. You could call new five times, and five object instances would be created. What if you wanted just one, and only one, instance of a class? That's where singleton patterns come into picture.

The purpose of the singleton pattern is to ensure that only one instance of a class is created.

The class implementing the singleton pattern not only ensures that only a single instance has been created, but also provides a way to access that instance. The single object instance under consideration is created only when it is requested for the first time.

A singleton pattern is useful when you are dealing with resource-intensive objects, or when the same object instance is to be passed and used in multiple places.

Design and Explanation

The overall design of the singleton pattern is shown in Figure 3-1.

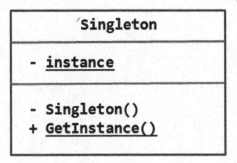

Figure 3-1. *Design of the singleton pattern*

Figure 3-1 shows a class, Singleton, that implements the singleton pattern. The class declares a static variable instance whose visibility is private. This way the instance can't be accessed directly by the external world.

Notice that the constructor of the class is private. This means you can't instantiate the Singleton class using the new keyword. However, you can still instantiate it from within the class.

GetInstance() is a public and static method that returns the instance to the caller. So, GetInstance() is an access point to the instance. It is the job of GetInstance() to instantiate Singleton if an instance doesn't already exist, otherwise it returns an existing instance.

In the figure it is assumed that the Singleton class won't be inherited by any other classes. What if, for some reason, you wished to inherit from Singleton? If so, you would need to make its constructor protected rather than private.

■ **Note**   The UML way to show static members is to underline them. Thus, the instance variable and the GetInstance() method are shown underlined in Figure 3-1.

Example

Now that you know what the singleton pattern is, let's try to implement it in an ASP.NET application. For the sake of this example, let's assume the following scenario:

You are building a blogging engine. Apart from the blog posts and their details, there is some data and settings that are applicable to the entire application. Such data can be called the metadata of the web application. For example, details such as contact e-mail, error-logging status, theme, and title of the blog are applicable application wide. Although these details are application wide, they might be needed in multiple places, such as layout pages, views, and components. Instead of creating an object instance in each of these locations, you can create it just once and then use the same instance everywhere. Obviously, the singleton pattern can be used here.

In this example you will create an ASP.NET application that simply displays application metadata, as shown in Figure 3-2.

Figure 3-2. *View displaying application metadata*

As you can see, the application displays website metadata such as title, administrator e-mail, default theme, and error-logging setting in a table. Of course, you won't do anything with this metadata as such. In a more realistic case you would use this metadata while developing various features of the application, such as a contact form or theme.

To begin developing this example, create a new ASP.NET web application using Visual Studio and configure it to use MVC and Entity Framework (see Chapter 1 for more details). Also store the database connection string of SingletonDb, the database used by the application, in the appsettings.json file.

Then add a class–WebsiteMetadata–in the Core folder and design it as shown in Listing 3-1.

Listing 3-1. WebsiteMetadata Class

```
[Table("WebsiteMetadata")]
public class WebsiteMetadata
{
    [DatabaseGenerated(DatabaseGeneratedOption.Identity)]
    public int Id { get; set; }
    [Required]
```

```
[StringLength(100)]
public string Title { get; set; }
[Required]
[StringLength(40)]
public string DefaultTheme { get; set; }
[Required]
[StringLength(50)]
public string AdminEmail { get; set; }
[Required]
public bool LogErrors { get; set; }
private static WebsiteMetadata instance;
private WebsiteMetadata()
{

}
public static WebsiteMetadata GetInstance()
{
    if(instance == null)
    {
        using (AppDbContext db = new AppDbContext())
        {
            if(db.Metadata.Count()==0)
            {
                db.Metadata.Add(new WebsiteMetadata() { Title = "My Application",
                AdminEmail = "admin@localhost", DefaultTheme = "Summer",
                LogErrors = true });
                db.SaveChanges();
            }
            instance = db.Metadata.SingleOrDefault();
        }
    }
    return instance;
}
}
```

The WebsiteMetadata class consists of five public properties—Id, Title, DefaultTheme, AdminEmail, and LogErrors—that represent the corresponding pieces of information. They are also decorated with data annotations such as [Required] and [StringLength]. Notice that the [Table] attribute maps the WebsiteMetadata class to the WebsiteMetadata table. What these pieces are and what they do is secondary to our example. What is important is that there is some metadata that needs to be accessed from multiple places. In this example, WebsiteMetadata is the class implementing the singleton pattern.

Then the code declares a static variable or instance of the WebsiteMetadata class. Declaring a variable of a type inside the type itself may sound a little odd, but this is an important part of the singleton. This variable, once assigned, stores the one and the only instance of WebsiteMetadata.

Next, the code defines a private constructor of WebsiteMetadata so that you can't instantiate it from the external world.

The GetInstance() static method is the access point of the instance. The GetInstance() method first checks whether the instance has been assigned any value. When you run the application for the first time, obviously the instance value will be null. If the instance value is null, the code connects with the database and retrieves the metadata information. This is done using AppDbContext, an Entity Framework data context class. Note that the code inserts some default values in the database if the WebsiteMetadata table is empty. If your table already contains some values (say you manually added them to the database), then you can remove the if statement that checks the count of records. The AppDbContext class will be discussed shortly.

The SingleOrDefault() method returns the single instance of the WebsiteMetadata class (remember that WebsiteMetadata is used as an entity in this example). You could have also created a new instance of WebsiteMetadata and assigned it the necessary values. The instance is then returned to the caller. The UML representation is shown in Figure 3-3.

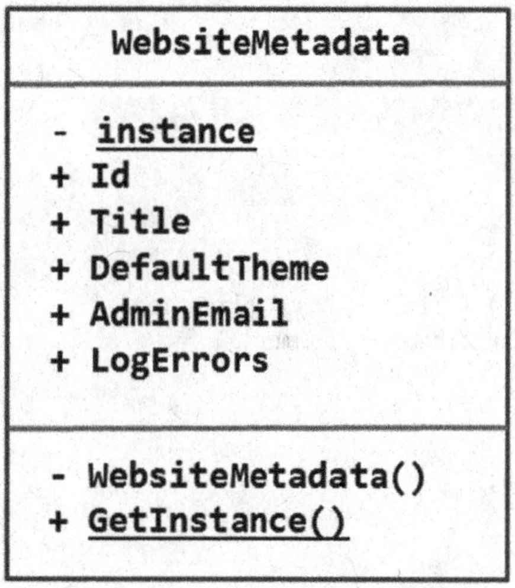

```
┌─────────────────────────────────────┐
│         WebsiteMetadata             │
├─────────────────────────────────────┤
│  -  instance                        │
│  +  Id                              │
│  +  Title                           │
│  +  DefaultTheme                    │
│  +  AdminEmail                      │
│  +  LogErrors                       │
│                                     │
├─────────────────────────────────────┤
│  -  WebsiteMetadata()               │
│  +  GetInstance()                   │
└─────────────────────────────────────┘
```

Figure 3-3. *UML class diagram for WebsiteMetadata class*

Compare this diagram with Figure 3-1 and try to relate what you learned earlier regarding the WebsiteMetadata class.

■ **Note** The preceding code doesn't create an instance of WebsiteMetadata using the new keyword because the Entity Framework is creating it for us. We simply grab the created instance using the SingleOrDefault() method. But from the application's point of view, WebsiteMetadata is creating the instance and supplying it wherever required. This is in fact the "logic of creation" that creational patterns intend to hide from the rest of the application.

Now add the AppDbContext class to the Core folder and modify it as shown in Listing 3-2.

Listing 3-2. AppDbContext Class

```
public class AppDbContext : DbContext
{
    public DbSet<WebsiteMetadata> Metadata { get; set; }

    protected override void OnConfiguring(DbContextOptionsBuilder optionsBuilder)
    {
        optionsBuilder.UseSqlServer(AppSettings.ConnectionString);
    }
}
```

The AppDbContext class defines a single DbSet–Metadata–that holds the WebsiteMetadata objects.

The overridden OnConfiguring() method sets the SQL Server database to be used, using the UseSqlServer() method.

Next, add HomeController to the Controllers folder and write the Index() action in it as shown in Listing 3-3.

Listing 3-3. Index() Action Using WebsiteMetadata Class

```
public IActionResult Index()
{
    WebsiteMetadata metadata = WebsiteMetadata.GetInstance();
    return View("Index",metadata);
}
```

The Index() action calls the GetInstance() static method of WebsiteMetadata and gets an instance of WebsiteMetadata. This instance is passed as a model to the Index view.

Finally, add the Index view to the Views/Home folder and write markup in it as shown in Listing 3-4.

Listing 3-4. Markup of Index View

```
@model Singleton.Core.WebsiteMetadata

<html>
...
<body>
    <h1>Website Metadata</h1>
    <table border="1" cellpadding="10">
        <tr>
            <td>Title :</td>
            <td>@Model.Title</td>
        </tr>
        <tr>
            <td>Administrator Email :</td>
            <td>@Model.AdminEmail</td>
        </tr>
```

```
        <tr>
            <td>Default Theme :</td>
            <td>@Model.DefaultTheme</td>
        </tr>
        <tr>
            <td>Log Errors :</td>
            <td>@Model.LogErrors</td>
        </tr>
    </table>
</body>
</html>
```

The Index view simply displays the Title, AdminEmail, DefaultTheme, and LogErrors properties in a table.

This completes the application. Before running the application you need to create the SingletonDb database (see Chapter 1 for more details).

Once the database is created, set a break point in the GetInstance() method and run the application. You will find that during the first run of the Index() action, the instance is null and hence you will see if blocks are getting executed. If you refresh the page (or open it in another tab) in the browser, you will find that the instance already exists from the previous run, and hence the code will simply return the existing instance to the caller.

Factory Method

At times you will have a set of classes performing a similar operation, but the exact class to be used to get the job done is dependent on some logic or condition. In such cases, a client doesn't know exactly which class from the available set has been instantiated. The client relies on some other classes to supply it the required object. These other classes in turn implement what is known as a factory method, which does the job of creating the required object instance.

As the name suggests, **the factory method pattern defines a way to create an object. And the subclasses decide which class to instantiate.** How do these subclasses decide which class to instantiate? This is quite application specific, and may involve some programmatic logic or configuration setting.

Design and Explanation

The UML diagram that shows the overall design of the factory method pattern is shown in Figure 3-4.

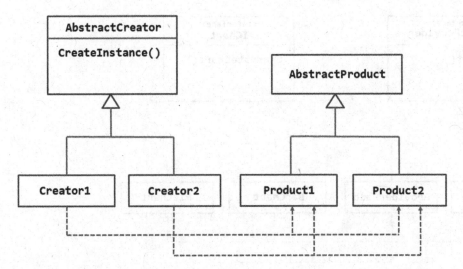

Figure 3-4. *Design of factory method pattern*

Figure 3-4 shows an abstract class, AbstractCreator, that defines the CreateInstance() method. This is the template of the factory method. AbstractCreator is inherited by two subclasses–Creator1 and Creator2. These subclasses implement the CreateInstance() method.

The implementation of CreateInstance() needs to decide whether to instantiate Product1 or Product2. The Product1 and Product2 classes are the subclasses of the AbstractProduct class.

The decision to instantiate Product1 or Product2 may depend on some application logic, the current application state, some condition, or merely a configuration setting.

The client (not shown in the figure) can consume Creator1 or Creator2. Invoking CreateInstance() on either will instantiate either Product1 or Product2 (depending on the instantiation logic), and that instance is supplied to the client.

Example

Suppose you are building a web application that deals with workers and time spent by them on a task. As a part of the system requirements, you are required to show number of hours worked on each day of the week in a graphical form. Your application can show two types of graphical charts–bar chart or pie chart. The decision to show bar chart or pie chart is dependent on the user preference.

Considering these requirements, you came up with a design, as shown in Figure 3-5.

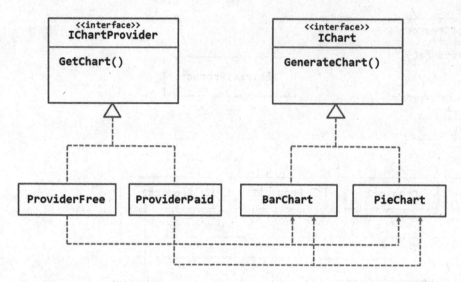

Figure 3-5. *GetChart() factory method returning a chart*

The figure shows an IChart interface that defines the GenerateChart() method. The GenerateChart() method is supposed to generate a chart based on X and Y coordinate values. The IChart interface is implemented by two classes–BarChart and PieChart.

The IChartProvider interface defines the factory method, GetChart(). The GetChart() method is supposed to return either BarChart or PieChart based on user's preference.

The IChartProvider interface is implemented by two classes, ProviderFree and ProviderPaid. These classes implement the GetChart() factory method.

It is not always necessary that you have multiple classes implementing GetChart(). There can be just one "creator" that implements GetChart() and returns BarChart or PieChart. However, at times you may need multiple "creators." Suppose that you have two types of user accounts–free and paid. If a user holds a free account, you want to use ProviderFree to generate the charts. If a user holds a paid account, you want to use ProviderPaid to generate the chart. You may create ProviderPaid so that it provides a richer representation of the data or renders the charts with fancy effects.

The client can use ProviderFree or ProviderPaid to get the IChart object. Once the IChart object is received, the client can assign X and Y coordinate values and generate the chart.

Now that you know the purpose of the factory method pattern, let's implement the preceding example in an ASP.NET application. Your application will look like Figure 3-6.

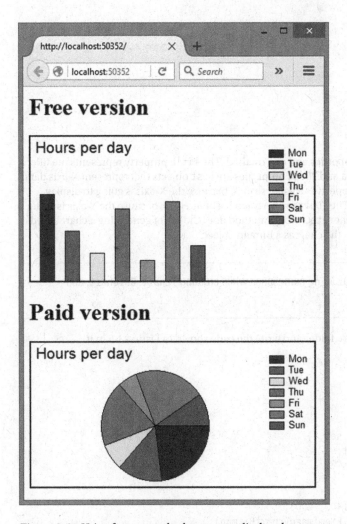

Figure 3-6. *Using factory method pattern to display charts*

As you can see, the application displays two charts–a bar chart in the top part and a pie chart in the bottom part of the page. The bar chart is rendered using a BarChart object returned by ChartProviderFree class, and the pie chart is rendered using a PieChart object returned by ChartProviderPaid class.

Begin by creating a new ASP.NET web application using Visual Studio and configure it to use MVC (see Chapter 1 for more details). Add a reference to the System.Drawing assembly. You will use classes from this assembly to generate the charts. Also delete the dnxcore50 entry from the frameworks section of the Project.json file.

Then add the IChart interface to the Core folder and modify it as shown in Listing 3-5.

Listing 3-5. IChart Interface

```
public interface IChart
{
    string Title { get; set; }
    List<string> XData { get; set; }
    List<int> YData { get; set; }
    Bitmap GenerateChart();
}
```

The IChart interface defines three properties and one method. The Title property represents the title of the chart under consideration. The XData and YData properties are List objects that represent X-axis data and Y-axis data, respectively. The XData property is a list of strings, because the X-axis is going to display days of the week (Monday, Tuesday, etc.). The YData property is a list of integers, because the Y-axis is going to display number of hours worked. The GenerateChart() method does the job of generating a chart based on the Title, XData, and YData and returns the chart as a Bitmap object.

■ **Note**   Make sure to import the System.Drawing namespace while creating IChart, BarChart, and PieChart classes.

Now, add the BarChart class to the Core folder and write the code shown in Listing 3-6 in it.

Listing 3-6. BarChart Class

```
public class BarChart:IChart
{
    public string Title { get; set; }
    public List<string> XData { get; set; }
    public List<int> YData { get; set; }

    public Bitmap GenerateChart()
    {
        var chartBitmap = new Bitmap(400, 200);
        var chartGraphics = Graphics.FromImage(chartBitmap);
        chartGraphics.Clear(Color.White);
        var titleFont = new Font("Arial", 16);
        var titleXY = new PointF(5, 5);
        chartGraphics.DrawString(Title, titleFont, Brushes.Black, titleXY);

        var spacing = 35;
        var scale = 10;
        for (var i = 0; i < YData.Count; i++)
        {
            var barBrush = new SolidBrush(ColorHelper.GetBrushColor(i));
            var barX = (i * spacing) + 15;
            var barY = 200 - (YData[i] * scale);
            var barWidth =20;
            var barHeight = (YData[i] * scale) + 5;
            chartGraphics.FillRectangle(barBrush, barX, barY, barWidth, barHeight);
            chartGraphics.DrawRectangle(Pens.Black, barX, barY, barWidth, barHeight);
        }
```

```
    var legendRect = new PointF(335, 20);
    var legendText = new PointF(360, 16);
    var legendFont = new Font("Arial", 10);
    for (var i = 0; i < XData.Count; i++)
    {
        var legendBrush = new SolidBrush(ColorHelper.GetBrushColor(i));
        chartGraphics.FillRectangle(legendBrush, legendRect.X, legendRect.Y, 20, 10);
        chartGraphics.DrawRectangle(Pens.Black, legendRect.X, legendRect.Y, 20, 10);
        chartGraphics.DrawString(XData[i], legendFont, Brushes.Black, legendText);
        legendRect.Y += 15;
        legendText.Y += 15;
    }

    var borderPen = new Pen(Color.Black, 2);
    var borderRect = new Rectangle(1, 1, 398, 198);
    chartGraphics.DrawRectangle(borderPen, borderRect);
    return chartBitmap;
    }
}
```

The BarChart class implements the IChart interface. The three properties–Title, XData, and YData are quite straightforward. The brain of the BarChart class is the GenerateChart() method. This method uses classes from the System.Drawing namespace to generate a bar chart. We won't go into the details of this method here, since the inner workings of this method are not directly connected to the factory method pattern. It is suffice to say that GenerateChart() renders the title, legends, and the bar chart as a Bitmap object. The Bitmap object is returned to the caller.

Next, add another class, PieChart, to the Core folder and write the code shown in Listing 3-7 in it.

Listing 3-7. PieChart Class

```
public class PieChart : IChart
{
    public string Title { get; set; }
    public List<string> XData { get; set; }
    public List<int> YData { get; set; }

    public Bitmap GenerateChart()
    {
        var chartBitmap = new Bitmap(400, 200);
        var chartGraphics = Graphics.FromImage(chartBitmap);
        chartGraphics.Clear(Color.White);
        var titleFont = new Font("Arial", 16);
        var titleXY = new PointF(5, 5);
        chartGraphics.DrawString(Title, titleFont, Brushes.Black, titleXY);

        var totalAngle = (float)0;
        var sweepAngle = (float)0;
        var startAngle = (float)0;
        for (var i = 0; i < YData.Count; i++)
        {
            totalAngle = totalAngle + YData[i];
        }
```

```
        for (var i = 0; i < YData.Count; i++)
        {
            var pieBrush = new SolidBrush(ColorHelper.GetBrushColor(i));
            var pieX = 100;
            var pieY = 40;
            var pieWidth = 150;
            var pieHeight = 150;
            sweepAngle = YData[i] / totalAngle * 360;
            chartGraphics.FillPie(pieBrush, pieX, pieY, pieWidth,pieHeight, startAngle,
            sweepAngle);
            chartGraphics.DrawPie(Pens.Black, pieX, pieY, pieWidth, pieHeight, startAngle,
            sweepAngle);
            startAngle += sweepAngle;
        }

        var legendRect = new PointF(335, 20);
        var legendText = new PointF(360, 16);
        var legendFont = new Font("Arial", 10);
        for (int i = 0; i < XData.Count; i++)
        {
            var legendBrush = new SolidBrush(ColorHelper.GetBrushColor(i));
            chartGraphics.FillRectangle(legendBrush, legendRect.X, legendRect.Y, 20, 10);
            chartGraphics.DrawRectangle(Pens.Black, legendRect.X, legendRect.Y, 20, 10);
            chartGraphics.DrawString(XData[i], legendFont, Brushes.Black, legendText);
            legendRect.Y += 15;
            legendText.Y += 15;
        }

        var borderPen = new Pen(Color.Black, 2);
        var borderRect = new Rectangle(1, 1, 398, 198);
        chartGraphics.DrawRectangle(borderPen, borderRect);
        return chartBitmap;
    }
}
```

The PieChart class implements the IChart interface. The PieChart class is quite similar to the BarChart class, except that the GenerateChart() method draws a pie chart instead of bar chart.

■ **Note** BarChart as well as PieChart classes use a helper class—ColorHelper. The ColorHelper class simply returns a color based on the supplied number. To save space, ColorHelper is not shown here. You can grab it from the code download of this chapter.

Next, add the IChartProvider interface to the Core folder as shown in Listing 3-8.

Listing 3-8. IChartProvider Interface

```
public interface IChartProvider
{
    IChart GetChart();
}
```

The IChartProvider interface contains a single method–GetChart()–that returns an IChart object. The IChartProvider interface is implemented by two classes, ChartProviderFree and ChartProviderPaid. These classes are shown in Listing 3-9.

Listing 3-9. ChartProviderFree and ChartProviderPaid Classes

```
public class ChartProviderFree:IChartProvider
{
    public IChart GetChart()
    {
        IChart chart = new BarChart();
        return chart;
    }
}

public class ChartProviderPaid : IChartProvider
{
    public IChart GetChart()
    {
        IChart chart = new PieChart();
        return chart;
    }
}
```

The ChartProviderFree class implements the GetChart() method. The GetChart() implementation returns an instance of BarChart to the caller. The ChartProviderPaid class implements the GetChart() method and returns an instance of the PieChart class. In this example there is no specific logic or condition for instantiating BarChart and PieChart. However, you can add such a logic to the GetChart() method. Nevertheless, the GetChart() method acts as the factory method.

Now, add HomeController to the Controllers folder. In this example, HomeController is the client to the ChartProviderFree and ChartProviderPaid classes. In addition to the Index() action, add two more actions to it–GetImageFree() and GetImagePaid(). These actions use ChartProviderFree and ChartProviderPaid, respectively, to generate charts. Since both of these methods are quite similar, only GetImageFree() is shown in Listing 3-10.

Listing 3-10. GetImageFree() Action Method

```
public IActionResult GetImageFree()
{
    ChartProviderFree cp = new ChartProviderFree();
    IChart chart = cp.GetChart();

    chart.Title = "Hours per day";

    List<string> xdata = new List<string>();
    xdata.Add("Mon");
    xdata.Add("Tue");
    xdata.Add("Wed");
    xdata.Add("Thu");
    xdata.Add("Fri");
    xdata.Add("Sat");
    xdata.Add("Sun");
```

```
        List<int> ydata = new List<int>();
        ydata.Add(12);
        ydata.Add(7);
        ydata.Add(4);
        ydata.Add(10);
        ydata.Add(3);
        ydata.Add(11);
        ydata.Add(5);

        chart.XData = xdata;
        chart.YData = ydata;

        Bitmap bmp = chart.GenerateChart();
        MemoryStream stream = new MemoryStream();
        bmp.Save(stream, ImageFormat.Png);
        byte[] data = stream.ToArray();
        stream.Close();
        return File(data, "image/png");
}
```

The GetImageFree() method is called from the Index view (this will be discussed shortly). It uses the ChartProviderFree class to grab an instance of IChart (from the FactoryMethod.Core namespace). Recollect that the GetChart() method of ChartProviderFree returns a BarChart.

The code then sets the Title of the chart to Hours per day. Then XData and YData properties are assigned values. In this case, the code uses sample values, but you can fetch them from the database if required.

Once Title, XData, and YData are assigned their respective values, the GenerateChart() method is called to generate a bar chart. The bar chart is returned as a Bitmap (from the System.Drawing namespace). To display this Bitmap on the view, the code saves it to a MemoryStream object (in the System.IO namespace). This is done using the Save() method of the Bitmap class. While saving the Bitmap to the MemoryStream, the format of image is set to PNG using the ImageFormat class. The ToArray() method of the MemoryStream is then used to retrieve the Bitmap as a byte array.

Finally, a FileContentResult object is constructed by using the File() method and passing the byte array to it. The second parameter of File() indicates the content type of the data (image/png in this case). The FileContentResult object is sent to the response stream.

Although not shown in Listing 3-10, you need to write the GetImagePaid() action along similar lines. The only difference between GetImageFree() and GetImagePaid() is that GetImagePaid() uses ChartProviderPaid instead of ChartProviderFree. Apart from this difference, the code is the same.

Now, add an Index view inside Views/Home folder and write the markup shown in Listing 3-11 in it.

Listing 3-11. Markup of Index View

```
<html>
<head>
    <title></title>
</head>
<body>
    <h1>Free version</h1>
    <img src="/home/getimagefree" />
    <h1>Paid version</h1>
    <img src="/home/getimagepaid" />
</body>
</html>
```

Notice the lines shown in bold letters. The markup consists of two <img> elements. The src attribute of the <img> elements point to /Home/GetImageFree and /Home/GetImagePaid, respectively.

This completes the application. Run the application in the browser and check whether the bar chart and pie chart are displayed as expected.

Prototype

When you create new objects of a class, the object instances are usually empty. The properties and data members of a class are not initialized yet (apart from their default values or constructor initializations). Although this is what you want in most cases, at times you may wish to create a new object by cloning an existing one. If this is your need, prototype pattern is the way to implement such functionality. **Prototype pattern allow you to create objects by cloning existing ones.** The existing object is used as a template or prototype for building the new one.

Why do we need to clone objects? A few reasons are as follows:

- You may want to pass an object to some other module for processing, and you want to ensure that the original instance is not accidently tampered with in the process.

- You may want to perform some "preview" operations on an object. You just want to get a feel of how the object will be after the changes, but you don't want to actually change the object.

- The new object and an existing one might closely match each other. So, you can clone the first one, modify just a few properties that are different, and then use the new instance the way you want.

- At times creating a new instance using the new keyword might add overhead to the object-creation process.

Design and Explanation

The UML diagram of the prototype pattern is shown in Figure 3-7.

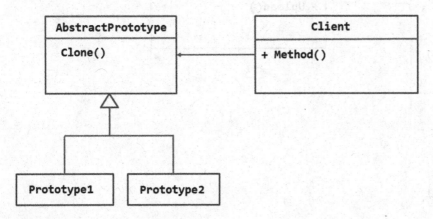

Figure 3-7. Design of prototype pattern

As shown in the figure, the prototype pattern has an abstract class or interface that defines a method for cloning the objects. In the figure, the Clone() method serves this purpose. The Clone() method is implemented by subclasses Prototype1 and Prototype2.

You might be aware that the .NET framework has an ICloneable interface in the System namespace. That's the .NET framework's way of implementing the prototype pattern. The ICloneable interface defines a single method–Clone(). The class implementing ICloneable needs to implement this method. Of course, you can always define your own interface or abstract class that does the same thing.

The cloning operation is of two types–shallow copy and deep copy. In the case of shallow copy, simple type fields of a class are copied into the cloned instance. For reference type fields, only the reference pointer is copied (the values they hold are not copied). This means the original as well as the cloned object points to the same reference. The shallow copy can be performed using the MemberwiseClone() method of the Object base class (every class in .NET is implicitly inherited from the Object base class).

In the case of deep copy, simple as well as reference type fields are copied into the cloned object. Thus, the original and the cloned object get independent copies of the reference type fields. The deep copy can be performed through a custom serialization technique (more on that later).

The prototype pattern by itself doesn't dictate whether you should create a shallow or a deep copy of an object. It's application specific, and as a developer you will need to decide which technique to use.

The Client class makes use of the AbstractPrototype class and its subclasses. The instances of Prototype1 and Prototype2 can call the Clone() method on themselves to create their own clones.

Example

Suppose you are building a web application that allows users to upload files to the server. The uploaded files are saved in the user's account, and the user can download them at any time. As a safety measure, you wish to implement an automatic backup feature for these files. Under this feature, a copy of the file being uploaded would be created by the backup system.

Considering these requirements, you come up with the design shown in Figure 3-8.

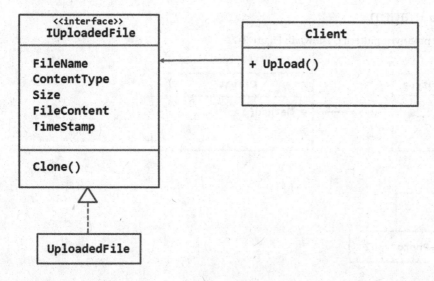

Figure 3-8. Backing up the uploaded files

As you can see, the IUploadedFile interface defines five properties—FileName, ContentType, Size, FileContent, and TimeStamp—that capture the corresponding details about a file being uploaded. Moreover, it defines the Clone() method. The UploadedFile class implements the IUploadedFile interface as well as the properties and the methods. In this example, UploadedFile creates a shallow copy of itself using the MemberwiseClone() method. The uploaded files could be very large in size, and performing deep copy might overburden the server. So, the example uses the shallow copy technique. The HomeController acts as a client and invokes the Clone() method to generate two copies of UploadedFile—one to be stored in the user account and the other to be supplied to the backup system. For the sake of simplicity the actual logic of file storage is omitted.

Let's put this design into action by developing an ASP.NET application. The main page of the application is shown in Figure 3-9.

Figure 3-9. *Uploading files to the server*

The application consists of a file-upload input field and a button. The user can select one or more files using the file-upload field and click on the Submit button to upload the file(s) to the server. Once the operation is complete, a success message is displayed at the bottom.

Begin by creating a new ASP.NET web application using Visual Studio and configure it to use MVC (see Chapter 1 for more details). Then add the IFileUploaded interface in the Core folder and write the code shown in Listing 3-12.

Listing 3-12. IUploadedFile Interface

```
public interface IUploadedFile
{
    string FileName { get; set; }
    long Size { get; set; }
    string ContentType { get; set; }
    DateTime TimeStamp { get; set; }
    byte[] FileContent { get; set; }

    IUploadedFile Clone();
}
```

The IUploadedFile interface defines five properties and one method. All the properties are self-explanatory. Note that the FileContent property is a byte array, because a file's contents can be text or binary. The Clone() method returns an IUploadedFile object.

Then add an UploadedFile class and implement the IUploadedFile interface in it. Listing 3-13 shows the completed UploadedFile class.

Listing 3-13. UploadedFile Class

```
public class UploadedFile : IUploadedFile
{
    public string FileName { get; set; }
    public long Size { get; set; }
    public string ContentType { get; set; }
    public DateTime TimeStamp { get; set; }
    public byte[] FileContent { get; set; }

    public IUploadedFile Clone()
    {
        return (IUploadedFile)this.MemberwiseClone();
    }
}
```

The Clone() method implemented in the UploadedFile class uses the MemberwiseClone() method of the Object base class and returns it to the caller.

Next, add HomeController to the Controllers folder and import the following namespaces into it:

```
using Prototype.Core;
using Microsoft.AspNet.Http;
using Microsoft.Net.Http.Headers;
using System.IO;
```

The Microsoft.AspNet.Http and Microsoft.Net.Http.Headers namespaces supply a few classes that are needed during the file-upload operation. Then add two action methods—Index() and Upload(). These actions are shown in Listing 3-14.

Listing 3-14. Index() and Upload() Actions

```
public IActionResult Index()
{
    return View();
}


[HttpPost]
public IActionResult Upload(IList<IFormFile> files)
{
    foreach (var file in files)
    {
        ContentDispositionHeaderValue header = ContentDispositionHeaderValue.Parse
        (file.ContentDisposition);
        string fileName = header.FileName;
        fileName = fileName.Trim('"');
        fileName = Path.GetFileName(fileName);
```

```
        MemoryStream ms = new MemoryStream();
        Stream s = file.OpenReadStream();
        s.CopyTo(ms);
        byte[] data = ms.ToArray();
        s.Close();
        ms.Close();

        UploadedFile primaryObj = new UploadedFile();
        primaryObj.FileName = fileName;
        primaryObj.ContentType = file.ContentType;
        primaryObj.Size = file.Length;
        primaryObj.TimeStamp = DateTime.Now;
        primaryObj.FileContent = data;

        IUploadedFile backupObj = primaryObj.Clone();

        //send primaryObj to main system
        //send backupObj to backup system
    }
    ViewBag.Message = files.Count +  " file(s) uploaded successfully!";
    return View("Index");
}
```

The Index() action simply returns an Index view (which will be discussed later). The Upload() action has a single parameter that receives the uploaded files as an IList of IFormFile objects. Each IFormFile object supplies more details about the file, such as ContentDisposition, ContentType, and Length.

A foreach loop iterates through the list of files. Each file's name is extracted from the ContentDisposition header. The filename contains the client-side path, and hence we just grab the filename and extension using the GetFileName() method.

The UploadedFile class expects the file content as a byte array. The code creates a new MemoryStream to store the file's contents. It then calls the OpenReadStream() method to get a handle on the underlying Stream object. The Stream obtained is copied to the MemoryStream object. Finally, the ToArray() method of MemoryStream is used to get the file contents as a byte array. The streams are then closed.

The code then proceeds to create an UploadedFile object and sets all of its properties. The primaryObj is intended to be used by the primary system (system dealing with user's account). To pass the file details to the backup system, the code creates another instance called backupObj using the Clone() method. The actual logic of storing the files is omitted for the sake of simplicity. Finally, a success message is passed to the view using ViewBag.

Next, add an Index view to the Views/Home folder and write the markup shown in Listing 3-15 into it.

Listing 3-15. Markup of Index View

```
<html>
<head>
    <title></title>
</head>
<body>
```

```
<h1>Select File(s) to Upload :</h1>
<form action="/home/upload" method="post" enctype="multipart/form-data">
    <input type="file" name="files" id="files" multiple />
    <input type="submit" value="Submit" />
</form>

<h4>@ViewBag.Message</h4>

</body>
</html>
```

The Index view consists of a <form> whose action attribute is set to /home/upload and enctype attribute is set to multipart/form-data. This way, the files will be POSTed to the Upload() action when submitted.

Inside, the view houses a file-input field and a Submit button. The success message from the ViewBag is displayed below the form.

This completes the application. Set a breakpoint in the Upload() action. Run it and check whether primaryObj gets cloned into backupObj as expected.

Implementing Deep Copy

In the preceding example you used the shallow copy technique to clone an object. What if you need to implement the deep copy technique? Let's discuss a technique that can be used in case you need to deep copy an object. This technique requires that the class under consideration (UploadedFile in this case) be serializable. Thus, you need to add the [Serializable] attribute on top of the UploadedFile class as follows:

```
[Serializable]
public class UploadedFile : IUploadedFile
{
    ...
}
```

Have a look at the code shown in Listing 3-16.

Listing 3-16. Deep Copy of UploadedFile Object

```
public IUploadedFile DeepCopy()
{
    if (!this.GetType().IsSerializable)
        throw new Exception("The object is not serializable!");

    BinaryFormatter formatter = new BinaryFormatter();
    MemoryStream ms = new MemoryStream();
    formatter.Serialize(ms, this);
    ms.Seek(0, SeekOrigin.Begin);
    IUploadedFile deepcopy = (IUploadedFile)formatter.Deserialize(ms);
    ms.Close();
    return deepcopy;
}
```

The DeepCopy() method first checks whether the object being deep copied is serializable or not. This is necessary, because the code uses the BinaryFormatter class from the System.Runtime.Serialization. Formatters.Binary namespace to serialize the object into a MemoryStream. If the object is not serializable, then an exception is thrown. Otherwise, a new BinaryFormatter and a new MemoryStream are created. The Serialize() method of BinaryFormatter is used to serialize the object into the MemoryStream; this way, an independent copy of the object gets created. To read this copied object back, the Deserialize() method of BinaryFormatter() is used. The MemoryStream is closed, and the cloned object is returned to the caller.

To create deep copy of an UploadedFile object you can now use the DeepCopy() method:

```
IUploadedFile backupObj = primaryObj.DeepCopy();
```

Summary

Creational patterns deal with object creation. This chapter discussed singleton, factory method, and prototype patterns. The singleton pattern is used to ensure that only one instance of a class is being created. The factory method pattern allows you create an instance of many subclasses based on some logic. The prototype pattern allows you to create an object instance by cloning an existing object.

You must have noticed that while implementing design patterns you often use one or more of the SOLID principles (such as SRP or OCP). Thus, SOLID principles and design patterns go hand in hand.

The next chapter covers the remaining two creational patterns: abstract factory and builder.

CHAPTER 4

■ ■ ■

Creational Patterns: Abstract Factory and Builder

In the previous chapter you learned three out of five creational patterns. This chapter will discuss the remaining two creational patterns, namely abstract factory and builder.

The factory method pattern discussed in the preceding chapter comes in handy when you wish to instantiate a class. However, at times you will need to create a family of objects that are related. That's where the abstract factory pattern comes into the picture.

Objects can be complex in nature. At times you will need to create complex objects such that the overall creation process is the same but the final object being created varies according to the requirement. The builder pattern can be used effectively in such situations.

This chapter will cover the following:

- Purpose and role of abstract factory and builder patterns

- UML structure and layout of these two patterns

- A proof of concept example for each that illustrates the implementation-level details of these patterns

- A few ways of storing the factory settings

Abstract Factory

The factory method pattern discussed in the preceding chapter allows a client to get an object without specifying the class name. It is the job of the factory method to create an object of the intended class and return it to the client. **The abstract factory pattern extends this further and allows you to create families of related objects.** A family of objects is a set of objects that are usually used together or a set of objects that are dependent on each other in some way.

As with the factory method pattern, the decision to instantiate a particular family of objects may depend on some configuration setting, business logic, or programmatic condition.

Design and Explanation

The UML diagram that follows in Figure 4-1 shows the overall design of abstract factory pattern.

B. Joshi, *Beginning SOLID Principles and Design Patterns for ASP.NET Developers*,
DOI 10.1007/978-1-4842-1848-8_4

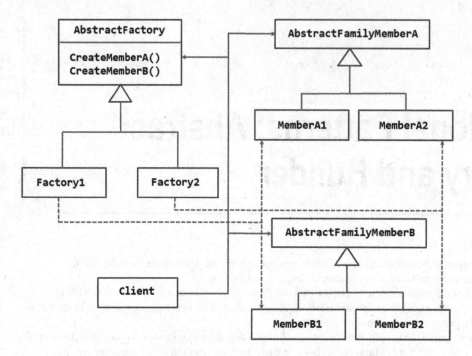

Figure 4-1. *Design of abstract factory pattern*

As you can see from the UML diagram, there are two families. The first family consists of two family members—MemberA1 and MemberB1. Along similar lines, the second family consists of two family members—MemberA2 and MemberB2.

The family members themselves are inherited from AbstractFamilyMemberA and AbstractFamilyMemberB, respectively.

There is an abstract class named AbstractFactory. This class provides the overall interface for creating the object families in the form of two methods—CreateMemberA() and CreateMemberB().

The methods of AbstractFactory are implemented by two concrete factories, namely Factory1 and Factory2. Factory1 creates objects belonging to the first family—MemberA1 and MemberB1. Similarly, Factory2 creates objects belonging to the second family—MemberA2 and MemberB2.

The client class uses either Factory1 or Factory2 (depending on some application-specific logic) and receives the corresponding family members. The client never uses the concrete family member names (MemberA1, MemberB1, MemberA2, MemberB2) in its code; rather, it uses their abstract types—AbstractFamilyMemberA and AbstractFamilyMemberB, respectively. This way, no matter which factory is being used the client code remains unchanged.

Example

Let's try to apply the abstract factory pattern to a real-world situation. Suppose that you are building a web application that will be used by different customers. Your primary choice of database is SQL Server, but you want to ensure that customers using other popular database engines are not left out. Thus, your web application's data-access layer should be such that it can work with SQL Server database or any other OLEDB-compliant database. As a result, you decide to use ADO.NET data providers for the sake of database connectivity and querying.

Considering these requirements, you come up with a design as shown in Figure 4-2.

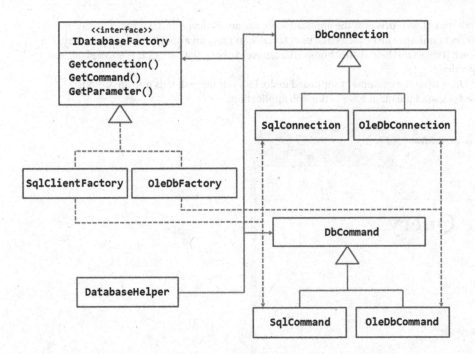

Figure 4-2. *Creating a database helper using the abstract factory pattern*

The .NET framework comes with two ADO.NET data providers—SqlClient and OleDb. These providers consist of objects such as connection, command, parameter, and data reader. As you might have guessed, the objects from these two data providers make families of related objects. Thus, SqlConnection, SqlCommand, SqlParameter, and SqlDataReader are the members of the SqlClient family. OleDbConnection, OleDbCommand, OleDbParameter, and OleDbDataReader are the members of the OleDb family. Notice that the figure shows only two family members for the sake of reducing the clutter.

Internally, the family members listed inherit from certain base classes residing in the System.Data. Common namespace. For example, the SqlConnection and OleDbConnection classes inherit from the DbConnection base class. The SqlCommand and OleDbCommand classes inherit from the DbCommand base class and so on.

■ **Note**   In this example, the classes making the families are available as the part of the .NET framework itself. So, your application need not create any family member classes as such. However, in other situations you will probably create the classes making the families yourself.

The interface IDatabaseFactory defines an interface for creating the factories and consists of three methods, namely GetConnection(), GetCommand(), and GetParameter(). Note that a data reader is always returned by a command, and hence there is no separate method for creating a data reader. The IDatabaseFactory is implemented by two concrete factory classes— SqlClientFactory and OleDbFactory.

The SqlClientFactory is responsible for creating the members of the SqlClient family, whereas the OleDbFactory is responsible for creating the members of the OleDb family.

The DatabaseHelper class represents the application's data-access layer, and it is the client for the factories and the object families. The DatabaseHelper class doesn't rely on a specific concrete factory or a specific family; rather, it relies on their abstractions—IDatabaseFactory, DbConnection, DbCommand, and DbParameter, respectively.

Now that you know what the example is supposed to do, let's put these details into an ASP.NET application. Figure 4-3 shows the main page of the web application.

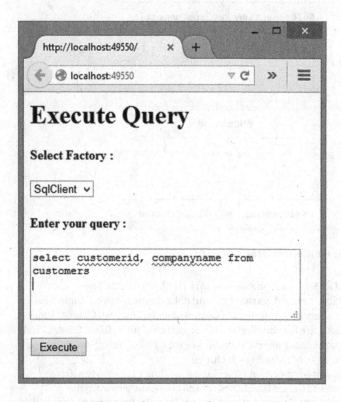

Figure 4-3. *Application that uses DatabaseHelper*

As you can see, the main page of the application consists of a dropdown list for selecting a factory to be used. It has two options, SqlClient and OleDb, representing the corresponding factory.

There is a text area for entering an SQL statement. The SQL statement can either be a query (SELECT) or action (INSERT / UPDATE / DELETE). Clicking on the Execute button executes the query against the Northwind database. If the query is a SELECT query the records returned by the query are displayed in a table, as shown in Figure 4-4.

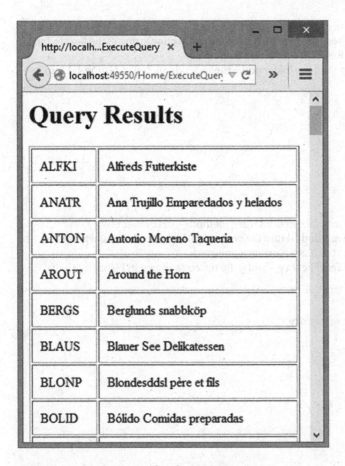

Figure 4-4. *Displaying results of a SELECT query*

However, if an action query is executed, the number of records affected are displayed, as shown in Figure 4-5.

Figure 4-5. *Displaying number of records affected by an action query*

115

To develop this application, begin by creating a new ASP.NET web application using Visual Studio and configure it to use MVC (see Chapter 1 for more details). Also store the connection string of the Northwind database in the appsettings.json file and load it in the AppSettings class.

Add the IDatabaseFactory interface in the Core folder and write the code shown in Listing 4-1 into it.

Listing 4-1. IDatabaseHelper Interface

```
public interface IDatabaseFactory
{
    DbConnection GetConnection();
    DbCommand GetCommand();
    DbParameter GetParameter();
}
```

As you can see, the IDatabaseFactory interface defines three methods—GetConnection(), GetCommand(), and GetParameter(). These methods return DbConnection, DbCommand, and DbParameter, respectively. So, make sure to import the System.Data.Common namespace.

Then add the first factory class—SqlClientFactory—and write the code shown in Listing 4-2 in it.

Listing 4-2. SqlClientFactory Class

```
public class SqlClientFactory:IDatabaseFactory
{
    public DbConnection GetConnection()
    {
        return new SqlConnection();
    }

    public DbCommand GetCommand()
    {
        return new SqlCommand();
    }

    public DbParameter GetParameter()
    {
        return new SqlParameter();
    }
}
```

The SqlClientFactory class implements IDatabaseFactory. The three methods GetConnection(), GetCommand(), and GetParameter() return new instances of SqlConnection, SqlCommand, and SqlParameter, respectively. These classes reside in the System.Data.SqlClient namespace, so make sure to import it into your class file. The SqlClientFactory is responsible for creating family members of the SqlClient family.

Now add an OleDbFactory class to the Core folder and write the code shown in Listing 4-3 in it.

Listing 4-3. OleDbFactory Class

```
public class OleDbFactory : IDatabaseFactory
{
    public DbConnection GetConnection()
    {
        return new OleDbConnection();
    }

    public DbCommand GetCommand()
    {
        return new OleDbCommand();
    }

    public DbParameter GetParameter()
    {
        return new OleDbParameter();
    }
}
```

The OleDbFactory class also implements IDatabaseFactory. The three methods GetConnection(), GetCommand(), and GetParameter() return a new instance of OleDbConnection, OleDbCommand, and OleDbParameter, respectively. These classes reside in the System.Data.OleDb namespace, so make sure to import it into your class file. The OleDbFactory is responsible for creating family members of the OleDb family.

Next, add the DatabaseHelper class to the Core folder. This class acts as the client of the factories and receives a factory through its constructor. This is shown in Listing 4-4.

Listing 4-4. Receiving a Factory in the DatabaseHelper

```
public class DatabaseHelper
{
    private IDatabaseFactory factory;

    public DatabaseHelper(IDatabaseFactory factory)
    {
        this.factory = factory;
    }
    ...
    ...
}
```

The DatabaseHelper constructor receives a parameter of type IDatabaseFactory. This parameter is stored in a factory private variable.

The DatabaseHelper class has four methods—two overloads of the ExecuteSelect() method and the two overloads of the ExecuteAction() method. The first set of methods is intended for executing SELECT queries while the second set of methods is intended for executing action queries. The overloads of ExecuteSelect() are shown in Listing 4-5.

Listing 4-5. Overloads of the ExecuteSelect() Method

```
public DbDataReader ExecuteSelect(string query)
{
    DbConnection cnn = factory.GetConnection();
    cnn.ConnectionString = AppSettings.ConnectionString;
    DbCommand cmd = factory.GetCommand();
    cmd.Connection = cnn;
    cmd.CommandType = CommandType.Text;
    cmd.CommandText = query;
    cnn.Open();
    return cmd.ExecuteReader(CommandBehavior.CloseConnection);
}

public DbDataReader ExecuteSelect(string query,DbParameter[] parameters)
{
    DbConnection cnn = factory.GetConnection();
    cnn.ConnectionString = AppSettings.ConnectionString;
    DbCommand cmd = factory.GetCommand();
    cmd.Connection = cnn;
    cmd.CommandType = CommandType.Text;
    cmd.CommandText = query;
    cmd.Parameters.AddRange(parameters);
    cnn.Open();
    return cmd.ExecuteReader(CommandBehavior.CloseConnection);
}
```

The first overload of ExecuteSelect() accepts a query, whereas the second overload accepts a query and an array of DbParameter objects. This way you can execute SELECT queries without and with parameters.

Inside, the code calls the GetConnection() method of the factory to retrieve a DbConnection object (make sure to import the System.Data and System.Data.Common namespaces). Depending on the factory passed into the constructor, this will be either an SqlConnection object or an OleDbConnection object. Then the ConnectionString property of the DbConnection is set to the ConnectionString from the AppSettings.

Then the GetCommand() method is called to get an instance of DbCommand. Again, depending on the factory, this would be either SqlCommand or OleDbCommand.

Then the Connection, CommandType, and CommandText properties of the DbCommand object are set to the corresponding values.

Finally, the connection is opened using the Open() method and the query is executed using the ExecuteReader() method. Notice that the CommandBehavior enumeration's CloseConnection value is passed to the ExecuteReader() method so that closing the data reader will also close the underlying connection. The ExecuteReader() method returns a DbDataReader object, which is returned to the caller.

The second overload of ExecuteSelect() is quite similar to the first one. The only difference is that it adds the supplied DbParameter objects into the Parameters collection of the DbCommand object. This is done using the AddRange() method of the Parameters collection.

The two overloads of ExecuteAction() are shown in Listing 4-6.

Listing 4-6. Overloads of ExecuteAction( )

```
public int ExecuteAction(string query)
{
    DbConnection cnn = factory.GetConnection();
    cnn.ConnectionString = AppSettings.ConnectionString;
    DbCommand cmd = factory.GetCommand();
    cmd.Connection = cnn;
    cmd.CommandType = CommandType.Text;
    cmd.CommandText = query;
    cnn.Open();
    int i = cmd.ExecuteNonQuery();
    cnn.Close();
    return i;
}

public int ExecuteAction(string query,DbParameter[] parameters)
{
    DbConnection cnn = factory.GetConnection();
    cnn.ConnectionString = AppSettings.ConnectionString;
    DbCommand cmd = factory.GetCommand();
    cmd.Connection = cnn;
    cmd.CommandType = CommandType.Text;
    cmd.CommandText = query;
    cmd.Parameters.AddRange(parameters);
    cnn.Open();
    int i = cmd.ExecuteNonQuery();
    cnn.Close();
    return i;
}
```

We won't discuss these methods in detail as they are quite similar to the ExecuteSelect() overloads. The ExecuteAction() overloads are intended to execute action queries, and hence they call the ExecuteNonQuery() method on the DbCommand object. Both of these methods return an integer indicating the number of records affected by the query.

■ **Note** While building a full-fledged data-access component you may also need to take into account other possibilities, such as executing scalar queries or executing stored procedures. We won't discuss all these possibilities here for the sake of simplicity.

Next, add the HomeController class to the Controllers folder. The HomeController will have two actions—Index() and ExecuteQuery(). The Index() action simply returns the Index view whereas the ExecuteQuery() action is invoked when the Execute button from the Index view is clicked (see the previous application screenshots). These actions are shown in Listing 4-7.

Listing 4-7. Actions of HomeController

```
public IActionResult Index()
{
    return View();
}


[HttpPost]
public IActionResult ExecuteQuery(string factorytype,string query)
{
    IDatabaseFactory factory = null;
    if (factorytype == "sqlclient")
    {
        factory = new SqlClientFactory();
    }
    else
    {
        factory = new OleDbFactory();
    }
    DatabaseHelper helper = new DatabaseHelper(factory);
    query = query.ToLower();
    if(query.StartsWith("select"))
    {
        DbDataReader reader = helper.ExecuteSelect(query);
        return View("ShowTable", reader);
    }
    else
    {
        int i = helper.ExecuteAction(query);
        return View("ShowResult", i);
    }
}
```

The ExecuteQuery() action receives two parameters—factorytype and query. These parameters are nothing but the selection made in the dropdown list and the query entered in the text area, respectively.

Inside, the code checks the factorytype value and accordingly creates either an SqlClientFactory or an OleDbFactory object. Notice that the factory variable is of type IDatabaseFactory.

■ **Note**   This example accepts SQL queries from the user and executes them without performing any validations. This can have several security implications and should be avoided in real-world applications. Here, we use it for the sake of simplicity.

Then the DatabaseHelper class is instantiated by passing the factory to its constructor.

If the query begins with "select" then the code assumes that it's a SELECT statement and the ExecuteSelect() method of DatabaseHelper is called by passing the query to it. In order to display the data fetched by the query, the DbDataReader object is passed to the ShowTable view.

If the query is an action query then the code calls the ExecuteAction() method of DatabaseHelper by passing the query to it. In order to display the number of records affected by the query, the return value of ExecuteAction() is passed to the ShowResult view.

Next, add an Index view to the Views/Home folder and write the markup shown in Listing 4-8 in it.

Listing 4-8. Markup of Index View

```
<html>
<head>
    <title></title>
</head>
<body>
    <h1>Execute Query</h1>
    <form asp-controller="Home" asp-action="ExecuteQuery" method="post">
        <h4>Select Factory :</h4>
        <select name="factorytype">
            <option value="sqlclient">SqlClient</option>
            <option value="oledb">OleDb</option>
        </select>
        <h4>Enter your query :</h4>
        <textarea name="query" rows="4" cols="40"></textarea>
        <br /><br />
        <input type="submit" value="Execute" />
    </form>
</body>
</html>
```

The Index view uses a form tag helper to render a form that submits to the ExecuteQuery action of the HomeController. The factorytype dropdown list contains two options, SqlClient and OleDb, that represent the corresponding factories. The query text area allows you to enter the query, and the Execute button submits the form.

Now add a ShowTable view to the Views/Home folder and write the markup shown in Listing 4-9 in it.

Listing 4-9. Markup of ShowTable View

```
@model System.Data.Common.DbDataReader

<html>
<head>
    <title></title>
</head>
<body>
    <h1>Query Results</h1>

    <table border="1" cellpadding="10">
        @while (Model.Read())
        {
            <tr>
                @for(int i=0;i<Model.FieldCount;i++)
                {
                    <td>@Model.GetString(i)</td>
                }
            </tr>
        }
```

121

```
    @{
        Model.Close();
    }
    </table>

</body>
</html>
```

The @model directive sets the model for the view to DbDataReader. In the main body of the view, a table is rendered by reading the data from DbDataReader. This is done using the Read() method and the @white block. Since the columns fetched by the query are not known at development time, a for loop iterates through all the columns of DbDataReader and renders table cells accordingly. The code assumes that the columns contain string data only and uses the GetString() method to retrieve the column content.

Finally, the DbDataReader is closed by calling its Close() method.

■ **Note**   Since this is just a proof of concept application, we simply passed the DbDataReader to the view. In a more real-world situation you may grab all the data from the DbDataReader into a data structure in the controller and pass that data to the view instead of to a data reader.

Now, add a ShowResult view to the Views/Home folder and write the markup shown in Listing 4-10 in it.

Listing 4-10. Markup of ShowResult View

```
<html>
<head>
    <title></title>
</head>
<body>
    <h1>Your query affected @Model record(s)!</h1>
</body>
</html>
```

This markup is quite straightforward. It simply displays the number of records affected by the action query to the user by outputting the Model value (an integer in this case).

This completes the application. Run the application and see whether it works as expected by switching the factories.

Storing Factory Settings

In the example that you just completed, you picked the factory to be used from a dropdown list. A similar technique was used in the example demonstrating the factory method pattern in the previous chapter. Although this is alright for demonstration, in a more realistic situation the factory to be used would be decided by some other means. Some possibilities are:

- Some business logic will decide which factory to use.

- You may store the factory to be used in the configuration file and then pick the settings from there for your code.

- You may store the class name of the factory class to be instantiated in the configuration file and then use .NET reflection to instantiate it.

The first approach is application specific and code centric. So, let's see how the other two approaches can be used.

Storing Factory Name in the Configuration File

In this technique you store the factory name to be used in the configuration file instead of in a dropdown list. Your code then reads these settings and accordingly instantiates a factory.

Open the appsettings.json file of the example that you just completed and modify it as per listing 4-11.

Listing 4-11. Storing Factory Name in Configuration File

```json
{
  "Data": {
    "DefaultConnection": {
      "ConnectionString": "Server=.;Database=Northwind;Trusted_Connection=True;"
    }
  },

  "AppSettings": {
    "Factory": "sqlclient"
  }
}
```

Notice the code shown in the bold letters. It creates an AppSettings section with a key—Factory. This key has a value of sqlclient indicating that you wish to instantiate the SqlClientFactory class. If you wish to use OleDbFactory you need to change this setting to oledb.

Next, open the Startup class and write the code to fill the AppSettings class with the setting just discussed (see Chapter 1 to know more). We won't discuss that code in too much detail here, but it will look like this:

```
public Startup(IHostingEnvironment env, IApplicationEnvironment appEnv)
{
    ...

    AppSettings.ConnectionString = config.Get<string>("Data:DefaultConnection:ConnectionString");
    AppSettings.Factory = config.Get <string>("AppSettings:Factory");
}
```

Finally, change the ExecuteQuery() action from the HomeController as shown in Listing 4-12.

Listing 4-12. Modified ExecuteQuery() Action

```
public IActionResult ExecuteQuery(string query)
{
    IDatabaseFactory factory = null;
    string factorytype = AppSettings.Factory;
    if (factorytype == "sqlclient")
    {
        factory = new SqlClientFactory();
    }
```

```
    else
    {
        factory = new OleDbFactory();
    }
    DatabaseHelper helper = new DatabaseHelper(factory);
    ...
    ...
}
```

As you can see, the code now checks the factory setting stored in the configuration file instead of in the dropdown list and instantiates a factory. The factory is then passed to the DatabaseHelper.

Storing Factory Type Name in the Configuration File

In the previous technique, although you stored the factory setting in the configuration type, you still needed the if block to check the setting and instantiate the factory type. If you wish to avoid such checking altogether, you can resort to .NET reflection and the Activator class.

Modify the appsettings.json file as shown in Listing 4-13.

Listing 4-13. Storing Factory Class Name in Configuration File

```
{
  "Data": {
    "DefaultConnection": {
      "ConnectionString": "Server=.;Database=Northwind;Trusted_Connection=True;"
    }
  },

  "AppSettings": {
    "FactoryType": "AbstractFactory.Core.SqlClientFactory"
  }
}
```

As you can see, this time you store the fully qualified type name of the factory class in the FactoryType key. Then modify your ExecuteQuery() method as shown in Listing 4-14.

Listing 4-14. Using Activator.CreateInstance() to Instantiate Factory

```
public IActionResult ExecuteQueryReflection(string query)
{
    IDatabaseFactory factory = null;
    string factorytype = AppSettings.FactoryType;
    ObjectHandle o = Activator.CreateInstance(Assembly.GetExecutingAssembly().FullName,
    factorytype);
    factory = (IDatabaseFactory)o.Unwrap();
    DatabaseHelper helper = new DatabaseHelper(factory);
    ...
    ...
}
```

The code assumes that the FactoryType key from the configuration file is loaded into the FactoryType property of the AppSettings class. The code shown in bold letters uses the CreateInstance() method of the Activator class. The CreateInstance() method takes two parameters. The first parameter is the Assembly (System.Reflection namespace) containing the factory type. In this example, the factories are part of the web application itself and hence the code passes the current assembly using the GetExecutingAssembly() method. The second parameter is the fully qualified type name that is to be instantiated. This parameter comes from the configuration file.

The CreateInstance() method returns a ObjectHandle (System.Runtime.Remoting namespace). To get the actual factory instance, the code calls the Unwrap() method on the ObjectHandle. The factory is then passed to the DatabaseHelper.

Builder

At times the object being constructed is complex in nature. It may consist of several other types. Moreover, multiple such complex objects might be needed in the system. So, you end up creating complex objects that have different representations but are constructed in a similar way. **The builder pattern allows you to isolate the construction process of an object from its representation.** The construction process under consideration can be used to create different representations.

A *representation* of an object means its overall structure and constituent parts. The complex object being constructed is represented by aggregation of one or more parts.

Design and Explanation

The UML diagram of the builder pattern is shown in Figure 4-6.

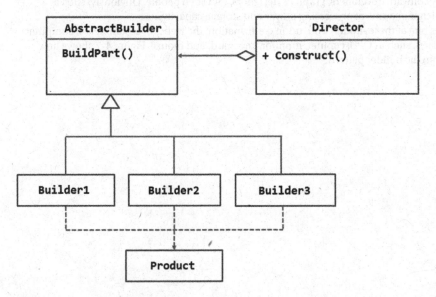

Figure 4-6. *Design of builder pattern*

As shown in the figure there is an abstraction of a builder in the form of the AbstractBuilder class. This class defines the BuildPart() method that is supposed to create a part of the complex object under consideration.

The AbstractBuilder is inherited by three builders—Builder1, Builder2, and Builder3. Each of the builder classes implements BuildPart(). Thus, each concrete builder class is responsible for creating the part it is assigned to build. The build process of all the three builder classes finally arrives at a finished Product. The Product is the complex object constructed by the builder. Thus, depending on the builder being used, the final Product will have parts added by Builder1, Builder2, or Builder3.

The process of constructing the Product is ordered by a class often called Director. Thus, the Director class initiates the Product construction process through its Construct() method.

■ **Note**   The Director and AbstractBuilder are connected through a line having an empty diamond facing the Director side and an arrow toward the AbstractBuilder side. The empty diamond indicates that the Director is doing an aggregation of parts created by the builder.

Example

Suppose you are building a website for a company that sells assembled personal computers. They want end users to select from three PC types—Home Computer, Office Computer, and Development Computer. The Home Computer contains parts that are suitable for home and student use. Obviously these parts are cheaper than the other types. The Office Computer is intended to be used in offices. Its parts are suitable for an office environment in terms of their power, capacity, and aesthetics. Finally, the Development Computer is intended to be used by software developers, graphics designers, and such people. Obviously, such a computer will be quite richer in terms of processing power and storage capacity.

The end user selects one of these models and, upon confirmation, the website "assembles" a computer by aggregating various parts, such as CPU, cabinet, monitor, keyboard, and mouse. Figure 4-7 shows how these requirements fit into the builder pattern.

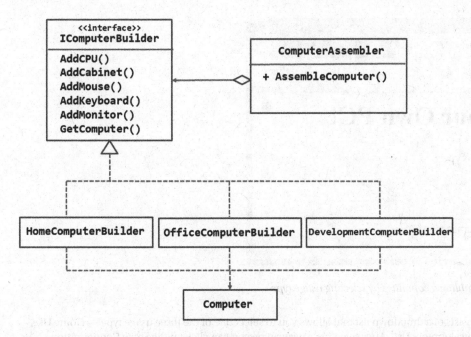

Figure 4-7. *Building a computer by aggregating its parts*

As you can see, the IComputerBuilder interface defines all six methods, namely AddCPU(), AddCabinet(), AddMouse(), AddKeyboard(), AddMonitor(), and GetComputer(). The first five methods add the corresponding parts to a computer, whereas the GetComputer() method returns a finished Computer. The IComputerBuilder interface is implemented by three builders—HomeComputerBuilder, OfficeComputerBuilder, and DevelopmentComputerBuilder. Thus, depending on the builder used to construct the computer, parts of the computer will vary.

The ComputerAssembler class is the director. It instructs that a computer be constructed through its AssembleComputer() method. The AssembleComputer() method calls the builder methods such as AddCPU() and AddKeyboard(). Thus, the process of building is defined by the ComputerAssembler class. The AssembleComputer() then returns the finished computer.

The user interface of this example is a page, as shown in Figure 4-8.

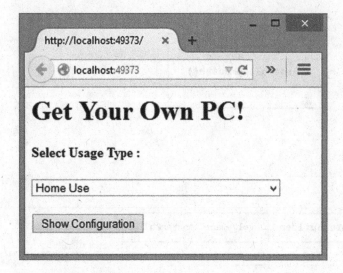

Figure 4-8. *Assembling a computer by selecting usage type*

The page consists of a dropdown list that allows you to select one of the three usage types—Home Use, Office Use, and Development Use. After selecting a usage type you can click on the Show Configuration button. Doing so assembles a computer and shows a list of parts used in it, as shown in Figure 4-9.

Figure 4-9. *Showing a computer's configuration*

Of course, the example uses sample part codes for the sake of testing, but you can add more descriptive and meaningful part codes.

To develop this example, begin by creating a new ASP.NET web application using Visual Studio and configure it to use MVC as well as Entity Framework (see Chapter 1 for more details).

Then add a ComputerPart class in the Core folder and write the code shown in Listing 4-15 in it.

Listing 4-15. ComputerPart Model Class

```
[Table("ComputerParts")]
public class ComputerPart
{
    [DatabaseGenerated(DatabaseGeneratedOption.Identity)]
    public int Id { get; set; }
    [Required]
    [StringLength(20)]
    public string UseType { get; set; }
    [Required]
    [StringLength(20)]
    public string Part { get; set; }
    [Required]
    [StringLength(50)]
    public string PartCode { get; set; }
}
```

The ComputerPart class has four properties—Id, UseType, Part, and PartCode. The UseType property indicates the usage type, such as HOME, OFFICE, or DEV. The Part property specifies the part name, such as CPU or KEYBOARD. The PartCode property holds the part code of a part. Notice that the ComputerPart class is mapped to the ComputerParts table.

The application DbContext that uses the ComputerPart class is shown in Listing 4-16.

Listing 4-16. DbContext of the Application

```
public class AppDbContext : DbContext
{
    public DbSet<ComputerPart> ComputerParts { get; set; }

    protected override void OnConfiguring(DbContextOptionsBuilder optionsBuilder)
    {
        optionsBuilder.UseSqlServer(AppSettings.ConnectionString);
    }
}
```

The AppDbContext class defines a single DbSet—ComputerParts. The overridden OnConfiguring() method sets the SQL Server database to be used by utilizing the UseSqlServer() method.

Now, add the Computer class to the Core folder. The Computer class represents the finished computer and is shown in Listing 4-17.

Listing 4-17. Computer Class

```
public class Computer
{
    public List<ComputerPart> Parts { get; set; }
}
```

The Computer class simply contains a list of ComputerPart objects.

Now, add an IComputerBuilder interface to the Core folder and write the code shown in Listing 4-18 in it.

Listing 4-18. IComputerBuilder Interface

```
public interface IComputerBuilder
{
    void AddCPU();
    void AddCabinet();
    void AddMouse();
    void AddKeyboard();
    void AddMonitor();
    Computer GetComputer();
}
```

The IComputerBuilder interface consists of six methods as discussed earlier. Notice that GetComputer() returns a Computer while other methods are void.

Next, add a HomeComputerBuilder class to the Core folder. The HomeComputerBuilder class implements IComputerBuilder and is shown in Listing 4-19.

Listing 4-19. HomeComputerBuilder Class

```
public class HomeComputerBuilder:IComputerBuilder
{
    private Computer computer;

    public HomeComputerBuilder()
    {
        computer = new Computer();
        computer.Parts = new List<ComputerPart>();
    }

    public void AddCPU()
    {
        using (AppDbContext db = new AppDbContext())
        {
            var query = from p in db.ComputerParts
                        where p.UseType == "HOME" && p.Part == "CPU"
                        select p;
            computer.Parts.Add(query.SingleOrDefault());
        }
    }

    public void AddCabinet()
    {
        using (AppDbContext db = new AppDbContext())
        {
            var query = from p in db.ComputerParts
                        where p.UseType == "HOME" && p.Part == "CABINET"
                        select p;
            computer.Parts.Add(query.SingleOrDefault());
        }
    }
```

```
public void AddMouse()
{
    using (AppDbContext db = new AppDbContext())
    {
        var query = from p in db.ComputerParts
                    where p.UseType == "HOME" && p.Part == "MOUSE"
                    select p;
        computer.Parts.Add(query.SingleOrDefault());
    }
}

public void AddKeyboard()
{
    using (AppDbContext db = new AppDbContext())
    {
        var query = from p in db.ComputerParts
                    where p.UseType == "HOME" && p.Part == "KEYBOARD"
                    select p;
        computer.Parts.Add(query.SingleOrDefault());
    }
}

public void AddMonitor()
{
    using (AppDbContext db = new AppDbContext())
    {
        var query = from p in db.ComputerParts
                    where p.UseType == "HOME" && p.Part == "MONITOR"
                    select p;
        computer.Parts.Add(query.SingleOrDefault());
    }
}

public Computer GetComputer()
{
    return computer;
}
}
```

The HomeComputerBuilder class declares a field of type Computer that holds a reference to the finished computer. The constructor simply initializes the Computer class and its Parts collection.

The AddCPU() method fetches the PartCode for the HOME usage type and adds it to the Parts collection of the Computer object. The other AddXXXX() methods are quite identical and hence are not discussed here to save some space.

Finally, the GetComputer() method returns the Computer object to the caller.

Just now you created a HomeComputerBuilder class. Add OfficeComputerBuilder and DevelopmentComputerBuilder classes along the same lines. They are not discussed here to save some space. You may also grab them from the code download of this book.

Next, add a ComputerAssembler class to the Core folder. The ComputerAssembler class is the Director and is shown in Listing 4-20.

Listing 4-20. ComputerAssembler Class

```
public class ComputerAssembler
{
    private IComputerBuilder builder;

    public ComputerAssembler(IComputerBuilder builder)
    {
        this.builder = builder;
    }

    public Computer AssembleComputer()
    {
        builder.AddCPU();
        builder.AddCabinet();
        builder.AddMonitor();
        builder.AddKeyboard();
        builder.AddMouse();

        return builder.GetComputer();
    }
}
```

The ComputerAssembler class has a member of type IComputerBuilder. This variable is assigned in the constructor. Since the constructor accepts a parameter of type IComputerBuilder, you can pass HomeComputerBuilder, OfficeComputerBuilder, or DevelopmentComputerBuilder—or any other class that implements IComputerBuilder.

The AssembleComputer() method calls methods on the builder such as AddCPU() and AddKeyboard(). Once all the parts are added, the finished Computer is retrieved by calling the GetComputer() method and is then returned to the caller.

Now let's move on to the controller and the views required by the application. Add HomeController to the Controllers folder and write two actions in it, as shown in Listing 4-21.

Listing 4-21. Build Action Uses ComputerAssembler

```
public IActionResult Index()
{
    return View();
}

public IActionResult Build(string usagetype)
{
    IComputerBuilder builder = null;
    switch(usagetype)
    {
        case "home":
            builder = new HomeComputerBuilder();
            break;
        case "office":
            builder = new OfficeComputerBuilder();
            break;
```

```
        case "development":
            builder = new DevelopmentComputerBuilder();
            break;
    }
    ComputerAssembler assembler = new ComputerAssembler(builder);
    Computer computer = assembler.AssembleComputer();
    return View("Success", computer);
}
```

The Index() action simply returns the Index view. The form from the Index view submits to the Build() action. The Build() action receives the usagetype. The switch statement checks the usagetype and accordingly one of the three classes implementing IComputerBuilder is instantiated.

Then a ComputerAssembler is created by passing the builder to its constructor. The AssembleComputer() method of the ComputerAssembler is called to assemble the computer. The finished Computer returned by the AssembleComputer() method is passed as a model to the Success view.

Now add an Index view to the Views/Home folder and write the markup shown in Listing 4-22 in it.

Listing 4-22. Markup of Index View

```html
<html>
<head>
    <title></title>
</head>
<body>
    <h1>Get Your Own PC!</h1>
    <form asp-controller="Home" asp-action="Build" method="post">
        <h4>Select Usage Type :</h4>
        <select name="usagetype">
            <option value="home">Home Use</option>
            <option value="office">Office Use</option>
            <option value="development">Software Development and Graphic Designing</option>
        </select>
        <br /><br />
        <input type="submit" value="Show Configuration" />
    </form>
</body>
</html>
```

The Index view uses a form tag helper to render a form that submits to the Build action of the HomeController. The form consists of a dropdown list with three usagetype values—home, office, and development. The Show Configuration button posts the form to the Build() action.

Then add a Success view to the Views/Home folder and write the markup shown in Listing 4-23 in it.

Listing 4-23. Markup of Success View

```html
@model Builder.Core.Computer

<html>
<head>
    <title>Success</title>
</head>
```

```
<body>
    <h1>Your computer has the following configuration :</h1>
    @foreach(var item in Model.Parts)
    {
        <h3>@item.PartCode</h3>
    }
</body>
</html>
```

The @model directive sets the model of the view to Computer. The main part of the view consists of a foreach loop that iterates through the Parts collection of the Model. Every iteration outputs the PartCode onto the page.

This completes the application. Before running the application, you need to create the BuilderDb database (see Chapter 1 to know more). Once the database and the table are created, add a few records for each of the computer parts (see the queries that you wrote earlier).

Now run the application and see whether the correct configuration is shown for various usage types. Can the Director class invoke the build process differently? Why not? For example, if you want to allow the user to pick all the parts except the monitor, then the Director class may not call the AddMonitor() method. Additionally, the sequence in which the object is constructed is decided by the Director class according to the application's requirements.

Summary

This chapter covered the remaining two creational patterns, namely abstract factory and builder. As you must have seen, these two patterns are slightly more complex than the other three creational patterns.

The abstract factory is useful when you wish to create a family of related or dependent objects. This is unlike the factory method pattern, where your concern is to instantiate only one class rather than a family.

The builder pattern allows you to separate the object being built and the process with which it is built. This way you can use the same process to build objects that have different representations. The builder pattern relies on a Director class to invoke the process of object creation.

The creational patterns deal with object creation, and your concern is how to instantiate an object under consideration. The structural patterns, the subject matter of the next chapter, deal with the overall structure and relationship between various classes.

■ ■ ■

CHAPTER 5

Structural Patterns: Adapter, Bridge, Composite, and Decorator

Structural patterns deal with the arrangement and relationship between the classes in the system. They focus on how classes and objects are composed so as to form larger and more complex structures. Obviously, structural patterns need to take into account all those classes that make up the system.

There are seven patterns in this category: adapter, bridge, composite, decorator, façade, flyweight, and proxy. This chapter will discuss the first four, and the next chapter will discuss the remaining three. Specifically, this chapter will include the following:

- An overview of structural patterns

- The purpose of adapter, bridge, composite, and decorator patterns

- The UML representation of each of these patterns

- A proof of concept example for each pattern that illustrates how the pattern is used

An Overview of Structural Patterns

As mentioned earlier, structural patterns concern themselves with the arrangement and relationship between the classes. Some of the tasks accomplished by structural patterns include:

- Control and grant access to an object

- Map calls intended for a class to another class with a different design

- Add new functionality or features to existing objects

- Utilize a small number of objects to serve a large number of requests

- Simplify access to a complex subsystem

Structural patterns can be used while designing a new application or while modifying an existing application. Some structural patterns, such as adapter, are mostly used while extending an existing system. In all there are seven structural patterns. Just for the sake of understanding their purpose, they are listed here:

- **Adapter:** Matches interfaces of classes that are otherwise incompatible

- **Bridge:** Separates abstraction from its implementation

- **Composite:** Allows you to create tree structures in a uniform way to deal with the items

- **Decorator:** Adds features or functionality to an object dynamically without inheritance

- **Façade:** Provides a simplified way to access complex subsystems

- **Flyweight:** Serves a large number of requests for an object by sharing existing instance(s)

- **Proxy:** Provides a placeholder for another object so as to control access to it

Out of these seven, adapter, bridge, composite, and decorator will be discussed in this chapter. The façade, flyweight, and proxy will be the subject of the next chapter.

Adapter

Sometimes it so happens that you build an application using a class (say, ClassA). This class has its own design (properties and methods), and the rest of the code is targeted for this design. During an extension of the application, you are required to use some another class (say, ClassB) in place of ClassA. However, more often than not the design of ClassB is different than that of ClassA. There can be many reasons for this mismatch. For example, ClassB might be supplied by a third-party system, or might have been developed for an altogether different system and now your application wants to use it, and so on. How does one deal with such incompatible classes? One obvious way is to make changes in all places where ClassA was used such that the code now uses ClassB. As you might have guessed, this might amount to a lot of rework and testing.

The adapter pattern comes to the rescue in such situations. It allows you to work with classes that have incompatible design. **The adapter converts the interface of a class into another interface as expected by the client application.** So, continuing the preceding example, an adapter will map the interface of ClassB to that of ClassA. This way the changes required will be quite a bit less. Although this may sound like a patchy work, the adapter allows us to use classes that we can't otherwise use due to a mismatch in their interfaces.

A real-world example of adapter is a mobile charger—it converts voltage from a higher value (say, 230 V AC) to some lower value (say, 5 V DV). These two interfaces can't be otherwise used together, but the adapter in the mobile charger makes this possible.

Design and Explanation

The overall design of the adapter pattern is shown in Figure 5-1.

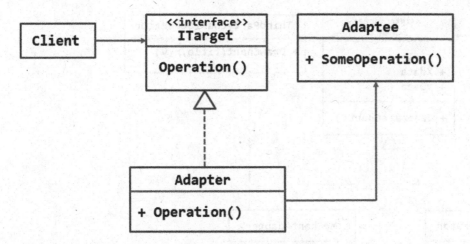

Figure 5-1. *UML diagram illustrating the adapter pattern*

The client is designed to work with one or more classes that have the interface ITarget. The ITarget interface has one method—Operation()—that is used by the client in its code. So, the client will have calls such as the following in its code:

```
ITarget obj = new OriginalTarget();
obj.Operation();
```

Here, OriginalTarget (not shown in the figure) is the class that adheres to ITarget. Now, during the extension of the application the Adaptee class comes into the picture. The Adaptee class is supposed to replace the OriginalTarget class. But Adaptee has the SomeOperation() method. Obviously, the two lines of code just shown need to be changed to in order to use the Adaptee class and its SomeOperation() method.

To simplify the change, the adapter class is used. The adapter class implements the ITarget interface. It also implements the Operation() method. The adapter class creates an instance of the Adaptee class. The Operation() method of adapter simply calls the SomeOperation() method of Adaptee. To code that uses the Adapter like this:

```
ITarget obj = new Adapter();
obj.Operation();
```

As you can see, the OriginalTarget can be easily substituted by adapter, thus causing minimal changes to the code.

Example

Now that you know what the adapter pattern does, let's apply this knowledge to a real-world scenario.

Suppose you developed a website that displays information in the form of a bar chart. While developing the application you created your own charting component instead of using a third-party component. After its release, the web application became quite popular and you now wish to replace your charting component with a richer third-party charting component. However, the designs of the third-party charting component and your charting component differ. To minimize the number of changes, you decided to create an adapter that maps the older interface with the new interface. Figure 5-2 shows the overall arrangement of the classes involved in the system.

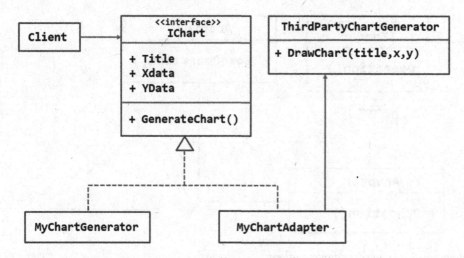

Figure 5-2. *Adapter for mapping charting components*

The application consists of an IChart interface. The IChart interface consists of three properties (Title, XData, and YData) and one method (GenerateChart()).

Originally, you created the MyChartGenerator class, which implemented the IChart interface. Hence, the original version of the application used MyChartGenerator everywhere. In this example, the controller acts as the client of IChart.

The ThirdPartyChartGenerator is the class that represents the third-party charting component. As you can see, the ThirdPartyChartGenerator has a single method, DrawChart(), that takes the title, x-axis data, and y-axis data.

Since MyChartGenerator and ThirdPartyChartGenerator have incompatible interfaces, an adapter is necessary. In this example, the MyChartAdapter class is such an adapter. The MyChartAdapter class implements the IChart interface so that its design conforms to the original requirements. The implementation of GenerateChart() in the MyChartAdapter class forwards the call to the DrawChart() method of the ThirdPartyChartGenerator.

Let's move ahead and put these details into an ASP.NET application. The main page of the application that you will develop is shown in Figure 5-3.

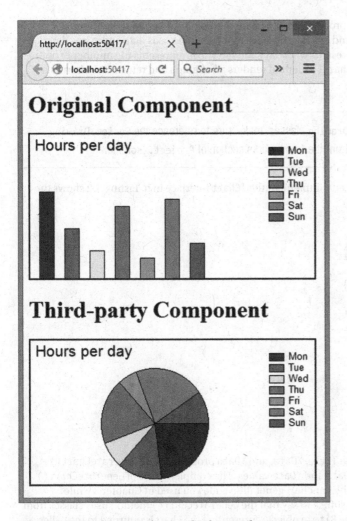

Figure 5-3. *Application adapting third-party charting component*

The application displays two charts—the top one using the MyChartGenerator class and the bottom one using the ThirdPartyChartGenerator class. Just for the sake of distinguishing the two charts, the MyChartGenerator renders a bar chart whereas the ThirdPartyChartGenerator renders a pie chart.

To develop this application, begin by creating a new ASP.NET web application using Visual Studio and configure it to use MVC (see Chapter 1 for more details).

Then, add the IChart interface to the Core folder and write the code in it as shown in Listing 5-1.

Listing 5-1. IChart Interface

```
public interface IChart
{
    string Title { get; set; }
    List<string> XData { get; set; }
    List<int> YData { get; set; }
    Bitmap GenerateChart();
}
```

The IChart interface consists of three properties and one method. The Title property represents the title rendered on the chart. The XData and YData properties represent the x-axis data and y-axis data, respectively. In this example, the x-axis represents weekdays and the y-axis represents the number of hours worked on a particular day. The GenerateChart() method renders a bar graph and returns the chart as a Bitmap object.

■ **Note**   Since this example uses System.Drawing classes, make sure to reference the System.Drawing assembly. Also, delete the dnxcore50 entry from the frameworks section of Project.json file.

Next, add the MyChartGenerator class and implement the IChart interface in it. Listing 5-2 shows the skeleton of MyChartGenerator.

Listing 5-2. MyChartGenerator Class

```
public class MyChartGenerator : IChart
{
    public string Title { get; set; }
    public List<string> XData { get; set; }
    public List<int> YData { get; set; }

    public Bitmap GenerateChart()
    {
        ...
        ...
        return chartBitmap;
    }
}
```

The MyChartGenerator implements the Title, XData, and YData properties. The GenerateChart() method renders a bar chart based on the XData and YData values. The complete code of GenerateChart() is not given here, since it's quite similar to the bar chart generation code you used in Chapter 3 while discussing the factory method pattern. It is suffice to say that the GenerateChart() method uses classes from System.Drawing to render the bar chart. The Bitmap object representing the chart is returned to the caller.

Now, add ThirdPartyChartGenerator class to the Core folder. Listing 5-3 shows the skeleton code of this class.

Listing 5-3. ThirdPartyChartGenerator Class

```
public class ThirdPartyChartGenerator
{

    public Bitmap DrawChart(string title,List<string> xData, List<int> yData)
    {
        ...
        ...
        return chartBitmap;
    }
}
```

The ThirdPartyChartGenerator has a DrawChart() method that accepts three parameters— title, xData, and yData. Inside, it uses System.Drawing classes to render a pie chart. The resulting Bitmap is returned to caller. The implementation of DrawChart() is not shown here since it's quite similar to the pie chart generation code you used in Chapter 3.

■ **Note**   To save you some time, you may grab the source code for this example from the code download of this book.

Next, add the MyChartAdapter class to the Core folder and write the code shown in Listing 5-4 in it.

Listing 5-4. MyChartAdapter Class

```
public class MyChartAdapter : IChart
{
    public string Title { get; set; }
    public List<string> XData { get; set; }
    public List<int> YData { get; set; }

    public Bitmap GenerateChart()
    {
        ThirdPartyChartGenerator chart = new ThirdPartyChartGenerator();
        return chart.DrawChart(Title, XData, YData);
    }
}
```

The MyChartAdapter class implements the IChart interface. Notice how it adapts the ThirdPartyChartGenerator. The GenerateChart() method creates an instance of ThirdPartyChartGenerator and calls DrawChart() on it. The Title, XData, and YData properties are passed as the values of the title, xData, and yData parameters, respectively. The Bitmap returned by the DrawChart() method is returned to the caller of GenerateChart().

Now, add HomeController to the Controllers folder. In addition to the Index() action, the HomeController has two more actions—one for rendering the chart using MyChartGenerator and one for rendering the chart using MyChartAdapter. The action that uses MyChartGenerator is shown in Listing 5-5.

Listing 5-5. Action That Uses MyChartGenerator

```
public IActionResult GetImageOwnComponent()
{
    IChart chart = new MyChartGenerator();

    chart.Title = "Hours per day";

    List<string> xdata = new List<string>();
    xdata.Add("Mon");
    xdata.Add("Tue");
    xdata.Add("Wed");
    xdata.Add("Thu");
    xdata.Add("Fri");
    xdata.Add("Sat");
    xdata.Add("Sun");
```

```
    List<int> ydata = new List<int>();
    ydata.Add(12);
    ydata.Add(7);
    ydata.Add(4);
    ydata.Add(10);
    ydata.Add(3);
    ydata.Add(11);
    ydata.Add(5);

    chart.XData = xdata;
    chart.YData = ydata;
    Bitmap bmp = chart.GenerateChart();
    MemoryStream stream = new MemoryStream();
    bmp.Save(stream, ImageFormat.Png);
    byte[] data = stream.ToArray();
    stream.Close();
    return File(data, "image/png");
}
```

The GetImageOwnComponent() action instantiates the MyChartGenerator class, sets its Title, XData, and YData properties, and then calls the GenerateChart() method.

The Bitmap is saved on a MemoryStream using its Save() method (make sure to import the Adapter. Core, System.Drawing, System.Drawing.Imaging, and System.IO namespaces). The content of the MemoryStream is obtained as a byte array and is returned to the response stream using the File() method.

The second action, GetImageThirdPartyComponent(), is shown in Listing 5-6.

Listing 5-6. Action That Uses MyChartAdapter

```
public IActionResult GetImageThirdPartyComponent()
{
    IChart chart = new MyChartAdapter();

    chart.Title = "Hours per day";

    List<string> xdata = new List<string>();
    xdata.Add("Mon");
    xdata.Add("Tue");
    xdata.Add("Wed");
    xdata.Add("Thu");
    xdata.Add("Fri");
    xdata.Add("Sat");
    xdata.Add("Sun");

    List<int> ydata = new List<int>();
    ydata.Add(12);
    ydata.Add(7);
    ydata.Add(4);
    ydata.Add(10);
    ydata.Add(3);
    ydata.Add(11);
    ydata.Add(5);
```

```
        chart.XData = xdata;
        chart.YData = ydata;
        Bitmap bmp = chart.GenerateChart();
        MemoryStream stream = new MemoryStream();
        bmp.Save(stream, ImageFormat.Png);
        byte[] data = stream.ToArray();
        stream.Close();
        return File(data, "image/png");
}
```

As you can see, MyChartGenerator is now substituted with MyChartAdapter. Recollect that the GenerateChart() method of MyChartAdapter actually invokes the DrawChart() method of ThirdPartyChartGenerator. The remaining code is quite similar to the previous action.

Next, add an Index view to the Views/Home folder and write the markup shown in Listing 5-7 in it.

Listing 5-7. Markup of Index View

```html
<html>
<head>
    <title></title>
</head>
<body>
    <h1>Original Component</h1>
    <img src="/home/GetImageOwnComponent" />
    <h1>Third-party Component</h1>
    <img src="/home/GetImageThirdPartyComponent" />
</body>
</html>
```

The Index view consists of two <img> elements—one pointing to the GetImageOwnComponent() action and the other pointing to the GetImageThirdPartyComponent() action. This way the image file content returned by these actions is displayed as an image in the browser.

This completes the application. Run the application and check whether it works as expected.

Object Adapter vs. Class Adapter

In the preceding example, how does the MyChartAdapter class adapt ThirdPartyChartGenerator? The GenerateChart() method creates an object of ThirdPartyChartGenerator and then calls its DrawChart() method. Since the adapter class uses an object of the adaptee, this type of adapter is called an *object adapter*.

There is one more way for the adapter to get the job done. The MyChartAdapter class can implement an IChart interface as well as inherit from a ThirdPartyChartGenerator class. Then the GenerateChart() method can call the DrawChart() method as shown in Listing 5-8.

Listing 5-8. Class Adapter

```
public class MyChartAdapter : ThirdPartyChartGenerator, IChart
{
    public string Title { get; set; }
    public List<string> XData { get; set; }
    public List<int> YData { get; set; }

    public Bitmap GenerateChart()
    {
        return this.DrawChart(Title, XData, YData);
    }
}
```

Since MyChartAdapter now inherits from ThirdPartyChartGenerator, there is no need to instantiate ThirdPartyChartGenerator. The GenerateChart() method can simply call the DrawChart() method of the base class. This type of adapter is called a *class adapter*.

Bridge

A complex system consists of several classes. Such systems often evolve over a period of time, resulting in multiple versions of the software. It is important to ensure that the clients who use the original version of the system do not break or alter its behavior when new versions are released. In other words, systems must keep their overall interfaces the same, even when the way they are implemented changes across different versions. The bridge pattern helps you achieve this goal. **The bridge pattern decouples an abstraction from its implementation so that they can evolve independently.**

Compare it with a real-life bridge joining two isolated pieces of land. The pieces of land are free to develop independently of one another. What joins these two independently developing pieces is the bridge. Another example is a photo-viewer application. In this case, the photo-viewer application and the image formats it supports can vary independently. Yet another example is a mobile phone and the SIM cards used in it. Again, each can evolve independently.

Thus, the bridge pattern involves two "sides"—one that represents the interfaces used by the clients and another that represents the implementations.

Design and Explanation

The UML diagram in Figure 5-4 illustrates the bridge pattern.

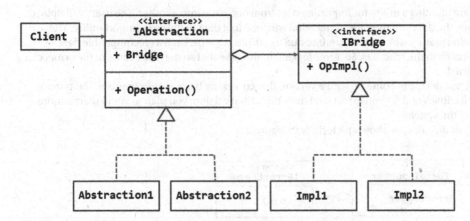

Figure 5-4. *UML diagram illustrating the bridge pattern*

The figure shows an interface, IAbstraction. This is the abstraction as seen by the client. The IAbstraction is implemented by two classes—Abstraction1 and Abstraction2. They represent two versions of the same abstraction. Abstraction1 and Abstraction2 form one side of the bridge.

The Operation() method of the abstractions use a component to get some work done. This component is represented by the IBridge interface. The IBridge interface is implemented by two classes—Impl1 and Impl2. These classes implement the OpImpl() method as per the requirement. The Impl1 and Impl2 classes form the other side of the bridge.

Notice that the aggregation symbol is used simply to hint that the classes implementing IAbstraction interface (Abstraction1 and Abstraction2) contain an object that implements IBridge. This object can be accessed through the Bridge property.

Suppose initially you came up with version 1.0 of the system just outlined. Version 1.0 has IAbstraction, and its concrete implementation is in the form of Abstraction1. It also has IBridge, and its concrete implementation is in the form of Impl1. Version 1.0 is being used by certain client applications.

Over a period of time, you decide to develop version 2.0 of the system. Version 2.0 will consist of IAbstraction, IBridge, and their respective concrete implementations—Abstraction2 and Impl2. The older clients can continue to use version 1.0 classes, whereas the newer clients will use version 2.0 classes. Thus, abstraction as well as implementation can vary independently.

At first glance you may find the bridge pattern to be quite similar to the adapter pattern. However, they are not the same. First, the adapter pattern usually comes into the picture on an ad-hoc basis. When something needs to be changed in a rather unexpected manner, and the new component needs to be fit into the existing system, adapter is used. However, the bridge pattern is consciously added into the system when you have anticipated that certain parts are going to evolve over a period of time. Second, the bridge has two clear-cut sides or branches that evolve independently as the system matures. Such a demarcation may not exist in the adapter.

Example

Now that you have an idea of what the bridge pattern is all about, let's make this more clear with a real-world example.

Suppose you are building a utility for importing data from one store into another. The users will upload a CSV file containing the data and then the application will feed that data to the data-import utility. The data-import operation may cause errors at runtime due to various reasons, such as incompatible data formats and a mismatch in the schemas. So, error logging is also essential so that the causes of the errors can be found out and fixed.

To begin with, you decide to come up with a version that covers the basic requirements of the system. Based on the user feedback and response received from this initial version, you plan to later create a more advanced version of the system.

The scenario just discussed is shown pictorially in Figure 5-5.

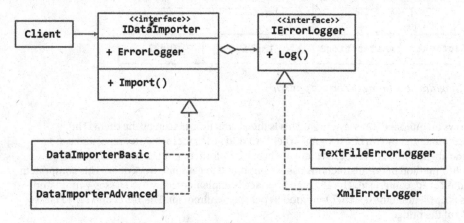

Figure 5-5. *Data importer and error logger components*

The IDataImporter interface represents the abstraction as seen by the client (a controller, in this example). The IDataImporter interface contains the ErrorLogger property and the Import() method. The ErrorLogger property is an object of IErrorLogger. The Import() method accepts a list of objects that are to be imported into the system. For the sake of simplicity, this example uses objects of the Customer class (not shown in the figure).

The IErrorLogger interface defines the Log() method. The Log() method accepts a message and logs it along with a timestamp.

The Import() method discussed earlier calls Log() whenever there is any error while importing the data.

The DataImporterBasic and TextFileErrorLogger classes represent the basic version of the utility. It might be that DataImporterBasic imports only the key fields, or it may lack any intelligent mapping between source and destination data types. For our proof of concept, the exact feature set is not important; what is important is to know that it's a basic version with limited functionality. Moreover, DataImporterBasic uses TextFileErrorLogger for the purpose of error logging. As the name suggests, the TextFileErrorLogger class logs the errors in a text file.

The DataImporterAdvanced and XmlErrorLogger classes represent the advanced version of the utility. DataImporterAdvanced might do some advanced operations that were not available in the basic version. Moreover, it logs the errors using the XmlErrorLogger class. XmlErrorLogger logs the errors in the XML format.

Now let's develop an ASP.NET application based on what we just discussed. The application you will develop is shown in Figure 5-6.

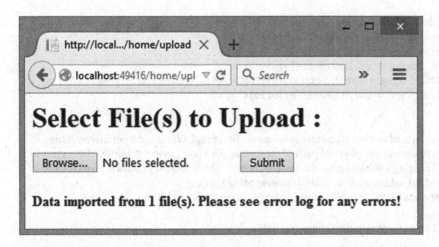

Figure 5-6. Application that uses data importer utility

As you can see, the application allows you to upload one or more CSV files using the file-input field. Once you select the files and click the Submit button, the data from the files is imported into the Customers table of the Northwind database by the data-importer utility discussed earlier. If there are any errors during the import operation they are logged to a file. A message is displayed on the page that informs the user of the completion of the import operation.

To develop this application, begin by creating a new ASP.NET web application using Visual Studio and configure it to use MVC and Entity Framework (see Chapter 1 for more details). Also store the connection string of the Northwind database in the appsettings.json file.

Then add the AppSettings class to the Core folder and write the code shown in Listing 5-9 in it.

Listing 5-9. AppSettings Class

```
public class AppSettings
{
    public static string ConnectionString { get; set; }
    public static string LogFileFolder { get; set; }
}
```

The AppSettings class consists of two static properties—ConnectionString and LogFileFolder. The ConnectionString property stores the database connection string, whereas LogFileFolder stores the folder inside which the log files are created. These properties are assigned from the Startup class as shown in Listing 5-10.

Listing 5-10. Setting the LogFileFolder Property

```
public Startup(IHostingEnvironment env, IApplicationEnvironment app)
{
    ConfigurationBuilder builder = new ConfigurationBuilder();
    builder.SetBasePath(app.ApplicationBasePath);
    builder.AddJsonFile("appsettings.json");
    IConfigurationRoot config = builder.Build();
    AppSettings.ConnectionString = config.Get<string>("Data:DefaultConnection:ConnectionString");
    AppSettings.LogFileFolder = env.MapPath("errorlogs");
}
```

Notice that the constructor of the Startup class receives an IHostingEnvironment parameter. This parameter can be used to figure out the physical path of the web application's wwwroot folder. This example stores the log files in the ErrorLogs folder under the wwwroot folder. The MapPath() method gives the full physical path to the ErrorLogs folder, such as C:\MyApp\wwwroot\errorlogs.

Then add a Customer class to the Core folder and write the code shown in Listing 5-11 in it.

Listing 5-11. Customer Class Mapped to the Customers Table

```
[Table("Customers")]
public class Customer
{
    public string CustomerID { get; set; }
    public string CompanyName { get; set; }
    public string ContactName { get; set; }
    public string Country { get; set; }
}
```

The Customer class consists of four properties—CustomerID, CompanyName, ContactName, and Country. The Customer class is mapped to the Customers table of the Northwind database. Note that the Customers table of the Northwind database contains many more columns. Here we use just four for the sake of simplicity.

Next, add the AppDbContext class to the Core folder and write the code shown in Listing 5-12 in it.

Listing 5-12. AppDbContext Class with Customers DbSet

```
public class AppDbContext : DbContext
{
    public DbSet<Customer> Customers { get; set; }

    protected override void OnConfiguring(DbContextOptionsBuilder optionsBuilder)
    {
        optionsBuilder.UseSqlServer(AppSettings.ConnectionString);
    }
}
```

The AppDbContext class defines the Customers DbSet and also configures the model to use the Northwind connection string using the UseSqlServer() method.

Now, add two interfaces—IDataImporter and IErrorLogger in the Core folder. Listing 5-13 shows the complete code of these interfaces.

Listing 5-13. IDataImporter and IErrorLogger Interfaces

```
public interface IErrorLogger
{
    void Log(string msg);
}

public interface IDataImporter
{
    IErrorLogger ErrorLogger { get; set; }
    void Import(List<Customer> data);
}
```

Notice that the Log() method accepts a string message that is logged to a file. The Import() method accepts a list of Customer objects.

Then add the two implementations of the IErrorLogger interface—TextFileErrorLogger and XmlErrorLogger into the Core folder. These classes are shown in Listing 5-14.

Listing 5-14. TextFileErrorLogger and XmlErrorLogger Classes

```
public class TextFileErrorLogger : IErrorLogger
{
    public void Log(string msg)
    {
        msg += $" [{DateTime.Now}]";
        msg += "\r\n";
        File.AppendAllText(AppSettings.LogFileFolder + "/errorlog.txt", msg);
    }
}

public class XmlErrorLogger : IErrorLogger
{
    public void Log(string msg)
    {
        msg = $"<error><message>{msg}</message><timestamp>{DateTime.Now}</timestamp></error>";
        File.AppendAllText(AppSettings.LogFileFolder + "/errorlog.xml", msg);
    }
}
```

The TextFileErrorLogger and XmlErrorLogger classes are quite similar in that both implement the Log() method. The Log() implementation of both classes adds a timestamp to the error message string. The resulting message is then appended to the respective log file using the AppendAllText() method of the File class (System.IO namespace).

The format and the file in which these classes log the data are different. The TextFileErrorLogger logs the errors in plain text format into an ErrorLog.txt file stored in the folder, as indicated by the LogFileFolder property.

The XmlErrorLogger logs the errors in XML format as shown in the code listing. The logs are written to an ErrorLog.xml file.

Next, add a DataImporterBasic class to the Core folder and write the code shown in Listing 5-15 in it.

Listing 5-15. DataImporterBasic Class Imports Data into Customers Table

```
public class DataImporterBasic : IDataImporter
{
    public IErrorLogger ErrorLogger { get; set; }

    public void Import(List<Customer> data)
    {
        using (AppDbContext db = new AppDbContext())
        {
            try
            {
                foreach (var item in data)
                {
                    db.Customers.Add(item);
                }
                db.SaveChanges();
            }
            catch(Exception ex)
            {
                ErrorLogger.Log(ex.Message);
            }
        }
    }
}
```

The Import() method accepts a list of Customer objects as the source data. Inside, the code iterates through the list and adds the Customer objects to the Customers DbSet. Calling the SaveChanges() method adds the newly added customers to the Customers table.

The try-catch block captures any exceptions during the import operation and logs the error(s) by calling the Log() method of the ErrorLogger object.

Now add a DataImporterAdvanced class to the Core folder and code it exactly like DataImporterBasic. This is just for the sake of simplicity. In a more realistic case the DataImporterAdvanced class will perform some advanced tasks not available in the DataImporterBasic.

Next, add a HomeController class to the Controllers folder. In addition to the Index() method, you need to add an action to deal with the uploaded files. This action is shown in Listing 5-16.

Listing 5-16. Dealing with Uploaded Files and Invoking Data Importer

```
[HttpPost]
public IActionResult Upload(IList<IFormFile> files)
{
    foreach (var file in files)
    {
        MemoryStream ms = new MemoryStream();
        Stream s = file.OpenReadStream();
        s.CopyTo(ms);
        byte[] data = ms.ToArray();
        s.Dispose();
        ms.Dispose();
```

```
        List<Customer> records = new List<Customer>();
        StringReader reader = new StringReader(System.Text.ASCIIEncoding.UTF8.
        GetString(data));
        while(true)
        {
            string record = reader.ReadLine();
            if (string.IsNullOrEmpty(record))
            {
                break;
            }
            else
            {
                string[] cols = record.Split(',');
                Customer obj = new Customer()
                {
                    CustomerID = cols[0],
                    CompanyName = cols[1],
                    ContactName = cols[2],
                    Country = cols[3]
                };
                records.Add(obj);
            }
        }
        IDataImporter importer = new DataImporterBasic();
        importer.ErrorLogger = new TextFileErrorLogger();
        importer.Import(records);
    }
    ViewBag.Message = "Data imported from " + files.Count + " file(s).
    Please see error log for any errors!";
    return View("Index");
}
```

The Upload() action receives a list of IFormFile objects (Microsoft.AspNet.Http namespace). These are the files uploaded by the user. The code then iterates through this list of uploaded files using a foreach loop and reads the contents of the file.

Inside the foreach loop, the code creates a new MemoryStream object. The Stream returned after calling the OpenReadStream() method of an IFormFile object is copied to the MemoryStream. The code does this in order to retrieve the file content as a byte array. The ToArray() method of the MemoryStream class does just that.

The next piece of code prepares a list of Customer objects by reading the byte array just obtained. The code converts the byte array into a string using the GetString() method of the UTF8 class. This string data is fed to the constructor of the StringReader class.

The while loop iterates through the StringReader object. The ReadLine() method reads a single line from the string data (in other words, a single entry from the CSV file) and constructs a Customer object by splitting it into an array and then reading the individual values of CustomerID, CompanyName, ContactName, and Country. If ReadLine() returns null the while loop is exited and the data-import operation begins.

An object of DataImporterBasic is created and its ErrorLogger property is set to an instance of the TextFileErrorLogger class. The Import() method is called on the importer object to import the list of Customer objects into the database.

A message is stored in the ViewBag that informs the user about the completion of the import operation.

The last piece of the application is the Index view, which allows the user to upload CSV files. Add the Index view to the Views/Home folder and write the markup shown in Listing 5-17 in it.

Listing 5-17. Markup of the Index View

```html
<html>
<head>
    <title>Import Data</title>
</head>
<body>
    <h1>Select File(s) to Upload :</h1>
    <form asp-controller="Home" asp-action="Upload" method="post" enctype="multipart/form-data">
        <input type="file" name="files" id="files" multiple />
        <input type="submit" value="Submit" />
    </form>
    <h4>@ViewBag.Message</h4>
</body>
</html>
```

The Index view consists of a form tag helper whose asp-action attribute points to the Upload() action and whose asp-controller attribute points to the Home controller. The enctype attribute is set to multipart/form-data because the application wants to upload files.

The form houses a file-input field and a Submit button. Just below the form, the message that was stored in the ViewBag is outputted.

This completes the application. In order to test the application you will need a sample CSV file containing dummy data. You can create this file manually or grab it from the code download for this book. You may deliberately add erroneous data (say, to have a CustomerID of more than five characters) so that the error logger gets a chance to log the errors. You will also need to create an ErrorLogs folder within the wwwroot folder. This is where the log files are placed.

Run the application, select the CSV file, and hit the Submit button. Since the application in its current form uses DataImporterBasic and TextFileErrorLogger you will see the ErrorLog.txt file within the ErrorLogs folder. Now, change the Upload() action to use DataImporterAdvanced and XmlErrorLogger and re-run the application. This time the errors will be logged in the ErrorLog.xml file.

Composite

Sometimes you need to deal with hierarchical data. Such data can be looked upon as a tree structure. Data from XML files is one example of such a tree structure, as are organizational hierarchies and user-interface components such as cascading menus and tree views. **The composite pattern allows you to organize the data in a tree structure such that a single item and a group of items from the tree can be treated in a uniform manner.**

Take, for example, a hypothetical tree-view control that displays an organizational hierarchy. The leaf-level item in this case is an employee. Moreover, an employee heading a particular department has certain number of subordinates. These subordinates might be exposed as, say, the ChildNodes collection of the control. No matter whether a tree node is an employee or department head, the tree view control offers the same set of methods—Add() and Remove(), for example—to deal with the data. Thus, individual objects and the composition of objects are dealt with in a similar way.

Design and Explanation

The UML diagram in Figure 5-7 illustrates the composite pattern.

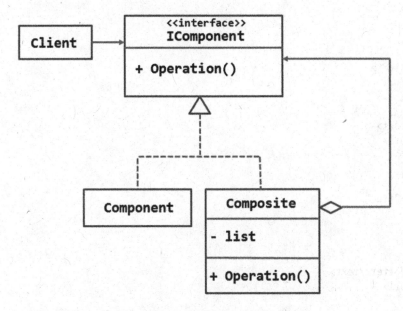

Figure 5-7. *UML diagram illustrating the composite pattern*

The IComponent interface represents the leaf-level item in the tree structure. In this figure it defines a single method—Operation()—but you can include all the methods that work on a leaf-level item. The IComponent interface is implemented in both the Component class and Composite class.

The Component class represents a concrete leaf-level item (such as an employee in the example discussed earlier).

The Composite class represents a composition or group of Component objects. The Composite class also implements the IComponent interface. Moreover, it can also have additional properties and methods of its own.

The Composite class maintains a list of Component objects as shown by the aggregation symbol. Although not shown in the figure, the Composite class can have its own properties and methods.

The client deals with Component objects as well as Composite objects based on the contract of IComponent.

Example

Let's see a realistic example of the composite pattern. Suppose you are building a web application that consists of a lot of menu items. Although a cascading menu is a user interface–level element, its source of data is often supplied by the server-side code. For example, you may store menu data in an XML file. Based on some condition or logic, you may load a particular XML file into a set of objects to form a tree structure and then supply the data to the user-interface element.

Consider the XML markup shown in Listing 5-18, which represents sample menu data.

Listing 5-18. Sample XML markup representing menu and menu items

```xml
<menuBar>
  <menu newwindownewWindow  ="false">
    <text>Categories</text>
    <url>/categories</url>
    <children>
      <menu>
        <text>Programming</text>
        <url>/programming</url>
      </menu>
      <menu>
        <text>Networking</text>
        <url>/networking</url>
      </menu>
    </children>
  </menu>
  <menu newwindownewWindow="true">
    <text>Subscribe</text>
    <url>/followus</url>
    <children>
      <menu>
        <text>Monthly Newsletter</text>
        <url>/newsletter</url>
      </menu>
      <menu>
        <text>Social Networks</text>
        <url>/social</url>
      </menu>
    </children>
  </menu>
</menuBar>
```

As you can see, the <menuBar> root element houses two <menu> elements. Each <menu> has a <text> element that represents the menu's text and a <url> element that points to a URL. The <children> element houses child menu items of the menu. The <children> element consists of one or more <menu> elements with a structure similar to the parent <menu> elements.

Assuming that this XML data is to be loaded into an object tree, you come up with the design shown in Figure 5-8.

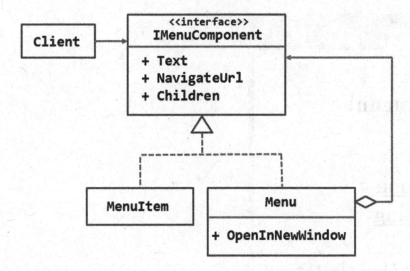

Figure 5-8. *Loading XML menu data using the composite pattern*

The IMenuComponent interface represents a leaf-level menu item. Thus, it corresponds to a leaf-level <menu> element from the XML markup discussed earlier. The IMenuComponent defines three properties— Text, NavigateUrl, and Children. The Text property corresponds to the value of the <text> element. The NavigateUrl property corresponds to the value of the <url> element. The Children property is a collection that can hold items of type IMenuComponent. The <menu> elements immediately inside the <menuBar> root node will have a Children collection filled by the corresponding child menu items.

The MenuItem class implements IMenuComponent and represents the concrete leaf-level menu item. The Menu class also implements IMenuComponent and represents a composition of MenuItem objects. In addition to the member defined by IMenuComponent, it has an OpenInNewWindow property. The OpenInNewWindow property governs whether the URL indicated by the NavigateUrl property should open in a new browser window or not. This property is set at the parent menu level so that all the children menu items exhibit the same behavior.

Now that you know how the menu example is going to work, let's move ahead and put these details into an ASP.NET application. The main page of the application that you will develop is shown in Figure 5-9.

Figure 5-9. *Menu loaded from XML markup*

Although Figure 5-9 doesn't show a fancy cascading menu, it does illustrate the composite pattern in action. The menu data from the XML file is displayed in nested bulleted lists. The top-level bulleted list items come from <menu> elements immediately below the <menuBar>, whereas the child menu items appear as their nested bulleted lists.

To develop this application, begin by creating a new ASP.NET web application using Visual Studio and configure it to use MVC (see Chapter 1 for more details). Add a reference to the System.Xml assembly because you need XmlDocument to read the XML file.

Then add an XML file to the wwwroot folder and key in the markup shown in Listing 5-18 earlier into it.

Now add the AppSettings class to the Core folder and write the following code in it:

```
public class AppSettings
{
    public static string MenuFilePath { get; set; }
}
```

The AppSettings class consists of a single property—MenuFilePath—that is intended to store the path of the menu XML file. This property will be set from the Startup class.

Now open the Startup class and set the MenuFilePath as shown in Listing 5-19.

Listing 5-19. Setting MenuFilePath Property

```
public Startup(IHostingEnvironment env, IApplicationEnvironment app)
{
    AppSettings.MenuFilePath = env.MapPath("menu.xml");
}
```

The code inside the constructor of the Startup class uses the MapPath() method of the IHostingEnvironment parameter to get a full physical path of the menu XML file. The preceding code assumes that the menu XML filename is menu.xml. Make sure to change it as per your filename.

Next, add the IMenuComponent interface to the Core folder and write the code shown in Listing 5-20 in it.

Listing 5-20. IMenuComponent Interface

```
public interface IMenuComponent
{
    string Text { get; set; }
    string NavigateUrl { get; set; }
    List<IMenuComponent> Children { get; set; }
}
```

The IMenuComponent interface consists of Text and NavigateUrl string properties. The Children collection property is a List of IMenuComponent objects.

Then add two classes, MenuComponent and Menu, to the Core folder. The complete code of these classes is shown in Listing 5-21.

Listing 5-21. MenuComponent and Menu Classes

```
public class MenuItem : IMenuComponent
{
    public string Text { get; set; }
    public string NavigateUrl { get; set; }
    public List<IMenuComponent> Children { get; set; }
}

public class Menu : IMenuComponent
{
    public string Text { get; set; }
    public string NavigateUrl { get; set; }
    public List<IMenuComponent> Children { get; set; }
    public bool OpenInNewWindow { get; set; }
}
```

The MenuComponent and Menu classes implement the IMenuComponent interface. Notice that the Menu class has an additional Boolean property—OpenInNewWindow.

Now it's time to load the XML file into these objects. This will happen in the client. So, add HomeController to the Controllers folder and write the following code in its Index() action.

Listing 5-22. Loading Menu and Menu Items from the XML File

```
public IActionResult Index()
{
    XmlDocument doc = new XmlDocument();
    doc.Load(AppSettings.MenuFilePath);
    List<Menu> menus = new List<Menu>();
    foreach (XmlNode nodeOuter in doc.DocumentElement.ChildNodes)
    {
```

157

```
            Menu menu = new Menu();
            menu.Text = nodeOuter.ChildNodes[0].InnerText;
            menu.NavigateUrl = nodeOuter.ChildNodes[1].InnerText;
            menu.OpenInNewWindow = bool.Parse(nodeOuter.Attributes["newWindow"].Value);
            menu.Children = new List<IMenuComponent>();
            foreach (XmlNode nodeInner in nodeOuter.ChildNodes[2].ChildNodes)
            {
                MenuItem menuItem = new MenuItem();
                menuItem.Text = nodeInner.ChildNodes[0].InnerText;
                menuItem.NavigateUrl = nodeInner.ChildNodes[1].InnerText;
                menu.Children.Add(menuItem);
            }
            menus.Add(menu);
        }
        return View(menus);
}
```

The code uses classes such as XmlDocument and XmlNode that reside in the System.Xml namespace. Make sure to import System.Xml into the controller.

The Index() action creates an object of XmlDocument and uses XmlDocument's Load() method to load the menu.xml file. A List of Menu objects is declared to store the menus. This List acts as the model for the Index view.

A foreach loop iterates through the ChildNodes collection of the root node (DocumentElement property). Each iteration of the loop creates a new Menu object. The Text and NavigateUrl properties of the Menu object are assigned the value of the InnerText property of the first and second child nodes. The OpenInNewWindow Boolean property is set to the value of the newWindow attribute of the <menu> element (see the XML file shown earlier).

The inner foreach loop is intended to populate the Children collection of a Menu object. The loop iterates through the ChildNodes collection of the third child of the parent <menu> element. Each iteration of the loop creates an instance of the MenuItem object. The Text and NavigateUrl properties of the MenuItem object are assigned as before, and the MenuItem is added to the Children collection of the Menu.

Finally, the List of Menu objects is passed to the Index view.

Now add the Index view to the Views/Home folder and write the markup shown in Listing 5-23 in it.

Listing 5-23. Markup of Index View

```
@model List<Composite.Core.Menu>

<html>
<head>
    <title>Menus</title>
</head>
<body>
  <h1>Here is your menu!</h1>
  <ul>
    @foreach (var item in Model)
    {
      <li>
        @if (item.OpenInNewWindow)
        {
          <a href="@item.NavigateUrl" target="_blank">@item.Text</a>
        }
```

```
  else
  {
    <a href="@item.NavigateUrl">@item.Text</a>
  }
  </li>
<ul>
@foreach (var subItem in item.Children)
{
  <li>
    @if (item.OpenInNewWindow)
    {
      <a href="@subItem.NavigateUrl" target="_blank">@subItem.Text</a>
    }
    else
    {
      <a href="@subItem.NavigateUrl">@subItem.Text</a>
    }
  </li>
}
</ul>
}
</ul>
</body>
</html>
```

The code iterates through the Model (List of Menu objects, in this case) and displays the menus in a bulleted list. Notice how the code checks the OpenInNewWindow property to set the target attribute of the hyperlinks to a value of _blank.

This completes the application. Run it and see whether the Index view shows the bulleted lists as expected. Try clicking on the individual links of the second menu to check whether they open in a new window.

Decorator

Sometimes you need to add extra functionality to an object dynamically. For example, consider an object that represents a photo. This object is the original object. Now you wish to add fancy effects to the photo, such as shadow and fading. If you inherit from the original class and add the respective functionality, the new photo object won't be the "original" one. It will be the object of the newly inherited class. This may not be acceptable, as the client is primarily interested in the "original" object, and fancy effects are optional features. The decorator pattern comes handy in such cases.

The decorator pattern allows you to dynamically attach additional functionality to a class. The class to which the additional functionality is being added doesn't know about this addition. It is added on the fly based on the system requirements. A decorator class is like a wrapper or topping—it wraps or covers the original object and adds extra functionality to it. If you don't want the decorator, that's fine. The original object is still there with you.

Design and Explanation

The UML diagram shown in Figure 5-10 illustrates the decorator pattern.

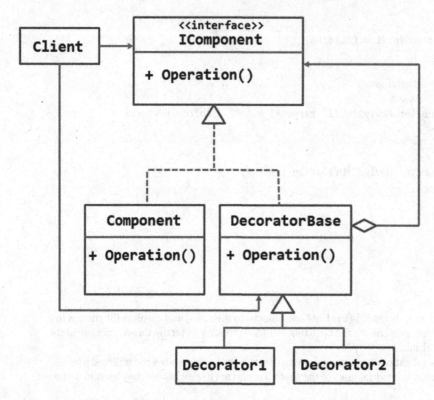

Figure 5-10. *UML diagram illustrating the decorator pattern*

The IComponent interface represents the interface of the primary class—the interface the client is interested in. The IComponent interface defines one method—Operation().

The Component class is the concrete implementation of IComponent. The client, by some means, has an instance of the Component class. Optionally, the client may want to decorate—add functionality dynamically—the object of the Component class. There can even be more than one type of decoration.

To accomplish this, the DecoratorBase class is introduced. DecoratorBase implements IComponent. Moreover, you can inherit this DecoratorBase to create multiple concrete decorations—Decorator1 and Decorator2. The concrete decorators will override the IComponent implementation of the DecoratorBase and add a specific functionality.

Notice that DecoratorBase is shown with a aggregation symbol, indicating that it holds an instance of IComponent. So, Decorator1 and Decorator2 are actually decorating this object instance.

The client will have an object of the Component class and can call the Operation() method on it. The client can pass the same object through any of the decorators and call Operation() of the decorators.

Example

Let's try to apply the decorator pattern to a real-world scenario. Suppose you are developing a website that deals with photos. As a means to indicate that the images are copyrighted you wish to add a watermark on the photos when they are displayed in the browser. However, you want to make this feature optional; the end users will decide whether to add a watermark to their photos. So, the addition of the watermark takes place on the fly.

In this case, the original photos won't have any watermark on them. Your application will need to decorate the original photos with a watermark. Thus, the application is a good candidate to use the decorator pattern. Figure 5-11 shows how the decorator pattern can be used in this specific example.

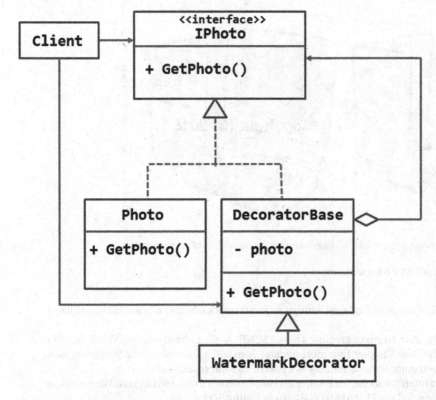

Figure 5-11. *WatermarkDecorator for adding watermark to photos*

The IPhoto interface defines a single method—GetPhoto(). The implementation of the GetPhoto() method is supposed to grab an image from a physical location and return it as a Bitmap object. The IPhoto is implemented in the Photo class.

The DecoratorBase class also implements IPhoto. It also holds an instance of the Photo class. This is the instance being decorated. The GetPhoto() method of the DecoratorBase class is marked as virtual so that it can be overridden by the child classes.

The DecoratorBase class is inherited by WatermarkDecorator. The WatermarkDecorator overrides the GetPhoto() method of the base class and adds a watermark to the photo wrapped by DecoratorBase.

The client, a controller in this case, creates an instance of Photo and passes it to the WatermarkDecorator for adding the watermark. Hence, the client is shown to be using IPhoto and DecoratorBase.

161

Now that you know the overall design of the system, let's put it into an ASP.NET application. The application you develop in this example looks as shown in Figure 5-12.

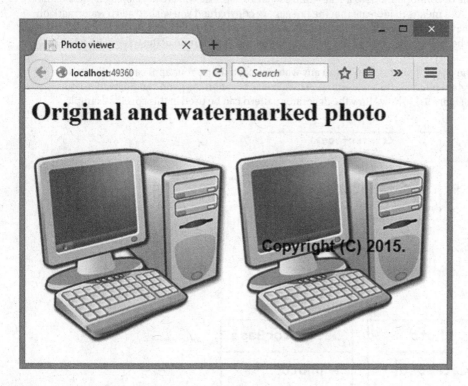

Figure 5-12. *A photo decorated with a watermark*

As you can see, the first image is displayed without any watermark whereas the second image has a watermark.

To develop this application, begin by creating a new ASP.NET web application using Visual Studio and configure it to use MVC (see Chapter 1 for more details). Also add a reference to the System.Drawing assembly because you need graphics functionality as a part of the watermark decorator.

Then add the IPhoto interface to the Core folder and implement it in the Photo class. The complete code of the IPhoto interface and the Photo class is shown in Listing 5-24.

Listing 5-24. IPhoto Interface Being Implemented in the Photo Class

```
public interface IPhoto
{
    Bitmap GetPhoto();
}

public class Photo : IPhoto
{
    private string fileName;
```

```
public Photo(string filename)
{
    this.fileName = filename;
}

public Bitmap GetPhoto()
{
    Bitmap bmp = (Bitmap)Image.FromFile(fileName);
    return bmp;
}
}
```

The IPhoto interface has a GetPhoto() method that returns a Bitmap object. The Photo class accepts a photo filename as a constructor parameter and stores it in a local fileName variable. The implementation of the GetPhoto() method calls the FromFile() method of the Image class to load the file specified by fileName into a Bitmap. The Bitmap object is returned to the caller.

Next, add the DecoratorBase class and implement the IPhoto interface in it (Listing 5-25).

Listing 5-25. DecoratorBase Implementing IPhoto

```
public abstract class DecoratorBase : IPhoto
{
    private IPhoto photo;

    public DecoratorBase(IPhoto photo)
    {
        this.photo = photo;
    }

    public virtual Bitmap GetPhoto()
    {
        return photo.GetPhoto();
    }
}
```

The DecoratorBase has a private variable of type IPhoto. This object holds a reference to the original photo that is to be decorated. The constructor of the DecoratorBase accepts IPhoto object and assigns it to the local photo variable.

The GetPhoto() method simply calls GetPhoto() on the IPhoto object passed earlier. Notice that GetPhoto() is marked as virtual so that it can be overridden in the child decorator classes.

Now add the WatermarkDecorator class in the Core folder and inherit from the DecoratorBase class (Listing 5-26).

Listing 5-26. WatermarkDecorator Adds a Watermark to IPhoto

```
public class WatermarkDecorator : DecoratorBase
{
    private string watermarkText;

    public WatermarkDecorator(IPhoto photo,string watermark) : base(photo)
    {
        this.watermarkText = watermark;
    }
```

```
public override Bitmap GetPhoto()
{
    Bitmap bmp = base.GetPhoto();
    Graphics g = Graphics.FromImage(bmp);
    Font font = new Font("Arial", 20, FontStyle.Bold, GraphicsUnit.Pixel);
    StringFormat sf = new StringFormat();
    sf.LineAlignment = StringAlignment.Center;
    sf.Alignment = StringAlignment.Center;
    float x = (float)bmp.Width / 2;
    float y = (float)bmp.Height / 2;
    g.DrawString(watermarkText, font, Brushes.Black, x, y, sf);
    g.Save();
    return bmp;
}
}
```

The constructor of the WatermarkDecorator accepts an object of IPhoto and a string to be displayed as the watermark. Note that the constructor passes the object of IPhoto to the base class constructor. The watermark text is stored in a local watermarkText variable.

The GetPhoto() method overridden does the job of decorating the original photo with a watermark. The code calls the GetPhoto() method of the base class to retrieve the Bitmap object of the photo image file.

A Graphics object is then created by calling the FromImage() method of the Graphics class and passing the Bitmap object as the parameter. The next few lines of code basically decide aspects such as font and location where the watermark is to be drawn.

Then the DrawString() method is called on the Graphics object by supplying details such as watermarkText, font, Brush, and location coordinates. The Save() method of the Graphics object saves the changes made to the image. The Bitmap object is then returned to the caller.

Now add a HomeController class to the Controllers folder. In the preceding examples you used AppSettings to store a file location. In this example, you will use dependency injection to grab an IHostingEnvironment object in the controller itself. Listing 5-27 shows how this is done.

Listing 5-27. Injecting IHostingEnvironment in the Controller

```
public class HomeController : Controller
{
    private IHostingEnvironment hostingEnvironment;

    public HomeController(IHostingEnvironment env)
    {
        this.hostingEnvironment = env;
    }
    ...
}
```

As you can see, the HomeController declares a variable of type IHostingEnvironment (Microsoft. AspNet.Hosting namespace). Moreover, the constructor accepts an IHostingEnvironment parameter, which is then stored in the local variable just declared. The IHostingEnvironment parameter is automatically injected for you by the MVC framework.

Next, in addition to the Index() action, you need two more actions—GetImageOriginal() and GetImageWatermarked()—to display the corresponding images. The GetImageOriginal() is shown in Listing 5-28.

Listing 5-28. GetImageOriginal() Action Displays an Image Without a Watermark

```
public IActionResult GetImageOriginal()
{
    string fileName = hostingEnvironment.MapPath("images/computer.png");
    IPhoto photo = new Photo(fileName);
    Bitmap bmp = photo.GetPhoto();
    MemoryStream stream = new MemoryStream();
    bmp.Save(stream, ImageFormat.Png);
    byte[] data = stream.ToArray();
    stream.Close();
    return File(data, "image/png");
}
```

The GetImageOriginal() action is supposed to display an image without any watermark. Notice how the code retrieves the physical filesystem path of computer.png using the MapPath() method of an hostingEnvironment object. Make sure that you have the computer.png image in the wwwroot/images folder of the application.

An instance of the Photo class is created by passing the photo filename to its constructor. The GetPhoto() method returns the image as a Bitmap object.

A MemoryStream (System.IO namespace) is then constructed, and the Bitmap object is saved into it using the Save() method of the Bitmap class.

The image saved in the MemoryStream is converted into a byte array using the ToArray() method. The byte array thus obtained is fed to the File() method to obtain a FileContentResult object. The FileContentResult is then returned from the action.

Now add a GetImageWatermarked() action and write the code shown in Listing 5-29 in it.

Listing 5-29. GetImageWatermarked() Displays an Image with a Watermark

```
public IActionResult GetImageWatermarked()
{
    string fileName = hostingEnvironment.MapPath("images/computer.png");
    IPhoto photo = new Photo(fileName);
    WatermarkDecorator decorator = new WatermarkDecorator(photo, "Copyright (C) 2015.");
    Bitmap bmp = decorator.GetPhoto();
    MemoryStream stream = new MemoryStream();
    bmp.Save(stream, ImageFormat.Png);
    byte[] data = stream.ToArray();
    stream.Close();
    return File(data, "image/png");
}
```

The code inside GetImageWatermarked() is quite similar to the one from the earlier action. However, it creates an object of WatermarkDecorator by passing the Photo object to it. The watermark text is also specified to a copyright message.

The GetPhoto() of WatermarkDecorator returns a Bitmap object on which the watermark is drawn. This Bitmap is converted to a byte array as before and passed to the File() method to obtain a FileContentResult.

Now it's time to create the Index view that displays both images. Add the Index view to the Views/Home folder and write the markup shown in Listing 5-30 in it.

Listing 5-30. Markup of Index View

```
<html>
<head>
    <title>Photo viewer</title>
</head>
<body>
    <h1>Original and watermarked photo</h1>
    <img src="/home/GetImageOriginal" />
    <img src="/home/GetImageWatermarked" />
</body>
</html>
```

The Index view consists of two image elements. The src attribute of the image elements point to the GetImageOriginal() and GetImageWatermarked() actions, respectively. This way the FileContentResult returned by these actions is displayed as the images on the page.

This completes the application. Run the application and see whether the watermark decorator works as expected.

Summary

The structural patterns deal with how classes and objects are arranged in a system. There are seven patterns in this category. This chapter discussed four of them, namely adapter, bridge, composite, and decorator.

The adapter pattern is used when you need to fit a new class into an existing system that otherwise wouldn't fit naturally into it. The adapter pattern is mostly applied on an ad-hoc basis.

The bridge pattern decouples the abstraction from its implementation so that both can vary independently. Applying a bridge pattern in a system is usually a conscious decision made by the developer.

The composite pattern allows you to work with tree structures such that individual items as well as group of items can be programmed in a uniform manner.

The decorator pattern decorates an object with some additional functionality. It does so dynamically by wrapping the original object and attaching more responsibilities to it.

The next chapter is going to discuss the remaining three structural patterns—façade, flyweight, and proxy.

CHAPTER 6

■ ■ ■

Structural Patterns: Façade, Flyweight, and Proxy

In the previous chapter, you learned the adapter, bridge, composite, and decorator design patterns. This chapter will discuss the remaining three structural patterns, namely façade, flyweight, and proxy. Specifically, this chapter will cover the following:

- The purpose of façade, flyweight, and proxy patterns

- The UML diagram and overall structure of these design patterns

- How the façade and proxy patterns allow you to shield complexities and grant access to an underlying subsystem

- How the flyweight pattern serves a large number of requests with a small set of objects

- Proof of concept example of each of these patterns

Façade

At times the client needs to interact with one or more subsystems, and these interactions might be quite complex. Consider, for example, an application that consumes a large number of third-party services. In this case, the client needs to know about details such as the data formats, the service metadata, the exact way to invoke the individual services, and so on. These details might be overwhelming for the client code–more so when such interactions are required at many places in the client code.

In such cases it would help if the complexities were isolated from the client code. Instead of dealing with these subsystems (and hence the complex operations involved) the client code would invoke some easy-to-use component. The component in turn would take care of the complex interactions with one or more subsystems. This component would act as an entry point or front gate–the façade–for the client code. **Thus the façade pattern provides a high-level, easy-to-use interface to the client by shielding the different interfaces of the subsystems**.

The façade pattern makes the interactions with the subsystems easy as well as uniform, freeing the client from those details.

© Bipin Joshi 2016
B. Joshi, *Beginning SOLID Principles and Design Patterns for ASP.NET Developers*,
DOI 10.1007/978-1-4842-1848-8_6

Design and Explanation

The UML diagram in Figure 6-1 illustrates the façade pattern.

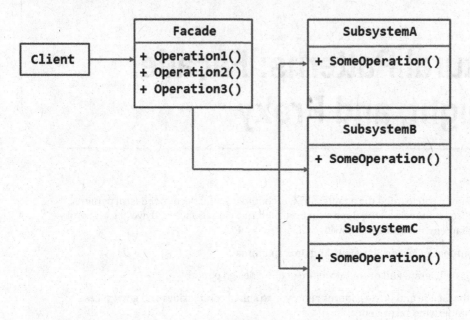

Figure 6-1. *UML diagram illustrating the façade pattern*

As you can see, the client wants to interact with three subsystems–SubsystemA, SubsystemB, and SubsystemC. These individual subsystems define their own set of operations–SomeOperation() in the figure. Although it may not be apparent from the figure, the overall interfaces of these subsystems can be quite different from one another. These subsystems might be libraries developed in-house or they can be third-party libraries.

The façade pattern shields these subsystems by providing a high-level, uniform, and simplified interface. In the figure this interface takes the form of three methods–Operation1(), Operation2(), and Operation3() - of the Facade class.

Instead of interacting with the subsystems directly, the client invokes one or more of the methods provided by the façade and gets the job done.

By high-level it is meant that the façade shields the complex interactions with the subsystems. By uniform it is meant that, although the design of each subsystem might be different from the other subsystems, the client is shielded from these differences. No matter which subsystem the client wants to interact with, the façade provides a consistent way to do so. By simplified it is meant that the client is shielded from the complexities involved in consuming the subsystems.

Example

Now that you know what the façade pattern is about, let's see a real-world example where it can be implemented.

Suppose you are building a website that allows visitors to search for books. The website accepts an ISBN from the end user. It then queries multiple services exposed by various book-selling websites and grabs the price of the book from the individual book sellers. The various book sellers may have different costs of shipping and discounts. So, your application compares the price offering of each seller and prepares a sorted list (lowest to highest) of the price offerings. Finally, the list is displayed to the end user.

Considering the preceding requirements, you conclude that the façade pattern can be quite useful here, because otherwise the client application will be overwhelmed by the complexity and differences in calling these third-party services. Figure 6-2 shows a possible arrangement after introducing the façade pattern.

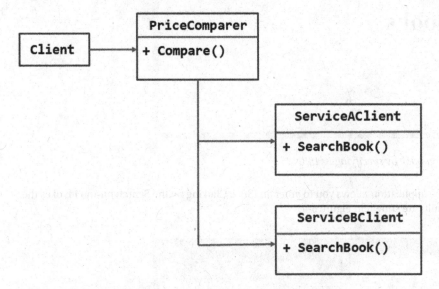

Figure 6-2. *The PriceComparer façade shielding the client from services*

The figure assumes that your application wants to consume two services—ServiceA and ServiceB— exposed by two independent book sellers. The actual services are not shown in the figure because they are hosted by some third-party providers. The ServiceAClient and ServiceBClient classes are the complex subsystems that invoke ServiceA and ServiceB, respectively. They have the SearchBook() method, which accepts an ISBN of a book and gets the offering by the specific book seller. So, from your application's point of view, interactions with ServiceAClient and ServiceBClient are shielded.

The PriceComparer class acts as the façade in this example. It provides a high-level method—Compare()—that internally calls the SearchBook() method of both the services and compares the price offerings.

The client class (a controller in this case) deals with the PriceComparer class only. The client need not know anything about the ServiceAClient and ServiceBClient subsystems.

Let's move ahead and develop an ASP.NET application demonstrating this design. Since you don't have any third-party services, you will create local Web APIs that return data from a local database. The application that you will develop looks as shown in Figure 6-3.

Figure 6-3. *Seaching for a book by specifying its ISBN*

The main page of the application allows you to enter an ISBN. Clicking on the Search button invokes the façade class, and the results are shown in Figure 6-4.

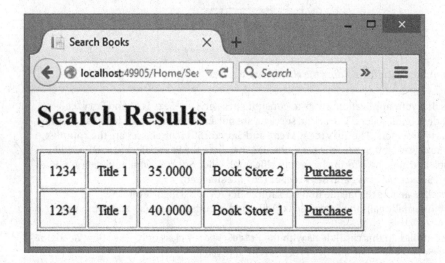

Figure 6-4. *Compaing prices from multiple sellers and displaying the results*

As you can see, the search for ISBN 1234 resulted in two records, and the data is displayed from lowest to highest. The "Purchase" link is supposed to take you to the book seller's purchase page for the specific book.

To develop this application, begin by creating a new ASP.NET web application named Façade using Visual Studio and configure it to use MVC and Entity Framework (see Chapter 1 for more details). Also store the database connection string of FacadeDb–the database used by the services–in the appsettings.json file.

Then add the AppSettings class to the Core folder and write the following code to it:

```
public class AppSettings
{
    public static string ConnectionString { get; set; }
}
```

The AppSettings class contains a single static property, ConnectionString, for storing the database connection string. Now open the Startup file and assign the ConnectionString property as shown in Listing 6-1.

Listing 6-1. Storing Connection String in the AppSettings Class

```
public Startup(IHostingEnvironment env, IApplicationEnvironment app)
{
...
...
  AppSettings.ConnectionString = config.Get<string>("Data:DefaultConnection:
  ConnectionString");
}
```

Next, add the Book class to the Core folder and write the code shown in Listing 6-2 in it.

Listing 6-2. Book Class Representing the Book Details

```
[Table("Books")]
public class Book
{
    public int Id { get; set; }
    public string ISBN { get; set; }
    public string Title { get; set; }
    public string Publisher { get; set; }
    public string Author { get; set; }
    public decimal Price { get; set; }
    public string Source { get; set; }
    public string PurchaseUrl { get; set; }
}
```

The Book class has eight properties, namely Id, ISBN, Title, Publisher, Author, Price, Source, and PurchaseUrl. Most of them are self-explanatory, except the last two. The Source property indicates the name of the book seller and the PurchaseUrl property indicates the URL where the book can be purchased. Also notice that the data type of the Price property is decimal.

Next, add AppDbContext to the Core folder and write the code shown in Listing 6-3 in it.

Listing 6-3. AppDbContext Class with Books DbSet

```
public class AppDbContext : DbContext
{
    public DbSet<Book> Books { get; set; }

    protected override void OnConfiguring(DbContextOptionsBuilder optionsBuilder)
    {
        optionsBuilder.UseSqlServer(AppSettings.ConnectionString);
    }
}
```

The AppDbContext class defines the Books DbSet that can be queried by the service clients.

Then add two Web API controllers–ServiceAController and ServiceBController–to the Core folder. In a more realistic case, these services would be developed and hosted by the third parties, and you would simply consume them. Here, you will develop them for the sake of completeness.

To add a Web API controller, right click on the Core folder and select Add ➤ New Item option. Then select Web API Controller Class from the Add New Item dialog (Figure 6-5).

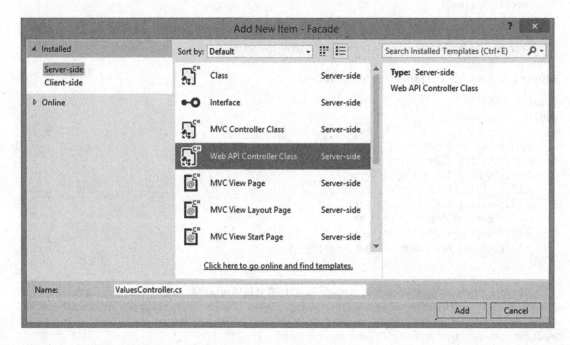

Figure 6-5. *Adding a Web API controller*

Name the Web API controllers ServiceAController and ServiceBController. The Web API controllers need to handle only the GET HTTP verb. The ServiceAController is shown in Listing 6-4.

Listing 6-4. ServiceAController Searching and Returning a Book

```
[Route("api/[controller]")]
public class ServiceAController : Controller
{
    [HttpGet("{isbn}")]
    public Book Get(string isbn)
    {
        using (AppDbContext db = new AppDbContext())
        {
            var query = from b in db.Books
                        where b.ISBN == isbn && b.Source=="Book Store 1"
                        select b;
            return query.SingleOrDefault();
        }
    }
}
```

Notice that the ServiceAController is decorated with a [Route] attribute to configure the routing for the Web API. It consists of a single method–Get()–that takes the ISBN as its parameter and returns a Book object representing the book. The Get() method is decorated with the [HttpGet] attribute to indicate that it handles the GET verb. The [HttpGet] attribute specifies the isbn route parameter so that the ISBN passed from the route can be mapped with the isbn parameter of the Get() method.

Inside, the code queries the Books DbSet in an attempt to search for a book with the specified ISBN and source (the source is also checked so that you can use just one table for the sake of testing). The result is returned to the caller.

Also write the same code inside the ServiceBController class. (Listing 6-5).

Listing 6-5. ServiceBController Searching and Returning a book

```
[Route("api/[controller]")]
public class ServiceBController : Controller
{

    [HttpGet("{isbn}")]
    public Book Get(string isbn)
    {
        using (AppDbContext db = new AppDbContext())
        {
            var query = from b in db.Books
                        where b.ISBN == isbn && b.Source == "Book Store 2"
                        select b;
            return query.SingleOrDefault();
        }
    }
}
```

The code is quite similar to the ServiceAController, except that the source is changed to "Book Store 2."

In order to consume the Web API services just developed, you will use an HttpClient component. So, open the Project.json file and add the entries shown in Listing 6-6 to the dependencies section.

Listing 6-6. Adding NuGet Packages for HttpClient

```
"dependencies": {
  ...
  ...
  "System.Net.Http": "4.0.1-beta-23516",
  "Newtonsoft.Json": "8.0.2"
}
```

■ **Note**   This example also uses Newtonsoft's `Json.Net` component—a popular JSON framework for .NET applications. You may also check for the latest versions of these packages.

Then add a ServiceAClient class to the Core folder and write the code shown in Listing 6-7 in it.

Listing 6-7. ServiceAClient Class Calling the ServiceAController Web API

```csharp
public class ServiceAClient
{
    public Book SearchBook(string isbn)
    {
        HttpClient client = new HttpClient();
        client.BaseAddress = new Uri("http://localhost:49905");
        client.DefaultRequestHeaders.Accept.Add(new MediaTypeWithQualityHeaderValue
        ("application/json"));
        HttpResponseMessage response = client.GetAsync("/api/ServiceA/" + isbn).Result;

        string jsonData = response.Content.ReadAsStringAsync().Result;
        Book book = JsonConvert.DeserializeObject<Book>(jsonData);
        return book;
    }
}
```

The ServiceAClient consists of a single method–SearchBook()–that takes the ISBN of a book as its parameter.

The SearchBooks() method uses the HttpClient (System.Net.Http namespace) class to invoke the ServiceAController Web API. The BaseAddress property points to the Uri where the Web API is hosted. In this case, the Web APIs are hosted in your application itself. Make sure to change the port number to meet your setup.

Then the Accept HTTP header is added to the DefaultRequestHeaders collection. This header uses application/json as its content type value.

The GetAsync() method invokes the ServiceA Web API by passing the ISBN as a route parameter. The GetAsync() returns HttpResponseMessage. This object wraps the actual Book object returned from the Web API. To retrieve the Book instance in the client code, you use the ReadAsStringAsync() method. This method returns a string that holds the data in JSON format. To convert this JSON data into a Book object, you use the Json.Net component. The DeserializeObject<T> generic method of the JsonConvert class (Newtonsoft.Json namespace) accepts the JSON string and returns a Book object. The Book object thus obtained is returned to the caller.

The code of ServiceBClient is quite similar to ServiceAClient with only one exception–it calls the ServiceBController Web API. Although this code won't be discussed, it is shown in Listing 6-8.

Listing 6-8. ServiceBClient Class Calling the ServiceBController Web API

```
public class ServiceBClient
{
    public Book SearchBook(string isbn)
    {
        HttpClient client = new HttpClient();
        client.BaseAddress = new Uri("http://localhost:49905");
        client.DefaultRequestHeaders.Accept.Add(new MediaTypeWithQualityHeaderValue
        ("application/json"));
        HttpResponseMessage response = client.GetAsync("/api/ServiceB/" + isbn).Result;

        string jsonData = response.Content.ReadAsStringAsync().Result;
        Book book = JsonConvert.DeserializeObject<Book>(jsonData);
        return book;
    }
}
```

Once the ServiceAClient and ServiceBClient classes are ready, proceed to create the façade class. Add the PriceComparer class to the Core folder and write the code shown in Listing 6-9 in it.

Listing 6-9. PriceComparer Acts as the Façade

```
public class PriceComparer
{
    public List<Book> Compare(string isbn)
    {
        ServiceAClient clientA = new ServiceAClient();
        Book bookA = clientA.SearchBook(isbn);

        ServiceBClient clientB = new ServiceBClient();
        Book bookB = clientB.SearchBook(isbn);

        List<Book> books = new List<Book>();
        books.Add(bookA);
        books.Add(bookB);

        books.Sort(delegate (Book b1, Book b2)
        {
            return b1.Price.CompareTo(b2.Price);
        });

        return books;
    }
}
```

The PriceComparer class consists of a single method—Compare(). The Compare() method accepts an ISBN of a book and returns a list of Book objects obtained from the services.

The Compare() method does four tasks:

- It calls ServiceA using ServiceAClient and obtains the details of a book as a Book object.

- It calls ServiceB using ServiceBClient and obtains the details of a book as a Book object.

- It adds these Book objects to a List so that they can be sent to the client.

- It sorts the List using a comparison delegate.

The first two tasks are performed by calling the SearchBook() method of the ServiceAClient() and ServiceBClient() classes, respectively. These calls each return a Book object. These Book objects are stored in the books List variable. The List is sorted using a comparison delegate. The delegate takes two Book objects and then compares their price using the CompareTo() method.

This completes the PriceComparer façade class. Now it's time to use the façade in the client code.

Add HomeController to the Controllers folder. In addition to the default Index() action, add a Search() action to it (Listing 6-10).

Listing 6-10. Search() Action Uses PriceComparer Class

```
public IActionResult Search(string isbn)
{
    PriceComparer comparer = new PriceComparer();
    List<Book> books = comparer.Compare(isbn);
    return View("Results",books);
}
```

The Search() method receives the ISBN entered by the user. It then calls the Compare() method of the PriceComparer class to retrieve a list of Book objects. This is the sorted list that needs to be displayed to the user. Hence, the List is passed as a model to the Results view.

Next, add an Index view to the Views/Home folder and write the markup shown in Listing 6-11 in it.

Listing 6-11. Markup of Index View

```
<html>
<head>
    <title>Search Books</title>
</head>
<body>
    <h1>Search Books</h1>
    <form asp-controller="Home" asp-action="Search" method="post">
        <strong>Enter Book ISBN :</strong>
        <br /><br />
        <input type="text" name="isbn" />
        <input type="submit" value="Search" />
    </form>
</body>
</html>
```

The Index view consists of a form that houses a textbox and a button. The form tag helper's asp-controller attribute points to the Home controller, and its asp-action attribute points to the Search action you just wrote.

The name of the textbox is set to isbn (this name and the Search() parameter name must match for proper model binding). The Search submit button posts the form.

Next, add a Results view to the Views/Home folder and write the markup shown in Listing 6-12 in it.

Listing 6-12. Markup of the Results View

```
@model List<Facade.Core.Book>
<html>
<head>
    <title>Search Books</title>
</head>
<body>
    <h1>Search Results</h1>
    <table border="1" cellpadding="10">
        @foreach(var item in Model)
        {
            <tr>
                <td>@item.ISBN</td>
                <td>@item.Title</td>
                <td>@item.Price</td>
                <td>@item.Source</td>
                <td><a href="@item.PurchaseUrl">Purchase</a></td>
            </tr>
        }
    </table>
</body>
</html>
```

The Results view specifies the model to be a List of Book objects using the @model directive. Make sure to change the namespace as per your setup.

The body of the view consists of a table rendered based on the List data. A foreach loop iterates through the List of Book objects and emits table rows filled with book's ISBN, title, price, and source. The PurchaseUrl is shown using an anchor tag.

This completes the application. Before running the application, you will need to create a FacadeDb database (see Chapter 1 for more details). Moreover, you will need to add a few dummy records for the sake of testing. Once that is done you can run the application and try searching for an ISBN. If all goes well you will be presented with a list of books sorted by the price (lowest to highest).

Flyweight

At times you will need to work with a large number of objects carrying the same state. But creating such a large number of object instances might be inefficient in terms of memory or resource consumption. To minimize the overhead on the system, you need to figure out whether multiple requests to the same set of data can reuse already-created object instances instead of recreating them.

You may achieve this by creating an object, filling its state, and reusing it across multiple requests. When a request asks for an object, the system first checks whether the state being requested is already available with an existing object. If yes, the existing object can be given to the requesting client. Otherwise a new object is created, its state is filled, and the object is stored somewhere for future reuse. It is also given to the client.

The flyweight pattern is used to implement such an efficient object-state reuse mechanism. **The flyweight pattern promotes the efficient use of memory and computing resources by sharing common state, thus avoiding duplication.**

The flyweight pattern identifies two distinct types of object state–intrinsic state and extrinsic state. The intrinsic state refers to the data that can be shared across a large number of requests. The extrinsic state refers to the data that can't be shared across multiple requests and hence needs to be computed on the fly. The class implementing the flyweight pattern provides additional methods by which to compute the extrinsic state.

■ **Note** The primary focus of the flyweight pattern is to avoid creating a large number of objects that store the same state by promoting the reuse of the object state. This should not be confused with object pooling, where the primary focus is to reuse the object instances, not necessarily the object state.

Design and Explanation

The UML diagram in Figure 6-6 illustrates the flyweight pattern.

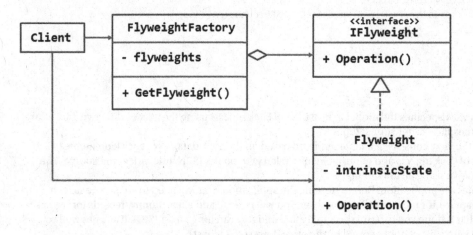

Figure 6-6. *UML diagram illustrating the flyweight pattern*

The client needs an instance of the Flyweight class to work with. Ordinarily, a client would have used the new keyword of C# to instantiate the Flyweight class. Here, the client gets an instance of the Flyweight class from the FlyweightFactory.

The FlyweightFactory maintains a list of unique Flyweight objects. This is indicated by the aggregation symbol in the figure. By unique it is meant that the Flyweight object holds a unique set of data that can be shared among a large number of requests. So, even though all the items stored in the list are of type Flyweight, each instance holds a unique set of data and can be used only by the requests that need the data it holds.

The client asks for a Flyweight object by calling the GetFlyweight() method of the FlyweightFactory. When a request for a specific set of data is received, GetFlyweight() checks whether a Flyweight object holding the requested data is already present in the list. If yes, the existing instance is returned to the caller. Otherwise a new Flyweight object is created and put in the list, and then its reference is returned to the caller.

The Flyweight object's interface is defined by the IFlyweight interface. Notice that the Flyweight class holds intrinsic state in a private intrinsicState member. The extrinsic state is computed by the Operation() method. Although the Flyweight shown in the figure has only one method, you can add more methods as per the application requirement.

Example

Now that you know what the flyweight pattern is, let's build an example that uses it.

Suppose you have developed a website that has large number of visitors. Now you wish to build a rich administrative interface that will be used by a team of administrators.

As a part of the administrative module, you need to develop a website analytics component that gives detailed information about the website activity, such as the number of page views, number of unique visitors, total bandwidth consumption, top search keywords, and other such information.

The analytics component is supposed to extract all this information from raw webserver logs generated up until the previous day. The webserver logs can be quite large in size, considering the highly trafficked nature of the website. So, the component is going to do a lot of complex and resource-intensive operations in order to extract and generate the statistical data just mentioned.

Now further imagine that there are many administrative pages, each dealing with some specific administrative task. Each of the administrative pages needs to display the website's analytical data in addition to the task-specific interface. This is done so that the administrators can, at a glance, get an idea of the usage statistics without leaving the page.

This will call for the creation of the website analytics object on every administrative page, even though all the instances are going to hold the same data. Thus the object holding the website analytical data is a good candidate to be a Flyweight object.

Now take this concept a step further. Assume that you have multiple subdomains under the main website, and such usage statistics are needed for each of the subdomains. So far you had only one set of data that needed to be shared across all the administrative pages. Now you have multiple sets of unique data (one per each subdomain, and the main website) that need to be shared.

Figure 6-7 shows how the flyweight pattern can be used to deal with this situation.

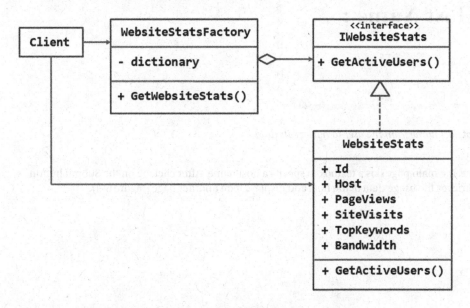

Figure 6-7. *WebsiteStats flyweight with intrinsic and extrinsic state*

The Flyweight object in this example is the WebsiteStats class. This class is supposed to generate the website analytics by reading and processing the webserver log files. Of course, for this example you will just put some dummy processing in this class. WebSiteStats implements the IWebsiteStats interface.

WebsiteStats implements six properties namely, Id, Host, PageViews, SiteVisits, TopKeywords, and Bandwidth. These properties hold the corresponding data and hence represent the intrinsic state of the flyweight pattern.

IWebsiteStats also requires that there should be some way to get the number of active users of the site at a given point of time. This information can't be extracted from the webserver logs, because it's a real-time piece of information. So, it needs to be computed on the fly using the GetActiveUsers() method. This data forms the extrinsic state of the flyweight class.

The WebsiteStatsFactory is the flyweight factory that is responsible for maintaining a dictionary of WebsiteStats objects. If you read the system requirements discussed earlier, you realize that the data is identical for a particular host. So, the dictionary will have host name as its key and the corresponding WebsiteStats object as its value.

Whenever the client needs an instance of the WebsiteStats object, it calls the GetWebsiteStats() method of the factory. This method checks whether a WebsiteStats object for a specified host already exists in the dictionary. If yes, that instance of WebsiteStats is returned to the client. If there is no entry for a given host, a new instance of WebsiteStats is created, its intrinsic state is filled, and the instance is stored in the dictionary. In any case, the client gets an instance from the dictionary.

Note that instead of creating the GetWebsiteStats() method, you can also create an indexer that does the same job (as you will do in the actual code later).

Now let's proceed to creating the ASP.NET application named Flyweight that illustrates what we discussed so far. Figure 6-8 shows the main page of the application.

Figure 6-8. *Accept host name from the user to retrieve its data*

As you can see, the main page has a textbox to specify a host name. After clicking on the Submit button the application retrieves the usage data of the host and displays it on another page (Figure 6-9).

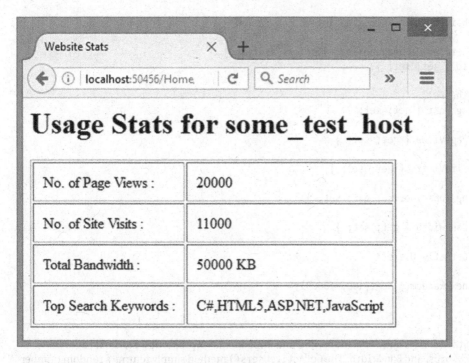

Figure 6-9. *Site usage data displayed to the user*

For the sake of simplicity this application won't use any webserver logs. Instead, it will simply pick values from a database table.

To develop this application, begin by creating a new ASP.NET web application using Visual Studio and configure it to use MVC and Entity Framework (see Chapter 1 for more details). Also store the database connection string of FlyweightDb—the database used to store site-usage data—in the appsettings.json file.

Add the AppSettings class to the Core folder and add the ConnectionString property to it. Then open the Startup class and assign the ConnectionString property of the AppSettings. You do this in exactly the same way as in the façade pattern example; we won't go into the details again.

Then add the IWebsiteStats interface and the WebsiteStats class to the Core folder. Also implement the IWebsiteStats interface in the WebsiteStats class. The complete code for both is shown in Listing 6-13.

Listing 6-13. IWebsiteStats Interface Implemented in WebsiteStats

```
public interface IWebsiteStats
{
    int Id { get; set; }
    string Host { get; set; }
    int PageViews { get; set; }
    int SiteVisits { get; set; }
    string TopKeywords { get; set; }
    int Bandwidth { get; set; }
    int GetActiveUsers();
}
```

```
public class WebsiteStats : IWebsiteStats
{
    [DatabaseGenerated(DatabaseGeneratedOption.Identity)]
    public int Id { get; set; }
    [Required]
    [StringLength(100)]
    public string Host { get; set; }
    [Required]
    public int PageViews { get; set; }
    [Required]
    public int SiteVisits { get; set; }
    [Required]
    public string TopKeywords { get; set; }
    [Required]
    public int Bandwidth { get; set; }

    public int GetActiveUsers()
    {
        return new Random().Next(100, 10000);
    }
}
```

The WebsiteStats class is quite straightforward and implements six properties–Id, Host, PageViews, SiteVisits, TopKeywords, and Bandwidth. The GetActiveUsers() method simply returns a random number between 100 and 10000. In a more realistic case this would be computed dynamically based on some application-specific logic. Various data annotations are added on top of the properties just to assist the entity framework migration commands in creating a proper table structure.

Next, add the AppDbContext class to the Core folder and write the code shown in Listing 6-14 in it.

Listing 6-14. AppDbContext with WebsiteStats DbSet

```
public class AppDbContext : DbContext
{
    public DbSet<WebsiteStats> WebsiteStats { get; set; }

    protected override void OnConfiguring(DbContextOptionsBuilder optionsBuilder)
    {
        optionsBuilder.UseSqlServer(AppSettings.ConnectionString);
    }
}
```

The AppDbContext class contains WebsiteStats DbSet. The code that you write later queries this DbSet to grab site-usage data for a host.

Now add the WebsiteStatsFactory class in the Core folder and write the code shown in Listing 6-15 in it.

Listing 6-15. WebsiteStatsFactory Giving Objects of WebsiteFactory

```
public class WebsiteStatsFactory
{
    private static Dictionary<string, WebsiteStats> dictionary = new Dictionary<string,
    WebsiteStats>();

    public IWebsiteStats this[string host]
    {
        get
        {
            if(!dictionary.ContainsKey(host))
            {
                using (AppDbContext db = new AppDbContext())
                {
                    var query = from stats in db.WebsiteStats
                                where stats.Host == host
                                select stats;
                    dictionary[host] = query.SingleOrDefault();
                }
            }
            return dictionary[host];
        }
    }
}
```

The WebsiteStatsFactory class declares a static Dictionary variable. The host name acts as the key, and the WebsiteStats object filled with that host's usage data is the value.

Notice that instead of the GetWebsiteStats() method, the WebsiteStatsFactory class defines an indexer to access the dictionary. This is done purely as a matter of convenient usage syntax.

The indexer accepts the host name string. Inside, the code checks whether the dictionary already contains the specified host name key. If the dictionary doesn't contain the host name key, the code fetches site-usage data for the specified host from the database. The data is retrieved as a WebsiteStats object using the SingleOrDefault() method and is stored in the dictionary. The indexer then returns the WebsiteStats object from the dictionary to the caller.

Next, add HomeController in the Controllers folder. In addition to the default Index() action, you need to add the ShowStats() action to it (Listing 6-16).

Listing 6-16. ShowStats() Action Asks for WebsiteStats Object

```
[HttpPost]
public IActionResult ShowStats(string host)
{
    WebsiteStatsFactory factory = new WebsiteStatsFactory();
    WebsiteStats stats = (WebsiteStats)factory[host];
    if (stats == null)
    {
        ViewBag.Message = "Invalid Host Name!";
        return View("Index");
    }
}
```

```
    else
    {
        return View(stats);
    }
}
```

The ShowStats() action receives a host name entered by the user as its parameter. Inside, it creates an instance of the WebsiteStatsFactory class. It then uses its indexer to grab an instance of WebsiteStats for the specified host. If the WebsiteStats object is obtained successfully, it is passed to the ShowStats view. If some invalid host name is entered, an error message is displayed to the user.

Now add the Index view to the Views/Home folder and write the markup shown in Listing 6-17 in it.

Listing 6-17. Markup of the Index View

```
<html>
<head>
    <title>Website Usage Data</title>
</head>
<body>

    <h1>Enter Host Name :</h1>
    <form asp-controller="Home" asp-action="ShowStats" method="post">
        <input type="text" name="host" />
        <input type="submit" value="Submit" />
    </form>
    <br />
    <strong>@ViewBag.Message</strong>
</body>
</html>
```

The Index view renders a form using the form tag helper. The asp-controller attribute of the form tag helper points to the Home controller, and its asp-action attribute points to the ShowStats action. The form houses a textbox and a button. The error message from the ViewBag is shown below the form.

Now add the ShowStats view to the Views/Home folder and write the markup shown in Listing 6-18 in it.

Listing 6-18. Markup of the ShowStats View

```
@model Flyweight.Core.WebsiteStats

<html>
<head>
    <title>Website Stats</title>
</head>
<body>

    <h1>Usage Stats for @Model.Host</h1>
    <table border="1" cellpadding="10">
        <tr>
            <td>No. of Page Views : </td>
            <td>@Model.PageViews</td>
        </tr>
```

```
    <tr>
        <td>No. of Site Visits : </td>
        <td>@Model.SiteVisits</td>
    </tr>
    <tr>
        <td>Total Bandwidth : </td>
        <td>@Model.Bandwidth KB</td>
    </tr>
    <tr>
        <td>Top Search Keywords : </td>
        <td>@Model.TopKeywords</td>
    </tr>
</table>
</body>
</html>
```

The @model directive specifies the model of the view to be the WebsiteStats class. Make sure to change the namespace of WebsiteStats as per your setup.

The markup then displays all the property values of the WebsiteStats instance in a table.

This completes the application. Before running the application, you will need to create a FlyweightDb database (see Chapter 1 for more details). Moreover, you will need to add a few dummy host name entries for the sake of testing. Once that is done, you can run the application and try retrieving the site-usage data for a host. Set a breakpoint in the index (WebsiteStatsFactory class) and see how multiple requests to the same host data are served by the WebsiteStats object already stored in the dictionary.

Proxy

Sometimes, instead of using an object directly, it is beneficial to use a placeholder for that object. A client invokes the methods of this placeholder. The placeholder in turn forwards the calls to the target object. Some of the situations in which such a placeholder is useful include when:

- you may want to allow controlled access to the target object and hence want to route all calls through a placeholder;

- you may want to hide the creation and configuration process of the target object from the client due the complexities involved;

- you may want to dynamically change the target object without affecting the client code; or

- the target object is not going to be available at development time and your application can connect with the target only at runtime.

If something of this sort is needed, the proxy pattern can be used as a solution. **The proxy pattern provides a placeholder or surrogate object that stands in for the target object and thus controls the access to it.** Since the proxy object is a placeholder for the target object, usually the proxy mimics the structure (properties and methods) of the target object.

If you ever developed ASMX web services or WCF services, then probably you are already familiar with the concept of a proxy. The service proxies used by ASMX and WCF services are based on the proxy pattern and are used to control and simplify access to the underlying service.

Design and Explanation

The UML structure of the proxy pattern is illustrated in Figure 6-10.

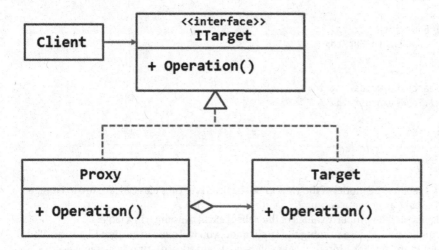

Figure 6-10. *UML diagram illustrating the proxy pattern*

The interface of the target object is represented by the ITarget interface. The ITarget interface contains one method–Operation().

The Target class implements the ITarget interface, and its Operation() method contains the code that performs the actual work.

The Proxy class also implements ITarget so as to mimic the Target object. As shown by the aggregation symbol, the Proxy class will have an instance of the Target (or will use the Target in some way). The Operation() method of the Proxy will forward the call to the Operation() method of the Target.

The client is interested in getting the work done from the Target. But it won't use an object of Target directly. Instead, the client will instantiate the Proxy and will invoke the operations of the Proxy. Since Proxy mimics the Target, the client code looks as if the calls are being made on the Target object itself.

Example

Now that you know what the proxy pattern does, let's see a real-world scenario in which you can use it.

Suppose that you are working on a web application that needs to consume a Web API to get some work done. Further, imagine that the Web API is being used at dozens of places in the application. Moreover, you expect that the same Web API will be hosted at different geographical locations and the client is going to use one based on some dynamic condition. Finally, the client needs to maintain a log of Web API calls made for the sake of administrative and monitoring purposes.

You can always use an HttpClient component in the client code to invoke the Web API. However, there are some constraints:

- The HttpClient component is designed to consume REST APIs and expects your code to supply details such as service end point and data formats (JSON or XML).

- Since the Web API is being used at many places in the application, you will need to repeat the similar code at all those places.

- The client code will need to figure out the URL of the target service from a set of URLs.

Considering these requirements and limitations, it would be beneficial if a proxy of the Web API is created instead of invoking the Web API directly. This way the client code simply needs to invoke the methods on the proxy. The proxy will take care of all the points just mentioned.

For the sake of this example, you will create a Web API that performs the CRUD (Create, Read, Update, and Delete) operations on the Customers table of the Northwind database.

The UML diagram for the scenario just explained is shown in Figure 6-11.

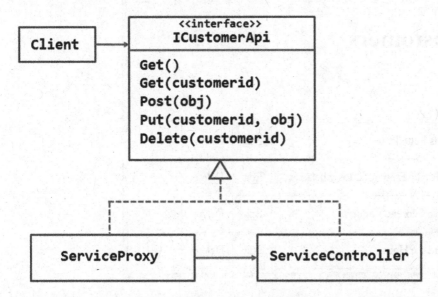

Figure 6-11. *Creating a proxy for calling the customer Web API service*

The ICustomerApi interface contains five methods that correspond to the HTTP verbs–GET, POST, PUT, and DELETE, respectively.

The Get() method has two variants–the parameter-less version returns a list of all the customers in the database, whereas the one taking a string parameter returns a single Customer matching the specified CustomerID.

The Post() method accepts a new Customer object as its parameter and attempts to add that Customer to the database.

The Put() method accepts a CustomerID that is being modified and a Customer object containing the modified values.

The Delete() method takes a CustomerID as its parameter and attempts to delete that customer.

The ICustomerApi interface is implemented in the ServiceController and ServiceProxy classes. The ServiceController class is a standard Web API controller, whereas the ServiceProxy is the proxy class.

The ServiceController handles the HTTP verbs and performs the CRUD operations on the underlying database.

The ServiceProxy invokes the ServiceController through HttpClient. The end point URL of the service is grabbed from the configuration file, but you can use any custom logic for deciding the URL (this is to resemble the application requirement). The Get(), Post(), Put(), and Delete() methods of the ServiceProxy forward the call to the corresponding methods of the Web API using the HttpClient component. Moreover, they log the calls to a text file.

The client (HomeController) creates an instance of the ServiceProxy and calls its methods to perform the respective operations.

The main page of the ASP.NET application that you develop in this section is shown in Figure 6-12.

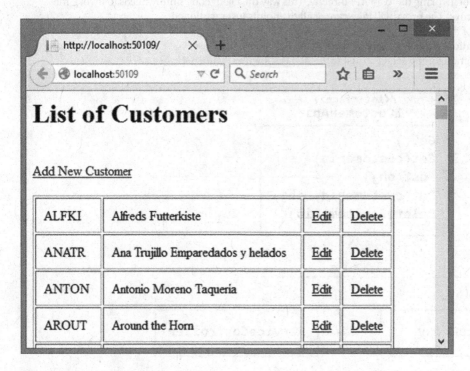

Figure 6-12. *List of customers*

The main page displays a list of existing customers in a table. For each customer record, "Edit" and "Delete" links are provided to perform the respective operations. The "Add New Customer" link above the table is used to add a new customer.

When you click on the "Edit" link an edit page is displayed (Figure 6-13) that allows you to modify that customer.

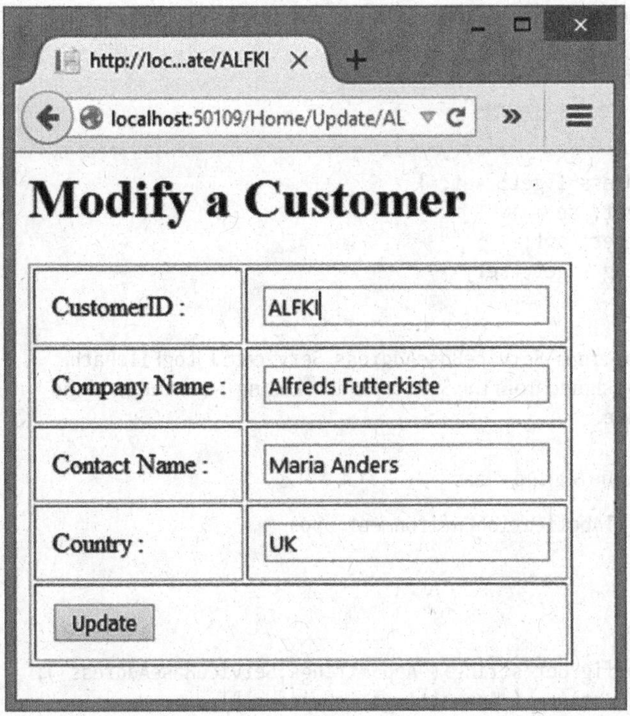

Figure 6-13. *Modifying an existing customer*

Adding a new customer works along similar lines, except that an empty data entry page is displayed to the user. Clicking on the "Delete" link deletes a customer and takes the user back to the main customer listing.

To develop this application, begin by creating a new ASP.NET web application named Proxy using Visual Studio and configure it to use MVC and Entity Framework (see Chapter 1 for more details). Also store the database connection string of the Northwind database in the appsettings.json file. Additionally, store the Web API end point and the log file path in appsettings.json as shown in Listing 6-19.

Listing 6-19. Storing Web API End Point URL in the Configuration File

```
{
  "AppSettings": {
    "ServiceBaseAddress": "http://localhost:50109",
    "ServiceUrl": "/api/service",
    "LogFilePath": "log.txt",
  },
  ...
  ...
}
```

The AppSettings section of the configuration file stores two settings—ServiceBaseAddress and ServiceUrl. The ServiceBaseAddress key points to the base address of the Web API, whereas the ServiceUrl key points to the actual path to the service. The combination of the two gives you the complete point URL of the Web API. Make sure to change the port number as your project setup requires.

Then add AppSettings class to the Core folder and write the code shown in Listing 6-20 in it.

Listing 6-20. AppSettings Class Storing Service End Point Details

```
public class AppSettings
{
    public static string ServiceBaseAddress { get; set; }
    public static string ServiceUrl { get; set; }
    public static string LogFilePath { get; set; }
    public static string ConnectionString { get; set; }
}
```

The AppSettings class contains three properties–ServiceBaseAddress, ServiceUrl, LogFilePath, and ConnectionString. These properties are assigned from the Startup class (Listing 6-21) and hold the corresponding values from the configuration file.

Listing 6-21. Assigning AppSettings Values in the Startup Class

```
public Startup(IHostingEnvironment env, IApplicationEnvironment app)
{
    ...
    ...

    AppSettings.ServiceBaseAddress = config.Get<string>("AppSettings:ServiceBaseAddress");
    AppSettings.ServiceUrl = config.Get <string>("AppSettings:ServiceUrl");
    AppSettings.LogFilePath = env.MapPath(config.Get<string>("AppSettings:LogFilePath"));
    AppSettings.ConnectionString = config.Get<string>("Data:DefaultConnection:
    ConnectionString");
}
```

Notice how LogFilePath has been constructed using the IHostingEnvironment object's MapPath() method. You need to make one more modification to the Startup class. You need to enable session state for your application, because you will be using the TempData dictionary in your code. TempData requires session state be enabled for an application. To do that you first need to add the Microsoft.AspNet.Session NuGet package in your application's Project.json file:

```
"dependencies": {
  ...

  "Microsoft.AspNet.Session": "1.0.0-rc1-final"
}
```

Secondly, you need to modify the ConfigureServices() and Configure() methods of the Startup class as shown in Listing 6-22.

Listing 6-22. Enabling Session State for the Application

```
public void ConfigureServices(IServiceCollection services)
{
    services.AddMvc();
    services.AddEntityFramework()
            .AddSqlServer();
```

```
    services.AddSession();
    services.AddCaching();
}

public void Configure(IApplicationBuilder app, IHostingEnvironment env, ILoggerFactory
loggerFactory)
{
    app.UseStaticFiles();
    app.UseSession();
    app.UseMvc(routes =>
    {
        routes.MapRoute(
            name: "default",
            template: "{controller=Home}/{action=Index}/{id?}");
    });
}
```

Notice the code marked in bold letters. The ConfigureServices() method adds session and caching services to the ASP.NET pipeline using the AddSession() and AddCaching() methods. And the Configure() method calls the UseSession() method to enable the session state.

Next, add the Customer class to the Core folder and write the code shown in Listing 6-23 in it.

Listing 6-23. Customer Model Class

```
[Table("Customers")]
public class Customer
{
    [Key]
    [StringLength(5)]
    public string CustomerID { get; set; }
    [Required]
    public string CompanyName { get; set; }
    [Required]
    public string ContactName { get; set; }
    [Required]
    public string Country { get; set; }
}
```

The Customer class is mapped to the Customers table using the [Table] attribute and contains four properties, namely CustomerID, CompanyName, ContactName, and Country. The data annotations added on top of the properties assist in model validation.

Then add AppDbContext class to the Core folder. This class has a Customers DbSet and is shown in Listing 6-24.

Listing 6-24. AppDbContext Class Exposing Customers DbSet

```
public class AppDbContext : DbContext
{
    public DbSet<Customer> Customers { get; set; }

    protected override void OnConfiguring(DbContextOptionsBuilder optionsBuilder)
    {
        optionsBuilder.UseSqlServer(AppSettings.ConnectionString);
    }
}
```

Now add the ICustomerApi interface to the Core folder as shown in Listing 6-25.

Listing 6-25. ICustomerApi Interface

```
public interface ICustomerApi
{
    List<Customer> Get();
    Customer Get(string customerid);
    void Post(Customer obj);
    void Put(string customerid, Customer obj);
    void Delete(string customerid);
}
```

The ICustomerApi interface consists of five methods—Get(), Get(customerid), Post(), Put(), and Delete().

Now add a Web API controller named ServiceController to the Core folder. This Web API controller will handle the GET, POST, PUT, and DELETE verbs and is shown in Listing 6-26.

Listing 6-26. ServiceController Web API Handling GET, POST, PUT, and DELETE Verbs

```
[Route("api/[controller]")]
public class ServiceController : Controller,ICustomerApi
{
    [HttpGet]
    public List<Customer> Get()
    {
        using (AppDbContext db = new AppDbContext())
        {
            return db.Customers.ToList();
        }
    }

    [HttpGet("{customerid}")]
    public Customer Get(string customerid)
    {
        using (AppDbContext db = new AppDbContext())
        {
            return db.Customers.Where(m => m.CustomerID == customerid).SingleOrDefault();
        }
    }
}
```

```
[HttpPost]
public void Post([FromBody]Customer obj)
{
    using (AppDbContext db = new AppDbContext())
    {
        db.Customers.Add(obj);
        db.SaveChanges();
    }
}

[HttpPut("{customerid}")]
public void Put(string customerid, [FromBody]Customer obj)
{
    using (AppDbContext db = new AppDbContext())
    {
        db.Entry(obj).State = EntityState.Modified;
        db.SaveChanges();
    }
}

[HttpDelete("{customerid}")]
public void Delete(string customerid)
{
    using (AppDbContext db = new AppDbContext())
    {
        Customer obj = db.Customers.Where(m => m.CustomerID == customerid).
        SingleOrDefault();
        db.Customers.Remove(obj);
        db.SaveChanges();
    }
}
}
```

The [Route] attribute configures the routing for the Web API. Notice that the ServiceController class not only inherits from the Controller base class but also implements the ICustomerApi interface.

The ServiceController contains all five actions:

- Get(): This method returns all the customers from the Customers table of the Northwind database.

- Get(customerid): This method receives a CustomerID from a route parameter and returns that single Customer to the caller.

- Post(obj): This method accepts a new Customer object and adds that customer to the Customers DbSet. The SaveChanges() method then saves the changes to the database.

- Put(customerid,obj): This method receives a CustomerID from a route parameter and a Customer object representing the modified values of the customer. It then saves the modified values to the database.

- Delete(customerid): This method receives a CustomerID from a route parameter. It then removes the Customer from the Customers DbSet and saves the changes to the database.

This completes the Web API. Now it's time to add the ServiceProxy to the Core folder. The complete code of the ServiceProxy class is shown in Listing 6-27.

Listing 6-27. The ServiceProxy Class Mimics the ServiceController

```
public class ServiceProxy : ICustomerApi
{
    private HttpClient client = new HttpClient();

    public ServiceProxy()
    {
        client.BaseAddress = new Uri(AppSettings.ServiceBaseAddress);
        client.DefaultRequestHeaders.Accept.Add(new MediaTypeWithQualityHeaderValue
        ("application/json"));
    }

    public List<Customer> Get()
    {
        HttpResponseMessage response = client.GetAsync(AppSettings.ServiceUrl).Result;
        string jsonData = response.Content.ReadAsStringAsync().Result;
        List<Customer> data = JsonConvert.DeserializeObject<List<Customer>> (jsonData);
        System.IO.File.AppendAllText(AppSettings.LogFilePath, $"Get() called on
        {DateTime.Now}");
        return data;
    }

    public Customer Get(string customerid)
    {
        HttpResponseMessage response = client.GetAsync(AppSettings.ServiceUrl +
        $"/{customerid}").Result;
        string jsonData = response.Content.ReadAsStringAsync().Result;
        Customer data = JsonConvert.DeserializeObject<Customer>(jsonData);
        System.IO.File.AppendAllText(AppSettings.LogFilePath, $"Get({customerid}) called on
        {DateTime.Now}");
        return data;
    }

    public void Post(Customer obj)
    {
        string jsonData = JsonConvert.SerializeObject(obj);
        StringContent content = new StringContent(jsonData);
        content.Headers.Clear();
        content.Headers.Add("Content-Type", "application/json");
        HttpResponseMessage response = client.PostAsync(AppSettings.ServiceUrl, content).
        Result;
        System.IO.File.AppendAllText(AppSettings.LogFilePath, $"Post() called on
        {DateTime.Now}");
    }
```

```
public void Put(string customerid, Customer obj)
{
    string jsonData = JsonConvert.SerializeObject(obj);
    StringContent content = new StringContent(jsonData);
    content.Headers.Clear();
    content.Headers.Add("Content-Type", "application/json");
    HttpResponseMessage response = client.PutAsync(AppSettings.ServiceUrl +
    $"/{customerid}", content).Result;
    System.IO.File.AppendAllText(AppSettings.LogFilePath, $"Put() called on
    {DateTime.Now}");
}

public void Delete(string customerid)
{
    HttpResponseMessage response = client.DeleteAsync(AppSettings.ServiceUrl +
    $"/{customerid}").Result;
    System.IO.File.AppendAllText(AppSettings.LogFilePath, $"Delete() called on
    {DateTime.Now}");
}
}
```

The ServiceProxy class implements ICustomerApi and hence contains all the five methods defined by the interface.

It declares an HttpClient object (System.Net.Http namespace) that is used by all the methods. Make sure to include the dependencies for System.Net.Http and Newtonsoft.Json in Project.json, as in the earlier example. The constructor of the ServiceProxy configures the HttpClient by setting its BaseAddress and Accept header. This code should be familiar to you, because you used it in an earlier example.

The Get(), Get(customerid), Post(), Put(), and Delete() methods of the ServiceProxy class invoke the corresponding methods of the ServiceController. This is done using the GetAsync(), PostAsync(), PutAsync(), and DeleteAsync() methods of the HttpClient, respectively. This code should look familiar to you, since you used it in an earlier example. Notice the use of the JsonConvert class to convert .NET objects into JSON strings.

Notice that all these methods also add a message to the log file. This is done using the AppendAllText() method of the File class (System.IO namespace). The log file is created at the location specified by the LogFilePath property.

Next, add the HomeController to the Controllers folder. The HomeController consists of six actions, as listed here:

- Index(): This method retrieves a list of Customer objects and passes it to the Index view for the sake of showing in a table.

- Update(id): This method is called when user clicks on the "Edit" link. It receives a CustomerID from the route parameter and fetches a Customer object for that CustomerID.

- Update(obj): This method is called when a user modifies the customer data and submits the form.

- Insert(): This method is called when a user clicks on the "Add New Customer" link. It displays the Insert view to the user.

- Insert(obj): This method is called when a user fills the Insert view and submits the form.

- Delete(id): This method is called when a user clicks on the "Delete" link.

The Index() action is shown in Listing 6-28.

Listing 6-28. Index() Action Fetches a List of Customers

```
public IActionResult Index()
{
    ServiceProxy proxy = new ServiceProxy();
    List<Customer> data = proxy.Get();
    return View(data);
}
```

The Index() action creates an instance of the ServiceProxy and calls its Get() method to retrieve a list of Customer objects. The customer data is passed to the Index view.

The two actions taking care of the update operation are shown in Listing 6-29.

Listing 6-29. Modifying Customer Details

```
public IActionResult Update(string id)
{
    ServiceProxy proxy = new ServiceProxy();
    Customer data = proxy.Get(id);
    return View(data);
}

[HttpPost]
public IActionResult Update(Customer obj)
{
    if (ModelState.IsValid)
    {
        ServiceProxy proxy = new ServiceProxy();
        proxy.Put(obj.CustomerID,obj);
        TempData["Message"] = "Customer modified successfully!";
        return RedirectToAction("Index");
    }
    else
    {
        return View(obj);
    }
}
```

The first version of the Update() method receives a CustomerID from the route. It then creates a ServiceProxy and calls its Get(customerid) method to retrieve a single Customer object matching the CustomerID. The Customer object thus obtained is passed to the Update view.

The second version of the Update() method receives a Customer object through model binding. Inside, it checks whether the Customer model contains valid data. This is done using the IsValid property of the ModelState. If the model is valid, the ServiceProxy is instantiated and its Put() method is called by passing the CustomerID and the Customer object.

An entry is added to the TempData dictionary with a key of Message. This key holds a success message that is displayed to the user.

The control is then redirected to the Index() action using the RedirectToAction() method.

If the ModelState is invalid, the Customer object is passed to the Update view so that the error(s) can be shown to the user.

The Insert() and Delete() actions are similar to the Update() actions except that they invoke the Post() and Delete() methods of the ServiceProxy. These actions are shown in Listing 6-30.

Listing 6-30. Inserting and Deleting a Customer

```
public IActionResult Insert()
{
    return View();
}


[HttpPost]
public IActionResult Insert(Customer obj)
{
    if (ModelState.IsValid)
    {
        ServiceProxy proxy = new ServiceProxy();
        proxy.Post(obj);
        TempData["Message"] = "Customer added successfully!";
        return RedirectToAction("Index");
    }
    else
    {
        return View(obj);
    }
}

public IActionResult Delete(string id)
{
    ServiceProxy proxy = new ServiceProxy();
    proxy.Delete(id);
    TempData["Message"] = "Customer deleted successfully!";
    return RedirectToAction("Index");
}
```

This completes the HomeController. Now it's time to create Index, Insert, and Update views. Add the Index view to the Views/Home folder. The markup of the Index view is shown in Listing 6-31.

Listing 6-31. Markup of Index View

```
@model List<Proxy.Core.Customer>

<html>
<head>
    <title>List of Customers</title>
</head>
```

```
<body>
    <h1>List of Customers</h1>
    @TempData["Message"]
    <br />
    <a asp-controller="Home" asp-action="Insert">Add New Customer</a>
    <br /><br />
    <table border="1" cellpadding="10">
        @foreach(var item in Model)
        {
            <tr>
                <td>@item.CustomerID</td>
                <td>@item.CompanyName</td>
                <td><a asp-controller="Home" asp-action="Update" asp-route-id=
                "@item.CustomerID">Edit</a></td>
                <td><a asp-controller="Home" asp-action="Delete" asp-route-id=
                "@item.CustomerID">Delete</a></td>
            </tr>
        }
    </table>
</body>
</html>
```

The @model directive sets the model of the Index view to a list of Customer objects. Make sure to change the model namespace to match your setup.

At the top, the markup outputs the success message stored in the TempData. It then displays a hyperlink using an anchor tag helper. The asp-controller attribute of the anchor tag helper points to the Home controller, and its asp-action attribute points to the Insert action.

Then a foreach loop iterates through the Model and renders a table onto the response stream. The table displays CustomerID and CompanyName properties and also shows the "Edit" and "Delete" links. Notice that the "Edit" link points to the Update() action, and the value of the id route parameter is passed to it using the asp-route-id attribute. Similarly, the "Delete" links point to the Delete() action.

Now add the Update view to the Views/Home folder and write the markup shown in Listing θ-32 in it.

Listing 6-32. Markup of the Update View

```
@model Proxy.Core.Customer

<html>
<head>
    <title>Modify a Cusotmer</title>
</head>
<body>
    <h1>Modify a Customer</h1>
    <form asp-controller="Home" asp-action="Update">
        <table border="1" cellpadding="10">
            <tr>
                <td><label asp-for="CustomerID">CustomerID :</label></td>
                <td><input asp-for="CustomerID" readonly="readonly" /></td>
            </tr>
```

```
        <tr>
            <td><label asp-for="CompanyName">Company Name :</label></td>
            <td><input asp-for="CompanyName" /></td>
        </tr>
        <tr>
            <td><label asp-for="ContactName">Contact Name :</label></td>
            <td><input asp-for="ContactName" /></td>
        </tr>
        <tr>
            <td><label asp-for="Country">Country :</label></td>
            <td><input asp-for="Country" /></td>
        </tr>
        <tr>
            <td colspan="2">
                <input type="submit" value="Update" />
            </td>
        </tr>
    </table>
</form>
<div asp-validation-summary="ValidationSummary.All"></div>
</body>
</html>
```

The @model directive sets the model of the Update view to the Customer class. The view displays a data-entry form in a table. This is done using form, label, and input tag helpers.

The asp-controller attribute of the form tag helper points to the Home controller, and its asp-action attribute points to the Update() action.

The asp-for attribute of the label and input tag helpers specify the model property being bound with the label or the input field.

The Update button posts the form to the Update() action. To display the model validation errors, a validation summary tag helper is used. The asp-validation-summary attribute of the <div> is set to ValidationSummary. All this is done so that all model errors are displayed.

Finally, add the Insert view to the Views/Home folder. The Insert view is quite similar to the Update view, except that it submits the form to the Insert() action. The markup of the Index view is shown in Listing 6-33.

Listing 6-33. Markup of the Insert View

```
@model Proxy.Core.Customer

<html>
<head>
    <title>Add a Customer</title>
</head>
<body>
    <h1>Add a Customer</h1>
    <form asp-controller="Home" asp-action="Insert">
        <table border="1" cellpadding="10">
            <tr>
                <td><label asp-for="CustomerID">CustomerID :</label></td>
                <td><input asp-for="CustomerID" /></td>
            </tr>
```

```
        <tr>
            <td><label asp-for="CompanyName">Company Name :</label></td>
            <td><input asp-for="CompanyName" /></td>
        </tr>
        <tr>
            <td><label asp-for="ContactName">Contact Name :</label></td>
            <td><input asp-for="ContactName" /></td>
        </tr>
        <tr>
            <td><label asp-for="Country">Country :</label></td>
            <td><input asp-for="Country" /></td>
        </tr>
        <tr>
            <td colspan="2">
                <input type="submit" value="Insert" />
            </td>
        </tr>
    </table>
</form>
<div asp-validation-summary="ValidationSummary.All"></div>
</body>
</html>
```

We won't go into the details of the Insert view, as it is quite similar to the Update view.

This completes the application. Run the application and check whether CRUD operations are being performed properly. Also open the log.txt file from the wwwroot folder and see whether the log of each operation is being added to it. The following are some of the sample log entries:

```
Get() called on 9/3/2015 11:53:04 AM
Get(ALFKI) called on 9/3/2015 11:53:30 AM
Put() called on 9/3/2015 11:53:36 AM
Get() called on 9/3/2015 11:53:36 AM
```

As you can see, the preceding log entries result from a single listing and update operation.

Summary

This chapter discussed three structural patterns, namely façade, flyweight, and proxy.

The façade pattern is used to shield the complex interactions between one or more subsystems. It presents a simplified view of the interactions to the client.

The flyweight pattern comes in handy when there are large numbers of objects carrying the same state. The flyweight pattern holds intrinsic state (the state that can be shared) and extrinsic state (the state that is required to be computed dynamically). The flyweight pattern reduces the overall memory footprint of the application by avoiding duplication.

The proxy pattern allows you to provide a placeholder object for another object so that the placeholder can stand in for the Target object. This way a proxy provides controlled access to the Target object.

This chapter and the previous chapter covered all seven structural patterns. Now, it's time to focus our attention on behavioral patterns. To that end, the next three chapters are going to discuss just that.

■ ■ ■

CHAPTER 7

Behavioral Patterns: Chain of Responsibility, Command, Interpreter, and Iterator

Now that we are done examining creational and structural patterns, this chapter will introduce you to a few behavioral patterns. As the name suggests, behavioral patterns concern themselves with how classes and objects behave, communicate, and message within a given system. This chapter will discuss four such patterns, namely chain of responsibility, command, interpreter, and iterator. It will include the following:

- Overview of behavioral patterns

- The purpose of chain of responsibility, command, interpreter, and iterator

- UML diagrams and overall structures of these design patterns

- Proof of concept example for each of these patterns

Behavioral Patterns

So far in this book you have learned about creational and structural patterns. The creational patterns deal with object creation, while the structural patterns deal with the arrangement of classes in a given system. Now it's time to look into the third category of GoF patterns–behavioral patterns.

Behavioral patterns concern themselves with the following:

- How classes and objects behave in a system

- How objects communicate and message with each other

- How different algorithms that a system relies upon are dealt with

In all there are eleven patterns in this category. They are as follows:

- **Chain of Responsibility:** Allows you to pass a request through a chain or series of objects, with each participant object performing some specific responsibility

- **Command:** Encapsulates an instruction or command in an object so that it can be played based on some application-specific logic

- **Interpreter:** Allows the defining and interpreting of an instruction set with specific notation and grammar

© Bipin Joshi 2016
B. Joshi, *Beginning SOLID Principles and Design Patterns for ASP.NET Developers*,
DOI 10.1007/978-1-4842-1848-8_7

- **Iterator:** Allows sequentially iterating and accessing items from a collection of items

- **Mediator:** Allows a simplified way of communicating between multiple objects by routing the communication through a specific object

- **Memento:** Allows the storing and restoring of an object's private state information without compromising the access scope of the state

- **Observer:** Allows the notifying of a number of objects when something happens in the system

- **State:** Allows altering the behavior of an object when its state changes

- **Strategy:** Allows encapsulating a number of algorithms in their own classes and the use of them interchangeably

- **Template Method:** Defines the skeleton of an algorithm and allows subclasses to redefine some or all of the steps

- **Visitor:** Defines an operation to be performed on elements of an object structure without affecting the elements

Out of these eleven patterns, this chapter will discuss chain of responsibility, command, interpreter, and iterator. The remaining patterns will be covered in the next two chapters.

Chain of Responsibility

A given task to be accomplished need not be performed by a single object. It can be handled by multiple objects, each contributing to the task completion in a specific and limited way.

Consider a loan application being submitted at a bank. From the point the request for a loan is received to the point it is sanctioned or rejected there might be many people contributing to the processing of that request. A clerk might check that the loan application is properly filled and all the supporting documents are attached. The clerk, however, doesn't have authority to approve the loan request. He then passes it to his supervisor. The supervisor may check the application in detail in terms of amount asked for, credibility of the requester, and so on. He may then send the application to the manager for approval. If the requested loan amount is within the limits that the manager can approve, he will approve it. Otherwise, he may send it to his senior for the approval. Finally, the application may get approved or rejected based on the bank's policies.

As you can see, the loan request passes through a series of handlers, and each handler performs a specific task and passes it to the next handler. This is where the chain of responsibility pattern can be used.

The chain of responsibility pattern allows you to pass a request through a series of handler objects. Thus a chain of objects is formed wherein one object receives the request, does some specific work, and passes the request to the next object in the chain. At the end of the chain the request is either successfully handled or an exception is generated.

Design and Explanation

The UML diagram in Figure 7-1 illustrates the chain of responsibility pattern.

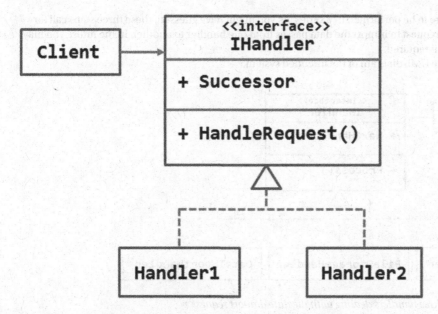

***Figure 7-1.** UML diagram illustrating chain of responsibility pattern*

The IHandler interface defines the members to be implemented in each handler class. In this case, the HandleRequest() method is supposed to act on the request and also pass it to the next handler in the chain.

Notice that the interface also defines a pointer to the successor object in the chain through the Successor property. This property when implemented in the handler classes holds a reference to the next handler in the chain.

The IHandler interface is implemented by two handlers–Handler1 and Handler2. The handlers are independent of one another except that one handler passes the request to the other.

The client decides on the initial handler to which the request is made. From that point onward, the request runs through the chain of handlers and results in its successful or erroneous completion. So, a sample run could be Client -> Handler1 -> Handler2 -> complete.

Note that the logic that decides the next handler in the chain is application specific. It is possible that based on some condition a request doesn't pass through certain handlers at all. Another possibility where all handlers may not get chance to act on the request is when an exception is raised while processing the request.

Example

Now that you know how the chain of responsibility pattern works, let's implement it in an example.

Suppose that you are building a web-based data-import utility. The end user will upload files with .txt or .csv extensions that are supposed to contain the data to be imported.

It is possible that the user may upload files with an incorrect extension or files containing data not adhering to the required structure. So, the application must validate these aspects before accepting the file as a valid source.

Once the file is accepted, it is copied to a folder as a record or as the original source of data. Then, the data is imported into an SQL Server table.

You can identify three responsibilities in the overall data-import operation:

- File-format and file-content validation

- Source-file storage on the server

- Importing data into the table

These operations are to be performed in a series. As you might have guessed, these three steps call for three handlers, and the request to import the data passes from one handler to another. In the future you may also add more handlers if required.

Figure 7-2 shows the UML diagram of the intended system.

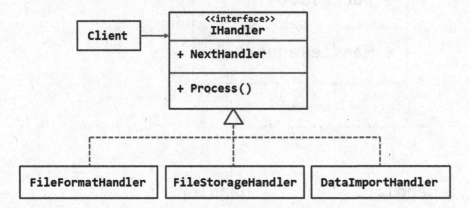

Figure 7-2. *A chain of three handlers dealing with the data-import request*

The IHandler interface consists of a property, NextHandler, and a method, Process(). The NextHandler property holds a reference to the next handler in the chain. The Process() method contains the processing logic that processes the request in some way. Moreover, Process() is also responsible for continuing the chain by invoking the Process() method on the NextHandler.

The IHandler interface is implemented by three classes, namely FileFormatHandler, FileStorageHandler, and DataImportHandler. Each of these handlers has specific responsibilities.

The FileFormatHandler checks whether the file extension is .txt or .csv. It also checks whether the data contained in the files matches with the expected structure. The FileStorageHandler does the job of storing a copy of the source file in a folder and also adds an entry for that file in a table. This is done for record-keeping purposes and tracking. The DataImportHandler class does the job of importing the source data into a database table. In addition to these handlers, you may have additional handlers as per your needs. Also notice that each handler is an independent class in itself and doesn't have any control as to what the next handler should be. It simply invokes the next handler (if any), but the wiring of the handlers is taken care of by the client code.

In this example, the client code invokes Process() on the FileFormatHandler since that is the first step in the chain.

Figure 7-3 shows what the main page of the application looks like.

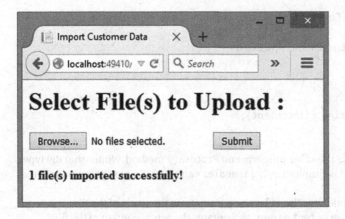

Figure 7-3. Uploading files to be imported

The page consists of a file-input field that allows you to select one or more files. After selecting the files you can click on the Submit button to start the file upload and import process. If the data from the files is imported successfully, a message is displayed confirming the successful completion of the process.

To develop this application, begin by creating a new ASP.NET web application project named COR using Visual Studio and configure it to use MVC and Entity Framework (see Chapter 1 for more details). Also store the database connection string of CorDb–the database used by the application–in the appsettings.json file.

Then add the AppSettings class to the Core folder and add two static properties to it, as shown in Listing 7-1.

Listing 7-1. AppSettings Class

```
public class AppSettings
{
    public static string StoragePath { get; set; }
    public static string ConnectionString { get; set; }
}
```

The StoragePath property holds the path to a folder where the uploaded files are stored. The ConnectionString property holds the database connection string of the CorDb database. These properties are assigned in the Startup class constructor, as illustrated in Listing 7-2.

Listing 7-2. Assigning StoragePath and ConnectionString

```
public Startup(IHostingEnvironment env, IApplicationEnvironment app)
{
    ...
    ...
    AppSettings.ConnectionString = config.Get<string>("Data:DefaultConnection:
    ConnectionString");
    AppSettings.StoragePath = env.MapPath("Uploads");
}
```

The code uses the MapPath() method of the IHostingEnvironment instance to compute the full physical path of the \wwwroot\Uploads folder. The path is then assigned to the StoragePath property of AppSettings. The database connection string is picked from appsettings.json and assigned to the ConnectionString property.

205

Now add the IHandler interface to the Core folder and write the code shown in Listing 7-3 in it.

Listing 7-3. IHandler Interface with NextHandler and Process( )

```csharp
public interface IHandler
{
    IHandler NextHandler { get; set; }
    void Process(string filename, string filecontent);
}
```

The IHandler interface consists of a NextHandler property and Process() method. Notice that the type of NextHandler is IHandler. This way any class implementing IHandler can act as the next participant in the chain.

The Process() method takes two parameters. The filename parameter is the name of the file containing the data to be imported. The filecontent parameter contains the actual content of the file.

Next, add the FileFormatHandler class to the Core folder and implement IHandler in it. The complete code of the FileFormatHandler class is shown in Listing 7-4.

Listing 7-4. FileFormatHandler Class

```csharp
public class FileFormatHandler : IHandler
{
    public IHandler NextHandler { get; set; }

    public void Process(string filename, string filecontent)
    {
        string ext = Path.GetExtension(filename);
        if (ext != ".txt" && ext != ".csv")
        {
            throw new Exception("Invalid file type!");
        }
        else
        {
            string[] records = filecontent.Split(new string[] { "\r\n" },
            StringSplitOptions.RemoveEmptyEntries);
            if (records == null || records.Length == 0)
            {
                throw new Exception("Invalid data!");
            }
            else
            {
                string[] cols = records[0].Split(',');
                if (cols.Length != 5)
                {
                    throw new Exception("Missing or incomplete data!");
                }
            }
        }
    }
```

```
        if (NextHandler != null)
        {
            NextHandler.Process(filename, filecontent);
        }
    }
}
```

The NextHandler property is quite straightforward. The Process() method does three things:

- It checks whether the file has a permitted extension.
- It detects whether the file is empty.
- And it also checks whether the file contains data that matches with the target table.

The code detects the file extension using the GetExtension() method of the Path class (System.IO namespace). If the file extension is anything other than .txt or .csv, the code throws an exception. If the file extension is alright, the code proceeds to validate the content.

Then the code checks whether the file content is empty. This is done by calling the Split() method on the file content. Notice that the content is split on the basis of \r\n so that all the CSV records are obtained in the records array. If records array is empty, it indicates that the file is empty, and an exception is thrown.

The final task is to check whether the file contains valid data. This example assumes that the data is to be imported into a Customers table with five columns. So, records from the file must contain four comma-separated values. To detect this, the code splits the first record and checks whether the cols array contains exactly five elements. If the number of elements is anything other than five, an exception is thrown.

Once FileFormatHandler does its job, it needs to hand over the control to the next handler object in the chain. Note that FileFormatHandler doesn't know which object will be handling the request next. All it can check is whether the NextHandler has been set or not. If it is set, the code calls the Process() method on the NextHandler object.

Now, add the FileStorageHandler class to the Core folder and implement the IHandler interface in it. Listing 7-5 shows the complete code of the FileStorageHandler class.

Listing 7-5. FileStorageHandler Class

```
public class FileStorageHandler : IHandler
{
    public IHandler NextHandler { get; set; }

    public void Process(string filename, string filecontent)
    {
        filename = AppSettings.StoragePath + "\\" + Path.GetFileNameWithoutExtension
        (filename) + DateTime.Now.ToString("yyyy-MM-dd") + Path.GetExtension(filename);
        System.IO.File.AppendAllText(filename, filecontent);
        using (AppDbContext db = new AppDbContext())
        {
            FileStoreEntry fse = new FileStoreEntry();
            fse.FileName = filename;
            fse.UploadedOn = DateTime.Now;
            db.FileStore.Add(fse);
            db.SaveChanges();
        }
```

```
        if (NextHandler != null)
        {
            NextHandler.Process(filename, filecontent);
        }
    }
}
```

FileStorageHandler does two things:

- It stores the uploaded file in a folder.

- It adds an entry in the FileStore table indicating that such-and-such file was uploaded to the server.

The filename received in the Process() method is just a filename of the uploaded file. So, the code computes its full path by appending the filename to the StoragePath property of AppSettings. Also notice that a date stamp is added to the filename so that one can easily know the date on which the file was uploaded.

The file content is written to the file, and the file is saved using the AppendAllText() method.

Then a database entry is added indicating that a new file was received by the system. This is done using a FileStoreEntry entity and FileStore DbSet (they are discussed later). The FileName and UploadedOn properties indicate the full path and filename of the file being saved and its time stamp, respectively.

The code then checks whether control needs to be handed over to NextHandler. If so, Process() is called on the NextHandler object.

Next, add the DataImportHandler class to the Core folder and implement the IHandler interface in it. The complete code of DataImportHandler is shown in Listing 7-6.

Listing 7-6. DataImportHandler Class

```
public class DataImportHandler : IHandler
{
    public IHandler NextHandler { get; set; }

    public void Process(string filename, string filecontent)
    {
        using (AppDbContext db = new AppDbContext())
        {
            string[] records = filecontent.Split(new string[] { "\r\n" },
            StringSplitOptions.RemoveEmptyEntries);
            foreach (string record in records)
            {
                string[] cols = record.Split(',');
                Customer obj = new Customer();
                obj.CustomerID = cols[0];
                obj.CompanyName = cols[1];
                obj.ContactName = cols[2];
                obj.Phone = cols[3];
                obj.Location = cols[4];
                db.Customers.Add(obj);
            }
            db.SaveChanges();
        }
```

```
        if (NextHandler != null)
        {
            NextHandler.Process(filename, filecontent);
        }
    }
}
```

The Process() method of DataImportHandler does the job of importing the content into the Customers table. The file content is split into a records array using the Split() method.

A foreach loop iterates through the records array and adds Customer entries to the Customers DbSet. This is done by splitting each record array element into a cols array and then setting the CustomerID, Companyname, ContactName, Phone, and Location properties of the Customer object (the Customer object and AppDbContext classes will be discussed later).

Once all the customers are added, SaveChanges() is called on the AppDbContext to save the data to the Customers table.

As before, DataImportHandler checks whether any NextHandler is available. If so, it invokes the Process() on it.

Note that although our requirements conclude that data import is the last step, the class still checks whether NextHandler is available and, if so, calls Process() on it. This design ensures that if additional handlers are wired in the future, the DataImportHandler class need not undergo any changes.

Now it's time to look into the Customer, FileStoreEntry, and AppDbContext classes. The Customer class represents a single customer from the Customers table, and the FileStoreEntry class represents a single file entry record from the FileStore table. These classes are shown in Listing 7-7.

Listing 7-7. Customer and FileStoreEntry Classes

```
[Table("Customers")]
public class Customer
{
    [Key]
    public string CustomerID { get; set; }

    [Required]
    [StringLength(40)]
    public string CompanyName { get; set; }

    [Required]
    [StringLength(40)]
    public string ContactName { get; set; }

    [Required]
    [StringLength(20)]
    public string Phone { get; set; }

    [Required]
    [StringLength(100)]
    public string Location { get; set; }

}
```

```
[Table("FileStore")]
public class FileStoreEntry
{
    [DatabaseGenerated(DatabaseGeneratedOption.Identity)]
    public int Id { get; set; }

    [Required]
    [StringLength(500)]
    public string FileName { get; set; }
    [Required]
    public DateTime UploadedOn { get; set; }

}
```

The Customer class is mapped to the Customers table using the [Table] attribute and contains five properties–CustomerID, CompanyName, ContactName, Phone, and Location. These properties also have some data annotations attached to them.

The FileStoreEntry class is mapped to the FileStore table using the [Table] attribute. It contains three properties–Id, FileName, and UploadedOn.

The properties of Customer and FileStore are quite straightforward and hold the respective pieces of information.

Now, add an AppDbContext class to the Core folder and write the code shown in Listing 7-8 in it.

Listing 7-8. AppDbContext with Customers and FileStore DbSets

```
public class AppDbContext:DbContext
{
    public DbSet<Customer> Customers { get; set; }
    public DbSet<FileStoreEntry> FileStore { get; set; }

    protected override void OnConfiguring(DbContextOptionsBuilder optionsBuilder)
    {
        optionsBuilder.UseSqlServer(AppSettings.ConnectionString);
    }
}
```

The AppDbContext class is the entity framework DbContext and contains two DbSets–Customers and FileStore.

Now it's time to code the client, HomeController. Add the HomeController class to the Controllers folder. In addition to the default Index() action, add the Upload() action to it as shown in Listing 7-9.

Listing 7-9. Upload() Method Starts the Chain

```
[HttpPost]
public IActionResult Upload(IList<IFormFile> files)
{
    foreach (var file in files)
    {
        ContentDispositionHeaderValue header = ContentDispositionHeaderValue.
        Parse(file.ContentDisposition);
        string fileName = header.FileName;
        fileName = fileName.Trim('"');
        fileName = Path.GetFileName(fileName);
```

```
            MemoryStream ms = new MemoryStream();
            Stream s = file.OpenReadStream();
            s.CopyTo(ms);
            byte[] data = ms.ToArray();
            s.Dispose();
            ms.Dispose();
            string fileContent = System.Text.ASCIIEncoding.ASCII.GetString(data);

            FileFormatHandler handler1 = new FileFormatHandler();
            FileStorageHandler handler2 = new FileStorageHandler();
            DataImportHandler handler3 = new DataImportHandler();

            handler1.NextHandler = handler2;
            handler2.NextHandler = handler3;
            handler3.NextHandler = null;

            handler1.Process(fileName, fileContent);
        }
        ViewBag.Message = files.Count + " file(s) imported successfully!";
        return View("Index");
    }
}
```

The Upload() method is called when a user clicks on the Submit button after selecting a file. The file uploaded by the user is received as a list of IFormFile objects.

A foreach loop then iterates through the uploaded files. This initial part of the code should be familiar to you, because you used it in earlier examples. It basically reads a file into a MemoryStream (System.IO namespace).

The MemoryStream contains data in binary form. This data is converted into a string using the GetString() method.

The code then instantiates the three handlers—FileFormatHandler, FileStorageHandler, and DataImportHandler (COR.Core namespace). The next three lines of code set the NextHandler properties. Notice that FileStorageHandler object acts as the NextHandler for FileFormatHandler, and the DataImportHandler object acts as the NextHandler for FileStoreHandler. The NextHandler for DataImportHandler is set to null because that is where the process ends.

Once the handlers are assigned, the Process() method of the first handler (FileFormatHandler) is invoked. Upon completion of processing, a Message is added to the ViewBag, indicating the successful completion of the data-import operation.

Finally, add an Index view to the Views/Home folder and write the markup shown in Listing 7-10 in it.

Listing 7-10. Markup of Index View

```
<html>
<head>
    <title>Import Customer Data</title>
</head>
<body>

    <h1>Select File(s) to Upload :</h1>
    <form asp-action="Upload" asp-controller="Home" method="post" enctype="multipart/
    form-data">
        <input type="file" name="files" id="files" multiple />
        <input type="submit" value="Submit" />
```

```
    </form>
    <h4>@ViewBag.Message</h4>
</body>
</html>
```

The Index view consists of a form that submits to the Upload action (asp-action attribute) of the HomeController (asp-controller attribute). Notice that the enctype attribute is set to multipart/form-data since the form is used to upload files.

The form consists of a file-input field and a Submit button. The Message from the ViewBag is also outputted at the end of the form.

This completes the application. Before you run and test the application, create the CorDb database, Customers table, and FileStore table (see Chapter 1 for more details). You will also need a sample .txt or .csv file containing the customer data to be imported. You can grab one from the code download of this chapter.

Set a breakpoint at the Process() method of each of the handler classes and run the application. Pick the file containing CSV data and click on the Submit button to upload the file. When the control halts at the break points, check and confirm the inner workings of all three handlers.

Command

Usually when one object invokes an operation on another object, the requested operation is performed immediately. At times, however, you will need to add a spacer between the object invoking a request and the object actually fulfilling the request.

Consider an example where you wish to send bulk mailing list emails to the respective recipients. When a client issues a "send" command, the bulk emailing system might already be busy sending emails from other senders. It might become necessary to queue your send request so that it can be executed at some later time when the bulk emailing system is available. The system may even need to route the request to a backup emailing system in case something goes wrong. This means there is a distance between the command invocation and actual command execution.

If your application needs such a feature, then the command pattern can come to the rescue. **The command pattern encapsulates a request or a command as an object. This object can be queued and played at a later time. One can even undo and redo the command if required.**

With the command pattern in place, a client doesn't invoke a request directly onto a target. Instead, a client makes use of an Invoker object. The Invoker object then decides when to play the command.

Design and Explanation

The UML diagram shown in Figure 7-4 illustrates the command pattern.

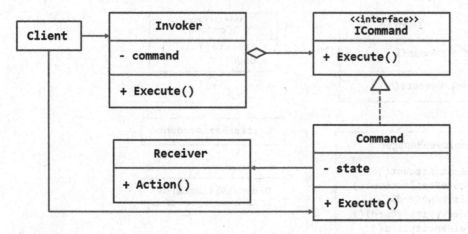

Figure 7-4. UML diagram illustrating command pattern

As shown in the figure, the ICommand interface represents an abstraction for a command. It has an Execute() method that is supposed to execute a requested operation on the targeted receiver.

The ICommand interface is implemented by the Command class. There can be many such implementations of ICommand depending on the application requirements. The Command class may hold some state specific to that command as indicated by the state private member. It also contains the implementation of the Execute() method. Execute() actually executes an operation on the target—the Receiver class.

The Receiver class is the actual object whose operation is to be invoked. The operation to be invoked is indicated by the Action() method.

The client doesn't call the Execute() method of the Command object directly. Instead, it makes use of the Invoker class, which holds one or more command objects as indicated by the aggregation symbol. The Execute() method of the Invoker decides when to invoke the Execute() method of the Command object(s) it holds. The Invoker may also do tasks such as queuing the command and redoing / undoing a command.

Notice that the Client is shown to be using the Invoker and Command objects. This is because the client needs to tell the Invoker which command(s) are to be invoked.

Example

Now that you know how the command pattern works, let's go ahead and develop an example that illustrates how it behaves.

Suppose you are developing a web application that is intended to be used by the human resources department of a company. When a newly selected candidate is about to join the company, the human resources department wants to ensure the timely availability of the employee's e-mail account, identity card, and visiting cards.

The human resources department employee initiates a request for all the three operations from a web interface. These three operations are, however, handled by three independent systems. For example, the request to create an e-mail account might be handled by the company's IT department whereas the request for printing the visiting cards might be handled by some third-party vendor or other department.

In order to simplify the overall tracking of these operations, it is decided that the three requests should be executed as a single transaction. If any part of the request fails for some reason, all the other requests should also be cancelled. This way all the operations are processed as a single bundle.

Considering these requirements, one may design the system as shown in Figure 7-5.

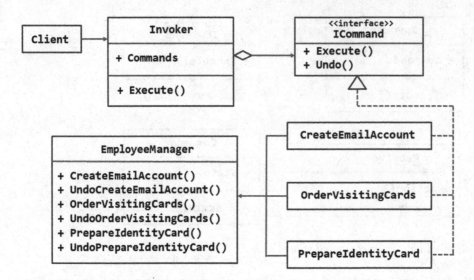

Figure 7-5. *Requesting employee operations through the command pattern*

As you can see, the ultimate Receiver object that performs the tasks is the EmployeeManager class. This class has six methods, namely CreateEmailAccount(), UndoCreateEmailAccount(), OrderVisitingCards(), UndoOrderVisitingCards(), PrepareIdentityCard(), and UndoPrepareIdentityCard(). As you might have guessed, the "Undo" methods cancel the corresponding tasks whereas the other methods perform the requested task.

The client shouldn't call these methods directly, because it might not be aware of the cancellation logic. The client should simply place the requests.

So, we need to encapsulate these three pairs of operations into the respective command objects. The classes CreateEmailAccount, OrderVisitingCards, and PrepareIdentityCard represent these commands.

The command classes are based on the ICommand interface, which consists of two methods—Execute() and Undo(). The Execute() method, when implemented, executes the requested operation on the EmployeeManager. The Undo() method, when implemented, cancels the preciously performed operation.

The Invoker class maintains a generic list of ICommand objects. This list is exposed as the Commands property. The Invoker needs a list because there could be more than one command to be executed. The Execute() method of the Invoker class executes the commands and contains logic to cancel the requests if something goes wrong.

Figure 7-6 shows the main page of the application that uses these classes.

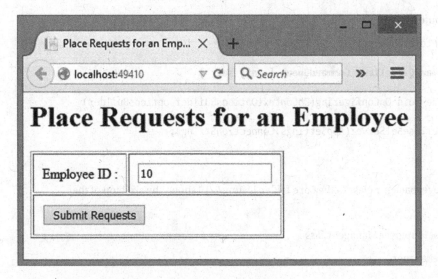

Figure 7-6. *Placing requests for employee accessories*

As you can see, the page accepts an employee ID. Upon entering the employee ID and clicking the Submit button, requests for e-mail address, visiting cards, and identity card are placed and a success message is displayed to the user.

To develop this application, begin by creating a new ASP.NET web application project named Command using Visual Studio and configure it to use MVC and Entity Framework (see Chapter 1 for more details). Also store the database connection string of CommandDb—the database used by the application—in the appsettings.json file.

Then add the AppSettings class to the Core folder and add the ConnectionString property to it. Also, set this property from the Startup class exactly like in the previous example.

Now, add the CommandQueueItem class to the Core folder and write the code shown in Listing 7-11 in it.

Listing 7-11. CommandQueueItem Class

```
[Table("CommandQueue")]
public class CommandQueueItem
{
    [DatabaseGenerated(DatabaseGeneratedOption.Identity)]
    public int Id { get; set; }

    [Required]
    public int EmployeeId { get; set; }

    [Required]
    public string CommandText { get; set; }
}
```

The CommandQueueItem class is mapped to the CommandQueue table and represents a single request to be processed by the processing system. It contains three properties—Id, EmployeeID, and CommandText. The CommandText property is merely a string indicating the requested operation. In a more realistic system, some separate system would be involved in processing the requested operation.

Next, add the AppDbContext class with the CommandQueue DbSet as shown in Listing 7-12.

Listing 7-12. AppDbContext Class

```
public class AppDbContext:DbContext
{
    public DbSet<CommandQueueItem> CommandQueue { get; set; }

    protected override void OnConfiguring(DbContextOptionsBuilder optionsBuilder)
    {
        optionsBuilder.UseSqlServer(AppSettings.ConnectionString);
    }
}
```

Then add the EmployeeManager class to the Core folder. Listing 7-13 shows the skeleton of the EmployeeManager class.

Listing 7-13. Skeleton of EmployeeManager Class

```
public class EmployeeManager
{
    private int employeeId;

    public EmployeeManager(int employeeid)
    {
        this.employeeId = employeeid;
    }

    public void CreateEmailAccount()
    {
    }

    public void UndoCreateEmailAccount()
    {
    }

    public void OrderVisitingCards()
    {
    }

    public void UndoOrderVisitingCards()
    {
    }

    public void PrepareIdentityCard()
    {
    }

    public void UndoPrepareIdentityCard()
    {
    }
}
```

The EmployeeManager class constructor accepts an employee ID and stores it in a private variable for later use. The EmployeeManager contains six methods, namely CreateEmailAccount(), UndoCreateEmailAccount(), OrderVisitingCards(), UndoOrderVisitingCards(), PrepareIdentityCard(), and UndoPrepareIdentityCard().

The "Do" methods perform the corresponding operation whereas the "Undo" methods cancel the request. For example, the CreateEmailAccount() method places a request for creating an e-mail account whereas the UndoCreateEmailAccount() method cancels the request.

These methods are quite similar in that the "Do" methods create a CommandQueueItem object and add an entry to the CommandQueue table, and the "Undo" methods remove an entry from the CommandQueue table. To save us some space, all the methods are not discussed here. The CreateEmailAccount() and UndoCreateEmailAccount() methods will be discussed. Listing 7-14 shows the CreateEmailAccount() method.

Listing 7-14. CreateEmailAccount() Method

```
public void CreateEmailAccount()
{
    using (AppDbContext db = new AppDbContext())
    {
        CommandQueueItem item = new CommandQueueItem();
        item.EmployeeId = this.employeeId;
        item.CommandText = "EMAIL_ACCOUNT";
        db.CommandQueue.Add(item);
        db.SaveChanges();
    }
}
```

The CreateEmailAccount() method creates a CommandQueueItem object and sets its EmployeeID and CommandText properties. The entry is then added to the CommandQueue DbSet and saved to the underlying table using the SaveChanges() method.

The UndoCreateEmailAccount() that cancels the request is shown in Listing 7-15.

Listing 7-15. UndoCreateEmailAccount() Method

```
public void UndoCreateEmailAccount()
{
    using (AppDbContext db = new AppDbContext())
    {
        CommandQueueItem item = db.CommandQueue.
                Where(i => i.EmployeeId == employeeId
                && i.CommandText == "EMAIL_ACCOUNT")
                .SingleOrDefault();
        if (item != null)
        {
            db.Entry(item).State = EntityState.Deleted;
            db.SaveChanges();
        }
    }
}
```

The UndoCreateEmailAccount() method grabs an entry matching a specific EmployeeID and CommandText (EMAIL_ACCOUNT, in this case) and then deletes the record from the table by setting its State property and calling the SaveChanges() method.

You can complete the other methods along similar lines just by changing the CommandText to the appropriate value. You may also grab the complete source code of the EmployeeManager class from the source code download of this book.

Then add a ICommand interface to the Core folder and write the code shown in Listing 7-16 in it:

Listing 7-16. ICommand Interface with TargetDate and Execute( )

```
public interface ICommand
{
    void Execute();
    void Undo();
}
```

The ICommand interface consists of two methods—Execute() and Undo().

Now, add three classes—CreateEmailAccount, OrderVisitingCards, and PrepareIdentityCard—to the Core folder. All of these classes implement the ICommand interface and call the respective methods on the EmployeeManager. Since these classes are quite identical to each other, all will not be not discussed here. The CreateEmailAccount class is shown in Listing 7-17.

Listing 7-17. CreateEmailAccount Class

```
public class CreateEmailAccount :ICommand
{
    private EmployeeManager manager;

    public CreateEmailAccount(EmployeeManager manager)
    {
        this.manager = manager;
    }

    public void Execute()
    {
        manager.CreateEmailAccount();
    }

    public void Undo()
    {
        manager.UndoCreateEmailAccount();
    }

}
```

The constructor of the CreateEmailAccount class accepts an EmployeeManager object as a parameter. A reference to the EmployeeManager is stored in a local variable for later use.

The Execute() method then calls the CreateEmailAccount() method on the EmployeeManager. Along the same lines, the Undo() method calls UndoCreateEmailAccount() on the EmployeeManager.

You can create the remaining two classes in a similar way by calling the respective pairs of methods on the EmployeeManager.

Next, add the Invoker class to the Core folder. Listing 7-18 shows the completed Invoker class.

Listing 7-18. Invoker Class Invoking the Commands

```
public class Invoker
{
    public List<ICommand> Commands { get; set; } = new List<ICommand>();

    public void Execute()
    {
        try
        {
            foreach (ICommand command in Commands)
            {
                command.Execute();
            }
        }
        catch
        {
            foreach (ICommand command in Commands)
            {
                command.Undo();
            }
        }
    }
}
```

The Invoker class maintains a list of ICommand objects. The client code adds the commands to this list as per the requirements. A try-catch block traps any exceptions that arise while placing the requests.

A foreach loop inside the try block iterates through the command list and invokes the Execute() method on each command object. If something goes wrong while placing the requests, another foreach loop from the catch block iterates through the command list and invokes the Undo() methods on the command objects.

Next, add the HomeController class to the Controllers folder. In addition to the default Index() action, add a ProcessEmployee() action to it, as shown in Listing 7-19.

Listing 7-19. ProcessEmployee() Action Initiates the Requests

```
[HttpPost]
public IActionResult ProcessEmployee(int employeeid)
{
    EmployeeManager manager = new EmployeeManager(employeeid);
    Invoker invoker = new Invoker();
    ICommand command = null;

    command = new CreateEmailAccount(manager);
    invoker.Commands.Add(command);
    command = new OrderVisitingCards(manager);
    invoker.Commands.Add(command);
    command = new PrepareIdentityCard(manager);
    invoker.Commands.Add(command);
```

```
    invoker.Execute();

    ViewBag.Message = $"Commands executed for employee #{employeeid}";
    return View("Index", employeeid);
}
```

The ProcessEmployee() action is called when a user clicks the Submit button on the Index view. It receives the employee ID entered by the user as its parameter. Inside, the code creates an EmployeeManager object by passing the employee ID to it. An instance of the Invoker class is also created.

Then a series of commands are added to the Commands list of the Invoker object. This code fragment adds all three commands—CreateEmailAccount, OrderVisitingCards, and PrepareIdentityCard—to the command list. Once the commands are added, the Execute() method of the Invoker is called. A message is set in the ViewBag to flag the success of the operation to the user.

Finally, add the Index view to the Views/Home folder and add the markup shown in the Listing 7-20 to it.

Listing 7-20. Markup of Index View

```
<html>
<head>
    <title>Place Requests for an Employee</title>
</head>
<body>
    <h1>Place Requests for an Employee</h1>
    <form asp-action="ProcessEmployee" asp-controller="Home" method="post">
        <table border="1" cellpadding="10">
            <tr>
                <td><label for="employeeid">Employee ID :</label></td>
                <td><input type="text" name="employeeid" value="@Model" /></td>
            </tr>
            <tr>
                <td colspan="2">
                    <input type="submit" value="Submit Requests" />
                </td>
            </tr>
        </table>
    </form>

    <h4>@ViewBag.Message</h4>

</body>
</html>
```

The Index view consists of a form that submits to the ProcessEmployee action (asp-action attribute) of the HomeController (asp-controller attribute). A textbox accepts the values of the employee ID, and a button submits the form. The success message from the ViewBag is also outputted at the bottom of the page.

This completes the application. Before you run and test the application, create the CommandDb database and CommandQueue table (see Chapter 1 for more details). Then set a breakpoint in the ProcessEmployee() action and run the application. Enter some test employee IDs and click the Submit button. Once the breakpoint is reached, step through the code to understand how the control flows from Invoker to commands and ultimately to the EmployeeManager.

Interpreter

While building .NET applications you rarely need to develop your own "language." Most commonly you utilize the features available in the framework and C# to accomplish your task. However, in some cases defining your own instruction set and then interpreting it within your code might become necessary.

Let's understand this with an example. Suppose you are developing a complex website that allows parts of the user interface to be stored in the database. This means the HTML markup that makes the user interface is pulled from some database table and then rendered on the user interface.

Going one step ahead, assume that now it is required that the staff managing the portal be allowed to define a part of the user interface as a part of its customization features. Further assume that the staff is not proficient in HTML or web markup in general. So, you will need to develop a simplified markup that they can easily understand and use. For example, to represent a date picker, the standard HTML uses this syntax:

```
<form action="/home/process" method="post">
 <input type="date" name="datepicker1" min="some_min_val" max="some_max_val" />
</form>
```

You may want to simplify this to:

```
[form postTo="process"]
 [datePicker minDate="some_val" maxDate="some_val" allowTime="false"]
[end]
```

The later piece of markup becomes the new "language" in the context of this application. Since this is a newly defined instruction set, an interpreter is necessary to decode its meaning for the rest of the system. That is where the interpreter pattern comes into the picture.

The interpreter pattern interprets a given instruction set in the context of a given application. The instruction set must have clearly defined rules of grammar so that the instructions are interpreted correctly. For instance, it must be clear to the system what possible values can be assigned to the allowTime attribute, or how date values are to be specified.

Design and Explanation

The UML diagram in Figure 7-7 illustrates the interpreter pattern.

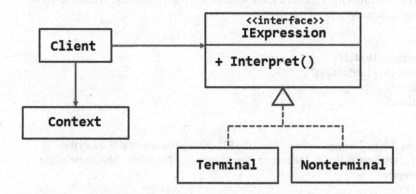

Figure 7-7. UML diagram illustrating the interpreter pattern

The IExpression interface represents an expression or a statement of the new language under consideration. It has the Interpret() method that, when implemented, is supposed to interpret the expression.

The two concrete classes, Terminal and Nonterminal, implement the IExpression interface. The Terminal class represents a single language statement to be interpreted, whereas the Nonterminal class represents a group of expressions (usually nested) that are to be interpreted. The Nonterminal class may use recursion or a similar technique to evaluate all the statements.

The Context class represents the global state that might be needed by the interpreter. This class is optional. If there is no global state to be used you can omit this class.

The Client class has the instruction set (a list of language statements or expressions) that is to be interpreted. How this instruction set is gathered depends on the application. For example, some applications may store the instruction set in a text file. Some other applications may accept it from the end user. And yet some other applications may pick it from the database.

Example

Now that you know the use of the interpreter pattern, let's apply this knowledge to an example.

Suppose that you are building a very big and complex website. You have created a set of class libraries that define various website management tasks, such as backing up the files and database, moving files from one location to another, deleting temporary files, and so on.

The administrator and the support staff have an administrative module at their disposal. The administrative module provides a user interface that calls the class libraries and gets the required task done.

Although the preceding arrangement works in most of the cases, at times the administrators find they need to define custom tasks that are not covered by the administrative module. Moreover, such tasks are quite unique in themselves, and modifying the administrative module to cover all the possibilities is impossible.

So, it is decided that there should be a way to invoke the APIs from the class libraries dynamically at runtime. A couple of possibilities could be:

- A command-line tool that accepts the assembly name, class name, method name, and method parameters and then invokes the said method using .NET reflection.

- A JSON file (*.json) that stores details such as assembly name, class name, method name, and method parameters. The JSON file can be uploaded onto the server and then handled using .NET reflection.

As an illustration we will use the JSON file approach just mentioned . To get an idea as to how the JSON might look, consider the following markup:

```
{
  "AssemblyName": "FileManagerLib.dll",
  "ClassName": "FileManagerLib.FileManager",
  "MethodName": "CreateFolder",
  "Parameters": [ "TestFolder" ]
}
```

This JSON fragment means this to the application—Load the FileManager assembly and call the CreateFolder method on its FileManagerLib. FileManager class by passing TestFolder (the name of the folder to be created) as a parameter.

■ **Note**   Don't worry too much at this stage if you find the JSON and the instruction bit complex to understand. Things will be clear as you proceed and develop the complete example.

As you can see, the instruction set defined by the JSON file is application specific and hence needs an interpreter that can decode it for the rest of the system. AssemblyName, ClassName, and MethodName become the vocabulary of the instruction set. And rules such as parameters must be in the same sequence as the actual methods become the grammar in the given context.

Figure 7-8 shows the arrangement that makes use of the interpreter pattern to achieve the goal.

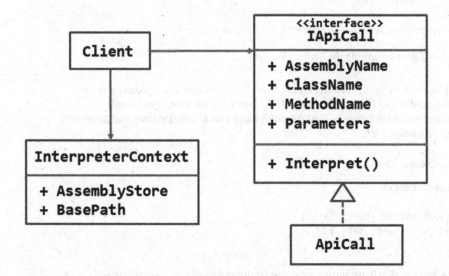

Figure 7-8. *ApiCall class interprets the JOSN and invokes the class library*

The IApiCall interface represents the abstraction for an API call. Here, an API call means invoking a method on a class residing in a particular assembly. The IApiCall interface consists of four properties—AssemblyName, ClassName, MethodName, and Parameters—and the Interpret() method. The properties represent the corresponding pieces of information. The implementation of the Interpret() method is supposed to load the assembly and make the API call. The IApiCall is implemented in the ApiCall class.

The InterpreterContext class holds two pieces of information that are needed by the ApiCall class—AssemblyStore and BasePath. The AssemblyStore property indicates the folder in which the assemblies (compiled class libraries) are stored. The BasePath property points to the full path to the wwwroot folder of the web application. This path is required for file system operations such as copying files and deleting files.

A controller acts as the Client, fills the InterpreterContext properties, and also loads a JSON file containing the instruction set. The instruction set is then fed to the ApiCall class.

The main page of the application you develop in this section simply allows you to pick one or more JSON files using a file-input field (Figure 7-9). Upon clicking the Submit button, the JSON files are processed, as discussed earlier.

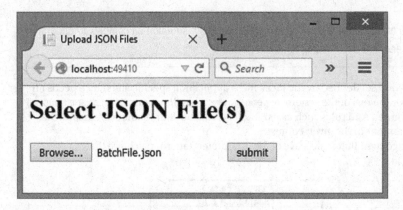

Figure 7-9. *Selecting *.json Files Containing the Instruction Set*

To develop this application, begin by creating a new ASP.NET web application project named Interpreter using Visual Studio and configure it to use MVC (see Chapter 1 for more details).

Then add an InterpreterContext class to the Core folder and add AssemblyStore and BasePath properties to it, as shown in Listing 7-21.

Listing 7-21. InterpreterContext Class

```
public class InterpreterContext
{
    public string AssemblyStore { get; set; }
    public string BasePath { get; set; }
}
```

The AssemblyStore and BasePath properties are quite straightforward and were discussed earlier.

Then add the IApiCall interface to the Core folder and add the property and method definitions shown in Listing 7-22.

Listing 7-22. IApiCall Interface

```
public interface IApiCall
{
    string AssemblyName { get; set; }
    string ClassName { get; set; }
    string MethodName { get; set; }
    List<string> Parameters { get; set; }

    void Interpret(InterpreterContext context);
}
```

The IApiCall interface consists of four properties—AssemblyName, ClassName, MethodName, and Parameters. Notice that the Parameters property is a generic list of strings. Each entry in this collection represents a parameter value of a method to be invoked. The parameters must be added in the order in which they appear in the method signature.

The Interpret() method accepts the InterpreterContext object as its parameter. This way information such as AssemblyStore and BasePath is made available to the code that interprets the instructions.

Next, add an ApiCall class to the Core folder and implement the IApiCall interface on it. The complete ApiCall class is shown in Listing 7-23.

Listing 7-23. ApiCall Class Interprets the Instructions

```
public class ApiCall : IApiCall
{
    public string AssemblyName { get; set; }
    public string ClassName { get; set; }
    public string MethodName { get; set; }
    public List<string> Parameters { get; set; }

    public void Interpret(InterpreterContext context)
    {
        Assembly assembly = Assembly.LoadFile(context.AssemblyStore + $"\\{AssemblyName}");
        Type type = assembly.GetType(ClassName);
        object obj = Activator.CreateInstance(type, context.BasePath);
        MethodInfo method = type.GetMethod(MethodName);
        method.Invoke(obj, Parameters.ToArray());
    }
}
```

The Interpret() method uses classes from the System.Reflection namespace (make sure to delete the dnxcore50 entry from the frameworks section of Project.json). First, it loads the assembly containing the classes and the methods to be invoked. This is done using the LoadFrom() static method of the Assembly class and by supplying the full path and name of the assembly (*.dll) file. Notice the use of the InterpreterContext AssemblyStore property in obtaining the path of the assembly.

The Type instance of the required class is then obtained using the GetType() method of the Assembly object.

This Type is then instantiated using the Activator.CreateInstance() method. The CreateInstance() method takes two parameters—the Type object whose instance is to be created and the constructor parameters (if needed). The code passes BasePath to the constructor.

So far you haven't created the FileManagerLib assembly. You will create it later. For now, it is suffice to say that the FileManager class constructor accepts the path of the website root folder as its parameter.

Once the object is obtained, the GetMethod() method is used to get a MethodInfo object describing the method as indicated by the MethodName property.

Finally, the method is invoked on the object using the Invoke() method of the MethodInfo instance. The Invoke() method accepts the object on which the method is to be invoked as well as an array of method parameters. In this case, method parameters are obtained from the Parameters generic list.

Now, add HomeController to the Controllers folder. In addition to the default Index() action, you need an action that deals with the uploaded JSON files. The ExecuteJSON() action that does this is shown in Listing 7-24.

Listing 7-24. ExecuteJSON() Action that Deals with the JSON Files

```
public IActionResult ExecuteJSON(List<IFormFile> files)
{
    foreach (IFormFile file in files)
    {
        ContentDispositionHeaderValue header = ContentDispositionHeaderValue.Parse(file.
ContentDisposition);
        string fileName = header.FileName;
        fileName = fileName.Trim('"');
        fileName = Path.GetFileName(fileName);
        string filePath = env.MapPath("BatchFiles\\" + fileName);
        file.SaveAs(filePath);

        List<ApiCall> apiCalls = JsonConvert.DeserializeObject<List<ApiCall>>(System.
IO.File.ReadAllText(filePath));
        InterpreterContext context = new InterpreterContext();
        context.AssemblyStore = env.MapPath("AssemblyStore");
        context.BasePath = env.WebRootPath;

        foreach (ApiCall call in apiCalls)
        {
            call.Interpret(context);
        }
    }
    ViewBag.Message = "API calls from the file(s) have been executed!";
    return View("Index");
}
```

The code saves the uploaded files to the wwwroot/BatchFiles folder. This code should be familiar to you since you used it many times in the previous examples.

Once the JSON file(s) is saved on the server, you need to read the JSON file and convert it into ApiCall objects. This is accomplished with the help of a Json.Net component. Make sure to add the NuGet package of Json.Net to your project before you write this code. Once added, you can use the JsonConvert class (Newtonsoft.Json namespace) to parse and read the JSON files. The DeserializeObject() generic method of the JsonConvert class accepts the JSON string data and returns a generic List of ApiCall objects. Notice that since the DeserializeObject() method requires a string, the uploaded JSON file is read in a string using the ReadAllText() method of the File class.

The InterpreterContext is then created and its AssemblyStore and BasePath properties are set to the /wwwroot/AssemblyStore folder and /wwwroot folder, respectively. This is done using the MapPath() method and the WebRoot property of the constructor injected IHostingEnvironment object.

A foreach loop iterates through the list of ApiCall objects and calls the Interpret() method on each ApiCall object. The InterpreterContext is also passed to the Interpret() method.

Once the foreach loop completes, a message is set in the ViewBag that indicates the successful completion of the operation.

Finally, add the Index view to the /Views/Home folder and write the markup shown in Listing 7-25 in it.

Listing 7-25. Markup of Index View

```html
<html>
<head>
    <title>Upload JSON Files</title>
</head>
<body>
    <h1>Select JSON File(s)</h1>
    <form asp-controller="Home" asp-action="ExecuteJSON" method="post" enctype="multipart/
form-data">
        <input type="file" name="files" id="files" multiple />
        <input type="submit" value="submit" />
    </form>
    <h2>@ViewBag.Message</h2>
</body>
</html>
```

This markup should be familiar to you since you used it in earlier examples. It basically consists of a form that houses a file-input field and a Submit button. The form is posted to the ExecuteJSON() action you wrote earlier.

Although this completes the web application, you still need to create the FileManagerLib class library that is being used by the web application. To create it, add a new Class Library project to the same solution and name the project as FileManagerLib. Then add the FileManager class to the project. Listing 7-26 shows the complete code of the FileManager class.

Listing 7-26. FileManager Class

```csharp
public class FileManager
{
    private string basePath;

    public FileManager(string basepath)
    {
        this.basePath = basepath;
    }

    public void CreateFolder(string location)
    {
        Directory.CreateDirectory(basePath + "\\" + location);
    }

    public void CopyFiles(string sourceFolder,string destinationFolder,string pattern)
    {
        sourceFolder = basePath + "\\" + sourceFolder;
        destinationFolder = basePath + "\\" + destinationFolder;

        string[] files = Directory.GetFiles(sourceFolder,pattern);
```

```
        foreach(string source in files)
        {
            string destination = destinationFolder + "\\" + Path.GetFileName(source);
            File.Copy(source, destination);
        }
    }

    public void DeleteFiles(string location,string pattern)
    {
        location = basePath + "\\" + location;
        string[] files = Directory.GetFiles(location, pattern);
        foreach (string file in files)
        {
            File.Delete(file);
        }
    }
}
```

We won't go into a detailed discussion of the FileManager class, because this class is used merely for testing purpose and performs the basic filesystem management tasks. It is suffice to note the following:

- The FileManager constructor takes a string parameter—the physical base path of the wwwroot folder. Recollect that the Interpret() method of ApiCall passes this parameter using reflection.

- The FileManager class contains three methods—CreateFolder(), CopyFiles(), and DeleteFiles(). The CreateFolder() method creates a new folder at a given location. The CopyFiles() method copies files from a source folder to a destination folder. The DeleteFiles() method deletes files from a folder. The CopyFiles() and DeleteFiles() methods allow you to specify a file-matching pattern (for example, *.png).

- The FileManagerLib assembly, FileManager class, and the three methods are specified in the JSON file.

Once you complete the FileManagerLib class library, compile it and copy its assembly (FileManagerLib.dll) to the AssemblyStore folder under wwwroot (you will need to create this folder). Also create the BatchFiles folders under wwwroot.

This completes the application; now it's time to test it. You will need to create a JSON file containing the instructions in order to test the application. You can do so either in Notepad or in Visual Studio. Listing 7-27 shows a sample JSON file.

Listing 7-27. BatchScript.json File Containing Instructions

```
[
  {
    "AssemblyName": "FileManagerLib.dll",
    "ClassName": "FileManagerLib.FileManager",
    "MethodName": "CreateFolder",
    "Parameters": [ "TestFolder" ]
  },
```

```
{
  "AssemblyName": "FileManagerLib.dll",
  "ClassName": "FileManagerLib.FileManager",
  "MethodName": "CopyFiles",
  "Parameters": ["Images","TestFolder","*.*"]
},
{
  "AssemblyName": "FileManagerLib.dll",
  "ClassName": "FileManagerLib.FileManager",
  "MethodName": "DeleteFiles",
  "Parameters": ["TestFolder","*.gif"]
}
]
```

As you can see, the BatchScript.json file consists of an array with three elements. Each array element specifies an AssemblyName, ClassName, MethodName, and Parameters. The Parameters themselves are specified in the form of a string array.

Notice that the JSON property names, such as AssemblyName and ClassName, must batch to the properties of the ApiCall class. This is because the JsonConvert class deserializes the JSON file into ApiCall objects based on this mapping.

The AssemblyName points to the assembly FileManagerLib.dll. The ClassName specifies the fully qualified name of the class—FileManagerLib.FileManager. The MethodName specifies the method to be invoked, such as CopyFiles. And the Parameters array specifies a list of parameter values as expected by the method. Then add a few files to the wwwroot/Images folder.

That's it! Now run the web application and upload the BatchScript.json file to the server. If everything goes well, you will find a TestFolder folder getting created under wwwroot. Files from the Images folder also get copied to the TestFolder. And all the GIF files (if any) get deleted from the TestFolder.

■ **Note**   In the preceding example, a JSON file acted as a source of the instruction set. However, that's not always necessary. You can even accept the instructions (AssemblyName, ClassName, MethodName, and Parameters) from a user interface and then invoke them using the Interpret() method of the ApiCall class.

Iterator

Many times your code will need to deal with a collection of objects. You are probably aware that the System.Collections and System.Collections.Generic namespaces provide many classes that represent a collection of objects. An ArrayList, List, and Dictionary are some of them.

Iterating through a collection of object is quite common in .NET applications. In C# the foreach loops simplify the overall access to the individual elements of a collection.

In many cases the built-in collection classes serve the purpose of iterating and accessing a collection sequentially quite well. However, in some cases you may want to devise your own way to iterate through a collection.

Suppose you have some data stored as a JSON file. The client wants to read and access the data—it must know how the JSON file is structured. The Iterator pattern can separate that logic away from the client and provide a simplified, cursor-like way to iterate through the JSON files.

In such situations the iterator pattern comes handy. **The iterator pattern allows your code to access the individual elements of an aggregate object sequentially.** In doing so, the client is shielded from knowing the internal details of the aggregate object.

Design and Explanation

The UML diagram in Figure 7-10 illustrates the iterator pattern.

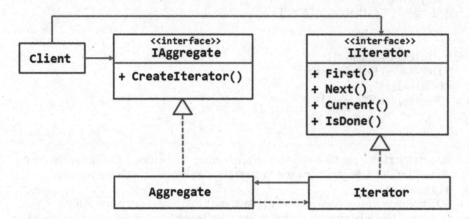

Figure 7-10. *UML diagram illustrating iterator pattern*

The IIterator interface defines the abstraction for the iterator. It has methods such as First(), Next(), Current(), and IsDone(). The First() method takes the cursor to the first element of the aggregate. The Next() method moves the cursor to the next element of the aggregate. The Current() method returns the element pointed to by the cursor at a given point in time. Finally, IsDone() indicates whether all the elements of the aggregate object have been iterated or not.

The Iterator class implements IIterator and provides the concrete implementation for the methods just mentioned.

The Iterator object simply iterates through an aggregate. The actual collection is represented by the IAggregate interface. The CreateIterator() method of the IAggregate interface, when implemented, is supposed to return an Iterator object for iterating through the aggregate.

The Aggregate class implements the IAggregate interface and represents the collection of elements to be iterated upon.

Notice the links between Aggregate and Iterator classes. The dashed arrow between Aggregate and Iterator represents the dependency of Aggregate on the Iterator. The solid arrow between Iterator and Aggregate represents an association between them.

The client uses both objects—IAggregate and IIterator.

Although the iterator pattern can be implemented in C# as shown in Figure 7-10, the .NET framework has a built-in way to implement it in the form of IEnumerable and IEnumerator interfaces. So, the next section will discuss and use that approach instead of the one just discussed.

Example

Suppose you have a database table with a very large number of records in it. To reduce the memory footprint of the code and for performance reasons, it is decided to use SqlDataReader instead of fetching the data and storing it in advance.

However, using SqlDataReader may make the client code a bit difficult and less readable due to the following reasons:

- To use SqlDataReader the client will also need to be aware of the table schema. The client needs to know the data types and column ordinals, or names, in order to use methods such as GetString() and GetInt32().

- The client code will have tight coupling with the SQL Server data provider, and any future changes in the data-access logic might need changes in the client code also.

- The client will need to take care of closing the SqlDataReader once done to ensure that the underlying database connection is closed properly.

So, it is decided that the client code should not use the SqlDataReader directly. The client code should look as if a standard collection is being iterated.

The scenario just described is a good candidate for using the iterator pattern. Figure 7-11 shows the design of the said system. The design assumes that the Orders table of the Northwind database is to be iterated using the implementation.

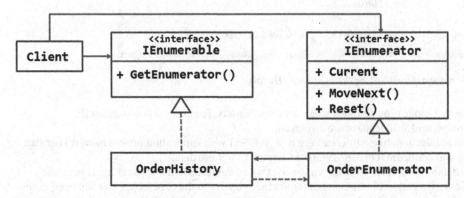

Figure 7-11. *Iterating through SqlDataReader using the iterator pattern*

The design shown in Figure 7-11 makes use of the .NET framework's built-in interfaces—IEnumerable and IEnumerator—for implementing the iterator pattern. These interfaces come in two flavors—generic and non-generic. The former flavor is available in the System.Collections.Generic namespace and the later flavor is available in the System.Collections namespace. Since generic collections are better than non-generic ones, we will use the generic interfaces in our implementation.

The IEnumerator interface consists of two methods—MoveNext() and Reset(). The OrderEnumerator class represents the concrete implementation of the IEnumerator interface. The MoveNext() implementation is responsible for shifting the current element pointer to the next Order. The Reset() method shifts the pointer back to the beginning of the collection. The *Current* property returns the current order pointed to by the iterator.

The IEnumerable interface can be implemented by any object that represents an aggregate or collection. In this example, OrderHistory is such an aggregate object and deals with all the orders from the Orders table. The IEnumerable interface requires the OrderHistory class to implement the GetEnumerator() method. GetEnumerator() returns an IEnumerator object (OrderEnumerator in this case) to the aggregate for iterating its elements.

The client code uses a foreach loop to iterate through the OrderHistory class. It can also access an order currently pointed to by the iterator.

The application that you build in this section looks a bit like the one shown in Figure 7-12.

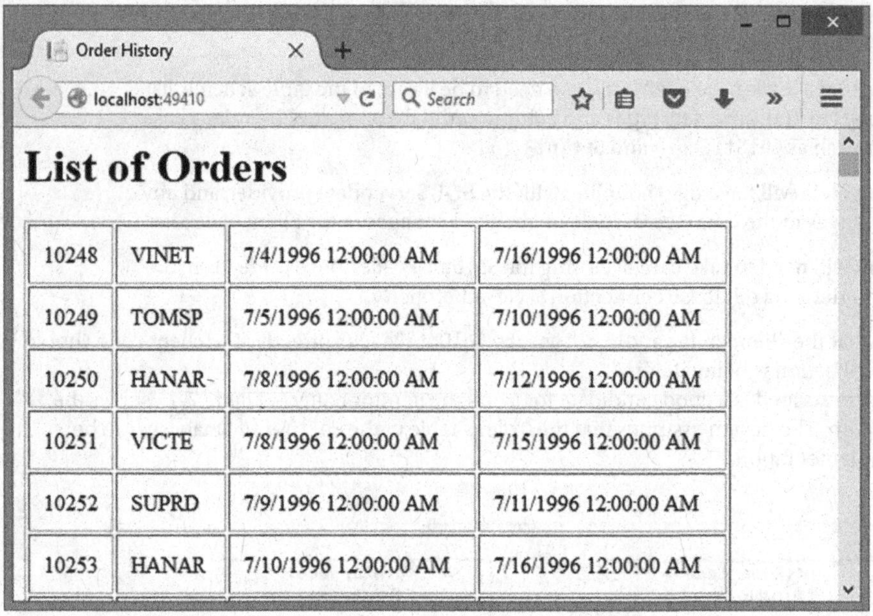

Figure 7-12. *Table rendered by iterating through OrderHistory*

As you can see, the application simply displays a table of orders. For every order, its OrderID, CustomerID, OrderDate, and ShippedDate are displayed.

To develop this application, begin by creating a new ASP.NET web application project named Iterator using Visual Studio and configure it to use MVC (see Chapter 1 for more details).

Also store the database connection string for the Northwind database in the appsettings.json file. Then add the AppSettings class with the ConnectionString property to the Core folder. You will need to set the ConnectionString property in the Startup class as you did for many of the earlier examples.

Then add the Order class to the Core folder. The Order class represents an element of the OrderHistory class and is shown in Listing 7-28.

Listing 7-28. Order Class Holding Details of an Order

```
public class Order
{
    public int OrderID { get; set; }
    public string CustomerID { get; set; }
    public DateTime OrderDate { get; set; }
    public DateTime ShippedDate { get; set; }
}
```

The Order class consists of four properties, namely OrderID, CustomerID, OrderDate, and ShippedDate. These properties correspond to the respective columns of the Orders table of the Northwind database.

Now add an OrderHistory class to the Core folder and implement the IEnumerable<T> interface in it. This complete, the code of the OrderHistory is shown in Listing 7-29.

Listing 7-29. OrderHistory Class Implementing IEnumerable<Order>

```
public class OrderHistory : IEnumerable<Order>
{
    public SqlDataReader Cursor { get; set; }

    public OrderHistory(bool openImmediately)
    {
        if (openImmediately)
        {
            this.OpenCursor();
        }
    }

    public void OpenCursor()
    {
        SqlConnection cnn = new SqlConnection(AppSettings.ConnectionString);
        SqlCommand cmd = new SqlCommand();
        cmd.Connection = cnn;
        cmd.CommandType = CommandType.Text;
        cmd.CommandText = "select OrderID,CustomerID,OrderDate,ShippedDate from orders where
        shippeddate is not null order by orderdate";
        cnn.Open();
        this.Cursor = cmd.ExecuteReader(CommandBehavior.CloseConnection);
    }

    public IEnumerator<Order> GetEnumerator()
    {
        return new OrderEnumerator(this);
    }

    private IEnumerator GetEnumerator1()
    {
        return this.GetEnumerator();
    }

    IEnumerator IEnumerable.GetEnumerator()
    {
        return GetEnumerator1();
    }
}
```

Before you write any code in the OrderHistory class, make sure to import System.Data, System.Data.SqlClient, System.Collections, and System.Collections.Generic namespaces at the top of the class file. You need to import both the System.Collections and the System.Collections.Generic namespaces because IEnumerable<T> from the latter namespace is based on IEnumerable from the former namespace.

The OrderHistory class implements the IEnumerable<T> interface and specifies Order as its generic type.

Then the OrderHistory class defines the Cursor public property. The Cursor property is an SqlDataReader and needs to be public because the OrderEnumerator class needs to iterate through it.

The Constructor of the OrderHistory class accepts a Boolean parameter, openImmediately, that indicates whether the SqlDataReader should be immediately created or not. If this parameter is true, the code calls the OpenCursor() private method.

The OpenCursor() private method opens a connection with the Northwind database and fires a SELECT statement using an SqlCommand object. The SELECT statement fetches OrderID, CustomerID, OrderDate, and ShippedDate column values from the database. Notice that the ExecuteReader() method specifies the CommandBehavior value to be CloseConnection. This way, calling the Close() method on the SqlDataReader will also close the underlying database connection.

The GetEnumerator() method returns IEnumerator<Order> in the form of an OrderEnumerator object (you will create OrderEnumerator shortly).

The next two methods—GetEnumerator1() and IEnumerable.GetEnumerator()—implement the GetEnumerator() method of IEnumerable privately. This is required because IEnumerable<T> itself inherits from the IEnumerable interface.

Next, add an OrderEnumerator class to the Core folder and implement IEnumerator<T> on it. The complete code of the OrderEnumerator class is shown in Listing 7-30.

Listing 7-30. OrderEnumerator Implementing IEnumerator<Order>

```
public class OrderEnumerator : IEnumerator<Order>
{
    private OrderHistory history;

    public OrderEnumerator(OrderHistory history)
    {
        this.history = history;
    }

    public bool MoveNext()
    {
        if(history.Cursor.IsClosed)
        {
            history.OpenCursor();
        }
        return history.Cursor.Read();
    }

    public void Reset()
    {
        history.Cursor.Close();
    }

    public Order Current
    {
        get
        {
            Order currentOrder = new Order();
            currentOrder.OrderID = history.Cursor.GetInt32(0);
            currentOrder.CustomerID = history.Cursor.GetString(1);
            currentOrder.OrderDate = history.Cursor.GetDateTime(2);
            currentOrder.ShippedDate = history.Cursor.GetDateTime(3);
            return currentOrder;
        }
    }
}
```

```
private object Current1
{
    get
    {
        return Current;
    }
}

object IEnumerator.Current
{
    get
    {
        return Current1;
    }
}

public void Dispose()
{
    if (history.Cursor != null && history.Cursor.IsClosed == false)
    {
        history.Cursor.Close();
    }
}
}
```

The OrderEnumerator class begins by declaring a private variable of OrderHistory. This variable is assigned in the constructor.

The MoveNext() method checks whether the SqlDataReader exposed by the Cursor property is open or not. If it is closed, the OpenCursor() method opens it so that the code can iterate through the records. The Read() method is then called on the SqlDataReader so that the record pointer is advanced to the next record. Note that initially the record pointer is placed before the beginning of the records. Thus, calling Read() for the first time moves it onto the first record. Subsequent calls to Read() advance the record pointer in the forward direction one record at a time.

The Reset() method closes the SqlDataReader by calling its Close() method. Recollect that earlier the CommandBehavior was set to CloseConnection. So, calling close on the SqlDataReader also closes the underlying connection.

The Current property is a read-only property and hence has only the get block. The code inside the get block creates a new Order object and populates it with the data from the SqlDataReader. Notice the use of the GetInt32(), GetString(), and GetDateTime() methods to read the integer, string, and DateTime column values, respectively. The newly created Order object is then returned to the caller.

The next two properties—Current1 and IEnumerable.Current—are required in order to implement the Current property of IEnumerable privately. This is because IEnumerator<T> inherits from IEnumerator.

The Dispose() method closes the SqlDataReader if it is open so that the underlying database connection is also closed.

Next, add HomeController in the Controllers folder. Modify its Index() action to include the code shown in Listing 7-31.

Listing 7-31. Iterating Through OrderHistory Collection

```
public IActionResult Index()
{
    OrderHistory history = new OrderHistory(true);
    List<Order> orders = new List<Order>();
    foreach (Order o in history)
    {
        orders.Add(o);
    }
    return View(orders);
}
```

The `Index()` action creates an instance of `OrderHistory`. The value of `true` passed to the constructor indicates that the cursor should be opened immediately.

Then a list of `Order` objects is created. This is purely for the sake of testing purposes. In a more realistic case you would iterate through the `OrderHistory`, access each and every `Order` object, and process it as per your requirement. Here, for the sake of testing, the code simply grabs `Order` objects from the `OrderHistory` and puts them into another collection. This is done using the `foreach` loop.

Notice that the `foreach` loop expects that the collection being iterated implements either the `IEnumerable` or the `IEnumerable<T>` interface. So, it works as expected with the history object.

The generic list of `Order` objects is then passed to the `Index` view to be displayed in a table.

Finally, add the `Index` view to the `Views/Home` folder and write the markup shown in Listing 7-32 in it.

Listing 7-32. Markup of Index View

```
@model List<Iterator.Core.Order>
...
<h1>List of Orders</h1>
<table border="1" cellpadding="10">
    @foreach(var item in Model)
    {
      <tr>
        <td>@item.OrderID</td>
        <td>@item.CustomerID</td>
        <td>@item.OrderDate</td>
        <td>@item.ShippedDate</td>
      </tr>
    }
</table>
...
```

The `Index` view is quite straightforward. It displays a table by iterating through the list of `Order` objects passed as the `Model`. The table displays the `OrderID`, `CustomerID`, `OrderDate`, and `ShippedDate` properties of each order.

This completes the application. You can run it and confirm whether the records are displayed as expected.

Summary

Behavioral patterns concern themselves with how a system behaves and communicates. This chapter covered four behavioral patterns, namely chain of responsibility, command, interpreter, and iterator.

The chain of responsibility pattern is used when a request is to be handled by multiple objects in a chain-like manner. The objects that handle the request can be wired by the client code. One handler, after completing its work, invokes the next handler in the chain.

The command pattern encapsulates a request as an object. Since a command is being represented as an object, operations such as queuing, redo, and undo can be easily performed.

The interpreter pattern is used to interpret a language or instruction set in an application's context. It allows you to define, parse, and execute an instruction set that is application specific.

The iterator pattern allows you to access individual elements of an aggregate object sequentially.

The next chapter will continue the discussion of behavioral patterns by discussing the mediator, memento, and observer patterns.

CHAPTER 8

■■■

Behavioral Patterns: Mediator, Memento, and Observer

Continuing our journey through behavioral patterns, this chapter will dissect the mediator, memento, and observer design patterns.

Sometimes you want objects of a system to communicate with each other. This communication can be one way or two way. The meditator and observer deal with how multiple objects send and / or receive messages to achieve communication.

The memento pattern concerns itself with the object's state. It handles the storing and retrieving of an object's state. To be specific, you will learn the following:

- Purpose and role of the mediator, memento, and observer design patterns

- UML structure and layout of these four patterns

- A proof of concept example for each illustrating the implementation of these patterns

Mediator

A system consisting of several different types of objects often needs a way for those objects to communicate with each other. If every interested object is supposed to communicate with the other objects directly, it can lead to complications. This is because each such object must know reasonable details about the object with which it is attempting to communicate.

Consider a real-life example. Suppose you wish to invest money in a variety of ways, such as fixed deposit schemes, insurance policies, debentures, and so on. Now, you can deal directly with each and every bank or company involved. As you might have guessed, doing so might be tedious, because you must know how to communicate with every bank or company you wish to invest your money with.

As an alternative, you may seek services from an investment agent who can do all the required communication on your behalf. So, you submit your application form and documents to this middleman, and he forwards them to the required bank or company. If the bank or company needs some more details from you, they convey that to the agent and the agent conveys the message to you. Thus, all the communication is routed through the mediator, and you are freed from knowing the internal workings of the individual parties involved.

© Bipin Joshi 2016

B. Joshi, *Beginning SOLID Principles and Design Patterns for ASP.NET Developers*,
DOI 10.1007/978-1-4842-1848-8_8

This is also how the mediator pattern works. **The mediator pattern defines a way for objects to interact with each other through a central coordinating object.** This central object takes care of routing the communication as required by the system. In doing so, the mediator pattern promotes loose coupling between the sender and receiver objects. Since sender and receiver objects don't need to know anything about each other, they can be modified independently without affecting each other.

■ **Note** At first glance you may find the mediator pattern to be similar to the proxy pattern discussed earlier. However, they are quite different. A proxy object mimics the target object, and your code uses the proxy as if it were using the target object. Here the mediator is a distinct and known object in the system. It doesn't pretend to be some other object.

Design and Explanation

The UML diagram in Figure 8-1 illustrates the mediator pattern.

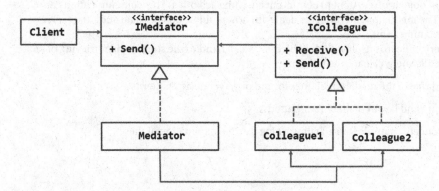

Figure 8-1. *UML diagram illustrating the mediator pattern*

As shown in the figure, there are two interfaces—one for the mediator object and the other for colleague objects. The colleague objects are the objects that wish to communicate with each other.

The IMediator interface has the Send() method. This method, when implemented, sends the communication from one colleague to the other. The Mediator class is the concrete implementation of the IMediator interface.

The IColleague interface consists of two methods—Receive() and Send(). The Receive() method, when implemented, receives a communication message from the mediator and processes it as per system requirements. The Send() method, when implemented, sends a message to a colleague through the mediator.

The IColleague interface is implemented in the Colleague1 and Colleague2 classes. Notice that the objects talking to each other may or may not be of the same type. Nevertheless they all implement the IColleague interface. For example, object A of Colleague1 may want to communicate with object B of Colleague2.

The Mediator class is shown to be using Colleague1 and Colleague2 because as a middleman it needs to interact with both of them.

Example

Now that you know how the mediator pattern works, let's implement it in an example.

Suppose you are building a big community forum application. As a part of the membership features you wish to allow members to chat with each other through some interface. As an initial step, a web interface will be developed for user-to-user chatting. But later you may develop alternatives such as a desktop version or a mobile version of the chat interface.

A user signs in to the system and can send messages to another user. If the target user is offline an exception is thrown; otherwise, the message is delivered to the other user.

Considering these requirements you can design the system as shown in Figure 8-2.

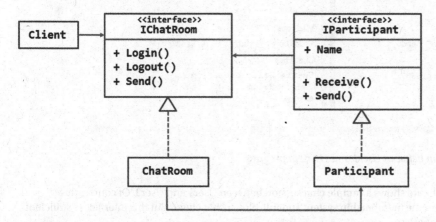

Figure 8-2. *A web-based chat implemented using the mediator pattern*

The IChatRoom interface represents the interface for the mediator. It consists of three methods–Login(), Logout(), and Send(). The Login() and Logout() methods control the entry and exit of a chat participant. The Send() method sends a chat message to its intended recipient. The ChatRoom class is the concrete implementation of the IChatRoom interface.

The IParticipant interface defines a chat participant. A participant has a name, as indicated by the Name property. The Receive() method receives a chat message from the ChatRoom. The Send() method sends a chat message to another participant through the ChatRoom. A chat message is represented by the ChatMessage class (not shown in the diagram). The Participant class represents a concrete implementation of IParticipant.

Notice that there is just one implementation of IParticipant in this example. However, you can have different implementations. For example, you may create IDesktopParticipant and IMobileParticipant that implement IParticipant. These participants form the colleagues in the system.

The web-based chat interface used by this application is shown in Figure 8-3.

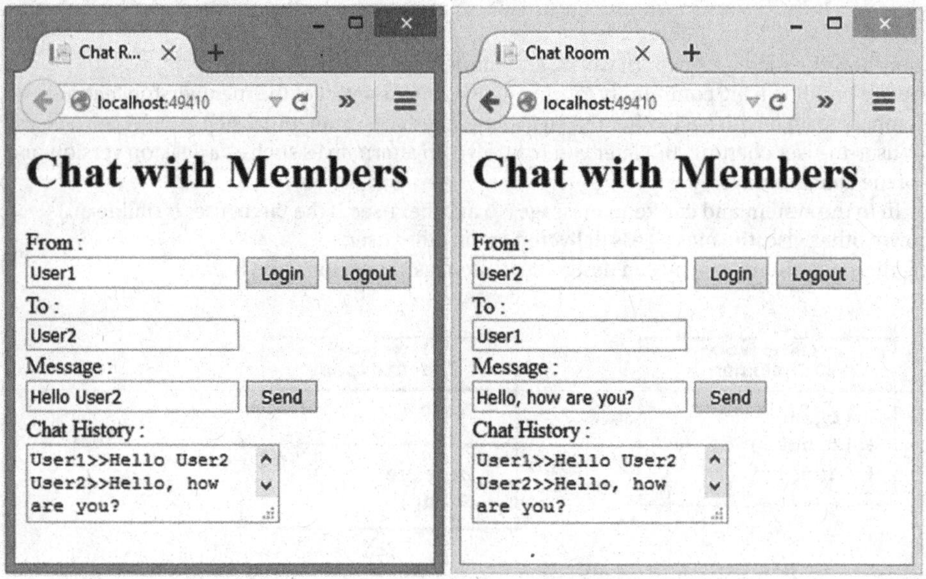

Figure 8-3. *A chat session between User1 and User2 in progress*

As you can see, the figure shows a sample chat session between User1 and User2. Of course, this example won't implement the membership system and full-blown chat client. But this interface is sufficient to illustrate the mediator pattern.

The interface consists of a textbox where a username can be entered. The Login and Logout buttons control the entry and exit of a user into the chat room.

There are textboxes for specifying the target user and a message. Upon specifying these details and clicking on the Send button, the message is sent to User2 through the ChatRoom mediator. The messages are stored in a database table for generating a chat history and accessing them later if required.

A text area displays a chat history of the current session. This text area is filled using jQuery code that polls the database periodically.

To develop this application, begin by creating a new ASP.NET web application project named Mediator using Visual Studio and configure it to use MVC and Entity Framework (see Chapter 1 for more details). Also store the database connection string of MediatorDb–the database used by the application–in the appsettings.json file.

Then add the AppSettings class to the Core folder. The AppSettings class needs to have the ConnectionString property that is assigned a value from the Startup class. Since this has been done many times in earlier examples, we won't go into those details here.

Then add a ChatMessage class to the Core folder. This class represents a single chat message and is shown in Listing 8-1.

Listing 8-1. ChatMessage Class Represents a Chat Message

```
[Table("ChatMessages")]
public class ChatMessage
{
    [DatabaseGenerated(DatabaseGeneratedOption.Identity)]
    public int Id { get; set; }
    [Required]
```

```
    [StringLength(20)]
    public string From { get; set; }
    [Required]
    [StringLength(20)]
    public string To { get; set; }
    [Required]
    public string Message { get; set; }
    [Required]
    public DateTime SentOn { get; set; }
}
```

The ChatMessage class contains five properties, namely Id, From, To, Message, and SentOn. The From and To properties indicate the usernames of the sender and the receiver of a message. The Message property holds the actual message text. The SentOn property indicates a date-time stamp of the message.

The [Table] attribute maps the ChatMessage class to the ChatMessages table. Although this example doesn't rely on data annotations such as [Required] and [StringLength] for data validation, they are useful while creating the ChatMessages table using entity framework migrations.

Now add an AppDbContext class to the Core folder and write the code shown in Listing 8-2 in it.

Listing 8-2. AppDbContext Class with ChatMessages DbSet

```
public class AppDbContext:DbContext
{
    public DbSet<ChatMessage> ChatMessages { get; set; }

    protected override void OnConfiguring(DbContextOptionsBuilder optionsBuilder)
    {
        optionsBuilder.UseSqlServer(AppSettings.ConnectionString);
    }
}
```

The AppDbContext class is a custom DbContext that has a single DbSet—ChatMessages.

Next, add an IParticipant interface to the Core folder (Listing 8-3).

Listing 8-3. IParticipant Folder Mediator Class

```
public interface IParticipant
{
    string Name { get; set; }
    void Send(string to, string message);
    void Receive(string from, string message);
    List<ChatMessage> GetChatHistory();
}
```

The IParticipant interface consists of one property and three methods. The Name property indicates the name of a user. The Send() method accepts a target username and a message as its parameters. The Receive() method receives chat messages intended for a participant. The GetChatHistory() method returns a generic list of ChatMessage objects. These messages indicate the chat history for that participant. The GetChatHistory() method is needed because the client code needs to display the chat history. It doesn't play any role in the mediator pattern as such. That's why it is not shown in the UML diagram.

Then add an IChatRoom interface to the Core folder and write the code shown in Listing 8-4 in it.

Listing 8-4. IChatRoom interface

```
public interface IChatRoom
{
    void Login(IParticipant participant);
    void Logout(IParticipant participant);
    void Send(string from, string to, string message);
}
```

The IChatRoom interface consists of three methods–Login(), Logout(), and Send(). The Login() and Logout() methods accept an IParticipant object and do the respective tasks for that participant. The Send() method accepts a sender, receiver, and message.

Now add the Participant class to the Core folder. The Participant class is the concrete implementation of IParticipant and is shown in Listing 8-5.

Listing 8-5. Participant Class Implementing IParticipant

```
public class Participant : IParticipant
{
    private IChatRoom chatroom;

    public string Name { get; set; }

    public Participant(string name, IChatRoom chatroom)
    {
        this.Name = name;
        this.chatroom = chatroom;
    }

    public void Send(string to, string message)
    {
        chatroom.Send(this.Name, to, message);
    }

    public void Receive(string from, string message)
    {
        ChatMessage msg = new ChatMessage();
        msg.From = from;
        msg.To = this.Name;
        msg.Message = message;
        msg.SentOn = DateTime.Now;
        using (AppDbContext db = new AppDbContext())
        {
            db.ChatMessages.Add(msg);
            db.SaveChanges();
        }
    }
}
```

```
public List<ChatMessage> GetChatHistory()
{
    using (AppDbContext db = new AppDbContext())
    {
        var query = from m in db.ChatMessages
                    where m.To == Name || m.From == Name
                    orderby m.SentOn ascending
                    select m;
        return query.ToList();
    }
}
}
```

The Participant class begins by declaring a local variable of type IChatRoom and a public Name property. This variable points to an object of the ChatRoom class. This variable is needed for sending a message to a target recipient. The IChatRoom variable and the Name property are assigned in the constructor of the class.

The Send() implementation calls the Send() method of the IChatRoom object and passes the Name, recipient, and message to it. The ChatRoom class is discussed shortly, but for now it is suffice to know that the Send() method of ChatRoom stores the message in the ChatMessages table.

The Receive() method is supposed to receive messages for the participant under consideration. These messages are received and then stored in the ChatMessages table. The Receive() method creates a new ChatMessage and sets its properties, such as From, To, Message, and SentOn. The ChatMessage is then added to the ChatMessages DbSet and saved to the database using the SaveChanges() method.

The GetChatHistory() method fetches all the ChatMessages records where recipient (To) or sender (From) is the same as the participant's Name property. These messages indicate the messages that were sent or received by the participant. The messages are then returned to the caller. In this example some jQuery code will call the GetChatHistory() method.

Next, add a ChatRoom class to the Core folder. This class consists of methods Login(), Logout(), Send(), and GetParticipant(). Listing 8-6 shows the skeleton of these methods.

Listing 8-6. Skeleton of the ChatRoom Mediator Class

```
public class ChatRoom : IChatRoom
{
    private static Dictionary<string, IParticipant> participants = new Dictionary<string,
IParticipant>();

    public void Login(IParticipant participant)
    {
    }

    public void Logout(IParticipant participant)
    {
    }

    public IParticipant GetParticipant(string name)
    {
    }

    public void Send(string from, string to, string message)
    {
    }
}
```

The ChatRoom class is the mediator class and implements the IChatRoom interface. It contains a private Dictionary object that holds the participants ready to participate in a chat. Note that this dictionary is static so that it can be accessed across multiple request-response cycles.

The Login() and Logout() methods keep track of users who are logged in to the chat room. These methods are shown in Listing 8-7.

Listing 8-7. Login() and Logout() Methods Keep Track of Users

```
public void Login(IParticipant participant)
{
    if (!participants.ContainsKey(participant.Name))
    {
        participants.Add(participant.Name, participant);
    }
}

public void Logout(IParticipant participant)
{
    if (participants.ContainsKey(participant.Name))
    {
        participants.Remove(participant.Name);
    }
}
```

The Login() method receives an IParticipant object–a participant wishing to join the chat room. Inside, the code checks whether the participant Name is already registered in the participants dictionary. If not, the participant is added to the dictionary indicating the logging-in operation. The participant's Name serves as the key and the IParticipant object serves as the value.

The Logout() method checks whether the participants dictionary contains any entry matching the supplied participant's Name. If yes, the participant is removed from the dictionary, indicating a logging-out operation.

Once logged in, participants can send messages. The Send() method handles the task of sending the messages, as shown in Listing 8-8.

Listing 8-8. Send() Method Stores Messages in Table

```
public void Send(string from, string to, string message)
{
    IParticipant target = participants[to];
    if (target != null)
    {

        target.Receive(from, message);
    }
    else
    {
        throw new Exception("Invalid chat participant!");
    }
}
}
```

The Send() method grabs the intended recipient of the message from the participants dictionary based on the to parameter. If the receiver user is found in the dictionary it indicates that the user is logged in and the message can be sent to him or her. Otherwise, an exception is thrown.

If a user is logged in, the target participant's Receive() method is invoked by passing the from and message values to it.

The ChatRoom class also needs an additional method (not defined in the IChatRoom interface) that grabs a specific participant and returns it to the caller. This method–GetParticipant()–is shown in Listing 8-9.

Listing 8-9. GetParticipant() Method Returns IParticipant Object

```
public IParticipant GetParticipant(string name)
{
    if (participants.ContainsKey(name))
    {
        return participants[name];
    }
    else
    {
        return null;
    }
}
```

The GetParticipant() method accepts a string username and attempts to find that user in the participants dictionary. If the username is found, the corresponding IParticipant object is returned to the caller; otherwise, the method returns null.

Now let's move our attention to the client code–HomeController. Add HomeController to the Controllers folder. In addition to the default Index() method, you need four more actions, namely Login(), Logout(), Send(), and GetHistory(). As you might have guessed, most of these actions are invoked by clicking the corresponding buttons. These methods in turn call methods on the ChatRoom and Participant classes. The following text discusses these methods.

Recollect that the application's user interface has Login and Logout buttons. These operations are performed through jQuery Ajax. The jQuery code (you will write it shortly) invokes the Login() and Logout() actions of the controller. These actions are shown in Listing 8-10.

Listing 8-10. Login() and Logout() Action Methods

```
[HttpPost]
public void Login([FromBody]ChatUser usr)
{
    ChatRoom room = new ChatRoom();
    IParticipant participant = new Participant(usr.Name, room);
    room.Login(participant);
}

[HttpPost]
public void Logout([FromBody]ChatUser usr)
{
    ChatRoom room = new ChatRoom();
    IParticipant participant = new Participant(usr.Name, room);
    room.Logout(participant);
}
```

Both of these method - Login() and Logout() - accept a parameter of type ChatUser. The ChatUser is simple view model class that simply holds the user's name and looks like this:

```
public class ChatUser
{
    public string Name { get; set; }
}
```

The Login() action creates an instance of the ChatRoom class and also an IParticipant object for the specified ChatUser. The Login() method of the ChatRoom is then invoked. This will add the participant to the logged-in users dictionary as discussed earlier.

The Logout() action is similar to Login(), but it calls the Logout() method on the ChatRoom object.

The Send() action that sends a chat message is shown in Listing 8-11.

Listing 8-11. Send( ) Action Sends a Chat Message

```
[HttpPost]
public IActionResult Send([FromBody]ChatMessage msg)
{
    ChatRoom room = new ChatRoom();
    IParticipant sender = room.GetParticipant(msg.From);
    IParticipant receiver = room.GetParticipant(msg.To);
    if (receiver != null)
    {
        sender.Send(msg.To, msg.Message);
        return Json(true);
    }
    else
    {
        return Json(false);
    }
}
```

The Send() action receives a ChatMessage object from a jQuery Ajax call. Inside, it creates an object of ChatRoom and also sender and receiver Participant objects. Notice the use of the GetParticipant() method in retrieving a reference to a logged-in participant. The code checks whether a participant is currently logged in. If yes, the ChatMessage is sent to the user by calling the Send() method on the sender participant object, and true is returned to the caller (in JSON format). Otherwise, false is returned to the caller (in JSON format).

Finally, add the GetHistory() action that retrieves the chat history for a participant. This method is shown in Listing 8-12.

Listing 8-12. GetHistory() Method Retrieves Chat History

```
[HttpPost]
public IActionResult GetHistory([FromBody]ChatUser usr)
{
    ChatRoom room = new ChatRoom();
    IParticipant participant = room.GetParticipant(usr.Name);
    if (participant != null)
```

```
    {
        return Json(participant.GetChatHistory());
    }
    else
    {
        return Json("");
    }
}
```

The GetHistory() action receives a ChatUser object as its parameter. Inside, it creates a ChatRoom object and gets a reference to the Participant object. This is done using the GetParticipant() method. If GetParticipant() returns a participant, it indicates that the participant is logged in and his chat history can be obtained. The GetChatHistory() method of the Participant object returns a list of ChatMessage objects. These messages are converted into their JSON equivalents using the Json() method and are returned to the calling jQuery code.

This completes the HomeController. Now, the final part that needs to be added is the Index view. Add the Index view to the Views/Home controller and place the markup shown in Listing 8-13 in it.

Listing 8-13. Markup of Index View

```
...
...
<body>
    <h1>Chat with Members</h1>
    <form>
        <div>From :</div>
        <input type="text" id="from" />
        <input type="button" id="login" value="Login" />
        <input type="button" id="logout" value="Logout" />
        <div>To :</div>
        <input type="text" id="to" />
        <div>Message :</div>
        <input type="text" id="message" />
        <input type="button" id="send" value="Send" />
        <div>Chat History :</div>
        <textarea id="history"></textarea>
    </form>
</body>
...
...
```

The Index view consists of three textboxes, three buttons, and a text area. The textboxes accept a sender's name, a recipient's name, and a message, respectively. The buttons initiate logging in, logging out, and send operations, respectively.

The click events of the buttons are handled by jQuery code. So, make sure to add a <script> reference to the jQuery library in the head section of the view. You may place the jQuery library file inside the Scripts folder under wwwroot and then drag and drop it in the <head> section of the view to generate the required <script> element.

Then add a new <script> block in the head section. This block will contain jQuery code. Just to give you an idea, the skeleton of the code that goes inside the script block is shown in Listing 8-14.

Listing 8-14. Skeleton of jQuery Code

```
<script src="~/scripts/jquery.min.js"></script>

<script type="text/javascript">

    $(document).ready(function () {
        var handle;

        $("#login").click(function () {
        });

        $("#logout").click(function () {
        });

        $("#send").click(function () {
    });

</script>
```

As you can see, the script block consists of a ready() callback. The callback in turn wires click event handlers of the Login, Logout, and Send buttons. The jQuery code periodically retrieves the chat history from the server. This is done using the setTimeout() JavaScript function. The handle variable declared at the top holds the handle returned by the setTimeout() call. The following text will discuss these methods in more detail.

■ **Note**   The following explanation assumes that you are familiar with jQuery library. If you are not familiar with jQuery and Ajax, consider reading some basics before continuing further. You may visit jQuery's official documentation at http://api.jquery.com

---

The Login button's click-event handler calls the Login() action of the HomeController and is shown in Listing 8-15.

Listing 8-15. Handling Click Event of Login Button

```
$("#login").click(function () {
    var options = {};
    options.url = "/home/login";
    options.type = "POST";
    options.data = JSON.stringify({ Name : $("#from").val() });
    options.contentType = "application/json";
    options.success = function () {
        alert("Logged in!");
        handle = setTimeout(GetHistory, 3000);
    };
    options.error = function () {
        alert("Error!");
    };
    $.ajax(options);
});
```

The code creates an options object–a JavaScript object that stores settings for an Ajax call.

The url property is set to the login action. The type property is set to POST, indicating that a POST Ajax request will be made to the server. The data property is set to an object with the Name property. Note that the structure of this JavaScript object must match with the structure of the ChatUser view model class. The JSON.stringify() method converts the JavaScript object into its JSON representation. The contentType property is set to application/json, indicating that JSON data is being sent along with the request.

The success callback is invoked upon the successful login attempt. The success callback displays an alert and also calls the setTimeout() method. The setTimeout() method calls the GetHistory() function after three seconds. The GetHistory() function is a custom JavaScript function that does the job of retrieving the chat history. This function will be discussed shortly.

The error callback simply displays an alert with an error message. Finally, the jQuery $.ajax() method is called by passing the options object to it as a parameter. The $.ajax() method makes an Ajax call to the Login() action of the controller.

The GetHistory() function just mentioned is shown in Listing 8-16.

Listing 8-16. GetHistory() Function Loads the History Text Area

```
function GetHistory() {
    var options = {};
    options.url = "home/gethistory";
    options.type = "POST";
    options.data = JSON.stringify({ Name: $("#from").val() });
    options.dataType = "json";
    options.contentType = "application/json";
    options.success = function (data) {
        var history = "";
        for (var i = 0; i < data.length; i++)
        {
            history += data[i].From + ">>" + data[i].Message + "\r\n";
        }
        $("#history").val(history);
        setTimeout(GetHistory, 3000);
    };
    $.ajax(options)
}
```

The code written inside the GetHistory() function is quite similar to what you wrote in the login click handler. There are only a few differences:

- The url property is pointing to the GetHistory() action of the HomeController.

- Since the GetHistory() function returns data in JSON format, the dataType property of the options is set to json.

- The success function receives an array of ChatMessage objects from the server. The code iterates through this array and stores all the messages in a variable. The history text area is then assigned this value using the val() method.

- The success function calls setTimeout() again so that polling can continue.

The click-event handler of the Logout button is quite similar to that of the Login button and is shown in Listing 8-17.

Listing 8-17. Handling Click Event of Logout Button

```
$("#logout").click(function () {
    var options = {};
    options.url = "/home/logout";
    options.type = "POST";
    options.data = JSON.stringify({ Name: $("#from").val() });
    options.contentType = "application/json";
    options.success = function () {
        alert("Logged out!");
        clearTimeout(handle);
    };
    options.error = function () {
        alert("Error!");
    };
    $.ajax(options);
});
```

This code is quite similar to what you wrote earlier except for two lines. This time the url property is set to call the Logout() action of the controller, and the success function calls the clearTimeout() function by passing the handle value to it. This way the polling stops when the user logs out of the chat room.

Finally, you need to complete the application by writing the click-event handler of the Send button. This event handler is shown in Listing 8-18.

Listing 8-18. Handling Click Event of the Send Button

```
$("#send").click(function () {
    var msg = {};
    msg.From = $("#from").val();
    msg.To = $("#to").val();
    msg.Message = $("#message").val();

    var options = {};
    options.url = "/home/send";
    options.type = "POST";
    options.data = JSON.stringify(msg);
    options.contentType = "application/json";
    options.success = function (flag) {
        if (flag) {
            alert("Message sent!");
        } else {
            alert(msg.To + " is offline!");
        }
    };
    options.error = function () {
        alert("Error!");
    };
    $.ajax(options);
    });
});
```

This code too is similar to what you wrote earlier. However, it differs in the following ways:

- The url property points to the Send() method of the HomeController.

- The Send() method of the controller expects a ChatMessage object. This object is formed at the beginning (msg object variable) and is then assigned to the data property.

- The success callback receives a Boolean value—true if the operation is successful, false otherwise—which is then checked. A success or error message is displayed to the user accordingly.

That's it! This completes the application. Since there are a lot of pieces that make up this example, you may want to consider grabbing the complete source code from the code download of this book.

Before you run the application, you will need to create the MediatorDb database with the ChatMessages table (see Chapter 1 for more details). Once the database is created, run the application in two browser tabs or windows and test it as outlined here:

- Switch to the first browser window or tab.

- Enter username as User1 in the From textbox and click on the Login button. If all goes well you will get a success alert.

- Switch to the second window or tab.

- Enter username as User2 in the From textbox and click on the Login button. If all goes well you will get a success alert.

- Switch to the first window or tab and enter User2 in the To textbox.

- Also enter some message in the Message textbox and click on the Send button.

- Switch to the second window or tab and confirm whether the message you just sent appears in the history textbox.

- Repeat the message-sending steps in the second window or tab by specifying User1 in the To textbox.

- Log out from any one window and try sending a message from the other window.

Stop the application and also have a look at the ChatMessages table of the MediatorDb database.

Memento

It is quite common for classes to have state that is private. Obviously, such state information is not accessible to the external world. This fits well with encapsulation—an important feature of object-oriented systems. However, at times this private state may need to cross the boundary of the class.

Consider a hypothetical e-mail application that allows users to create and send e-mail messages. Such systems usually provide a "save as draft" option that allows the user to save the message without sending to the intended recipient. The message can be loaded back later, completed, and then sent to the recipient.

In this case, the e-mail object's internal state, such as sender, receiver, and message, needs to be saved to some external storage medium. Later the e-mail object is to be reconstructed from this saved state.

If your application calls for such an externalization of an object's internal state, the memento pattern can be used. **The memento pattern allows you to save an object's state external to the object and also allows you to restore the object's state when needed.** The memento pattern does this saving and restoring without breaking any of the encapsulation rules set while designing the class. You may think of the memento pattern as a way to create and restore snapshots of one or more objects in the system.

Design and Explanation

The UML diagram in Figure 8-4 illustrates the memento pattern.

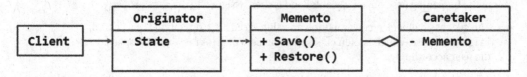

Figure 8-4. *UML diagram illustrating the memento pattern*

As shown in the figure, the `Originator` is a class whose internal state is to be saved and restored.

The `Memento` class provides two methods—`Save()` and `Restore()`—that perform the tasks of saving and restoring the `Originator` object's state. The medium where the object's state is saved is dependent on the application. For example, an application may save the state to a physical disk file or database table, or even to an in-memory store.

The `Caretaker` class holds a reference to the `Memento` object as indicated by the aggregation symbol. The `Caretaker` may even maintain a list of `Memento` objects rather than a single object. The `Memento` objects can be used to restore the object's state to that particular snapshot.

The `Client` class simply creates the `Originator` and may initiate save and restore operations on the `Memento`.

Example

Now that you know how the memento pattern works, let's see a realistic example where it can be used.

Suppose you are building a website that provides certain services to its users. Getting frequent feedback from the users is important so as to improve the services, and hence the website needs to have a survey module.

The survey module presents certain survey questions to the user and attempts to grab the responses to these questions. Upon beginning the survey, the user might want to discontinue and then resume the survey at some later time. Thus, allowing a user to save the already entered responses and restoring them once the user resumes is critical for the overall functionality of the survey module.

When a user decides to save the survey responses, they are stored in a separate, user-specific file. This is done to avoid polluting the main database tables from stray or incomplete surveys.

Considering these requirements, you can design the system shown in Figure 8-5.

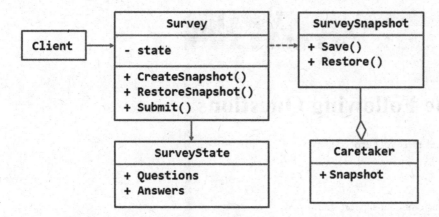

Figure 8-5. *Survey module saves and restores survey snapshots to a file*

As you can see, the Survey object is the class whose state is to be saved and restored. Its state is held in a private member–state. The state member is of type SurveyState. The SurveyState is basically a list of survey questions and their answers as entered by the user.

The Survey class has a CreateSnapshot() method that saves the current state of a Survey object. This is done by calling the Save() method of the SurveySnapshot class. Along the same lines, the RestoreSnapshot() method restores a previously saved snapshot by calling the Restore() method of the SurveySnapshot class. Thus, the SurveySnapshot class acts as the Memento object.

The Caretaker class simply holds a reference to the Snapshot object (if any). The client code can later access this snapshot for restoring the survey state.

The Submit() method of the Survey class persists all the user responses to a database table.

Figure 8-6 shows the main page of the application that you will build as a part of this example.

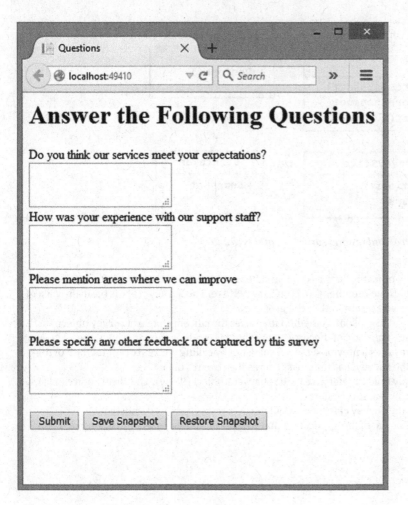

Figure 8-6. *Main page of the survey module*

The application displays a list of questions to the user. The user can type the answers to the questions in the respective text area fields. There are three buttons at the bottom–Submit, Save Snapshot, and Restore Snapshot.

Clicking on the Submit button saves the survey responses into the Answers table. Clicking on the Save Snapshot button creates a snapshot of the answers entered by the user and saves them into a disk file. Clicking on the Restore Snapshot button restores the answers from the disk file into the survey object and also into the text area fields.

For the sake of simplicity we won't develop a user-authentication system. The snapshot is created in a file with a fixed name. In a more realistic application, you would create files for each user, and depending on the current authenticated user you would load the corresponding file.

To develop this application, begin by creating a new ASP.NET web application project using Visual Studio and configure it to use MVC and Entity Framework (see Chapter 1 for more details). Also store the database connection string of MementoDb–the database used by the application–in the appsettings.json file.

Then add the AppSettings class to the Core folder and add the two properties to it as shown in Listing 8-19.

Listing 8-19. AppSettings Class Stores Snapshot Filename

```
public class AppSettings
{
    public static string StoragePath { get; set; }
    public static string ConnectionString { get; set; }
}
```

The StoragePath property holds a filename of the snapshot file. This property, along with the ConnectionString property, is set in the Startup class, as shown in Listing 8-20.

Listing 8-20. Setting the StoragePath Property

```
public Startup(IHostingEnvironment env, IApplicationEnvironment app)
{
    ...
    ...
    AppSettings.ConnectionString = config.Get<string>("Data:DefaultConnection:ConnectionString");
    AppSettings.StoragePath = env.MapPath("Snapshots/snapshot.dat");
}
```

For this example, the StoragePath property is set to wwwroot/Snapshots/Snapshot.dat. Make sure to create the Snapshot folder under wwwroot.

Then add a SurveyState class into the Core folder (Listing 8-21).

Listing 8-21. SurveyState Class Stores Wuestions and Answers

```
[Serializable]
public class SurveyState
{
    public List<int> Questions { get; set; }
    public List<string> Answers { get; set; }
}
```

The SurveyState class consists of two properties–Questions and Answers. The Questions property stores a List of question IDs from the database. The Answers property stores a List of answers entered by the user for each question ID in the Questions property.

Notice that the SurveyState class is marked with the [Serializable] attribute. This is required, because the Memento object serializes the SurveyState objects to disk files using .NET framework's binary formatter.

Next, add the SurveySnapshot class to the Core folder and write the code from Listing 8-22 in it.

Listing 8-22. SurveySnapshot Saves and Restores the Survey State

```
public class SurveySnapshot
{
    private string fileName;

    public SurveySnapshot(string filename)
    {
        this.fileName = filename;
    }
```

```
    public void Save(SurveyState state)
    {
        FileStream stream = new FileStream(fileName, FileMode.Create);
        BinaryFormatter formatter = new BinaryFormatter();
        formatter.Serialize(stream, state);
        stream.Close();
    }

    public SurveyState Restore()
    {
        FileStream stream = new FileStream(fileName, FileMode.Open);
        BinaryFormatter formatter = new BinaryFormatter();
        object obj = formatter.Deserialize(stream);
        stream.Close();
        return (SurveyState)obj;
    }
}
```

The SurveySnapshot class begins by declaring a private string variable that holds the snapshot filename. Since it is common to vary the snapshot filenames based on some logic, the code doesn't use AppSettings class directly. Instead, it allows the filename to be passed through the constructor.

The Save() method accepts a SurveyState object as its parameter. Inside, it creates a FileStream object (System.IO namespace) by specifying the filename captured earlier. A BinaryFormatter (System.Runtime.Serialization.Formatters.Binary namespace) is then created. The Serialize() method of the BinaryFormatter class accepts a Stream object to which the data is to be saved as well as the object that is to be saved. The stream is then closed (also be sure to remove the entry for the .NET core from the frameworks section of Project.json).

The Restore() method does the job of reading the previously stored snapshot file. It does so by opening a FileStream on the filename. This time BinaryFormatter's Deserialize() method is used to deserialize the object state from the file into an object. The Deserialize() method returns an object, and hence the code typecasts it to SurveyState and then returns to the caller.

Now add a Survey class to the Core folder and write the code shown in Listing 8-23 in it.

Listing 8-23. Survey Class Is the Class Whose State Is to Be Saved

```
public class Survey
{
    private SurveyState state;

    public Survey(SurveyState state)
    {
        this.state = state;
    }

    public SurveySnapshot CreateSnapshot()
    {
        SurveySnapshot snapshot = new SurveySnapshot(AppSettings.StoragePath);
        snapshot.Save(this.state);
        return snapshot;
    }
}
```

```
public void RestoreSnapshot(SurveySnapshot snapshot)
{
    this.state = snapshot.Restore();
}

public List<string> GetAnswers()
{
    return this.state.Answers;
}

public void Submit()
{
    using (AppDbContext db = new AppDbContext())
    {
        for (int i = 0; i < state.Questions.Count; i++)
        {
            Answer ans = new Answer();
            ans.QuestionId = state.Questions[i];
            ans.AnswerText = state.Answers[i];
            ans.SubmittedOn = DateTime.Now;
            db.Answers.Add(ans);
        }
        db.SaveChanges();
    }
}
}
```

The Survey class maintains its state in a private variable of type SurveyState. This state is assigned through the constructor of the class.

The CreateSnapshot() method creates a memento SurveySnapshot object by passing the StoragePath to it. The Save() method of the Memento object is then called to save the private state of the Survey to a file. The SurveySnapshot object is returned to the caller so that the restore operation can be done at some later stage.

The RestoreSnapshot() method accepts an existing SurveySnapshot object and invokes its Restore() method. The state obtained from the Restore() method is assigned to the private state variable. This way the Survey object's state is loaded with the previously persisted state.

The GetAnswers() method is needed by the controller code. It simply returns the answers to the caller. These answers are needed for displaying them on the view. GetAnswers() doesn't participate in the functioning of the memento in any way.

The Submit() method saves all the answers by the user to the Answers table of the database. The code iterates through the Questions list of the SurveyState object. Each iteration creates a new Answer object and adds it to the Answers DbSet. The SaveChanges() method of the AppDbContext saves the data to the Answers table.

The application needs AppDbContext, Answer, and Question classes in order to save and retrieve data into a database table. The Question class is shown in Listing 8-24.

Listing 8-24. Question Class Represents a Survey Question

```
[Table("Questions")]
public class Question
{
    [DatabaseGenerated(DatabaseGeneratedOption.Identity)]
    public int QuestionId { get; set; }

    [Required]
    [StringLength(100)]
    public string QuestionText { get; set; }
}
```

The Question class represents a survey question and maps to the Questions table. It consists of two properties–QuestionId and QuestionText. The QuestionId property is an integer, and QuestionText holds the actual question.

The Answer class represents an answer to a survey question and is shown in Listing 8-25.

Listing 8-25. Answer Class Represents a Survey Answer

```
[Table("Answers")]
public class Answer
{
    [DatabaseGenerated(DatabaseGeneratedOption.Identity)]
    public int AnswerId { get; set; }

    [Required]
    public int QuestionId { get; set; }

    [Required]
    [StringLength(100)]
    public string AnswerText { get; set; }

    [Required]
    public DateTime SubmittedOn { get; set; }
}
```

The Answer class maps to the Answers table and contains four properties–AnswerId, QuestionId, AnswerText, and SubmittedOn. These properties are quite straightforward.

The AppDbContext class that represents entity framework DbContext is shown in Listing 8-26.

Listing 8-26. AppDbContext Class with Questions and Answers DbSets

```
public class AppDbContext:DbContext
{
    public DbSet<Question> Questions{ get; set; }
    public DbSet<Answer> Answers { get; set; }

    protected override void OnConfiguring(DbContextOptionsBuilder optionsBuilder)
    {
        optionsBuilder.UseSqlServer(AppSettings.ConnectionString);
    }
}
```

The AppDbContext class defines two DbSets–Questions and Answers.

Now add the Caretaker class to the Core folder and write the code shown in Listing 8-27 in it.

Listing 8-27. Caretaker Class Holds Memento Object

```
public class Caretaker
{
    public static SurveySnapshot Snapshot { get; set; }
}
```

The Caretaker class consists of a single property–Snapshot–that holds a SurveySnapshot object. Notice that the Snapshot property is static so that it can be accessed across multiple requests. Of course, you may think of saving the snapshots in the user's session, or devise some alternative in order to support multiuser scenarios. For this example, it is sufficient to store the snapshots in the static Snapshot property.

So far you have developed classes specific to the implementation of the memento pattern. Now, let's consume these classes in a controller.

Add HomeController to the Controller folder. The Index() action of the controller should fetch all the survey questions from the Questions table and send them to the Index view as its model. The Index() action is shown in Listing 8-28.

Listing 8-28. Index() Action Fetches Survey Questions

```
public IActionResult Index()
{
    using (AppDbContext db = new AppDbContext())
    {
        return View(db.Questions.ToList());
    }
}
```

The code inside the Index() is quite straightforward. It simply fetches all the questions from the Questions table and sends a List of Question objects to the Index view.

You need to write another action–ProcessForm()–that is invoked when any of the three buttons–Submit, Save Snapshot, and Restore Snapshot–are called. The ProcessForm() action is shown in Listing 8-29.

Listing 8-29. ProcessForm() Action Deals with the Survey Responses

```
[HttpPost]
public IActionResult ProcessForm(List<int> question,List<string> answer,string submit,string
save,string restore)
{
    SurveyState state = new SurveyState();
    state.Questions = question;
    state.Answers = answer;
    Survey survey = new Survey(state);

    if (submit != null)
    {
        Caretaker.Snapshot = null;
        survey.Submit();
        ViewBag.Message = "Survey data submitted!";
    }
```

```
    if (save != null)
    {
        Caretaker.Snapshot = survey.CreateSnapshot();
        ViewBag.Message = "Snapshot created!";
    }

    if (restore!=null)
    {
        survey.RestoreSnapshot(Caretaker.Snapshot);
        ViewBag.Message = "Survey restored!";
    }

    ViewBag.Answers = survey.GetAnswers();

    using (AppDbContext db = new AppDbContext())
    {
        List<Question> model = db.Questions.ToList();
        return View("Index", model);
    }
}
```

The ProcessForm() method has five parameters. The Questions and Answers are lists that represent the question IDs and answers entered by the user. The next three parameters correspond to the three buttons. They are used by the code to detect which of the three buttons was clicked.

Inside, the code creates a SurveyState object and sets its Questions and Answers properties. The SurveyState object is then passed to the constructor of the Survey class.

The next three if statements decide which of the three buttons was clicked. For example, if the Save Snapshot button is clicked, the Save parameter won't be null. It will contain the value of the button. The same is applicable to the other buttons.

If the Submit button is clicked, the Submit() method of the Survey object is called and survey data is stored in the database. Since the survey is now saved to the database, the Caretaker is also set to null, erasing any previously created snapshot.

If the Save Snapshot button is clicked, a snapshot of the current survey state is created by calling the CreateSnapshot() method on the Survey object. The SurveySnapshot object thus returned is stored by the Caretaker object.

If the Restore Snapshot button is clicked, a previously stored snapshot is loaded into the Survey object. This is done by calling the RestoreSnapshot() method on the Survey object.

All three if statements also set a message in the ViewBag. This message is displayed on the view.

The Index view needs a list of questions and the answers (if any). The questions can be directly obtained from the Questions table. The answers are passed through the Answers ViewBag property. This is done by calling the GetAnswers() method of the Survey object and assigning the returned List to the Answers property.

Finally, add the Index view to the Views/Home folder. Listing 8-30 shows the markup of the Index view.

Listing 8-30. Markup of Index View

```
@model List<Memento.Core.Question>

...
<body>
    <h1>Answer the Following Questions</h1>
    <form asp-action="ProcessForm" asp-controller="Home" method="post">
        @for(int i=0;i<Model.Count;i++)
```

```
    {
        <input type="hidden" name="question[@i]" value="@Model[i].QuestionId" />
        <div>@Model[i].QuestionText</div>
        <textarea name="answer[@i]">
        @if(ViewBag.Answers!=null)
        {
            @ViewBag.Answers[i]
        }
        </textarea>
    }
    <br /><br />
    <input type="submit" name="submit" value="Submit" />
    <input type="submit" name="save" value="Save Snapshot" />
    <input type="submit" name="restore" value="Restore Snapshot" />
</form>
<h4>@ViewBag.Message</h4>
...
```

A List of Question objects acts as the model for the Index view. A form tag helper is used to render a form that submits to the ProcessForm() action (asp-action attribute) of the HomeController (asp-controller attribute).

Inside, the form displays a series of questions in <div> elements by iterating through the Model. A hidden field also stores the QuestionId for each question. Recollect that the ProcessForm() action requires the question parameter. If hidden input fields are not used, that parameter won't be populated with the QuestionId values. A text area displays the answer if it was saved previously.

The three buttons–Save, Save Snapshot, and Restore Snapshot–invoke the corresponding operations. Notice that the name attribute of these buttons matches the corresponding parameters of the ProcessForm() action.

The Message assigned from the if statements is also outputted at the bottom of the view.

This completes the application. Before you test it, you will need to create the MementoDb database with Questions and Answers tables (see Chapter 1 for more details). You will also need to enter a few sample questions in the Questions table. Once the database is ready, run the application and test the behavior of the Save Snapshot and Restore Snapshot buttons.

Observer

Sometimes you need to notify many objects in the system about something interesting happening in the application. Think of it as a radio broadcasting, where a radio station broadcasts signals and people interested in listening tune in their radio sets to the desired frequency.

Such a model of sending and receiving notifications is also called a publisher-subscriber model. One or more subscriber objects subscribe to receive notifications from the publisher. And the publisher sends out notifications to all the subscribed objects. Obviously this is an example of a one-to-many communication.

If your intention is to broadcast notifications as mentioned, the observer pattern can be put to use. **The observer pattern defines one-to-many dependency between objects so that when one object changes its state all the others are notified about the change.** Moreover, the other objects can be updated upon receiving the notification.

The discussion of the observer pattern might remind you of the delegate-based event handling of C#. For example, a Windows Forms control may raise events such as click or double-click and act as an event publisher. The one or more event handlers wired to an event represent the subscribers. The observer pattern can be implemented using delegates and events. However, for our illustration we won't go with that approach.

■ **Note**   Apparently the mediator and observer patterns sound similar in that both communicate between multiple objects. However, the mediator offers two-way communication while the observer offers one-way broadcasting.

Another example of observer is the FileSystemWatcher class available in the System.IO namespace. This class keeps an eye on filesystem operations such as file or folder creation. It has events such as Changed, Created, Deleted, and Renamed that can be handled by the interested parties. Once it detects the operations, it notifies all the event subscribers by raising the appropriate event.

Design and Explanation

The UML diagram in Figure 8-7 illustrates the observer pattern.

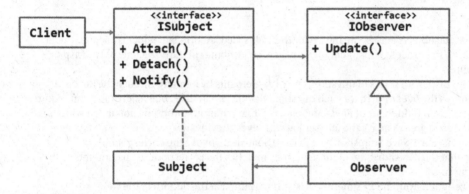

Figure 8-7.   *UML diagram illustrating the observer pattern*

As shown in the figure, the IObserver interface is the abstraction for the classes wanting to receive notifications. It consists of an Update() method. The Update() method is called automatically when the state changes, and it is responsible for performing post–state change operations. The operations could be anything, such as refreshing the user interface, saving something in the database, sending e-mails, and so on.

The Observer class is the concrete implementation of IObserver. There could be multiple Observer classes. As long as they implement IObserver, they can subscribe to receive the notifications.

The ISubject interface represents the abstraction for the object wanting to send the notifications. The concrete implementation of ISubject maintains a collection of IObserver objects–the observers interested in receiving the notifications. The Attach() and Detach() methods subscribe and unsubscribe the observers by adding or removing them from the Observers collection. The Notify() method sends out the notifications to the subscribers.

The Subject class is the concrete implementation of ISubject. Notice that there is an association between ISubject and IObserver just as there is between Observer and Subject.

The Client code does the job of instantiating the Subject object and one or more Observer objects.

Example

Now that you how the observer pattern works, let's illustrate with an example.

Suppose you are building a discussion forum for the developer community at large. To ensure quality and to avoid marketing SPAM, an administrator will monitor the forum posts as and when they are made.

As soon a new forum post arrives in the system you need to notify the administrator about the new post. Moreover, you also need to notify an activity tracker about the post. The activity tracker module is supposed to track the user activity over a period of time and allot users certain badges and prizes.

The notification feature required by the system can be implemented using the observer pattern. Figure 8-8 shows a possible design.

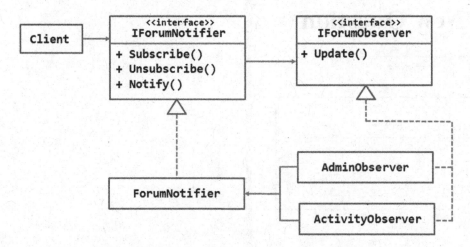

Figure 8-8. *Sending notifications when a new forum post is available*

The IForumObserver interface is the interface implemented by the observer classes–AdminObserver and ActivityObserver.

The AdminObserver class represents the administrator interested in getting notified when a new forum post is made. The Update() implementation of AdminObserver adds an entry to the Notification database table. The ActivityObserver class represents the activity tracker interested in tracking user activity. The Update() implementation of ActivityObserver adds an entry to the Activity database table. Of course, you can do any other application-specific operation in these implementations.

The IForumNotifier interface is implemented by the publishers of the notifications. The concrete implementation of IForumNotifier maintains a list of IForumObserver objects. The objects are added to this list using the Subscribe() method and are removed from the list using the Unsubscribe() method. The Notify() method sends a notification to all the subscribers when a new forum post is added to the system.

The ForumNotifier represents the concrete implementation of the IForumNotifier interface.

The Client–a controller in this example–sets up the ForumNotifier instance by wiring subscribers. Thus, AdminObserver and ActivityObserver objects depend on the ForumNotifier to receive the notifications.

The main page of the application you are going to build is shown in Figure 8-9.

Figure 8-9. *Posting a new question in the forum*

The page allows you to post a new forum question. It consists of three textboxes that accept user's name, question's title, and the descriptive question text. The Submit button adds the post to the ForumPosts database table.

There are two hyperlinks at the bottom of the page–"Show Notifications" and "Show Activity Log." Clicking on the "Show Notifications" link displays a list of all the notification received so far. Similarly, clicking on the "Show Activity Log" link shows the records from the ActivityLog table.

To develop this application, begin by creating a new ASP.NET web application project named Observer using Visual Studio and configure it to use MVC and Entity Framework (see Chapter 1 for more details). Also store the database connection string of ObserverDb–the database used by the application–in the appsettings.json file.

The application needs to store data in three tables–ForumPosts, Notifications, and Activity. So, the application needs the corresponding entities and the DbContext. Moreover, the AppSettings class with the ConnectionString property is also needed (AppSettings is not discussed here, since you already used it many of the earlier examples).

Add the ForumPost class to the Core folder and write the code shown in Listing 8-31 in it.

Listing 8-31. ForumPost Class Represents a Forum Post

```
[Table("ForumPosts")]
public class ForumPost
{
    [DatabaseGenerated(DatabaseGeneratedOption.Identity)]
    public int Id { get; set; }

    [Required]
    [StringLength(20)]
    public string UserName { get; set; }

    [Required]
    [StringLength(100)]
    public string Title { get; set; }

    [Required]
    public string Description { get; set; }

    [Required]
    public DateTime PostedOn { get; set; }

}
```

The ForumPost class is mapped to the ForumPosts table using the [Table] attribute. It contains five properties—Id, UserName, Title, Description, and PostedOn. This example won't implement the user authentication as such, but the UserName property stores the username of the user who added a forum post. The Title and Description properties represent the title and descriptive text of a forum post. The PostedOn property is the timestamp for the time at which the post was added.

Then add a Notification class to the Core folder and write the code from Listing 8-32 in it.

Listing 8-32. Notification Class Stores Notification Details

```
[Table("Notifications")]
public class Notification
{
    [DatabaseGenerated(DatabaseGeneratedOption.Identity)]
    public int Id { get; set; }

    [Required]
    [StringLength(100)]
    public string Description{ get; set; }

    [Required]
    public DateTime ReceivedOn { get; set; }
}
```

The Notification class represents a notification and maps to the Notifications table. It consists of three properties—Id, Description, and ReceivedOn. These properties are quite straightforward and represent the corresponding pieces of information about a notification.

Now add the Activity class to the Core folder. Listing 8-33 shows the ActivityLog class.

Listing 8-33. ActivityLog Class Tracks User Activities

```
[Table("ActivityLog")]
public class Activity
{
    [DatabaseGenerated(DatabaseGeneratedOption.Identity)]
    public int Id { get; set; }

    [Required]
    [StringLength(100)]
    public string Description{ get; set; }

    [Required]
    public DateTime TimeStamp { get; set; }
}
```

The Activity class maps to the ActivityLog table and contains three properties—Id, Description, and TimeStamp.

Next, add an AppDbContext class to the Core folder and define the DbSet properties as shown in Listing 8-34.

Listing 8-34. AppDbContext with Three DbSet Properties

```
public class AppDbContext:DbContext
{
    public DbSet<ForumPost> ForumPosts{ get; set; }
    public DbSet<Notification> Notifications { get; set; }
    public DbSet<Activity> ActivityLog { get; set; }

    protected override void OnConfiguring(DbContextOptionsBuilder optionsBuilder)
    {
        optionsBuilder.UseSqlServer(AppSettings.ConnectionString);
    }
}
```

The AppDbContext class defines three DbSet properties, namely ForumPosts, Notifications, and ActivityLog. They hold entities for the corresponding tables.

Next, add an IForumObserver interface to the Core folder (Listing 8-35).

Listing 8-35. IForumObserver Interface

```
public interface IForumObserver
{
    void Update(ForumPost post);
}
```

The IForumObserver interface contains the Update() method, which receives a ForumPost object as its parameter.

Then add AdminObserver and ActivityObserver classes to the Core folder. Both of these classes implement IForumObserver and are quite similar. Listing 8-36 shows the AdminObserver class.

Listing 8-36. AdminObserver Class Implements IForumObserver

```
public class AdminObserver:IForumObserver
{
    public void Update(ForumPost post)
    {
        using (AppDbContext db = new AppDbContext())
        {
            Notification notification = new Notification();
            notification.Description = $"New forum post - {post.Title} - received on
{DateTime.Now}";
            notification.ReceivedOn = DateTime.Now;
            db.Notifications.Add(notification);
            db.SaveChanges();
        }
    }
}
```

The `AdminObserver` class implements the `Update()` method defined in the `IForumObserver` interface. The `Update()` method adds an entry to the `Notifications` table. This is done by creating a `Notification` object and setting its `Description` and `ReceivedOn` properties to the appropriate values. Notice the use of the `ForumPost` parameter in forming the `Description`. The entry is added to the table by calling the `SaveChanges()` method.

The `ActivityObserver` class is quite similar to the `AdminObserver` class except that its `Update()` method adds an entry to the `ActivityLog` table. For the sake of saving space, the `ActivityObserver` class will not be discussed here.

Next, add an `IForumNotifier` interface to the Core folder and define the methods in it as shown in Listing 8-37.

Listing 8-37. IForumNotifier Interface

```
public interface IForumNotifier
{
    void Subscribe(IForumObserver observer);
    void Unsubscribe(IForumObserver observer);
    void Notify(ForumPost post);
}
```

The `IForumNotifier` interfaces defines `Subscribe()`, `Unsubscribe()`, and `Notify()` methods. The `Subscribe()` and `Unsubscribe()` methods accept an `IForumObserver` object as their parameter. The `Notify()` method accepts a `ForumPost` object as its parameter.

Then add a `ForumNotifier` class to the Core folder and implement the `IForumNotifier` interface on it as shown in Listing 8-38.

Listing 8-38. ForumNotifier Class Acts as the Publisher

```
public class ForumNotifier:IForumNotifier
{
    private static List<IForumObserver> observers;

    static ForumNotifier()
    {
        observers = new List<IForumObserver>();
    }
```

```
    public void Subscribe(IForumObserver observer)
    {
        observers.Add(observer);
    }

    public void Unsubscribe(IForumObserver observer)
    {
        observers.Remove(observer);
    }

    public void Notify(ForumPost post)
    {
        foreach(IForumObserver observer in observers)
        {
            observer.Update(post);
        }
    }
}
```

The ForumNotifier class begins by declaring a private generic List to hold IForumObserver objects. Notice that this variable is static so that the subscribers can live across multiple request-response cycles.

The Subscribe() method adds the IForumObserver object received as the parameter to the observers list. Along the same lines, the Unsubscribe() method removes the specified IForumObserver object from the subscribers list.

The Notify() method iterates through the subscribers list and notifies each subscriber by invoking the subscriber's Update() method. The ForumPost object is passed to the Update() method.

Now it's time to create the client–HomeController. Add the HomeController class to the Controllers folder. The HomeController class needs four actions–Index(), AddPost(), ShowNotifications(), and ShowActivityLog(). The Index() action sets up the publisher and the subscriber objects and is shown in Listing 8-39.

Listing 8-39. Index() Action Configures Publisher and Subscribers

```
public IActionResult Index()
{
    AdminObserver observer1 = new AdminObserver();
    ActivityObserver observer2 = new ActivityObserver();
    ForumNotifier notifier = new ForumNotifier();

    notifier.Subscribe(observer1);
    notifier.Subscribe(observer2);

    return View();
}
```

The Index() action creates instances of AdminObserver and ActivityObserver. It also instantiates a ForumNotifier object.

The AdminObserver and ActivityObserver are wired as the subscribers using the Subscribe() method. When a user adds a new forum post, the AddPost() action is invoked. This action is shown in Listing 8-40.

Listing 8-40. AddPost( ) Action Adds a Forum Post

```
public IActionResult AddPost(ForumPost post)
{
    post.PostedOn = DateTime.Now;
    using (AppDbContext db = new AppDbContext())
    {
        db.ForumPosts.Add(post);
        db.SaveChanges();
    }
    ViewBag.Message = "Post submitted successfully!";
    ForumNotifier notifier = new ForumNotifier();
    notifier.Notify(post);
    return View("Index", post);
}
```

The AddPost() action receives a ForumPost object through model binding. It then adds the ForumPost to the ForumPosts DbSet using the Add() method. The ForumPost is saved to the ForumPosts table by calling SaveChanges() on the DbContext. A success message is set in the ViewBag and is rendered on the view.

A new ForumNotifier object is created. Recollect that since the subscribers collection of ForumNotifier is marked as static, the previously added subscribers are available to the new instance of ForumNotifier. Then Notify() is called on the ForumNotifier object so as to send notifications to all the subscribers.

The ShowNotifications() and ShowActivityLog() actions simply retrieve all the notifications and activity log entries from the respective tables and pass them to the corresponding views. These methods are shown in Listing 8-41.

Listing 8-41. ShowNotifications( ) and ShowActivityLog( ) Actions

```
public IActionResult ShowNotifications()
{
    using (AppDbContext db = new AppDbContext())
    {
        List<Notification> notifications = db.Notifications.ToList();
        return View(notifications);
    }
}

public IActionResult ShowActivityLog()
{
    using (AppDbContext db = new AppDbContext())
    {
        List<Activity> activitylog = db.ActivityLog.ToList();
        return View(activitylog);
    }
}
```

This completes the HomeController. Now the final step is to create three views—Index, ShowNotifications, and ShowActivityLog.

Begin by adding the Index view to the Views/Home folder and then write the markup shown in Listing 8-42 in it.

Listing 8-42. Markup of Index View

```
@model Observer.Core.ForumPost

...
<body>
    <h1>Post a New Question</h1>
    <form asp-action="AddPost" asp-controller="Home" method="post">
        <table border="1" cellpadding="10">
            <tr>
                <td><label asp-for="UserName">Username :</label></td>
                <td><input type="text" asp-for="UserName" /></td>
            </tr>
            <tr>
                <td><label asp-for="Title">Title :</label></td>
                <td><input type="text" asp-for="Title" /></td>
            </tr>
            <tr>
                <td><label asp-for="Description">Description :</label></td>
                <td><textarea asp-for="Description"></textarea></td>
            </tr>
            <tr>
                <td colspan="2">
                    <input type="submit" name="submit" value="Submit" />
                </td>
            </tr>
        </table>
    </form>
    <h4>@ViewBag.Message</h4>
    <br />
    <a asp-action="ShowNotifications" target="_blank">Show Notifications</a>
    <br /><br />
    <a asp-action="ShowActivityLog" target="_blank">Show Activity Log</a>
...
```

The Index view consists of a form that submits to the AddPost() action (asp-action attribute) of the HomeController (asp-controller attribute). The form houses a table that represents a data-entry screen for adding a forum post.

There are three labels, two textboxes, one text area, and a button. Notice how the labels and textboxes are model bound using the asp-for attribute of the respective tag helpers. The success message is also outputted at the bottom of the table.

At the bottom of the view there are two hyperlinks—one that points to the ShowNotifications() action (asp-action attribute) and one that points to the ShowActivityLog() action.

Then add ShowNotifications and ShowActivityLog views to the Views/Home folder. Both of these views are quite identical except that their model is different. Listing 8-43 shows the markup of ShowNotifications view.

Listing 8-43. ShowNotifications View

```
@model List<Observer.Core.Notification>

<html>
<head>
    <title>List of Notifications</title>
</head>
<body>
    <h1>List of Notifications</h1>
    @foreach(var item in Model)
    {
        <h2>@item.Description</h2>
    }
</body>
</html>
```

The ShowNotifications view receives a List of Notification objects as its model. A foreach loop iterates through the Model and displays the Description property of the Notification objects onto the response stream.

The ShowActivityLog view is similar, but its model is a List of Activity objects. The ShowActivityLog view is not discussed here to save some space.

This completes the application. Before you run the application you will need to create the ObserverDb database (see Chapter 1 for more details) with the required tables. Once the database is ready, run the application and try adding a new forum post.

After adding a forum post, open the "Show Notifications" and "Show Activity Log" links in new tab. This will display the notifications and activity log confirming the working of the publisher as well as the subscribers.

Summary

This chapter discussed three behavioral patterns, namely mediator, memento, and observer. The mediator pattern provides a way for objects to perform bi-directional communication. It simplifies the overall interaction between the objects, because one object need not know anything about the other object. The Mediator object takes care of passing on the communication messages between them.

The memento pattern allows you to save and restore the internal state of an object without compromising the encapsulation. The memento pattern can be used in situations where you need to save a snapshot of one or more objects to some medium and wish to reload the snapshot at a later stage.

The observer pattern offers a publisher-subscriber model such that one or more objects can subscribe to receive notifications. The publisher broadcasts the notifications when something interesting happens in the system. The subscribers are notified and updated accordingly.

The next chapter will continue our journey of behavioral patterns by discussing the remaining four patterns—state, strategy, template method, and visitor.

CHAPTER 9

■ ■ ■

Behavioral Patterns: State, Strategy, Template Method, and Visitor

This chapter will cover the remaining behavioral patterns, namely state, strategy, template method, and visitor.

The state pattern uses the internal state of an object to alter its behavior. The strategy and template method patterns deal with algorithms.

The strategy pattern allows you to work with a family of algorithms such that the algorithms can be used in an interchangeable manner. The template method defines a skeleton of an algorithm such that one or more steps can be altered.

The visitor pattern is used to perform an operation on the elements of an object structure. The operation is independent of the object structure, and you can define additional operations without modifying the object structure.

Specifically, this chapter will cover the following aspects of these four patterns:

- Purpose and role of the state, strategy, template method, and visitor patterns

- UML structure and layout of these four patterns

- A proof of concept example illustrating the implementation of each of these patterns

State

At times your processing logic depends upon the internal state of an object. A usual approach to handling such state-dependent processing is to have a series of if statements or a switch statement that checks for the state, and then depending on the state certain processing is triggered.

This approach may pose difficulties when there is a reasonable amount of state-specific processing. Any changes to the processing logic of a state will cause the whole class to be modified and retested. Moreover, the addition of state values will also cause the class to be modified.

The state pattern can help you in such situations. **The state pattern allows an object to change its behavior when its internal state changes. This change in behavior is accomplished by utilizing a set of possible state objects.**

© Bipin Joshi 2016
B. Joshi, *Beginning SOLID Principles and Design Patterns for ASP.NET Developers*,
DOI 10.1007/978-1-4842-1848-8_9

The state pattern solves the problem described earlier by isolating each state-specific piece of processing into its own class. This way a state is represented by an object that also encapsulates the processing belonging to that state. Additional state objects can be easily added without affecting the main class. Modification to the existing state-specific processing causes only that state class to undergo change.

Consider a workflow application that has states such as Documents Verified, Sent for Review, Pending Approval, Approved, and Rejected. Now each of these states might have specific processing that is required, and hence can be represented by a separate class. These state objects have a common base class or implement a common interface. The main workflow class uses polymorphic behavior to invoke the processing.

Design and Explanation

The UML diagram in Figure 9-1 illustrates the state pattern.

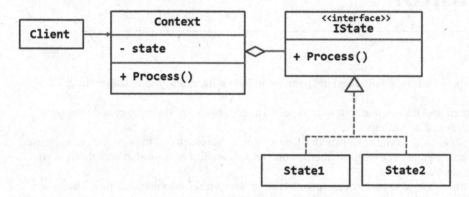

Figure 9-1. *UML diagram illustrating the state pattern*

The IState interface provides the abstraction for the state objects. The Process() method, when implemented, does the processing for a particular state. It takes a Context object as its parameter so that a new state can be assigned after the desired processing.

The State1 and State2 classes represent the concrete implementations of the IState interface.

The Context class is the application-specific class that holds an instance of the state object. The state member can point to State1 or State2 depending on the application flow. The Context class also has the Process() method, which does its work and calls the Process() on the state member.

The Client class instantiates the Context and also specifies the initial state of the Context.

Example

Now that you know the purpose and design of the state pattern, let's put this knowledge to use in an example.

Suppose you are developing a web application that allows you to create and track marketing campaigns. The whole process from campaign creation to completion is a workflow that progresses as follows:

- The marketing personnel come up with an idea for a marketing campaign.

- These ideas are added to the application, and a campaign is created. The campaign, however, requires approval from a proper authority.

- The campaign idea is then reviewed by a manager, and if found suitable it is approved.

- Once a campaign is approved, all the material required for the campaign is prepared. This may include things such as banners, boardings, pamphlets, digital advertisements, and videos.

- Once all the material for a campaign is prepared, it is ready to get executed.

- The campaign is run, and the whole cycle can be repeated for another campaign.

As you might have guessed from the preceding workflow, there are certain states through which the campaign goes: Campaign Creation, Campaign Approval, Campaign Material Preparation, and Campaign Execution. Once a campaign is run, the workflow resets to the initial state.

The web application should allow for creating the campaign and also for processing the campaign through these states.

Considering this workflow of a marketing campaign, one may come up with a design like that shown in Figure 9-2.

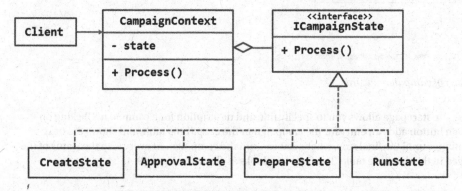

Figure 9-2. *A marketing campaign with four states*

The ICampaignState interface represents an abstraction for a campaign state. It consists of a single method—Process().

The ICampaignState interface is implemented by four state classes, namely CreateState, ApprovalState, PrepareState, and RunState. The Process() implementation of these four classes does some processing that is specific to that state. For our example, the code simply changes the status in the Campaigns database table, but it could be any simple-to-complex processing belonging to that state. Moreover, additional states can also be added at a later date.

The CampaignContext class represents the context class and contains a member variable that holds a reference to one of the four ICampaignState implementations.

The Process() of the CampaignContext triggers the workflow. In this case the initial state of a campaign will be CreateState. Each call to the Process() method of the context calls the Process() method on the state object. The state member then changes its pointer to the next state in the workflow. This way it appears that calls to the same method—Process()—are behaving as if the underlying class has been changed.

The Client—HomeController—creates the CampaignContext, sets its initial state, and begins the workflow like a wizard does.

Figure 9-3 shows the initial page of the application.

Figure 9-3. *First step of campaign wizard*

As you can see, the start page allows you to specify title and description for a campaign. Clicking on the Create Campaign button adds an entry for the campaign in the Campaigns table and shows the next step. This flow continues until the final step, where you can run the campaign. At every step the status of the campaign is changed in the database table. The final step looks as shown in Figure 9-4.

Figure 9-4. *Campaign wizard completes when a campaign is run*

When you click on the Run Campaign button, the wizard resets to the initial page, and you can enter details for another campaign.

For the sake of simplicity we won't provide any facility to exit the workflow in between and resume it later. However, in a more realistic and full-fledged implementation, you should provide that as well.

To develop this application, begin by creating a new ASP.NET web application project named State using Visual Studio and configure it to use MVC and Entity Framework (see Chapter 1 for more details). Also store the database connection string of StateDb—the database used by the application—in the appsettings.json file.

Then add the AppSettings class to the Core folder. The AppSettings class needs to have the ConnectionString property and is assigned a value from the Startup class. Since this has been done many times in earlier examples, we won't go into those details here.

Now, add the Campaign class to the Core folder and write the code shown in Listing 9-1 in it.

Listing 9-1. Campaign Entity Represents Campaign Details

```
[Table("Campaigns")]
public class Campaign
{
    [DatabaseGenerated(DatabaseGeneratedOption.Identity)]
    public int Id { get; set; }
    [Required]
    [StringLength(100)]
    public string Title { get; set; }
    [Required]
    public string Description { get; set; }
    [Required]
    [StringLength(100)]
    public string Status { get; set; }
}
```

The Campaign entity class is mapped to the Campaigns table using the [Table] attribute. The Campaign class consists of four properties, namely Id, Title, Description, and Status. They represent the title of a campaign, its description, and its current status, respectively. The Status property is changed by individual state classes, as you will see later.

Then, add the AppDbContext class to the Core folder and define the Campaigns DbSet as shown in Listing 9-2.

Listing 9-2. AppDbContext with Campaigns DbSet

```
public class AppDbContext:DbContext
{
    public DbSet<Campaign> Campaigns { get; set; }

    protected override void OnConfiguring(DbContextOptionsBuilder optionsBuilder)
    {
        optionsBuilder.UseSqlServer(AppSettings.ConnectionString);
    }
}
```

Next, add the CampaignContext class to the Core folder and write the code shown in Listing 9-3 in it.

Listing 9-3. CampaignContext Holds Reference to State Object

```
public class CampaignContext
{
    public ICampaignState State { get; set; }
    public Campaign Campaign { get; set; }
```

```
public CampaignContext(ICampaignState state)
{
    this.State = state;
}

public void Process()
{
    State.Process(this);
}
}
```

The CampaignContext class has two public properties, namely State and Campaign. The State property holds an object that implements the ICampaignState interface (which will be discussed shortly). This property is public, because you need to change it from the individual state classes (you will see that shortly). The Campaign property represents campaign information as encapsulated by the Campaign entity class.

The constructor of the CampaignContext class sets the initial state of the campaign. The Process() method calls the Process() method of the ICampaignState object, thus triggering the workflow.

Then, add an ICampaignState interface to the Core folder (Listing 9-4).

Listing 9-4. ICampaignState Interface

```
public interface ICampaignState
{
    void Process(CampaignContext context);
}
```

The ICampaignState interface is a simple interface with just one method—Process(). The Process() method accepts a CampaignContext object. This way the individual state objects can access and change the State property of the CampaignContext. They can also access the Campaign object if needed.

Now add four classes—CreateState, ApprovalState, PrepareState, and RunState—to the Core folder and implement ICampaignState on all of them. These classes are quite similar. So, for the sake of saving some space, only CreateState (Listing 9-5) and RunState will be discussed.

Listing 9-5. CreateState Class

```
public class CreateState : ICampaignState
{
    public void Process(CampaignContext context)
    {
        using (AppDbContext db = new AppDbContext())
        {
            context.Campaign.Status = "Campaign has been created";
            db.Campaigns.Add(context.Campaign);
            db.SaveChanges();
        }
        context.State = new ApprovalState();
    }
}
```

The CreateState class represents the campaign creation state. The Process() implementation sets the Status of the Campaign object and adds it to the Campaigns DbSet. Then, SaveChanges() is called to save the campaign details to the Campaigns table.

Since the campaign is now awaiting approval, the State property of the CampaignContext is changed from CreateState (the initial state) to ApprovalState.

You can create ApprovalState and PrepareState classes along similar lines. Just change the Status property of the existing Campaign object to some appropriate text and call SaveChanges() to save the changed status. These classes are not discussed here. You can grab their code from the code download of this book.

The RunState class resets the state to CreateState again and is shown in Listing 9-6.

Listing 9-6. RunState Class Resets the Campaign Workflow

```
public class RunState : ICampaignState
{
    public void Process(CampaignContext context)
    {
        using (AppDbContext db = new AppDbContext())
        {
            Campaign campaign = db.Campaigns.Where(o => o.Id == context.Campaign.Id).
            SingleOrDefault();
            campaign.Status = "Campaign has been successfully run";
            db.SaveChanges();
        }
        context.State = new CreateState();
    }
}
```

The RunState gets a hold of the existing Campaign object and changes its Status as shown in the code. The Status is saved by calling the SaveChanges() method.

The context State is set to CreateState() so that the workflow is reset to its initial state and a new campaign can be created.

This completes the state classes. Now let's focus on the HomeController that instantiates and walks a user through the workflow. Begin by adding the HomeController class to the Controllers folder.

The HomeController needs to store the CampaignContext object across multiple requests. Hence, it uses in-memory cache to do that. Of course, you could use other options, such as session, in order to support multiuser scenarios.

To use the in-memory cache, open the Startup class and modify the ConfigureServices() method as shown in Listing 9-7.

Listing 9-7. Enabling Caching in Startup Class

```
public void ConfigureServices(IServiceCollection services)
{
    services.AddMvc();
    services.AddEntityFramework()
            .AddSqlServer();
    services.AddCaching();
}
```

The code calls the AddCaching() method to add in-memory caching to the registered services. Then, you can use a constructor injection to get a MemoryCache object (Listing 9-8).

Listing 9-8. Constructor Injection to Receive MemoryCache

```
public class HomeController : Controller
{
    private IMemoryCache cache;

    public HomeController(IMemoryCache cache)
    {
        this.cache = cache;
    }
...
...
}
```

The HomeController begins by declaring a variable of type IMemoryCache (Microsoft.Framework. Caching.Memory namespace). This variable is assigned from the constructor of the HomeController. The constructor receives the IMemoryCache object through ASP.NET's DI framework and it is then stored in the local cache variable.

The HomeController has five actions—Index(), Create(), Approve(), Prepare(), and Run()—that process individual stages of the workflow. These actions will be discussed next.

Listing 9-9 shows the Index() action that triggers the campaign workflow.

Listing 9-9. Index() Starts the Campaign Workflow

```
public IActionResult Index()
{
    ICampaignState initialState = new CreateState();
    CampaignContext context = new CampaignContext(initialState);
    cache.Set("context", context);
    return View();
}
```

The Index() action creates a new instance of the CreateState class and also the CampaignContext class. The CreateState object is passed to the constructor of the CampaignContext object. This way the initial state of the context is set.

The CampaignContext object needs to be preserved across multiple requests. Thus, it is stored in the MemoryCache using the Set() method. The Set() method accepts a key and a value to be stored.

The Index() action then returns the Index view to the browser.

Once a user fills in the campaign details, such as title and description, and clicks on the Create Campaign button, Create() action takes over (Listing 9-10).

Listing 9-10. Create() Action Stores the Campaign Details in the Table

```
[HttpPost]
public IActionResult Create(Campaign obj)
{
    CampaignContext context = cache.Get<CampaignContext>("context");
    context.Campaign = obj;
    context.Process();
    return View("Approve", obj);
}
```

The Create() action grabs the CampaignContext object stored in the MemoryCache. The Campaign property of the CampaignContext is assigned to the Campaign object that was obtained through model binding. The Process() method is called to process the campaign. Since the State of the campaign is CreateState, the Process() method will add an entry to the Campaigns table, and the State will be changed to ApprovalState. The Create() action sends the Approve view to the browser.

When a user clicks on the Approve Campaign button from the Approve view, the Approve() action takes over; it is shown in Listing 9-11.

Listing 9-11. Approve() Action

```
[HttpPost]
public IActionResult Approve()
{
    CampaignContext context = cache.Get<CampaignContext>("context");
    context.Process();
    return View("Prepare", context.Campaign);
}
```

The Approve() action grabs the CampaignContext object stored in the MemoryCache and calls its Process() method. This time the State property is pointing to the ApprovalState object, and hence calling the Process() method will change the Status of the campaign and also set the State to PrepareState. The Approve() action sends the Prepare view to the browser.

The Prepare() and Run() actions are quite similar to Approve(). They also get a hold of the CampaignContext object from the MemoryCache and call its Process() method. This will change the State property of the context to PrepareState and RunState, respectively. The Prepare() and Run() actions send the Prepare view and Index view to the browser, respectively. These methods are not discussed here to save some space.

Now, it's time to create the views—Index, Approve, Prepare, and Run. Begin by adding an Index view to the Views/Home folder and write the markup shown in Listing 9-12 in it.

Listing 9-12. Markup of Index View

```
@model State.Core.Campaign
...
<body>
    <h1>Create a New Campaign</h1>
    <form asp-action="Create" asp-controller="Home" method="post">
        <table border="1" cellpadding="10">
            <tr>
                <td><label asp-for="Title">Title :</label></td>
                <td><input type="text" asp-for="Title" /></td>
            </tr>
            <tr>
                <td><label asp-for="Description">Description :</label></td>
                <td><textarea asp-for="Description"></textarea></td>
            </tr>
            <tr>
                <td colspan="2">
                    <input type="submit" name="submit" value="Create Campaign" />
                </td>
```

```
            </tr>
        </table>
    </form>
</body>
...
```

The Campaign class acts as the model for the Index view, as indicated by the @model directive. The Index view consists of a form tag helper that posts to the Create() action (asp-action attribute) of the HomeController (asp-controller attribute).

The form consists of two labels, a textbox, a text area, and a button. The textbox and the text area are bound with the Title and Description properties of the model, respectively. The Create Campaign button submits the form.

Next, add an Approve view to the Views/Home folder and write the markup shown in Listing 9-13 in it.

Listing 9-13. Markup of Approve View

```
@model State.Core.Campaign
<html>
<head>
    <title>Approval</title>
</head>
<body>
    <h1>@Model.Title</h1>
    <div>@Model.Description</div>
    <h2>To approve the campaign click on the following button.</h2>
    <form asp-action="Approve" asp-controller="Home" method="post">
        <input type="submit" value="Approve Campaign" />
    </form>
</body>
</html>
```

The Approve view is quite straightforward. It simply displays the Title and Description of the model (Campaign object) and provides a button to approve the campaign. The form tag helper submits the form to the Approve() action (asp-action attribute) of the HomeController (asp-controller attribute).

The Prepare and Run views are quite similar to the Approve view. The only difference is that they submit the form to the Prepare() and Run() actions, respectively. These views are not discussed here to save some space.

This completes the application. Before you run the application, create the StateDb database with the Campaigns table (see Chapter 1 for more details). Once the database is created, run the application and try running the complete campaign workflow. At each stage, check the status of the campaign as stored in the database. Also notice how clicking the Run Campaign button of the Run view runs the campaign and takes you to the Index view again to create another campaign.

Strategy

A class might be dependent upon different ways of accomplishing a task. These different ways form the strategies or algorithms that are needed to do some work. A usual approach is to put all these algorithms into a single class and utilize one of them based on some condition or logic.

This approach of putting all strategies into a single class suffers from the same drawbacks that were given as reasons to use the state pattern. A recommended approach, therefore, is to separate each algorithm into its own class. The client can then decide which class to instantiate and utilize to get the job done. This way, any changes to an algorithm are isolated to a single class. Moreover, additional algorithms can be added at a later time.

The strategy pattern allows you to do just that. **The strategy pattern defines a family of strategies or algorithms. Each algorithm is encapsulated in its own class. The different algorithms forming the family can be used in an interchangeable way.** Additional algorithms can be added to the family at a later time without affecting the existing code.

At first glance you may find the strategy pattern to be quite similar to the state pattern since both isolate pieces of processing into separate classes. However, they are not the same, for the following reasons:

- The state pattern is inherently associated with the internal state of a class. The strategy pattern is about a strategy or algorithm that is used to do something. It need not be associated with the state of a class as such.

- A State object in the state pattern manipulates the state of the Context class. So, usually State classes need a pointer to the Context object. This is not necessary in the strategy pattern. A class encapsulating an algorithm is a standalone class in itself, and it may not manipulate anything from the client class.

- The strategy pattern is about accomplishing a task using one of several algorithms. The state pattern is about doing different tasks based on a state.

Consider the chart example we discussed in earlier chapters. Suppose an application needs to display a bar chart or a pie chart. The selection of the type of chart is based on some configuration setting or condition. One can encapsulate the logic required to process data and generate the chart in two classes—BarChart and PieChart. So, the algorithms for generating bar charts and pie charts are now isolated into their own classes. The client can simply use one of them to accomplish the task of displaying a chart. At a later date, additional chart types can be added to the system by encapsulating algorithms of those chart types into their own classes.

Design and Explanation

The UML diagram in Figure 9-5 illustrates the strategy pattern.

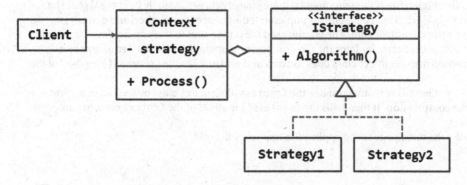

Figure 9-5. *UML diagram illustrating the strategy pattern*

As shown in the figure, the IStrategy interface represents the abstraction for the algorithm. It consists of the Algorithm() method. When implemented, the Algorithm() method does some work based on the processing strategy it represents.

The IStrategy interface is implemented by two strategy classes—Strategy1 and Strategy2. These two classes encapsulate different strategies that are interchangeable. They form a family of algorithms.

The Context class holds an instance of one of the implementations of IStrategy. Its Process() method invokes the Algorithm() method of the Strategy object.

The Client class instantiates and uses the Context class as and when needed.

Example

Now, let's put our knowledge of the strategy pattern to use in an example.

Suppose you are developing a website that allows users to download certain files. To simplify the download operation, you want to provide a file-compression feature. This feature will allow the user to pick a file from a list of files and specify the file-compression algorithm they want to use. The possible compression algorithms are Deflate, GZip, and Zip.

Considering these requirements, you come up with the design shown in Figure 9-6.

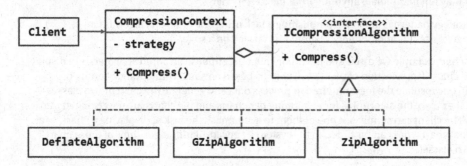

Figure 9-6. *Compression files based on three algorithms*

The ICompressionAlgorithm interface represents the common contract implemented by all the strategy classes. It has one method—Compress()—that when implemented does the job of compressing a file.

The ICompressionAlgorithm is implemented by three strategy classes, namely DeflateAlgorithm, GZipAlgorithm, and ZipAlgorithm. These classes implement the Compress() method and compress a source file using the respective algorithm. The compressed file is then sent to the browser for downloading.

The CompressionContext class initiates the file-compression operation. It holds a strategy object. The Compress() method of the Context class does its work and also invokes the Compress() method of the Strategy object.

The Client—HomeController—instantiates the CompressionContext class by passing it a Strategy object to use for the compression. It then calls the Compress() method of the Context class to compress the file.

Figure 9-7 shows the main page of the application that you will build.

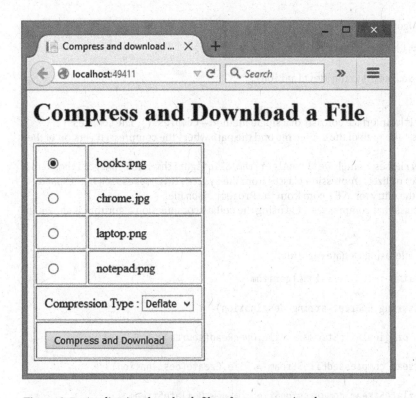

Figure 9-7. *Application downloads files after compressing them*

The application presents a list of files that can be downloaded to the user. A user can pick one file at a time, select the compression type from the dropdown list, and then click on the Compress and Download button. Doing so will compress the selected file using the specified algorithm; the user is then prompted to save the compressed file.

To develop this application, begin by creating a new ASP.NET web application project named Strategy using Visual Studio and configure it to use MVC (see Chapter 1 for more details).

Then, add the AppSettings class to the Core folder. The AppSettings class needs to have two properties—SourceFolder and DestinationFolder—that represent the source-file location and the compressed-file location, respectively. Since you have created AppSettings many times in earlier examples, we won't go into those details here. The Startup constructor that sets these two properties is shown in Listing 9-14.

Listing 9-14. Setting the Source and Destination Locations

```
public Startup(IHostingEnvironment env)
{
    AppSettings.SourceFolder = env.MapPath("SourceFolder");
    AppSettings.DestinationFolder = env.MapPath("DestinationFolder");
}
```

As shown in the code, the SourceFolder and DestinationFolder properties are set to wwwroot/SourceFolder and wwwroot/DestinationFolder, respectively.

Now add the ICompressionAlgorithm interface to the Core folder and write the code shown in Listing 9-15 in it.

287

Listing 9-15. ICompressionAlgorithm interface

```
public interface ICompressionAlgorithm
{
    void Compress(string source, string destination);
}
```

The ICompressionAlgorithm interface consists of a single method—Compress(). The Compress() method takes two parameters—the path of the source file and the path where the compressed version of the file is to be stored.

Next, add three Strategy classes, namely DeflateAlgorithm, GZipAlgorithm, and ZipAlgorithm, to the Core folder. These three classes utilize compression classes from the System.IO.Compression namespace. You will also need to remove the entry for .NET core from the Project.json file.

The DeflateAlgorithm class that compresses a file using the deflate compression algorithm is shown in Listing 9-16.

Listing 9-16. Compressing a File Using Deflate Algorithm

```
public class DeflateAlgorithm : ICompressionAlgorithm
{
    public void Compress(string source, string destination)
    {
        using (FileStream originalFileStream = File.OpenRead(source))
        {
            using (FileStream compressedFileStream = File.Create(destination))
            {
                using (DeflateStream compressionStream = new DeflateStream
                (compressedFileStream, CompressionMode.Compress))
                {
                    originalFileStream.CopyTo(compressionStream);
                }
            }
        }
    }
}
```

The DeflateAlgorithm implements the Compress() method that was defined in the ICompressAlgorithm interface. The Compress() method opens the source file in read mode using the originalFileStream object. The compressedFileStream object represents the FileStream for the destination file (the compressed file).

The file content is read from the originalFileStream, is compressed, and is then written to the compressedFileStream object. To accomplish this task, the DeflateStream class is used. The constructor of the DeflateStream class accepts the compressedFileStream and CompressionMode objects. CompressionMode is set to Compress since our intension is to compress the file. Then, the content from the originalFileStream object is copied to the compressionStream object using the CopyTo() method.

Use of the using blocks ensures that all the streams are closed when the using block completes.

Now, add the code shown in Listing 9-17 to the GZipAlgorithm class.

Listing 9-17. GZipAlgorithm Class

```
public class GZipAlgorithm : ICompressionAlgorithm
{
    public void Compress(string source, string destination)
    {
        using (FileStream originalFileStream = File.OpenRead(source))
        {
            using (FileStream compressedFileStream = File.Create(destination))
            {
                using (GZipStream compressionStream = new GZipStream(compressedFileStream,
                CompressionMode.Compress))
                {
                    originalFileStream.CopyTo(compressionStream);
                }
            }
        }
    }
}
```

The GZipAlgorithm class is quite similar to the DeflateAlgorithm class. The only difference is that GZipAlgorithm uses the GZipStream class instead of the DeflateStream class.

Next, open the ZipAlgorithm class and write the code shown in Listing 9-18 in it.

Listing 9-18. ZipAlgorithm Class

```
public class ZipAlgorithm : ICompressionAlgorithm
{
    public void Compress(string source, string destination)
    {
        using (ZipArchive zip = ZipFile.Open(destination, ZipArchiveMode.Create))
        {
            zip.CreateEntryFromFile(source, Path.GetFileName(source));
        }
    }
}
```

The ZipAlgorithm class uses the ZipArchive class to create a ZIP destination file. This is done by using the Open() method and setting ZipArchiveMode to Create. A ZipArchive can contain one or more files. The CreateEntryFromFile() method adds the compressed version of the source file to the ZipArchive. The second parameter of CreateEntryFromFile() specifies the name of the entry being added.

Next, add the CompressionContext class to the Core folder and write the code shown in Listing 9-19 in it.

Listing 9-19. CompressionContext Class

```
public class CompressionContext
{
    private ICompressionAlgorithm strategy;

    public CompressionContext(ICompressionAlgorithm strategy)
    {
        this.strategy = strategy;
    }
```

```
    public void Compress(string source, string destination)
    {
        strategy.Compress(source, destination);
    }
}
```

The CompressionContext class defines a Strategy private variable of type ICompressionAlgorithm. This variable is assigned from the Constructor code.

The Compress() method accepts the source and destination filenames as its parameters. Inside, it calls the Compress() method of the strategy object by passing the source and destination parameters to it.

Now, let's move on to the Client—HomeController. Add HomeController to the Controllers folder and modify its Index() action as shown in Listing 9-20.

Listing 9-20. Index() Action Sends a List of Files That Can Be Downloaded

```
public IActionResult Index()
{
    string[] files = Directory.GetFiles(AppSettings.SourceFolder);
    List<string> fileNames = new List<string>();
    foreach(string file in files)
    {
        fileNames.Add(Path.GetFileName(file));
    }
    return View(fileNames);
}
```

The Index() action uses the GetFiles() method of the Directory class (System.IO namespace) to get a list of files from the SourceFolder. The GetFiles() method returns an array of filenames. The filenames are fully qualified paths. A foreach loop iterates through this array and adds an entry to the fileNames generic List that contains just the filename (without the full path). The fileNames list acts as the model for the Index view.

When a user clicks on the Compress and Download button from the Index view, the CompressFile() action is invoked. This action is shown in Listing 9-21.

Listing 9-21. CompressFile() Action Compresses the Selected File

```
[HttpPost]
public IActionResult CompressFile(string selectedfile, string compressiontype)
{
    string extension = "";
    string contentType = "";
    CompressionContext context = null;
    switch (compressiontype)
    {
        case "Deflate":
            extension = ".cmp";
            contentType = "application/deflate";
            context = new CompressionContext(new DeflateAlgorithm());
            break;
        case "GZip":
            extension = ".gz";
            contentType = "application/gzip";
            context = new CompressionContext(new GZipAlgorithm());
            break;
```

```
        case "Zip":
            extension = ".zip";
            contentType = "application/zip";
            context = new CompressionContext(new ZipAlgorithm());
            break;
    }
    string source = AppSettings.SourceFolder + $"\\{selectedfile}";
    string destination = AppSettings.DestinationFolder + $"\\{Path.GetFileNameWithoutExtensi
on(selectedfile)}{extension}";
    context.Compress(source, destination);
    return File(destination, contentType, Path.GetFileName(destination));
}
```

The CompressFile() method receives two things from model binding–name of the selected file and compression type to be used.

Inside, the code declares a variable of type CompressionContext. Two local variables are also declared to hold the target file extension and the content type. The content type is needed at the time of downloading the file.

A switch statement checks the compressiontype value. If the compression type is Deflate, the file extension is set to .cmp, its content type is set to application/deflate, and the context variable is instantiated by passing the DeflateAlgorithm object as its parameter.

If the compression type is GZip, the file extension is set to .gz, its content type is set to application/gzip, and the context variable is instantiated by passing the GZipAlgorithm object as its parameter.

If the compression type is Zip, the file extension is set to .zip, its content type is set to application/zip, and the context variable is instantiated by passing the ZipAlgorithm object as its parameter.

Then the source path of the selected file is determined by appending the selected filename to the SourceFolder property of AppSettings. Along the same lines, the destination path of the compressed file is determined by extracting just the filename and attaching the compression-specific extension.

Then the Compress() method of the CompressionContext class is called by passing the source and destination path to it.

The compressed file is sent to the browser for download using the File() method of the Controller base class. The File() method accepts three parameters. The first parameter is the path of the file to be sent for the download, the second parameter is the content type of the file, and the third parameter is the name to be displayed in the file download dialog of the browser.

The final piece of the application is the Index view. Add the Index view to the Views/Home folder and write the markup shown in Listing 9-22 in it.

Listing 9-22. Markup of the Index View

```
@model List<string>

...
<body>
    <h1>Compress and Download a File</h1>
    <form asp-action="CompressFile" asp-controller="Home" method="post">
        <table border="1" cellpadding="10">
            @foreach (var file in Model)
            {
                <tr>
                    <td><input type="radio" name="selectedfile" value="@file" /></td>
                    <td>@file</td>
                </tr>
            }
```

```
        <tr>
            <td colspan="2">Compression Type :
                <select name="compressiontype">
                    <option>Deflate</option>
                    <option>GZip</option>
                    <option>Zip</option>
                </select>
            </td>
        </tr>
        <tr>
            <td colspan="2">
                <input type="submit" value="Compress and Download" />
            </td>
        </tr>
    </table>
  </form>
...
</html>
```

The Index view receives a list of filenames that can be downloaded as its model. It consists of a form tag helper that submits to the CompressFile() action (asp-action attribute) of the HomeController (asp-controller attribute). Inside the form, a foreach loop iterates through the Model and displays a table of these filenames. Each entry of the table has a radio button whose name is selectedfile, which has a value that is the same as the filename. This way all the radio buttons have the same name and they act as a single group (only one can be selected at a time). There is also a dropdown list with three options–Deflate, GZip, and Zip. The Compress and Download button submits the form.

This completes the application. Before running the application, create SourceFolder and DestinationFolder folders under wwwroot and also place a few files inside the SourceFolder. Then run the application and try downloading the files by picking their compression type.

Template Method

Sometimes an operation consisting of several steps needs to deviate from a few steps depending on some condition. Consider a data-import utility like the one we discussed in earlier chapters. Suppose that this data-import utility does the job of importing data in the following steps: get source information, validate source data, validate destination information, read data from the source, prepare it as per required destination format, write data to the destination. Now, although these steps remain the same for any kind of source data, the actual implementation may vary. For example, if the source data is CSV, then the validation step needs to check for the commas, number of fields, and such things, whereas if the source data is XML, the validation step needs to ensure that the data is well-formed and conforms to some XSD schema.

If you need to deal with such situations, the template method pattern comes in handy. **The template method pattern allows you to define a skeleton of an algorithm in an operation such that some steps of the algorithm can be deferred to subclasses.** The overall structure of the operation remains the same, but some steps are redefined by the subclasses.

Design and Explanation

The UML diagram in Figure 9-8 illustrates the template method pattern.

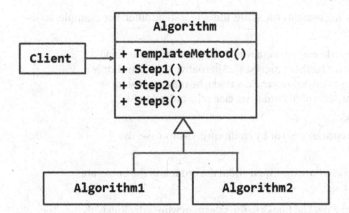

Figure 9-8. *UML diagram illustrating the template method pattern*

The Algorithm abstract class outlines the skeleton of the operation in terms of steps: Step1(), Step2(), and Step3(). These three steps are abstract methods. The TemplateMethod() calls the steps required to complete the operation.

The two classes, Algorithm1 and Algorithm2, inherit from the Algorithm base class. Notice that since Algorithm1 and Algorithm2 inherit from the Algorithm class, the arrow is indicated with solid lines. These two implementations redefine Step1(), Step2(), and Step3() as per their requirements. They, however, cannot redefine TemplateMethod(), since it's not an abstract method.

■ **Note** In most of the examples that were covered earlier, you used interfaces to define a contract for the classes Here you use abstract class to do that. You could have used an interface here also, but in this case abstract classes are more suitable than interfaces.

The Client can instantiate Algorithm1 or Algorithm2 and invoke the TemplateMethod() to perform the intended operation.

Example

Now that you know how the template method pattern works, let's develop an example that illustrates the code-level details.

Suppose you are building a web application for a bookstore. The bookstore plans to sell books in two ways–through the physical bookstore and through their website. In the first model, the customer personally visits the bookstore, whereas the second mode consists of a shopping cart–driven online purchase facility.

Irrespective of the mode of purchase, an order needs to be processed in the following steps:

- The order needs to be validated in terms of availability of the title and requested number of copies.

- The payment needs to be accepted.

- The books need to be packed.

- The books need to be sent to the customer.

Although the skeleton of order processing remains the same, the actual steps differ. For example, an in-person order is processed as follows:

- A customer visits the bookstore. He can personally pick the books from the racks and take them to the salesman for further processing. Alternatively, he can simply request one or more book titles to the salesman. Moreover, he may request more copies of some title. Once all aspects of the order are clear, the order can be considered as a valid order.

- The customer may pay the amount by cash or by credit card. In any case, the payment must be made in full.

- Packing personnel available in store are informed about the order and the books are packed and put inside a carry bag.

- Packing personnel hand over the packed books to the salesman who is dealing with the customer. The books are then handed over to the customer.

An online order is processed as follows:

- A customer visits the bookstore's website. He logs in to the system and adds desired books to the shopping cart. Upon placing the order, the titles and their quantity are checked for availability. The online orders are handled differently, and the books are stocked at a different location than at the store. So, availability of the books is to be confirmed through some external system.

- The payments are accepted only through credit cards. A third-party payment gateway securely processes the payment.

- The packing department handling the packaging of online orders is informed about the order by the system sending some notification to their external system. The packing department packs the books and hands them over to the shipping department.

- The shipping department utilizes services of some courier company to deliver the books to the customer.

As you can see, both "algorithms" of order processing vary at certain steps, but the overall skeleton remains the same.

Considering these requirements, one may come up with arrangement shown in Figure 9-9.

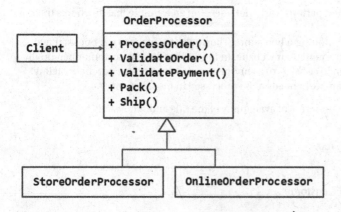

Figure 9-9. *OrderProcessing by store and online website*

The OrderProcessor is an abstract class that consists of four abstract methods–ValidateOrder(), ValidatePayment(), Pack(), and Ship()–and one concrete method–ProcessOrder().

The StoreOrderProcessor and OnlineOrderProcessor classes inherit from the OrderProcessor base class. They redefine all four abstract methods by overriding them and writing their respective implementation. In a realistic situation there would be a lot of code, including a product catalog and a shopping cart, and also third-party systems would be involved while implementing them. Of course, you won't build all those pieces here. For the sake of this example, the implementations will simply log messages to a database table.

The main page of the application that you will develop is shown in Figure 9-10.

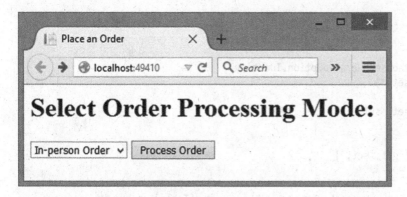

Figure 9-10. *Initiating the order processing*

There is a dropdown list that allows you to select the order-processing mode: In-person order or Online order. Clicking on the Process Order button processes the order as per the selection. The processing steps are logged into the OrderLog database table. Those logs are displayed to the user as shown in Figure 9-11.

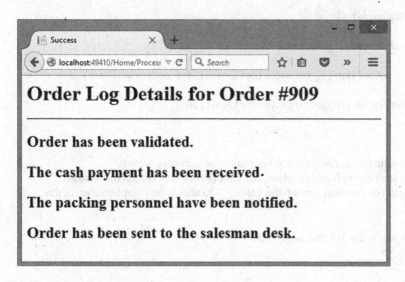

Figure 9-11. *Displaying order logs to the user*

295

To develop this application, begin by creating a new ASP.NET web application project named TemplateMethod using Visual Studio and configure it to use MVC and Entity Framework (see Chapter 1 for more details). Also store the database connection string of TemplateMethodDb–the database used by the application–in the appsettings.json file.

Then add the AppSettings class to the Core folder. The AppSettings class needs to have the ConnectionString property and is assigned a value from the Startup class. Since this has been done many times in earlier examples, we won't go into those details here.

Now add the OrderLog entity class to the Core folder and write the code shown in Listing 9-23 in it.

Listing 9-23. OrderLog Class

```
[Table("OrderLog")]
public class OrderLog
{
    [DatabaseGenerated(DatabaseGeneratedOption.Identity)]
    public int Id { get; set; }
    [Required]
    public int OrderId { get; set; }
    [Required]
    [StringLength(200)]
    public string Status { get; set; }
}
```

The OrderLog entity class is mapped to the OrderLog table using the [Table] attribute. It consists of three properties: Id, OrderId, and Status. The OrderLog class and the OrderLog table are used simply to log messages about a specific OrderId as and how the order processing happens.

Then add AppDbContext class to the Core folder and write the code shown in Listing 9-24 in it.

Listing 9-24. AppDbContext with OrderLog DbSet

```
public class AppDbContext:DbContext
{
    public DbSet<OrderLog> OrderLog { get; set; }

    protected override void OnConfiguring(DbContextOptionsBuilder optionsBuilder)
    {
        optionsBuilder.UseSqlServer(AppSettings.ConnectionString);
    }
}
```

The AppDbContext class is quite straightforward and consists of an OrderLog DbSet.

Next, add the OrderProcessor class to the Core folder. The OrderProcessor class is the abstract base class that defines the skeleton of the order processing. Listing 9-25 shows the complete code of the OrderProcessor class.

Listing 9-25. OrderProcessor Class is the Abstract Base Class

```
public abstract class OrderProcessor
{
    protected int orderId;

    public abstract void ValidateOrder();
    public abstract void ValidatePayment();
```

```
    public abstract void Pack();
    public abstract void Ship();

    public void ProcessOrder(int orderid)
    {
        this.orderId = orderid;
        ValidateOrder();
        ValidatePayment();
        Pack();
        Ship();
    }

}
```

The OrderProcessor abstract class begins by declaring a protected variable for holding an order ID. It is made protected because the derived classes need to access the order ID while performing their operations.

Then the class defines four abstract methods, namely ValidateOrder(), ValidatePayment(), Pack(), and Ship(). These four abstract methods represent the individual steps of the order-processing algorithm. Their intended purpose is quite clear from their respective names. Since these methods are abstract, the derived classes need to provide concrete implementations for them.

The ProcessOrder() method is a concrete method that defines the skeleton of the order-processing algorithm. It receives an order ID from the client and assigns it to the orderId protected variable. The ProcessOrder() method then calls the other four abstract methods in a specific order. Since ProcessOrder() is concrete, the derived types can't override it, thus keeping the skeleton unchanged.

Now add the StoreOrderProcessor class to the Core folder and inherit it from the OrderProcessor base class. Listing 9-26 shows the outline of the StoreOrderProcessor class.

Listing 9-26. Outline of the StoreOrderProcessor Class

```
public class StoreOrderProcessor : OrderProcessor
{
    public override void ValidateOrder()
    {
    }

    public override void ValidatePayment()
    {
    }

    public override void Pack()
    {
    }

    public override void Ship()
    {
    }
}
```

The StoreOrderProcessor class overrides each of the four abstract methods from the OrderProcessor base class. The concrete implementations of these methods simply add an entry to the OrderLog table. For example, the concrete implementation of ValidateOrder() is shown in Listing 9-27.

Listing 9-27. ValidateOrder() Method Adding OrderLog Entry

```
public override void ValidateOrder()
{
    using (AppDbContext db = new AppDbContext())
    {
        OrderLog log = new OrderLog();
        log.OrderId = this.orderId;
        log.Status = "Order has been validated.";
        db.OrderLog.Add(log);
        db.SaveChanges();
    }
}
```

The ValidateOrder() method creates a new OrderLog object and sets its OrderId and Status properties. The OrderLog object is then added to the OrderLog DbSet. SaveChanges() is called to save the OrderLog entry to the OrderLog table.

The other three overridden methods are quite similar to ValidateOrder(). The only change is that they add a different status as per the operation under consideration. These methods are not discussed here to save some space.

Now add the OnlineOrderProcessor class to the Core folder. The OnlineOrderProcessor is quite similar to StoreOrderProcessor and is outlined in Listing 9-28.

Listing 9-28. OnlineOrderProcessor Processes Online Orders

```
public class OnlineOrderProcessor : OrderProcessor
{
    public override void ValidateOrder()
    {
    }

    public override void ValidatePayment()
    {
    }

    public override void Pack()
    {
    }

    public override void Ship()
    {
    }
}
```

The OnlineOrderProcessor is not discussed here due to space-saving reasons. You can grab the complete source code of StoreOrderProcessor and OnlineOrderProcessor classes from the code download of this book.

Next, add HomeController to the Controllers folder. In addition to the default Index() action, you need to add one more action, ProcessOrder(),to it. The ProcessOrder() action is shown in Listing 9-29.

Listing 9-29. ProcessOrder() Initiates Order Processing

```
[HttpPost]
public IActionResult ProcessOrder(string type)
{
    OrderProcessor processor = null;

    if(type=="store")
    {
        processor = new StoreOrderProcessor();
    }
    else
    {
        processor = new OnlineOrderProcessor();
    }
    int orderId = new Random().Next(100, 1000);
    processor.ProcessOrder(orderId);
    using (AppDbContext db = new AppDbContext())
    {
        List<OrderLog> logs = db.OrderLog.Where(o => o.OrderId == orderId).ToList();
        return View("Success", logs);
    }
}
```

The Process Order button from the Index view submits the form to the ProcessOrder() action. ProcessOrder() receives the order-processing mode selected from the dropdown list through the type parameter.

Inside, the OrderProcessor local variable is declared. If type is store, a new instance of StoreOrderProcessor is created; otherwise, a new instance of OnlineOrderProcessor is created. Notice that here the code uses polymorphic behavior through inheritance.

A random order ID is then generated using the Random class and is passed to the ProcessOrder() method of the OrderProcessor class.

A List of OrderLog entries belonging to the order ID under consideration is fetched from the OrderLog table and is passed to the Success view.

Now add the Index view to the Views/Home folder and write the markup shown in Listing 9-30 in it.

Listing 9-30. Markup of Index View

```
<html>
<head>
    <title>Place an Order</title>
</head>
<body>
    <h1>Select Order Processing Mode:</h1>
    <form asp-action="ProcessOrder" asp-controller="Home" method="post">
        <select name="type">
            <option value="store">In-person Order</option>
            <option value="online">Online Order</option>
        </select>
        <input type="submit" name="submit" value="Process Order" />
    </form>
</body>
</html>
```

The Index view consists of a form tag helper that submits to the ProcessOrder() action (asp-action attribute) of the HomeController (asp-controller attribute). It houses a type dropdown list with two options: In-person Order and Online Order. The Process Order button submits the form.

Finally, add a Success view to the Views/Home folder and write the markup shown in Listing 9-31 in it.

Listing 9-31. Success View Shows OrderLog Entries

```
@model List<TemplateMethod.Core.OrderLog>

<html>
<head>
    <title>Success</title>
</head>
<body>
    <h1>Order Log Details for Order #@Model.First().OrderId</h1>
    <hr />
    @foreach(var item in Model)
    {
        <h2>@item.Status</h2>
    }
</body>
</html>
```

The Success view simply iterates through the List of OrderLog objects received as the Model. All the log entries are outputted to the response stream.

This completes the application. Before you run the application, create the TemplateMethodDb database with the OrderLog table (see Chapter 1 for more details). Once the database is created, run the application, select an order-processing mode, and click on the Process Order button. Repeat with the other mode and check the OrderLog entries in the database to confirm that the respective order-processing class was being used.

Visitor

At times you need to perform an operation on all the elements of an object structure. The operation by itself is not directly linked with the elements or the object structure, but the operation requires details of these elements.

Consider a shopping cart that is filled with one or more items. Now the shopping cart may have assorted items–groceries, vegetables, fruits, tinned food, packaged raw food, household accessories, and more. The shopping cart is an object structure consisting of several elements or items.

Now suppose you wish to apply a certain holiday discount on the items purchased. Obviously, the tax and discount would be item specific. Fruits and vegetables will have a different discount than household accessories. Moreover, since the discount is holiday-specific, it can't be part of the main object structure or items.

In order to arrive at the total discount, you need to iterate through the shopping cart, consider each item therein, and calculate the discount for that item's category. This discount calculation is external to the object structure and doesn't directly interfere with it.

The visitor pattern can be used in such cases. **The visitor pattern defines an operation that is to be performed on all the elements of an object structure. Additional operations can be defined at any time without changing the object structure under consideration.** As the name suggests, the visitor pattern visits the elements of an object structure and performs some operation on them.

In the preceding example of a shopping cart, a discount visitor would have iterated through all the items in the cart and applied a category-specific discount to them. In the future another visitor, say, a tax visitor, can be created that visits all the items to figure out tax amount based on their type. The discount visitor as well as the tax visitor don't need to change the original object structure.

Design and Explanation

The UML diagram in Figure 9-12 illustrates the visitor pattern.

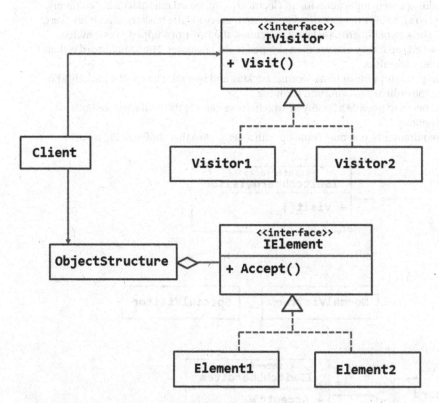

Figure 9-12. *UML diagram illustrating the bisitor pattern*

As shown in the figure, ObjectStructure is the class on which some operation is to be performed. It consists of one or more IElement objects as shown by the aggregation notation. The ObjectStructure can hold IElement objects in any manner; it could be a simple list, a tree structure, or any recursive arrangement.

The IElement interface represents the common interface implemented by all the elements forming the ObjectStructure. It has single method–Accept().

Element1 and Element2 represent the concrete implementations of IElement. The implementation of Accept() from these classes accepts a visitor object–an implementation of IVisitor–that is supposed to access the element.

The IVisitor interface represents the common interface for all the visitors and consists of the Visit() method. Visitor1 and Visitor2 are the concrete implementations of IVisitor. The implementation of the Visitor() method receives an IElement object that is to be operated upon.

Thus, the Accept() method of the element objects receive a visitor object. Accept() then invokes the Visit() method of the visitor object and passes a reference to itself. The Visit() method includes the logic of the operation to be performed on the element.

The Client creates a visitor object required to perform the operation. It also instantiates and arranges the ObjectStructure as per the application requirements. The visitor is passed to the ObjectStructure so that it can be utilized further.

Example

Now that you have reviewed the basics of the visitor pattern, let's examine how it works with an example.

Suppose you are building a web application for an electrical switchboard manufacturing company. An electrical switchboard consists of several assorted items, such as enclosure, busbars, circuit breakers, transformers, and so on. Since switchboards are larger structures, they are not shipped in assembled form. All the items are packed separately and are then shipped to the customer. The switchboard is then assembled on the customer's premises.

There are two packing and shipping options–normal packing and special. The special packing and shipping costs more than the ordinary packing and shipping.

The web application needs to provide a facility by which a user can see the final costs for both packaging and shipping options.

Considering these requirements, one may come up with a design like that shown in Figure 9-13.

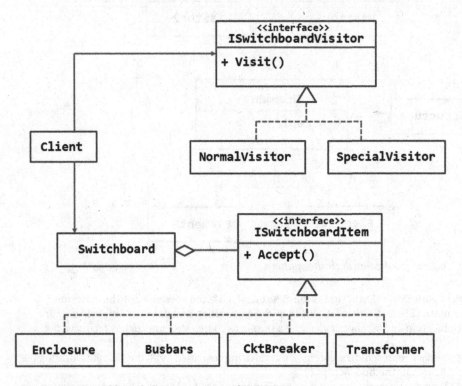

Figure 9-13. *Switchboard object structure with two visitors*

The Switchboard class represents an electrical switchboard consisting of one or more items. The switchboard items are based on a common interface–ISwitchboardItem. There are four concrete switchboard items, namely Enclosure, Busbars, CircuitBreaker, and Transformer. All of them implement the Accept() method defined by the ISwitchboardItem.

The ISwitchboardVisitor interface represents a common interface for any switchboard visitor. As far as this example is concerned, two concrete implementations are available: NormalVisitor and SpecialVisitor. The NormalVisitor class represents a visitor that determines the cost of packing and shipping under normal mode. The SpecialVisitor class represents a visitor that determines the cost of packing and shipping under special mode.

These classes have four overloads of the Visit() implementations—one for each ISwitchboardItem implementation.

The Client—HomeController—builds a Switchboard object structure by capturing items going in it from the user. It also instantiates a visitor object and passes it to the Switchboard object during its construction. The Client calls the Calculate() method on the Switchboard (not shown in the figure) to perform the packing and shipping cost calculation.

The main page of the application that you will develop is shown in Figure 9-14.

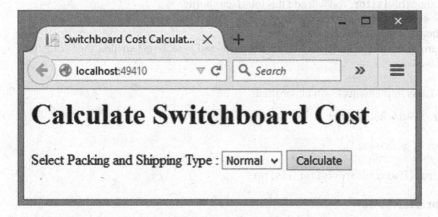

Figure 9-14. *Application allows a user to build a switchboard*

A user can pick the type of packing and shipping—Normal or Special. Upon clicking the Calculate button, a visitor calculates the total cost of the switchboard and displays it as shown in Figure 9-15.

Figure 9-15. *Determining the total cost of a switchboard*

To develop this application, begin by creating a new ASP.NET web application project named Visitor using Visual Studio and configure it to use MVC (see Chapter 1 for more details).

Then add the ISwitchboardItem interface to the Core folder and write the code shown in Listing 9-32 in it.

Listing 9-32. ISwitchboardItem Interface

```
public interface ISwitchboardItem
{
    double Accept(ISwitchboardVisitor visitor);
}
```

The ISwitchboardItem interface consists of a single method: Accept(). The Accept() method accepts a parameter of type ISwitchboardVisitor. You will add this interface shortly.

Then add four classes–Enclosure, Busbars, CircuitBreaker, and Transformer–to the Core folder and implement the ISwitchboardItem interface on all of them.

All of these classes are quite similar, and hence all are not discussed here. To get an idea, the Enclosure class is shown in Listing 9-33.

Listing 9-33. Enclosure Class Implements ISwitchboardItem

```
public class Enclosure:ISwitchboardItem
{
    public double Cost { get; set; }

    public double Accept(ISwitchboardVisitor visitor)
    {
        return visitor.Visit(this);
    }
}
```

The Enclosure class implements the ISwitchboardItem interface. It consists of a Cost property that indicates the cost of the enclosure. The Accept() implementation receives a visitor in the form of an object implementing ISwitchboardVisitor. Inside, the Visit() method is called on the visitor object, and a reference to the Enclosure object is passed to it. This way a visitor can access the members of the Enclosure object (Cost in this case).

Once all the four classes are ready, proceed to creating the ISwitchboardVisitor interface as shown in Listing 9-34.

Listing 9-34. ISwitchboardVisitor Interface

```
public interface ISwitchboardVisitor
{
    double Visit(Enclosure item);
    double Visit(Busbars item);
    double Visit(CircuitBreaker item);
    double Visit(Transformer item);
}
```

The ISwitchboardVisitor interface defines one Visit() method for every concrete implementation of the ISwitchboardItem interface. All the Visit() methods return a double value–the cost of packing and shipping that item. This way each Visit() gets to do the item-specific operation, if any. Moreover, this design ensures that the concrete visitor implementations take into account all the switchboard items.

Next, add NormalVisitor and SpecialVisitor classes to the Core folder and implement the ISwitchboardVisitor interface on them. These two implementations are quite similar, and hence only NormalVisitor is discussed here (Listing 9-35).

Listing 9-35. NormalVisitor Implements ISwitchboardVisitor

```
public class NormalVisitor:ISwitchboardVisitor
{
    public double Visit(Enclosure item)
    {
        return (item.Cost * 1.1);
    }

    public double Visit(Transformer item)
    {
        return (item.Cost * 1.1);
    }

    public double Visit(Busbars item)
    {
        return (item.Cost * 1.1);
    }

    public double Visit(CircuitBreaker item)
    {
        return (item.Cost * 1.1);
    }
}
```

The NormalVisitor class is quite straightforward. All the Visit() methods assume that the cost of packing and shipping the item under consideration is 1.1 times the original cost of the item. Of course, in a more realistic application this logic could be quite complex, but this simple calculation is sufficient for our example.

You can create SpecialVisitor along similar lines or grab it from the code download of this book. Next, add a Switchboard class to the Core folder and write the code shown in Listing 9-36 in it.

Listing 9-36. Switchboard Class Represents the Object Structure

```
public class Switchboard
{
    private ISwitchboardVisitor visitor;

    public List<ISwitchboardItem> Items { get; set; } = new List<ISwitchboardItem>();

    public Switchboard(ISwitchboardVisitor visitor)
    {
        this.visitor = visitor;
    }

    public double Calculate()
    {
        double totalCost = 0;
        foreach (ISwitchboardItem item in Items)
```

```
    {
        totalCost += item.Accept(visitor);
    }
    return totalCost;
    }
}
```

The Switchboard class represents the object structure to be processed by the visitors. It begins by declaring a private variable of type ISwitchboardVisitor. This variable is assigned in the constructor of the class. The Items public property holds a list of switchboard items making the switchboard. The items are added by the client code.

The Calculate() method iterates through the Items list and invokes Accept() on each item. The visitor object is passed to the Accept() method. The cost returned by Accept() is incrementally stored in the totalCost local variable. Once all the items are visited, the totalCost is returned to the caller.

Now add HomeController to the Controllers folder. In addition to the default Index() action, you need to add one action, Calculate(), to the controller. The Calculate() action is shown in Listing 9-37.

Listing 9-37. Calculate() Action Determines the Total Cost

```
[HttpPost]
public IActionResult Calculate(string visitortype)
{
    ISwitchboardVisitor visitor = null;
    if (visitortype == "Normal")
    {
        visitor = new NormalVisitor();
    }
    else
    {
        visitor = new SpecialVisitor();
    }
    Switchboard switchboard = new Switchboard(visitor);
    switchboard.Items.Add(new Enclosure() { Cost = 50000 });
    switchboard.Items.Add(new Transformer() { Cost = 10000 });
    switchboard.Items.Add(new Busbars() { Cost = 5000 });
    switchboard.Items.Add(new CircuitBreaker() { Cost = 20000 });
    double totalCost = switchboard.Calculate();
    ViewBag.PackingShippingType = visitortype;
    ViewBag.TotalCost = totalCost;
    return View();
}
```

The Calculate() action is called when the Calculate button from the Index view is clicked. It receives a visitor type–Normal or Special–through model binding.

The if statement checks the visitor type and accordingly instantiates either NormalVisitor or SpecialVisitor. This instance is stored in the visitor local variable.

Then a new Switchboard object is created by passing the visitor object to the Switchboard's constructor. All four switchboard items are added to the Switchboard object using its Items collection property. Notice that while instantiating the switchboard items such as Enclosure, Busbars, CircuitBreaker, and Transfer, the cost property is also set to a hard-coded value. In a more realistic case the cost would come from a database table.

Once all the items are added to the Switchboard object, its `Calculate()` method is called to calculate the total cost of the switchboard. The packing and shipping type as well as the total cost are stored in ViewBag properties and the Calculate view is returned.

Next, add an Index view to the Views/Home folder and write the markup shown in Listing 9-38 in it.

Listing 9-38. Markup of Index View

```html
<html>
<head>
    <title>Switchboard Cost Calculator</title>
</head>
<body>
    <h1>Calculate Switchboard Cost</h1>
    <form asp-action="Calculate" asp-controller="Home" method="post">
        Select Packing and Shipping Type :
        <select name="visitortype">
            <option>Normal</option>
            <option>Special</option>
        </select>
        <input type="submit" value="Calculate" />
    </form>
</body>
</html>
```

The Index view markup is quite straightforward. It consists of a form tag helper that submits to the `Calculate()` action (asp-action attribute) of the HomeController (asp-controller attribute). The form houses a dropdown list and a button. The dropdown list allows a user to select the type of packing and shipping. The Calculate button submits the form.

Finally, add the Calculate view to the Views/Home folder and write the markup as shown in Listing 9-39 in it.

Listing 9-39. Markup of the Calculate View

```html
<html>
<head>
    <title>Switchboard Cost</title>
</head>
<body>
    <h2>
        Total cost with @ViewBag.PackingShippingType
        packing and shipping is
        Rs. @ViewBag.TotalCost.
    </h2>
</body>
</html>
```

The Calculate view simply forms a message informing the user of the total cost of the selected packing and shipping type. This is done by outputting PackingShippingType and TotalCost ViewBag properties.

This completes the application. Run the application, select desired packing and shipping type, and click on the Calculate button. You should get the total cost depending on the type selected in the dropdown list.

Summary

This chapter covered the remainder of the behavioral patterns, namely state, strategy, template method, and visitor.

The state pattern allows an object to change its behavior when its internal state changes. This change in the behavior is accomplished by utilizing a set of possible state objects.

The strategy pattern isolates an algorithm or strategy to accomplish something in its own class. The different strategies can be used in an interchangeable manner.

The template method pattern outlines the skeleton of the algorithm such that some of the steps involved in the operation can be redefined by subclasses.

The visitor pattern defines an operation that is to be performed on all the elements of an object structure. Additional operations can be defined at any time without changing the object structure under consideration.

The chapters so far have covered all the GoF design patterns. The next chapter is going to discuss some of the Patterns of Enterprise Application Architecture that are commonly used with ASP.NET applications.

■■■

Patterns of Enterprise Application Architecture: Repository, Unit of Work, Lazy Load, and Service Layer

Thus far in this book you have learned the SOLID principles of object-oriented software design and GoF design patterns. This chapter will discuss select patterns of enterprise application architecture.

You were introduced to these patterns of enterprise application architecture in Chapter 1. It's time to delve into a few of those most commonly used in ASP.NET applications in more detail. To that end this chapter will discuss the following patterns along with proof of concept examples:

- Repository

- Unit of Work

- Lazy Load

- Service Layer

The catalog of Patterns of Enterprise Application Architecture includes many other patterns. Due to space constraints this chapter won't cover them all. The idea is to make you familiar with some of these patterns so that you can explore more. The preceding selection of patterns doesn't imply that other patterns are unimportant or are not used in ASP.NET applications. The mentioned patterns are selected simply because they are commonly used in real-world ASP.NET applications.

Overview of P of EAA

Before we go into the details of the patterns mentioned earlier, let's quickly see what an enterprise application is and how these patterns are organized. In his book, *Patterns of Enterprise Application Architecture*, Martin Fowler discusses several characteristics of an enterprise application. It would be worthwhile to take a look at some of them before discussing the P of EAA.

© Bipin Joshi 2016
B. Joshi, *Beginning SOLID Principles and Design Patterns for ASP.NET Developers*,
DOI 10.1007/978-1-4842-1848-8_10

Enterprise Applications are usually large-scale data-driven applications used by a business to get its job done. They include applications such as a payroll system, web-based order-processing system, or an accounting system. Such applications often exhibit the following characteristics:

- They deal with large amounts of data. This data pertains to the business domain. It could be customer records, order history, inventory details, or any such application-specific data. Whatever may be the case, the amount of data the application needs to handle is quite large. Of course, there can't be a precise measure of "large," since each system and business is unique in itself.

- They store data in some data store. The data handled by these applications is quite important for the functioning of the business. Obviously, it needs some persistent storage, such as an RDBMS or a NoSQL database. The database engine is usually separate from the main application. This way the same data can be consumed by many applications if required.

- The data is used in multiuser environment. These applications are usually multiuser systems. That means at a given point in time many users might access the same data. It is possible to overwrite changes made by someone without even knowing anything about it. So, dealing with concurrency and concurrency violations is often required in such applications.

- These applications rely on certain business rules that are known to the business domain experts. These applications capture those rules and translate them into code. The business rules can change at any time. So, even these applications need to be changed or upgraded to take into account the modified or new business rules.

- A business usually performs many operations of varying sizes, and each operation deals with a set of data. The data pertaining to an operation is displayed and manipulated by many pages. So, such applications usually have a lot of user-interface pages.

- All the operations of a business might not be taken care of by a single application. Multiple applications cater to the business, and these applications might need to interact with each other. Thus, application integration might also be required by such systems.

If you review the preceding characteristics, you will find that they basically talk about three distinct areas–data management, business rules, and user interface. That's why modern applications divide the whole application into three conceptual layers:

- Data-access layer

- Business-logic layer

- User-interface or presentation layer

An application that is divided into these three layers can be pictorially represented as shown in Figure 10-1.

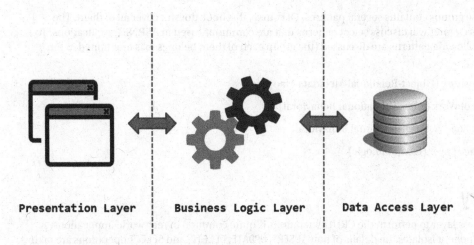

Presentation Layer   Business Logic Layer   Data Access Layer

Figure 10-1. *An application conceptually divided into three layers*

As shown in the figure, the entire application is divided into three conceptual layers. The data-access layer deals with the data store–specific operations, such as Create-Read-Update-Delete (CRUD) and stored procedures. The business-logic layer encapsulates the business-specific processes and rules. It also communicates with the data-access layer to read and write business data to the persistent data store. The presentation layer consists of a user interface (a browser-based user interface in the case of ASP.NET) that displays the data to the end user and also accept input from the end user.

Since each layer deals with a specific task, modifications, extensions, and maintenance of such systems becomes easier. As far as an ASP.NET application is concerned, you may create the data-access layer using ADO.NET, Entity Framework, and class libraries. The business-logic layer usually consists of class libraries or services. And the presentation layer consists of views, Web Forms, or even HTML pages.

It must be noted that this division is said to be conceptual because all three pieces can reside on a single server. For larger systems these layers might be deployed onto different physical servers, resulting in a distributed system. In the latter case they are called tiers. The term *3-tier* is often used to cover both the architectures.

Martin Fowler's book, *Patterns of Enterprise Application Architecture*, groups the patterns in such a way that they can be associated with one of these three layers. The grouping of these patterns is as follows:

- Domain logic patterns
- Data source architectural patterns
- Object-relational behavioral patterns
- Object-relational structural patterns
- Object-relational metadata mapping patterns
- Web presentation patterns
- Distribution patterns
- Offline concurrency patterns
- Session state patterns
- Base patterns

Each of these groups contains several patterns. Of course, this book doesn't cover all of them. The remainder of this chapter will discuss select patterns that are commonly used in ASP.NET applications. To be specific, the following patterns are discussed (the group each of them belongs to is mentioned in the bracket):

- Repository (Object-Relational Metadata Mapping)

- Unit of Work (Object-Relational Behavioral)

- Lazy Load (Object-Relational Behavioral)

- Service Layer (Domain Logic)

Repository

Using a data-access layer to perform the CRUD operations is quite common in real-world applications. A data-access component isolates the details of how INSERT, UPDATE, DELETE, and SELECT operations are taking place in the system. This data-access component is generic in nature because it is used by many other parts of the system.

Now imagine a situation in which you need to perform a same-database operation (say, a complex set of queries) from multiple places. Although a data-access component encapsulates the basic CRUD operations, it won't offer any help in avoiding duplication of these operations. So, you may end up writing the same code in multiple places.

In such cases you can introduce a layer between your domain classes and the data-access layer. This layer will take care of encapsulating operations that can be reused again and again. This layer comes in the form of the repository pattern. **The repository pattern mediates between the data-access layer and the rest of the system. Moreover, it does so by providing collection-like access to the underlying data.**

Once the repository pattern is implemented, the client code won't invoke the data-access component directly. Instead, it will invoke the repository to get the job done. The repository offers a collection interface by providing methods to add, modify, remove, and fetch domain objects.

It is interesting to know that Entity Framework already implements the repository pattern. For example, you can add, modify, remove, and access entities from a DbSet, which is quite similar to a collection. Your code never needs to bother with dealing with ADO.NET objects such as SqlConnection and SqlCommand on its own. You simply use the DbSet and perform the desired operation on it.

As far as ASP.NET applications are concerned, they may use ADO.NET objects or Entity Framework for the database operations. If the application uses ADO.NET objects, the repository pattern is definitely beneficial.

If Entity Framework has already implemented the repository pattern, do you need to implement it again? In simple applications you may not, but in real-world systems adding one more layer between the client code and Entity Framework is beneficial due to the following reasons:

- If you use EF directly in your client, the LINQ queries will be embedded in the client / business-logic layer. This might be undesirable.

- With repository in place, all querying code is isolated from the rest of the application, promoting loose coupling between various layers.

- If you are doing unit testing with a mock data store, you can simply plug in a mock repository instead of the real repository (the one that uses EF). This way the rest of the application code remains unchanged even after switching the repositories.

Design and Explanation

To understand the role of the repository pattern in Entity Framework–driven applications, see Figure 10-2 and Figure 10-3.

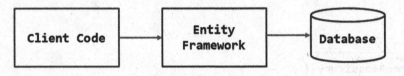

Figure 10-2. *Data access without a repository*

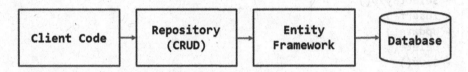

Figure 10-3. *Data access with a repository*

Figure 10-2 shows an application that doesn't implement its own repository. The client code directly invokes operations on the Entity Framework such as LINQ to Entities queries, Add(), Remove(), and SaveChanges(). The Entity Framework then communicates with the underlying database to get the job done. The client code just mentioned could be a business-logic layer or any other piece of code that needs to perform database operations. This setup can be modified to use a repository, as shown in Figure 10-3.

Figure 10-3 shows a repository that sits between the client code and the Entity Framework. In this case the repository encapsulates all the LINQ to Entities queries as well as Add(), Remove(), and SaveChanges() calls. The client invokes methods on the repository. The repository translates those methods into corresponding Entity Framework operations. The Entity Framework then communicates with the underlying database.

Example

Now that you know what the repository pattern is meant for, let's develop an example that builds on this knowledge.

Suppose you are building a data-driven web application that allows its users to add, modify, and delete customers from a database. You wish to facilitate the unit testing and to hide all the querying logic from the client. You decide to implement the repository pattern. Considering these requirements, you can design the system shown in Figure 10-4.

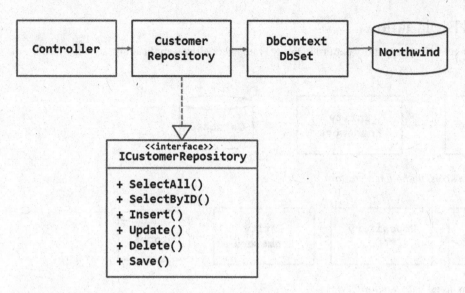

Figure 10-4. *Customer repository mediates between controller and EF*

As shown in the figure, the CustomerRepository sits between the controller and the Entity Framework. Of course, in a larger application you may have a business layer that talks with the repository. What is more important is to know the role of the CustomerRepository.

The CustomerRepository implements the ICustomerRepository interface. The ICustomerRepository interface defines six methods, namely SelectAll(), SelectByID(), Insert(), Update(), Delete(), and Save(). These methods perform the respective tasks. For example, the SelectAll() method executes a LINQ to Entities query against the Customers DbSet and fetches all the Customer entities from the database. Similarly, the Insert() method adds a new Customer to the Customers DbSet.

Note that the ICustomerRepository interface was created so that there can be multiple repository classes that implement it. For example, you can create a mock repository that implements ICustomerRepository and can be used during unit testing.

The CustomerRepository communicates with the Northwind database through Entity Framework DbContext and DbSet.

The application you will develop in this section is shown in Figure 10-5.

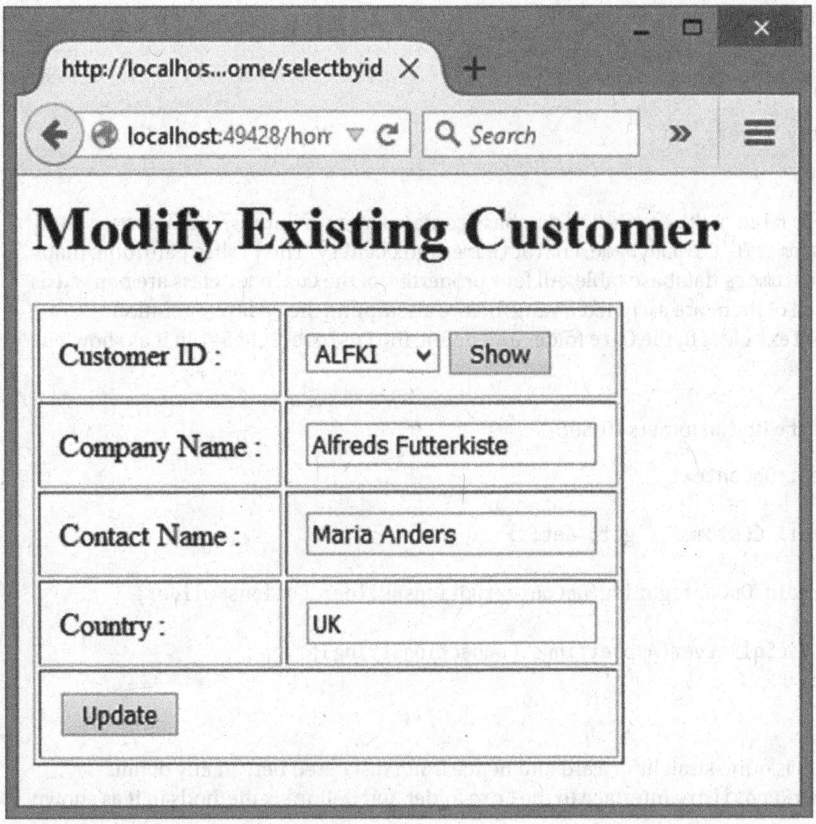

Figure 10-5. *Modifying an existing customer*

Although the CustomerRepository allows us to perform insert, update, as well as delete operations on the Customers table, for the sake of simplicity the application only performs modifications.

The application displays a list of all the CustomerIDs in a dropdown list. Clicking on the Show button displays CompanyName, ContactName, and Country for the selected CustomerID. You can modify the customer details and click on the Update button to save the changes back to the database.

To develop this application, begin by creating a new ASP.NET web application project using Visual Studio and configure it to use MVC and Entity Framework (see Chapter 1 for more details). Also store the database connection string of the Northwind database in the appsettings.json file.

Then add the AppSettings class to the Core folder and add the ConnectionString static property to it. Open the Startup class and write the code to set the ConnectionString property to the one stored in the appsettings.json file. You are already familiar with this piece of code, and hence it's not discussed here.

Now add the Customer class to the Core folder and write the code shown in Listing 10-1 into it.

Listing 10-1. Customer Entity

```
[Table("Customers")]
public class Customer
{
    [Key]
    public string CustomerID { get; set; }
    [Required]
```

315

```
    public string CompanyName { get; set; }
    [Required]
    public string ContactName { get; set; }
    [Required]
    public string Country { get; set; }
}
```

Although the Customers table of the Northwind database contains many columns, the Customer entity uses only four of them: CustomerID, CompanyName, ContactName, and Country. The [Table] attribute maps the Customer class to the Customers database table. All four properties of the Customer class are marked as [Required] to ensure that all of them are assigned a value before attempting the update operation.

Next, add the AppDbContext class to the Core folder and define the Customers DbSet in it as shown in Listing 10-2.

Listing 10-2. AppDbContext with Customers DbSet

```
public class AppDbContext:DbContext
{
    public DbSet<Customer> Customers{ get; set; }

    protected override void OnConfiguring(DbContextOptionsBuilder optionsBuilder)
    {
        optionsBuilder.UseSqlServer(AppSettings.ConnectionString);
    }
}
```

The AppDbContext class is quite straightforward and hence is not discussed here in any detail.

Next, add the ICustomerRepository interface to the Core folder and define six methods in it as shown in Listing 10-3.

Listing 10-3. ICustomerRepository Interface

```
public interface ICustomerRepository
{
    List<Customer> SelectAll();
    Customer SelectByID(string id);
    void Insert(Customer obj);
    void Update(Customer obj);
    void Delete(string id);
    void Save();
}
```

The SelectAll() method, when implemented, is supposed to return a List of Customer entities to the caller. The SelectByID() method accepts a CustomerID as its parameter and returns the Customer matching that ID. The Insert() and Update() methods accept a Customer object and add or update it in the Customers DbSet. The Delete() method accepts a CustomerID and removes a Customer matching that ID from the Customers DbSet. The Save() method propagates the changes made to the Customers DbSet back to the database.

In addition to these six methods, you can add more methods that perform specific tasks.

Now add CustomerRepository class in the Core folder and implement ICustomerRepository interface on it. Listing 10-4 shows the complete code of the CustomerRepository class.

Listing 10-4. CustomerRepository Class Implements ICustomerRepository

```
public class CustomerRepository:ICustomerRepository,IDisposable
{
    private AppDbContext db;

    public CustomerRepository()
    {
        this.db = new AppDbContext();
    }

    public CustomerRepository(AppDbContext db)
    {
        this.db = db;
    }

    public List<Customer> SelectAll()
    {
        return db.Customers.ToList();
    }

    public Customer SelectByID(string id)
    {
        return db.Customers.Where
        (c => c.CustomerID == id).SingleOrDefault();
    }

    public void Insert(Customer obj)
    {
        db.Customers.Add(obj);
    }

    public void Update(Customer obj)
    {
        db.Entry(obj).State = EntityState.Modified;
    }

    public void Delete(string id)
    {
        Customer obj = db.Customers
            .Where(c => c.CustomerID == id)
            .SingleOrDefault();
        db.Customers.Remove(obj);
    }

    public void Save()
    {
        db.SaveChanges();
    }
```

```
public void Dispose()
{
    db.Dispose();
}
}
```

The CustomerRepository class begins by declaring a variable of AppDbContext. This variable, db, is instantiated in the parameter-less constructor of the class. There is also a constructor that accepts an instance of AppDbContext. This way you can either instantiate AppDbContext locally or supply it from outside.

Then the CustomerRepository implements all six methods as defined by the ICustomerRepository interface. The implementation of these methods is quite straightforward and hence is not discussed here. You have already used these Entity Framework operations in previous examples.

Notice how the implementation calls the Add(), Remove(), and SaveChanges() methods on the DbContext. Also notice how modifications are done by setting the State property to EntityState.Modified.

The CustomerRepository also implements IDisposable so that the AppDbContext instance can be disposed of.

Now that our CustomerRepository is ready, let's add the controller that utilizes it.

Add HomeController to the Controllers folder. You need to add three actions–Index(), SelectByID(), and Update()–to the HomeController. The Index() action is shown in Listing 10-5.

Listing 10-5. Index() Fetches All the Customers from the Database

```
public IActionResult Index()
{
    using (CustomerRepository repository = new CustomerRepository())
    {
        List<Customer> customers = repository.SelectAll();
        ViewBag.Customers = from c in customers
                            select new SelectListItem()
                            {
                                Text = c.CustomerID,
                                Value = c.CustomerID
                            };
        return View();
    }
}
```

The Index() action instantiates the CustomerRepository and invokes its SelectAll() method. In order to display a list of CustomerIDs in a dropdown, you need a list of SelectListItem objects (Microsoft. AspNet.Mvc.Rendering namespace). So, a LINQ query is executed that creates SelectListItem objects from the customers List. The Text and Value properties of the SelectListItem class represent the text to be displayed in the dropdown list and its value, respectively.

The list of SelectListItem objects is stored in the Customers ViewBag property so that it can be accessed on the view.

When you select a CustomerID from the dropdown list and click on the Show button, the SelectByID() action is invoked (Listing 10-6).

Listing 10-6. SelectByID() Fetches a Single Customer

```
[HttpPost]
public IActionResult SelectByID(string customerid)
{
    using (CustomerRepository repository = new CustomerRepository())
    {
        Customer data = repository.SelectByID(customerid);
        List<Customer> customers = repository.SelectAll();
        ViewBag.Customers = from c in customers
                            select new SelectListItem()
                            {
                                Text = c.CustomerID,
                                Value = c.CustomerID
                            };
        return View("Index", data);
    }
}
```

The SelectByID() action receives a customerid selected in the dropdown list through model binding. Inside, the code creates a CustomerRepository object and calls its SelectByID() method by passing the customerid value to it. The Customer data variable, thus obtained, acts as the model for the Index view. A list of SelectListItem objects is created as before.

Once the Customer details such as CompanyName, ContactName, and Country are displayed, you can modify them and click on the Update button. At this point the Update() action is called (Listing 10-7).

Listing 10-7. Update() Action Persists the Changes

```
[HttpPost]
public IActionResult Update(Customer obj)
{
    using (CustomerRepository repository = new CustomerRepository())
    {
        repository.Update(obj);
        repository.Save();
        List<Customer> customers = repository.SelectAll();
        ViewBag.Customers = from c in customers
                            select new SelectListItem()
                            {
                                Text = c.CustomerID,
                                Value = c.CustomerID
                            };
        ViewBag.Message = "Customer modified successfully!";
        return View("Index", obj);
    }
}
```

The Update() action receives a Customer object to be modified through model binding. Inside, the code creates a CustomerRepository object and calls its Update() method by passing the Customer object to it. Then the Save() method is called to save the changes to the database. A list of SelectListItem objects is created as before (you could have avoided this duplication by creating a private helper method). A success message is assigned to the Message ViewBag property for displaying on the view.

This completes the controller. Now add an Index view to the Views/Home folder and write the markup shown in Listing 10-8 in it.

Listing 10-8. Markup of the Index View

```
@model Repository.Core.Customer

<h1>Modify Existing Customer</h1>
<form asp-action="Update" asp-controller="Home">
    <table border="1" cellpadding="10">
        <tr>
            <td><label asp-for="CustomerID">Customer ID :</label></td>
            <td>
                <select asp-for="CustomerID" asp-items="@ViewBag.Customers"></select>
                <input type="submit" value="Show" formaction="/home/selectbyid" />
            </td>
        </tr>
        <tr>
            <td><label asp-for="CompanyName">Company Name :</label></td>
            <td><input asp-for="CompanyName" /></td>
        </tr>
        <tr>
            <td><label asp-for="ContactName">Contact Name :</label></td>
            <td><input asp-for="ContactName" /></td>
        </tr>
        <tr>
            <td><label asp-for="Country">Country :</label></td>
            <td><input asp-for="Country" /></td>
        </tr>
        <tr>
            <td colspan="2"><input type="submit" value="Update"/></td>
        </tr>
    </table>
    @ViewBag.Message
</form>
```

The @model directive sets the model for the Index view to the Customer class. The main view consists of a form tag helper that submits the form to the Update() action (asp-action attribute) of the HomeController (asp-controller attribute).

The form consists of a series of labels, a dropdown list, four textboxes, and two buttons. Notice how these tag helpers are bound with the corresponding properties of the Customer model class. Also, notice how the dropdown list is filled with the SelectListItem objects passed through the Customers ViewBag property. This is done using the asp-items attribute of the dropdown list tag helper.

The Show submit button overrides the form's action by submitting the form to the SelectByID() action. This is done by setting its formaction attribute to /home/selectbyid.

Finally, the Message ViewBag property is outputted at the bottom of the page that displays the message assigned from the Update() action.

This completes the application. Run the application and check whether customer details can be modified successfully.

Creating repositories based on a generic interface

In the preceding example you created an ICustomerRepository that was specifically designed with the Customer entity in mind. What if you have many other entities (say Product, Employee, and Order) that also require the same set of methods? Of course, you can create a separate interface for each of them. But you may end up with lots of interfaces that are quite similar in nature (IProductRepository, IEmployeeRepository, IOrderRepository, and so on). In such cases you can create a generic interface that allows you to specify the entity class during its implementation.

Consider the code shown in Listing 10-9.

Listing 10-9. IRepository Is a Generic Interface

```
public interface IRepository<T1,T2> where T1:class
{
    List<T1> SelectAll();
    T1 SelectByID(T2 id);
    void Insert(T1 obj);
    void Update(T1 obj);
    void Delete(T2 id);
    void Save();
}
```

The IRepository interface accepts two generic types: T1 and T2. T1 has a constraint that it must be a class. T1 is the entity class, such as Customer or Employee. T2 is the data type of the primary key. T2 is needed in the SelectByID() and Delete() methods. T2 might be an integer or a string or some other type.

Once created, IRepository can act as a repository interface for many repositories. For example, CustomerRepository can implement IRepository like this:

```
public class CustomerRepository:IRepository<Customer,string>
{
    ...
    ...
}
```

Some other repository, say EmployeeRepository, can implement IRepository like this:

```
public class EmployeeRepository:IRepository<Employee,int>
{
    ...
    ...
}
```

Notice that this time the Employee class is being specified as T1 and integer as T2.

Unit of Work

A business operation may involve multiple steps while it is required that, as a whole, the operation be treated as a single batch or unit. You can resort to database transactions and accomplish the task as follows:

- Begin a database transaction.

- Perform all the steps of the operation one by one against the database.

- Commit or roll back the transaction.

Although this sounds quite straightforward, there is a catch–you are performing individual steps of the operation directly onto the database. So, if an operation involves ten steps, you are creating ten database write operations. Such a large number of small database operations can affect the overall performance of the system.

Wouldn't it be better if you could capture individual steps and then send them to the database engine at once and execute them in a single transaction? That's the idea behind the unit of work pattern. **The unit of work pattern keeps track of your business transaction that is supposed to alter the database in some way. Once the business transaction is over, the tracked steps are played onto the database in a transaction so that the database reflects the desired changes.** Thus the unit of work pattern tracks a business transaction and translates it into a database transaction, wherein steps are collectively run as a single unit.

The good news is that Entity Framework already implements the change tracking for you and also performs the INSERT, UPDATE, and DELETE operations in a transactional batch.

Suppose you have a DbContext housing two DbSet objects, say, Orders and OrderDetails. The Orders DbSet contains information pertaining to an order as a whole, such as OrderID, CustomerID, OrderDate, and ShippingAddress. The OrderDetails DbSet contains details about various items of an order, such as ProductID and Quantity.

Obviously, saving a newly added Order and its details should happen in a transaction. When you add a new Order object to the Orders DbSet, Entity Framework tracks this operation. Similarly, the addition of OrderDetail objects is also tracked. Finally, when you are done you call the SaveChanges() method on the DbContext. At this point, all the changes tracked so far are converted into a batch query. A database transaction is started, the batch is executed, and the transaction is committed (or rolled back if there are any errors). Thus, Entity Framework change tracking and the SaveChanges() method implement the unit of work pattern.

Design and Explanation

In the preceding section you learned the basics of the unit of work pattern. You are also aware that Entity Framework implements this pattern. Now let's see why and how you may still need to implement this pattern in your application.

Consider Figure 10-6, which shows an application with two repositories.

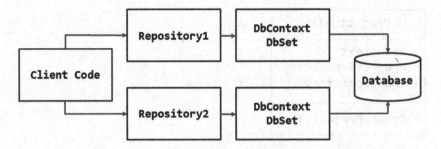

Figure 10-6. *Repositories with independent DbContext objects*

The application consists of two repositories: Repository1 and Repository2. Let's assume that Repository1 and Repository2 handle all the database operations as two independent entities. These repositories instantiate their own DbContext, perform operations on the desired DbSet, and once done call the SaveChanges() method.

So far, so good. Now let's assume that operations performed by Repository1 and Repository2 are to be executed as a single unit of work. The preceding design will fail to achieve that because each repository is using its own DbContext, and each DbContext will create its own transaction when SaveChanges() is called on it.

If you wish to execute a business transaction utilizing these two repositories, they must share the same DbContext. Figure 10-7 shows the modified design of the system.

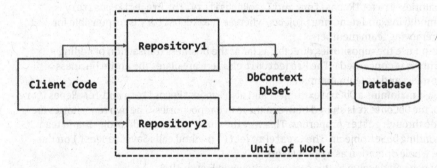

Figure 10-7. *Implementing unit of work with repositories*

The modified design consists of Repository1 and Repository2 sharing the same DbContext object and DbSet objects. Changes made by Repository1 and Repository2 are tracked under a single DbContext and hence form a batch. Moreover, when you invoke SaveChanges() a single database transaction executes the entire batch, making it a unit of work.

Example

Now that you understand how the unit of work pattern works, let's develop an example that implements the design discussed in the preceding section.

Suppose you are building a web application that maintains details about projects executed by a company and about the team members working on those projects. The application allows a user to add a project and its team members. The project details and the team member details are stored in two different database tables–Projects and TeamMembers. You want the addition of a project and its team members to be treated as a unit of work. Considering these requirements, you design the system shown in Figure 10-8.

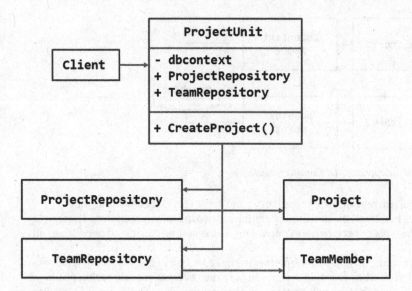

Figure 10-8. *Adding a project and team members as a unit*

The application consists of two entities–Project and TeamMember. The DbContext houses two DbSets, namely Projects and TeamMembers, that hold the respective entities.

There are two repositories–ProjectRepository and TeamRepository. The ProjectRepository is responsible for adding, modifying, and removing projects, whereas TeamRepository is responsible for adding, modifying, and removing team members.

The client code doesn't use the repositories directly (as far as the business transaction of adding a project and its team members is concerned). The ProjectUnit class encapsulates the entire business transaction of adding a project and its team members.

The ProjectUnit class maintains a DbContext object and also ProjectRepository and TeamRepository objects. More important, the DbContext is shared between these two repositories. The two repositories are exposed to the client code through getter properties. This way the client code can add projects and team members to the corresponding DbSet objects. The CreateProject() method calls SaveChanges() on the DbContext executing the whole operation as a unit of work.

The application that you will develop in this section is shown in Figure 10-9.

Figure 10-9. *Adding a new project and its team members*

The application allows you to specify a project name and the names of team members working on it. Upon clicking the Create Project button, data is added to the Projects and TeamMembers tables respectively.

To develop this application, begin by creating a new ASP.NET web application project using Visual Studio and configure it to use MVC and Entity Framework (see Chapter 1 for more details). Also store the database connection string for UnitOfWorkDb–the database used by the application–in the appsettings.json file.

Then add the AppSettings class to the Core folder and add a ConnectionString static property to it. Open the Startup class and write the code to set the ConnectionString property to the one stored in the appsettings.json file. You are already familiar with this piece of code, and hence it's not discussed here.

Now add Project and TeamMember classes to the Core folder and write the code shown in Listing 10-10 in them.

Listing 10-10. Project and TeamMember Entities

```
[Table("Projects")]
public class Project
{
    [Key]
    public Guid ProjectID { get; set; }
    [Required]
    public string ProjectName { get; set; }
}

[Table("TeamMembers")]
public class TeamMember
{
    [DatabaseGenerated(DatabaseGeneratedOption.Identity)]
    public int TeamMemberID { get; set; }
```

325

```
[Required]
public Guid ProjectID { get; set; }
[Required]
public string Name { get; set; }
}
```

The Project class consists of two properties, namely ProjectID and ProjectName. Note that ProjectID is a Guid and serves as the primary key. The Project entity is mapped to the Projects table using [Table] attribute.

The TeamMember class consists of three properties, namely TeamMemberID, ProjectID, and Name. TeamMemberID is an identity column. The [Table] attribute maps the TeamMember class to the TeamMembers table.

Next, add the AppDbContext class to the Core folder and define two DbSet objects in it as shown in Listing 10-11.

Listing 10-11. AppDbContext with Projects and TeamMembers DbSet Objects

```
public class AppDbContext:DbContext
{
    public DbSet<Project> Projects { get; set; }
    public DbSet<TeamMember> TeamMembers { get; set; }

    protected override void OnConfiguring(DbContextOptionsBuilder optionsBuilder)
    {
        optionsBuilder.UseSqlServer(AppSettings.ConnectionString);
    }
}
```

The AppDbContext class is quite straightforward and contains two DbSet objects–Projects and TeamMembers.

Now add a repository interface–IRepository–to the Core folder. Instead of creating two different interfaces for the repositories, this example uses a generic interface as shown in Listing 10-12.

Listing 10-12. IRepository Is a Generic Repository Interface

```
public interface IRepository<T1,T2> where T1:class
{
    List<T1> SelectAll();
    T1 SelectByID(T2 id);
    void Insert(T1 obj);
    void Update(T1 obj);
    void Delete(T2 id);
    void Save();
}
```

You learned about the utility of generic repository interfaces while discussing the repository pattern. Here, you need to create two repositories–ProjectRepository and TeamRepository–that implement the IRepository interface. The complete code of ProjectRepository is shown in Listing 10-13.

Listing 10-13. ProjectRepository Deals with Projects

```
public class ProjectRepository:IRepository<Project,Guid>,IDisposable
{
    private AppDbContext db;

    public ProjectRepository(AppDbContext db)
    {
        this.db = db;
    }

    public List<Project> SelectAll()
    {
        return db.Projects.ToList();
    }

    public Project SelectByID(Guid id)
    {
        return db.Projects.Where(c => c.ProjectID == id)
                        .SingleOrDefault();
    }

    public void Insert(Project obj)
    {
        db.Projects.Add(obj);
    }

    public void Update(Project obj)
    {
        db.Entry(obj).State = EntityState.Modified;
    }

    public void Delete(Guid id)
    {
        Project obj = db.Projects
                        .Where(c => c.ProjectID == id)
                        .SingleOrDefault();
        db.Entry(obj).State = EntityState.Deleted;
    }

    public void Save()
    {
        db.SaveChanges();
    }

    public void Dispose()
    {
        db.Dispose();
    }
}
```

The ProjectRepository class implements IRepository by specifying Project as T1 and Guid as T2. Moreover, the constructor of ProjectRepository accepts an AppDbContext from outside and stores it in a local variable–db. This is important, because you wish to share the same DbContext among multiple repositories.

Further, the class implements all six methods of the IRepository–SelectAll(), SelectByID(), Insert(), Update(), Delete(), and Save(). These methods should look familiar to you, because you worked with them while learning the repository pattern.

The TeamRepository can be developed along similar lines. It will use TeamMember as T1 and int as T2. For the sake of saving some space, the TeamRepository class will not be discussed here. You can grab the complete code of the TeamRepository class from this book's code download.

Now, add a ProjectUnit class to the Core folder and write the code shown in Listing 10-14 in it.

Listing 10-14. ProjectUnit Class

```
public class ProjectUnit
{
    private AppDbContext db;
    private ProjectRepository projectRepository;
    private TeamMemberRepository teamRepository;

    public ProjectUnit()
    {
        db = new AppDbContext();
        projectRepository = new ProjectRepository(db);
        teamRepository = new TeamMemberRepository(db);
    }

    public ProjectRepository ProjectRepository
    {
        get
        {
            return this.projectRepository;
        }
    }

    public TeamMemberRepository TeamRepository
    {
        get
        {
            return this.teamRepository;
        }
    }

    public void CreateProject()
    {
        db.SaveChanges();
    }
}
```

The ProjectUnit class begins by declaring three private variables–AppDbContext, ProjectRepository, and TeamRepository. These variables are instantiated in the constructor of the class. Notice that db is passed to the constructor of both ProjectRepository and TeamRepository. This way both repositories share the same DbContext.

The two public properties–ProjectRepository and TeamRepository–expose the respective private objects to the external world. This way the client code can add the entities to the respective DbSet objects.

The CreateProject() method calls the SaveChanges() method on the AppDbContext object. This is where a database transaction gets created and a batch of operations is executed. Once the execution is complete, the transaction is committed by saving the changes to the database.

Now it's time to create the HomeController, the client to the ProjectUnit class. Add HomeController to the Controllers folder. In addition to the default Index() action, you need to add the CreateProject() action. This action is shown in Listing 10-15.

Listing 10-15. CreateProject() Action

```
[HttpPost]
public IActionResult CreateProject(Project project, List<TeamMember> members)
{
    ProjectUnit unit = new ProjectUnit();
    project.ProjectID = Guid.NewGuid();
    unit.ProjectRepository.Insert(project);
    foreach (var item in members)
    {
        item.ProjectID = project.ProjectID;
        unit.TeamRepository.Insert(item);
    }
    unit.CreateProject();
    ViewBag.Message = "Project created successfully!";
    return View("Index");
}
```

The CreateProject() action is invoked when you click on the Create Project button on the Index view. It receives a Project object and a List of TeamMember objects through model binding.

Inside, the code creates an instance of the ProjectUnit class. The ProjectID property of the Project object is assigned a Guid through the NewGuid() method of the Guid structure.

Then the Project object is added to the Projects DbSet using ProjectRepository. At this time, the Project object gets added to the Projects DbSet, but it is not yet added to the database.

A foreach loop iterates through the members List and adds the TeamMember objects to the TeamMembers DbSet using TeamRepository.

Once all team members are added, the CreateProject() method of the ProjectUnit class is called to save all the changes back to the database. A success message is also stored in the ViewBag.

Let's complete the application by adding the Index view. Add the Index view to the Views/Home folder and write the markup shown in Listing 10-16 in it.

Listing 10-16. Markup of the Index View

```
<h1>Add New Project</h1>
<form asp-action="CreateProject" asp-controller="Home" method="post">
    <table border="1" cellpadding="10">
        <tr>
            <td>Project Name : </td>
            <td><input name="ProjectName" type="text"/></td>
        </tr>
```

```
        <tr>
            <td>Team Members : </td>
            <td>
                <input name="members[0].Name" type="text" />
                <br /><br />
                <input name="members[1].Name" type="text" />
            </td>
        </tr>
        <tr>
            <td colspan="2"><input type="submit" value="Create Project"/></td>
        </tr>
    </table>
    @ViewBag.Message
</form>
```

The Index view consists of a form rendered through form tag helper. The form is submitted to the CreateProject() action (asp-action attribute) of the HomeController (asp-controller attribute).

The form houses a textbox for entering the ProjectName, two textboxes for specifying team member names, and a Submit button. Of course, in a more realistic application you would have the ability to enter as many team members as you wanted. Notice the naming convention used with the textboxes accepting team member names. This naming convention ensures that the model-binding framework converts the values into a List of TeamMember objects.

The Message assigned from the CreateProject() action is outputted at the bottom of the page.

This completes the application. Before running the application, you will need to create the UnitOfWorkDb database with Projects and TeamMembers tables (refer Chapter 1 for more details). Once the database and tables are created, run the application and try adding a new project.

Lazy Load

Usually when you receive an object from a data-access layer or a service, it contains all the data exposed by its properties. Consider a data-access layer that returns a list of Customer objects based on the customer data stored in the database. Each Customer object from this list represents a customer, and details such as CustomerID, CompanyName, ContactName, and Country are loaded into the respective properties of the object.

This is what is expected in most situations. However, at times you may want to deviate from this behavior. Suppose, the Customer class contains a collection property named Orders. The Orders collection is supposed to contain a list of all the orders placed by that Customer in the form of Order objects. Under normal circumstances, the Orders collection would also be filled in with the required data and returned from the data-access layer. However, imagine a situation where only Customer contact details are required. The orders placed by the customer are not needed at all. Obviously, loading the Orders collection at the time of Customer instantiation is wasteful. It would be nice to load order information only if it is needed. In fact, that's the idea behind the lazy load pattern.

The lazy load pattern is used to load data required by an object after it is instantiated. So, an object instance is available to your code, but all of its properties may not contain the data they are supposed to expose. The object knows how to load that data whenever required. Usually, the data is loaded only when a property is accessed for the first time. All the properties of an object may not support lazy loading. The properties that are resource intensive or hold bulky data are loaded in a lazy manner whereas the others are loaded as usual.

Design and Explanation

Although the fundamental idea behind the lazy load pattern is to load data after an object has been initialized, there are various ways to implement this idea. The common techniques used to implement the lazy load pattern are listed here:

- **Lazy initialization:** In this technique a class field that is to be lazy loaded is initially kept empty. Every time the field is accessed it is checked as to whether it is empty or not. If it is empty then data is fetched and loaded into the field. This requires you to shield the field inside a getter property. The getter property does the checking and loading of data as explained previously.

- **Virtual proxy:** A virtual proxy is an object that closely resembles the original object but doesn't hold any data. The data is loaded only when any of its methods are called.

- **Value holder:** A value holder is an object that wraps the actual object to be used. Initially the object is empty. You need to ask the value holder for its value. At that time the value holder checks whether the object has been loaded or not and loads the data if not already loaded.

- **Ghost:** A ghost is the actual object needed by the application with only partially loaded data. Initially the ghost contains only the ID (or whatever the primary key is) of the object. Whenever the code attempts to access any field of the object, the object is loaded with the complete data.

This chapter will not cover all of these techniques. The first one—lazy initialization—is a simple technique that can be implemented in your applications and hence will discussed here. The .NET Framework supports lazy initialization through the System.Lazy class. That is also discussed in later sections.

To understand how the lazy load pattern works through lazy initialization, see Figure 10-10.

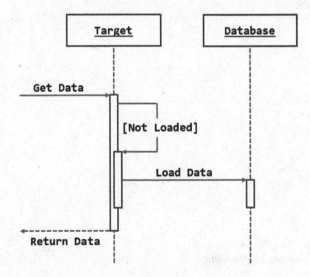

Figure 10-10. *Lazy load pattern through lazy initialization*

Suppose there is an object—Target— that has a public property—say, Data. The Data property exposes a private field, _data, that is intended to hold the data from the database. Further assume that the data to be stored in the _data field is quite bulky and hence needs to be loaded in lazy manner.

Initially, when the client code creates the Target object the _data field is empty. When the client code accesses the Data public property, the property checks whether _data is empty or not. It could be a simple check against a null value. If _data is not loaded yet, a query is executed, and the required data is fetched from the database. The returned data is then loaded into the _data field, and the Data property returns that data to the caller.

When the Data property is accessed again, the data is already loaded in the _data field and hence can be returned to the caller immediately. Thus, the Data property is lazy initialized, and the Target object supports the lazy load pattern.

Example

Now that you know what the lazy load pattern is, let's build an example that illustrates how it works.

Suppose you are building a web application that deals with customers and their orders. The orders are grabbed by employees of the company and are placed into the system through a web interface.

The employee data is needed by the human resources department of the company for various purposes. Most of the time, employee details such as name, designation, and phone number are needed. However, during performance reviews or pay increases, details about the orders brought in by an employee are necessary.

As you might have guessed, all attributes of an employee other than orders are required very frequently. It makes sense to make them available as soon as an employee object is created. The orders data, however, can be loaded if and when required. So, orders data is a good candidate for the lazy load pattern. In this case, you will go for lazy initialization of the property returning orders.

Considering these requirements, you may load the orders as shown in Figure 10-11.

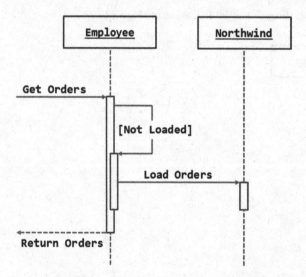

Figure 10-11. *Loading orders placed by an employee using lazy loading*

This example uses the Northwind database as its data store. The Employees table of the Northwind database contains employee information such as EmployeeID, FirstName, and LastName. The Orders table contains a list of orders placed in the system. Each order has the EmployeeID of the employee who placed that order. So, for a single EmployeeID there could be zero or more orders. The Orders property of the Employee class implements lazy initialization.

Initially, when an Employee object is created, the Orders property is set to null. When the client code accesses the Orders property for the first time, a database query is fired, and all the orders placed by that employee are fetched. The data that is returned is stored in a private collection variable. The Orders property then returns the collection to the caller. Subsequent calls to the Orders property simply return the orders already fetched from the database.

The application that you will develop in this section is shown in Figure 10-12.

Figure 10-12. *Application loading orders using lazy initialization*

The application consists of a textbox to enter an EmployeeID. Clicking on the Show button displays a list of orders placed by that employee.

To develop this application, begin by creating a new ASP.NET web application project using Visual Studio and configure it to use MVC (see Chapter 1 for more details). This example doesn't use Entity Framework. Instead, it uses an ADO.NET object model for data access. So, store the database connection string of the Northwind database in the appsettings.json file.

Then add the AppSettings class to the Core folder and add the ConnectionString static property to it. Open the Startup class and write the code to set the ConnectionString property to the one stored in the appsettings.json file. You are already familiar with this piece of code, and hence it will not be discussed here.

Now, add the Order class to the Core folder and define properties as shown in Listing 10-17.

Listing 10-17. Order Class

```
public class Order
{
    public int OrderID { get; set; }
    public DateTime OrderDate { get; set; }
}
```

Although the Orders table contains many more columns, the Order class contains only two properties—OrderID and OrderDate.

Then add the Employee class to the Core folder. The skeleton of the Employee class is shown in Listing 10-18.

Listing 10-18. Skeleton of the Employee Class

```
public class Employee
{
    private List<Order> orders = null;

    public int EmployeeID { get; set; }
    public string FirstName { get; set; }
    public string LastName { get; set; }
    public string Title { get; set; }

    public Employee(int id)
    {
      ...
    }

    public List<Order> Orders
    {
      ...
    }

}
```

The Employee class consists of a constructor and five public properties. The code begins by declaring a private List of Order objects. Initially, the orders list is null.

Then the class defines four properties—EmployeeID, FirstName, LastName, and Title. These properties are loaded in the constructor of the class.

The constructor of the class accepts an employee ID and loads data into the preceding four properties. The orders list is not filled at this point in time. The Orders public property lazy initializes the orders list and will be discussed shortly.

The code that loads EmployeeID, FirstName, LastName, and Title properties in the constructor is shown in Listing 10-19.

Listing 10-19. Loading Properties During Object Initialization

```
public Employee(int id)
{
    this.EmployeeID = id;

    SqlConnection cnn = new SqlConnection(AppSettings.ConnectionString);
    SqlCommand cmd = new SqlCommand("select employeeid,firstname,lastname,title from
    employees where employeeid=@id", cnn);
```

```
        cmd.Parameters.Add(new SqlParameter("@id",id));
        cnn.Open();
        SqlDataReader reader = cmd.ExecuteReader();
        while(reader.Read())
        {
            this.FirstName = reader.GetString(1);
            this.LastName = reader.GetString(2);
            this.Title = reader.GetString(3);
        }
        cnn.Close();
}
```

The code sets the EmployeeID property to the id passed to the constructor. Then a new SqlConnection object (System.Data.SqlClient namespace) is created, and the connection string of the Northwind database is passed to its constructor.

Then an SqlCommand object is created by specifying a SELECT query and the SqlConnection object created earlier. The SELECT query fetches EmployeeID, FirstName, LastName, and Title columns from the Employees table for a specific employee ID. The query is parameterized and hence an SqlParameter object containing the EmployeeID value is added to the command's Parameters collection.

The database connection is opened using the Open() method, and the query is executed by calling the ExecuteReader() method of SqlCommand. The ExecuteReader() method returns an SqlDataReader object.

A while loop and Read() method iterate through the SqlDataReader, and the FirstName, LastName, and Title properties of the Employee object under consideration are loaded. Note that the code uses the GetString() method to read values of columns because all the columns contain string data.

The database connection is then closed. At this point in time all the properties except Orders contain the desired data.

The Orders property that loads the orders list is shown in Listing 10-20.

Listing 10-20. Loading Orders by Lazy Initialization

```
public List<Order> Orders
{
    get
    {
        if(this.orders==null)
        {
            SqlConnection cnn = new SqlConnection(AppSettings.ConnectionString);
            SqlCommand cmd = new SqlCommand("select orderid,orderdate from orders where
            employeeid=@id", cnn);
            cmd.Parameters.Add(new SqlParameter("@id", this.EmployeeID));
            cnn.Open();
            SqlDataReader reader = cmd.ExecuteReader();
            if(reader.HasRows)
            {
                this.orders = new List<Order>();
            }
            while(reader.Read())
            {
                Order order = new Order()
                {
                    OrderID = reader.GetInt32(0),
                    OrderDate = reader.GetDateTime(1)
                };
```

```
                this.orders.Add(order);
            }
            cnn.Close();
        }
        return this.orders;
    }
}
```

The Orders property contains only a getter block. Notice the code marked in bold letters. The if statement checks whether the orders list is null or not. Recollect that the orders list is assigned a null value at the time of variable declaration.

If the Orders property is being accessed for the first time, the orders list will be null and the code from the if block gets executed. The code is quite similar to what you wrote in the constructor earlier, with a few differences.

The code executes a SELECT statement that fetches all the orders (OrderID and OrderDate columns) where EmployeeID is same as the EmployeeID property. Then the HasRows property of the SqlDataReader is checked to see whether any rows have been returned. If there are rows in the SqlDataReader, the orders list is initialized to a new List of Order objects.

A while loop and Read() method are used to read the order data. For every order row, an Order object is created, and its OrderID and OrderDate properties are set to the values gotten from the respective columns. Notice that the code uses GetInt32() for the OrderID column because OrderID is an integer, and uses GetDateTime() for the OrderDate column since it holds date and time data.

All the orders for an EmployeeID are added to the orders list, and the database connection is closed. The Orders property then returns the orders list to the caller.

Next, add HomeController to the Controllers folder. In addition to the Index() action, you need to add the GetDetails() action as shown in Listing 10-21.

Listing 10-21. GetDetails() Action Causes Orders to Load

```
public IActionResult GetDetails(int employeeid)
{
    Employee emp = new Employee(employeeid);
    return View("Index",emp);
}
```

The GetDetails() action is called when you click the Show button. It receives an employee ID as entered in the textbox through model binding. An Employee object is then created by supplying this employee ID. At this point in time, the Orders property is not yet loaded. The Employee object thus created is passed to the Index view as its model.

Now add the Index view to the Views/Home folder and write the markup shown in Listing 10-22 in it.

Listing 10-22. Markup of the Index View

```
@model LazyLoad.Core.Employee

<h2>Employee ID :</h2>
<form asp-action="GetDetails" asp-controller="Home" method="post">
    <input type="text" name="employeeid" />
    <input type="submit" value="Show" />
    <br />
    <br />
```

```
@if (Model != null)
{
<h4>Orders placed by @Model.FirstName @Model.LastName (@Model.Title)</h4>
<div>
    <table border="1" cellpadding="10">
        @foreach (var item in Model.Orders)
        {
            <tr>
                <td>#@item.OrderID</td>
                <td>@item.OrderDate</td>
            </tr>

        }
    </table>
</div>
}
</form>
```

The Index view renders a form using a form tag helper. The form houses the EmployeeID textbox and the Show button. The Show button submits the form to the GetDetails() action (asp-action attribute) of the HomeController (asp-controller attribute).

Then the if statement checks whether the Model property is null. Initially, when the view is rendered for the first time, the Model property will be null and hence no table is rendered.

When you enter an employee ID and click the Show button, GetDetails() is invoked and an Employee object is sent to the view. The employee details, such as FirstName, LastName, and Title are displayed at the top of the table. The foreach loop iterates through the Orders property of the Employee model object. This is where the orders list gets populated. Each Order's OrderID and OrderDate are displayed in a table.

This completes the application. Run the application and enter a valid employee ID in the textbox. Upon clicking the Show button, the view should display a list of orders placed by that employee.

Using .NET Framework's System.Lazy Class

The .NET Framework's Lazy class readily provides support for lazy initialization of objects. To use this class, you create an instance of the Lazy class, specifying the type you wish to be lazy initialized. The actual class is instantiated when you access the Value property of the Lazy object for the first time. This way, object instantiation is deferred until you actually need the object.

The Lazy class comes in handy when you are dealing with resource-intensive objects that may or may not be used by your code. Instantiating such objects in advance may prove to be wasteful if, during the course of processing, they aren't used at all. The Lazy class also allows you to execute resource-intensive initialization code while creating the object.

To understand how the Lazy class works, consider the following code fragment:

```
Lazy<Customer> lazyObj = new Lazy<Customer>();
...
Customer obj = lazyObj.Value;
```

The first line of code creates an instance of the Lazy class by specifying Customer as the generic target type. At this line, the object of Customer is not created. Somewhere later in the code, when you actually need the Customer object, the code accesses the Value property of the Lazy object. Since it is the first time the Value is being accessed, the Lazy object creates an object of Customer and returns it to the calling code. Subsequent calls to the Lazy object will return the Customer object that has already been created.

The Lazy class also allows you to specify an initialization code that creates the target object. The following code fragment will make this usage clear:

```
Lazy<Customer> lazyObj = new Lazy<Customer>(()=>{
    Customer obj = new Customer();
    //do something more with obj
    return obj;
});
```

As you can see, this time the constructor of the Lazy class takes a factory method in the form of a lambda expression. The factory method creates the Customer object and may perform some processing on it. The Customer object is then returned from the method.

Just to understand the usefulness of the Lazy class, consider a hypothetical report-generator class. The report generator generates three reports—Customer Listing, Order History, and Employee Listing—through three independent methods. Let's assume that the Customer data required by the report generator comes from some resource-intensive operation.

One may think of designing the report generator shown in Listing 10-23.

Listing 10-23. Report Generator Using Local CustomerData Object

```
public class ReportGenerator
{
    public void GenerateCustomerReport()
    {
        CustomerData data = new CustomerData();
        //use data to generate report
    }

    public void GenerateOrderHistoryReport()
    {
        CustomerData data = new CustomerData();
        //use data to generate report
    }

    public void GenerateEmployeeReport()
    {
        //no need of Customer data
        //generate employee report
    }
}
```

As you can see, two methods, namely GenerateCustomerReport() and GenerateOrderHistoryReport(), are creating local objects of the CustomerData class. If the client code needs to generate both these reports, it will be creating the resource-intensive CustomerData object twice. This is undesired.

To rectify this problem one may change the design as shown in Listing 10-24.

Listing 10-24. Creating Global CustomerData Object

```
public class ReportGenerator
{
    private CustomerData data = new CustomerData();
```

```
public void GenerateCustomerReport()
{
    //use data to generate report
}

public void GenerateOrderHistoryReport()
{
    //use data to generate report
}

public void GenerateEmployeeReport()
{
    //no need of Customer data
    //generate employee report
}
}
```

In this case, the CustomerData object is created even though the client code may not use it all. For example, the client code may generate just the third report by using the GenerateEmployeeReport() method. Thus, the CustomerData object gets created but is never used.

Using the Lazy class can solve both these issues, as shown in Listing 10-25.

Listing 10-25. Using Lazy to Lazy Initialize CustomerData

```
public class ReportGenerator
{
    Lazy<CustomerData> lazyObj = new Lazy<CustomerData>();

    public void GenerateCustomerReport()
    {
        CustomerData data = lazyObj.Value;
        //use data to generate report
    }

    public void GenerateOrderHistoryReport()
    {
        CustomerData data = lazyObj.Value;
        //use data to generate report
    }

    public void GenerateEmployeeReport()
    {
        //no need of Customer data
        //generate employee report
    }
}
```

In this case, a Lazy object is created as a class-level member. At this point, the CustomerData object is not yet created.

If you call GenerateCustomerReport() or GenerateOrderHistoryReport(), CustomerData gets instantiated. That's because their code accesses the Value property of lazyObj. Moreover, if you call both of these methods, the same instance (created when Value was accessed for the first time) would be used by both of them.

If you call only the third method—GenerateEmployeeReport()—no CustomerData object gets created because the Value property of lazyObj has not been accessed.

Service Layer

An application being accessed over the web need not have only a web-based user interface. In addition to the web-based user interface, it may have a Windows (desktop) interface or a mobile interface. In such cases, it is helpful to encapsulate and expose the functionality of the application as one or more services. The services are then accessed by multiple clients, including web, Windows, and mobile clients.

The service layer pattern is useful in such situations. **The service layer pattern exposes an application's functionality as a layer of services, thus defining the boundary of the application for the clients.** The services expose the operations the client can invoke and also take care of the nitty-gritties of those operations, such as data access, business logic, and workflow.

The client applications need not know the internals of the services or how they function. All they need to know is a set of operations that can be invoked to get the job done. The data involved in the operations is not directly exposed to the clients; rather, a business operation or task is exposed to them.

The service layer pattern can be useful even if there is just the web interface to an application. Consider a Single-Page Application (SPA) or an application that heavily uses Ajax to function. In such cases the client-side JavaScript code needs to invoke server-side business functionality through Ajax calls. The server-side functionality can be encapsulated in one or more services. The services can then be consumed by the client-side JavaScript.

The service layer pattern can be used to expose application functionality that is shared by multiple web applications. For example, a company with expertise in a business domain may expose certain functionality as services, thus allowing their clients to consume it in their respective applications.

Design and Explanation

The overall design of the service layer pattern is shown in Figure 10-13.

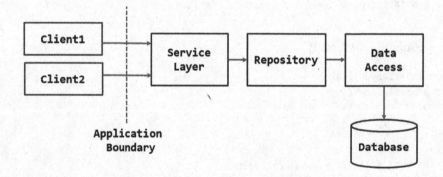

Figure 10-13. *Using the service layer in ASP.NET applications*

All the data access needed in a given business operation is handled by the repositories. Of course, it is not mandatory for a service layer to use repositories. Since many ASP.NET applications use the repository pattern, it is assumed here that repositories are being used for data manipulation.

The service layer deals with the repository and performs data-centric operations. These could be simple CRUD operations or complex data-centric operations.

Where would the business logic go? There are two possible ways to invoke the business logic involved in the operation:

- The domain objects themselves can include the associated business logic.

- The service layer can include the required business logic.

If an application is using the former way to encapsulate the business logic, the service layer will simply call the appropriate methods on the domain objects. On the other hand, if an application is using the latter approach, the service includes the code to perform the business processing involved in an operation. The figure assumes this latter approach.

The client applications Client1 and Client2 access the service layer to perform an operation. All they know is a set of operations exposed by the service layer. They don't need to know the internals (such as repositories, data access, and database) of the service layer.

Example

Now that you know what the service layer pattern is, let's illustrate it with an example.

Suppose you are building an application for a stock-trading company. The application performs two basic operations—buy stocks and sell stocks. Multiple client applications need to invoke these operations:

- A Windows-based desktop application is used by the staff of the company. They take buy / sell orders from their clients over the phone and invoke them as and when required.

- A web application is used by their customers. The customers log on to the web application and buy / sell stocks themselves.

- A mobile application is also made available to the customers. They can buy /sell stocks conveniently using a smartphone.

Considering these requirements, it makes sense to expose the business operations needed by the application as a service. The service can then be consumed over the web by all client types. Figure 10-14 shows the overall setup of the application.

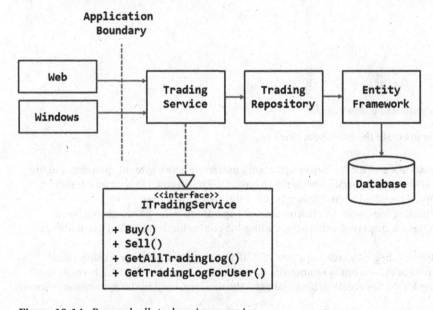

Figure 10-14. *Buy and sell stocks using a service*

The operations that need to be exposed to the clients are encapsulated by a service—the `TradingService`. The service is based on an interface, `ITradingService`, consisting of four operations—`Buy()`, `Sell()`, `GetAllTradingLog()`, and `GetTradingLogForUser()`.

The implementation of the `Buy()` method buys a specified number of shares of a stock. The `Sell()` method sells a specified number of shares of a stock. For the sake of simplicity, this example simply adds a database entry in the database signifying the buy or sell operation. Of course, in a more realistic application many more steps might be involved.

The `GetAllTradingLog()` method returns all the buy / sell transaction-log entries. This method is called by the staff of the company (Windows client). The `GetTradingLogForUser()` method returns the transaction log only for a specific user. This method is used by the end customers (web and mobile clients) to see their past transaction history.

The `TradingService` relies on the `TradingRepository` to perform the database operations. The `TradingRepository` in turn uses Entity Framework for data access.

For the sake of simplicity, this example will build only the web client and will use jQuery Ajax to invoke the `TradingService`. The application you will develop in this example is shown in Figure 10-15.

Figure 10-15. *Application to invoke the TradingService*

The application consists of a series of textboxes that accept username, stock symbol, quantity, and unit price. The dropdown list allows you to specify whether it's a buy or sell operation. Clicking on the Submit button invokes the appropriate method of the `TradingService` through jQuery Ajax.

You can also see the trading-log entries by click on the Get Log button. If the associated textbox is kept empty, all the log entries are displayed; otherwise, trading-log entries for the specified username are displayed.

To develop this application, begin by creating a new ASP.NET web application project using Visual Studio and configure it to use MVC and Entity Framework (see Chapter 1 for more details). Also store the database connection string for the `ServiceLayerDb` database—the database used by the application—in the `appsettings.json` file.

Then add the AppSettings class to the Core folder and add the ConnectionString static property to it. Open the Startup class and write the code to set the ConnectionString property to be the one stored in the appsettings.json file. You are already familiar with this piece of code, and hence it will not be discussed here.

Now add the StockTradingEntry class to the Core folder and define the properties in it as shown in Listing 10-26.

Listing 10-26. StockTradingEntry Class

```
[Table("StockTradingLog")]
public class StockTradingEntry
{
    [DatabaseGenerated(DatabaseGeneratedOption.Identity)]
    public int Id { get; set; }
    [Required]
    [StringLength(20)]
    public string UserName { get; set; }
    [Required]
    [StringLength(40)]
    public string Symbol { get; set; }
    [Required]
    public decimal UnitPrice { get; set; }
    [Required]
    public int Quantity { get; set; }
    [Required]
    public DateTime TimeStamp { get; set; }
    [Required]
    [StringLength(10)]
    public string Operation { get; set; }
}
```

The StockTradingEntry class is mapped to the StockTradingLog table and consists of seven properties, namely Id, UserName, Symbol, UnitPrice, Quantity, TimeStamp, and Operation.

The Id property is the primary key (identity value). The UserName property indicates the name of the user performing the buy or sell operation. The Symbol and UnitPrice properties indicate the stock symbol and the unit price of that stock, respectively. The Quantity property indicates the number of stocks purchased or sold during the Operation (BUY / SELL). The TimeStamp property is the date and time at which the operation took place.

Next, add the AppDbContext class that defines the StockTradingLog DbSet, as shown in Listing 10-27.

Listing 10-27. AppDbContext Class with StockTradingLog DbSet

```
public class AppDbContext:DbContext
{
    public DbSet<StockTradingEntry> StockTradingLog { get; set; }

    protected override void OnConfiguring(DbContextOptionsBuilder optionsBuilder)
    {
        optionsBuilder.UseSqlServer(AppSettings.ConnectionString);
    }
}
```

343

Next, add the ITradingRepository interface to the Core folder and modify it as shown in Listing 10-28.

Listing 10-28. ITradingRepository Defines an Interface for the Repository

```
public interface ITradingRepository
{
    List<StockTradingEntry> SelectAll();
    List<StockTradingEntry> SelectForUser(string user);
    void Insert(StockTradingEntry obj);
    void Update(StockTradingEntry obj);
    void Delete(int id);
}
```

The ITradingRepository interface contains definitions for five methods, namely SelectAll(), SelectForUser(), Insert(), Update(), and Delete(). We won't go into the details of repository interfaces and the repository, since you are already familiar with the repository pattern.

Then add the TradingRepository class to the Core folder and implement the ITradingRepository interface in it (Listing 10-29).

Listing 10-29. TradingRepository Repository Class

```
public class TradingRepository:ITradingRepository
{
    public List<StockTradingEntry> SelectAll()
    {
        using (AppDbContext db = new AppDbContext())
        {
            return db.StockTradingLog.ToList();
        }
    }

    public List<StockTradingEntry> SelectForUser(string user)
    {
        using (AppDbContext db = new AppDbContext())
        {
            return db.StockTradingLog.Where(i => i.UserName == user).ToList();
        }
    }

    public void Insert(StockTradingEntry obj)
    {
        using (AppDbContext db = new AppDbContext())
        {
            db.StockTradingLog.Add(obj);
            db.SaveChanges();
        }
    }

    public void Update(StockTradingEntry obj)
    {
        throw new NotImplementedException();
    }
```

```
public void Delete(int id)
{
    throw new NotImplementedException();
}
}
```

The TradingRepository class is quite straightforward and implements all the methods defined by the ITradingRepository interface. Notice that there is no separate Save() method here. The Insert(), Update(), and Delete() methods themselves call SaveChanges(). For this specific example, the code skips the implementation of Update() and Delete() by throwing a NotImplementedException. That's because this example doesn't need to perform update and delete operations. Also notice that both select methods return a List of StockTradingEntry objects–all entries or entries for a specific user, respectively.

The StockTradingEntry entity is the internal representation of the data. The client applications send an object of the BuySellDetails class to the TradingService. The BuySellDetails class is shown in Listing 10-30.

Listing 10-30. Clients Use BuySellDetails Class to Pass Data

```
public class BuySellDetails
{
    public string UserName { get; set; }
    public string Symbol { get; set; }
    public decimal UnitPrice { get; set; }
    public int Quantity { get; set; }
    public DateTime TimeStamp { get; set; }
}
```

The BuySellDetails class is a simple class and consists of properties, namely UserName, Symbol, UnitPrice, Quantity, and TimeStamp.

Now you are ready to build the TradingService service. The TradingService is based on the ITradingService interface. So, add it to the Core folder and define the methods in it as shown in Listing 10-31.

Listing 10-31. ITradingService Interface Is the Dervice Interface

```
public interface ITradingService
{
    bool Buy(BuySellDetails obj);
    bool Sell(BuySellDetails obj);
    List<StockTradingEntry> GetAllTradingLog();
    List<StockTradingEntry> GetTradingLogForUser(string user);
}
```

The ITradingService interface outlines four methods, namely Buy(), Sell(), GetAllTradingLog(), and GetTradingLogForUser().

The Buy() and Sell() methods perform the respective operations. They pass to the service a BuySellDetails object that contains the details about the operation, such as stock to be purchased and quantity. These methods return a Boolean value indicating the success (true) or failure (false) of the operation.

The GetAllTradingLog() and GetTradingLogForUser() methods return a List of StockTradingEntry objects to the caller. The former method returns all the entries from the database, whereas the latter method accepts a username whose log entries are to be returned.

Before you go ahead and implement the ITradingService interface, note the following:

- There are different approaches to creating a service. For example, one can use the REST-style Web API service. You can also create a controller and invoke its actions from a client. We won't go into the pros and cons of these approaches. It is sufficient to say that this example uses the latter approach.

- This example uses a controller as a service. The controller class acting as a service can be placed inside the Controllers folder.

- The service can be invoked by using either Ajax or HttpClient (or similar) component. The choice between the two depends on the type of the client you need to develop. For example, if you wish to call the service from the web pages of the same application, then Ajax is more suitable since both the service and the client pages belong to the same origin. However, if the service and the client are part of different web applications, HttpClient is more suitable.

Now, add the StockTradingServiceController class to the Controllers folder. Listing 10-32 shows the skeleton of this service class.

Listing 10-32. Skeleton of TradingService Class

```
public class TradingServiceController : Controller,ITradingService
{
    public bool Buy(BuySellDetails obj)
    {
    }

    public bool Sell(BuySellDetails obj)
    {
    }

    public List<StockTradingEntry> GetAllTradingLog()
    {
    }

    public List<StockTradingEntry> GetTradingLogForUser(string user)
    {
    }
}
```

The TradingService controller inherits from the Controller class and also implements the ITradingService interface. The implementation of the Buy() operation is shown in Listing 10-33.

Listing 10-33. Implementing the Buy() Operation

```
public bool Buy(BuySellDetails obj)
{
    TradingRepository repository = new TradingRepository();
    StockTradingEntry entry = new StockTradingEntry();
    entry.UserName = obj.UserName;
    entry.Symbol = obj.Symbol;
    entry.Quantity = obj.Quantity;
    entry.UnitPrice = obj.UnitPrice;
```

```
    entry.Operation = "BUY";
    entry.TimeStamp = obj.TimeStamp;
    repository.Insert(entry);
    return true;
}
```

The Buy() operation receives a BuySellDetails object as its parameter. Inside, the code instantiates a TradingRepository object and also a StockTradingEntry object. It then transfers the data from the BuySellDetails object to the StockTradingEntry object. The Operation property of StockTradingEntry is set to BUY since this is a buy operation. The StockTradingEntry object is saved to the database by calling the Insert() method on the TradingRepository.

The Buy() method simply returns true, indicating that the operation was successful. In a more realistic situation you would have some error trapping or business processing that decides the outcome of the operation.

The Sell() operation implementation is quite similar to that of Buy(). The only difference is that the Operation property of StockTradingEntry is set to SELL. The Sell() operation will not be discussed here so as to save some space.

The GetAllTradingLog() and GetTradingLogForUser() operations are quite straightforward and are shown in Listing 10-34.

Listing 10-34. Returning Trading Log Entries

```
public List<StockTradingEntry> GetAllTradingLog()
{
    TradingRepository repository = new TradingRepository();
    return repository.SelectAll();
}

public List<StockTradingEntry> GetTradingLogForUser(string user)
{
    TradingRepository repository = new TradingRepository();
    return repository.SelectForUser(user);
}
```

The GetAllTradingLog() method creates a TradingRepository object and invokes the SelectAll() method on it. Similarly, the GetTradingLogForUser() method invokes the SelectForUser() method by passing the username as its parameter.

This completes the TradingService. To create the client, first add HomeController to the Controllers folder and then add an Index view to the Views/Home folder.

The Index view consists of two <form> elements—the one that calls buy / sell operations and the other that lists the trading-log entries. The first <form> is shown in Listing 10-35.

Listing 10-35. Form That Allows Buy / Sell of Stocks

```
<form>
    <table>
        <tr>
            <td>User Name : </td>
            <td><input id="username" type="text" /></td>
        </tr>
```

```
    <tr>
        <td>Symbol : </td>
        <td><input id="symbol" type="text" /></td>
    </tr>
    <tr>
        <td>Quantity : </td>
        <td><input id="quantity" type="text" /></td>
    </tr>
    <tr>
        <td>Unit Price : </td>
        <td><input id="unitprice" type="text" /></td>
    </tr>
    <tr>
        <td>Buy or Sell :</td>
        <td>
            <select id="operation">
                <option>Buy</option>
                <option>Sell</option>
            </select>
        </td>
    </tr>
    <tr>
        <td colspan="2">
            <input type="button" id="buysell" value="Submit" />
        </td>
    </tr>
    </table>
</form>
```

The form houses a table containing four textboxes, a dropdown list, and a button. The textboxes accept UserName, Symbol, Quantity, and UnitPrice. The dropdown list allows you to select the operation–Buy or Sell. The button is used to initiate the selected operation.

The other form is quite straightforward and is shown in Listing 10-36.

Listing 10-36. Form That Displays Trading-Log Entries

```
<form>
    <div>Get Trading Log For :</div>
    <input type="text" id="tradingloguser" />
    <input type="button" id="getlog" value="Get Log" />
</form>
<div id="tradinglog"></div>
```

The form consists of a textbox and a button. The textbox accepts a username whose trading log is to be displayed. The Get Log button initiates the service operation. The <div> placed just below this form displays the trading-log entries returned by the service.

Since the client calls the TradingService using jQuery Ajax, make sure to add a <script> reference to the jQuery library in the head section of the view. The code from Listing 10-37 shows how the Buy() or Sell() operations of the TradingService can be invoked using jQuery.

Listing 10-37. Invoking Buy() or Sell() Operations

```
$("#buysell").click(function () {
    var obj = {};
    obj.UserName = $("#username").val();
    obj.Symbol = $("#symbol").val();
    obj.Quantity = $("#quantity").val();
    obj.UnitPrice = $("#unitprice").val();
    obj.TimeStamp = new Date().toISOString();

    var options = {};
    if ($("#operation").val() == "Buy") {
        options.url = "/TradingService/buy";
    }
    else {
        options.url = "/TradingService/sell";
    }
    options.type = "POST";
    options.data = obj;
    options.dataType = "json";
    options.success = function (flag) {
        alert(flag);
    }
    options.error = function (jqXHR, error, status) {
        alert(status);
    }
    $.ajax(options);
});
```

The Buy() or Sell() operation is invoked the click-event handler of the Buy Sell button. The code creates a new JavaScript object (obj) and sets five properties on it, namely UserName, Symbol, Quantity, UnitPrice, and TimeStamp. The obj represents the BuySellDetails object expected by the Buy() and Sell() actions of the TradingService controller. Note that these property names must be the same as those of the BuySellDetails class. The UserName, Symbol, Quantity, and UnitPrice properties get their values from the respective textboxes (val() method of jQuery) whereas the TimeStamp is set to the current date and time values.

Then the code proceeds to create another JavaScript object–options–that holds the settings required to make the Ajax call. Depending on the option selected in the dropdown list, the url property of the options object is either set to /TradingService/buy (Buy) or /TradingService/sell (Sell).

The type property indicates the HTTP verb used to invoke the operation–POST in this case. The data property holds the data that is to be sent while invoking a service method. In this case the obj object created earlier is set as the data. The dataType property indicates the kind of data returned by the service–json in this case.

The success callback function is called when the service is successfully invoked. It receives the return value of the service method (Boolean in this case) as its parameter. The code simply displays the return value in an alert.

The error callback function gets called if there is any error when calling the service. The error function simply displays the HTTP status in an alert.

Finally, the TradingService is invoked using the $.ajax() method of jQuery. The options object is passed to $.ajax() as its parameter.

The click-event handler of the Get Log button contains jQuery code to invoke the GetAllTradingLog() and GetTradingLogForUser() actions. This code is shown in Listing 10-38.

Listing 10-38. Invoking GetAllTradingLog() and GetTradingLogForUser()

```
$("#getlog").click(function () {
    var options = {};
    if ($("#tradingloguser").val() == "") {
        options.url = "/TradingService/GetAllTradingLog";
    }
    else {
        options.url = "/TradingService/GetTradingLogForUser";
        var obj = {};
        obj.user = $("#tradingloguser").val();
        options.data = obj;
    }
    options.type = "POST";
    options.dataType = "json";
    options.success = function (data) {
        var html = "<table border='1' cellpadding='10'>";
        for (var i = 0; i < data.length; i++) {
            html += "<tr><td>" + data[i].UserName + "</td>";
            html += "<td>" + data[i].Symbol + "</td>";
            html += "<td>" + data[i].Quantity + "</td>";
            html += "<td>" + data[i].UnitPrice + "</td>";
            html += "<td>" + data[i].TimeStamp + "</td>";
            html += "<td>" + data[i].Operation + "</td></tr>";
        }
        html += "</table>";
        $("#tradinglog").html(html);
    }
    options.error = function (jqXHR, error, status) {
        alert(status);
    }
    $.ajax(options);
});
```

The code creates a JavaScript object–options–as before. Then it checks whether a username is specified in the tradingloguser textbox. If the textbox is empty, the url property is set to /TradingService/GetAllTradingLog. Otherwise, the url is set to /TradingService/GetTradingLogForUser. In the latter case, another JavaScript object (obj) is also created that holds the value of the user parameter of the GetTradingLogForUser() service method.

The type and dataType properties are set to POST and json, respectively. The success callback function receives an array of StockTradingEntry objects. A for loop iterates through the data array, and an HTML table is formed. The table displays UserName, Symbol, Quantity, UnitPrice, TimeStamp, and Operation properties of the StockTradingEntry object. Once the HTML table is created, the markup is added to the tradinglog <div> element. This is done using the html() method of jQuery.

The error callback function displays the error (if any) as before. Finally, the $.ajax() method is used to invoke the service.

This completes the application. Before you run the application, make sure to create the ServiceLayerDb database (see Chapter 1 for more details). Once the ServiceLayerDb database and StockTradingLog table are ready, run the application and try performing Buy() or Sell() operations. Then also test the working of GetAllTradingLog() and GetTradingLogForUser() operations.

Injecting Repositories Through Dependency Injection

In the preceding examples in this chapter, you used repositories in several places. You instantiated the repositories as and when needed and disposed of them once their job was over. You could have also injected these repositories into the controllers using the dependency injection (DI) features of ASP.NET.

Dependency injection is a technique for developing loosely coupled software systems. This objective is accomplished by supplying or injecting the dependencies of a class from some external source. This way a class can be created using interfaces of its dependencies rather than of concrete classes. The DI framework can then inject the concrete implementations of the dependencies into the class. Although we won't discuss DI in detail, it would be worthwhile to get acquainted with it through an example.

Let's assume that you wish to inject the `CustomerRepository` into the `HomeController` using the DI features of ASP.NET. To accomplish this goal you need to register the `AppDbContext` and `CustomerRepository` classes with the DI framework. This is done inside the `ConfigureServices()` method of the `Startup` class, as shown in Listing 10-39.

Listing 10-39. Registering DbContext and Repository with DI Framework

```
public void ConfigureServices(IServiceCollection services)
{
    services.AddMvc();
    services.AddCaching();

    services.AddEntityFramework()
            .AddSqlServer()
            .AddDbContext<AppDbContext>(options =>
            options.UseSqlServer(AppSettings.ConnectionString));
    services.AddScoped<ICustomerRepository, CustomerRepository>();
}
```

Notice the code marked in bold letters. It calls the `AddDbContext()` method to register the `AppDbContext` class with the DI framework. Notice how the database connection string is being assigned while registering the `AppDbContext` (since the connection string is being assigned here, you can remove the `OnConfiguring()` method from `AppDbContext`). This is necessary, because the `CustomerRepository` needs an `AppDbContext` object in order to work (it has a constructor to receive an `AppDbContext` object).

The code then uses the `AddScoped()` method to register the `CustomerRepository` implementation of `ICustomerRepository`. A type to be injected is called a *service*. The DI framework does two basic tasks for the service type:

- It instantiates an object of said service and supplies it to the controllers. The dependencies can be injected through constructor injection or through property injection.

- It handles the lifetime (when to create an object and when to dispose of it) of the injected object.

There are four lifetime modes for a service being injected:

- **Singleton:** An object of a service is created and supplied to all the requests to that service. So, basically all requests get the same object to work with.

- **Scoped:** An object of a service is created for each and every request. So, each request gets its a new instance of a service to work with.

- **Transient:** An object of a service is created every time an object is requested.

- **Instance:** In this case you are responsible for creating an object of a service. The DI framework then uses that instance in the singleton mode mentioned earlier.

The preceding example uses the lifetime mode of scoped. Other lifetime modes can be used through the respective methods: AddSingleton(), AddTransient(), and AddInstance().

The HomeController needs to be modified to receive the injected service. Assuming you wish to use constructor injection, the constructor of the HomeController will look like Listing 10-40.

Listing 10-40. Constructor Injection in HomeController

```
public class HomeController : Controller
{

    private ICustomerRepository repository;

    public HomeController(ICustomerRepository repository)
    {
        this.repository = repository;
    }
    ...
    ...
}
```

The code declares a member variable of ICustomerRepository. The constructor takes one parameter of ICustomerRepository. This parameter will be injected by the DI framework and is stored in the repository variable for later use.

Since the HomeController receives the repository through DI, the Index() method doesn't need to instantiate it. Listing 10-41 shows the modified Index() action.

Listing 10-41. Index() Action Uses Injected Repository

```
public IActionResult Index()
{
    List<Customer> customers = repository.SelectAll();
    ViewBag.Customers = from c in customers
                        select new SelectListItem()
                        {
                            Text = c.CustomerID,
                            Value = c.CustomerID
                        };
    return View();
}
```

As you can see, the Index() action uses the repository object received earlier instead of instantiating the CustomerRepository.

Summary

This chapter covered a few patterns of enterprise application architecture. The P of EAA are organized based on the layers they belong to. To be specific, this chapter covered four important patterns: repository, unit of work, lazy load, and service layer.

The repository pattern mediates between the data-access layer and the rest of the system. Moreover, it does so by providing a collection-like access to the underlying data.

The unit of work pattern keeps track of business transactions that are supposed to alter the database in some way. Once the business transactions are over, the tracked steps are played onto the database in a transaction so that the database reflects the desired changes.

The lazy load pattern is used to load data required by an object after it is instantiated. So, an object instance is available to your code, but all of its properties may not contain the data they are supposed to expose. The object knows how to load the data whenever required.

The service layer pattern exposes an application's functionality as a layer of services, thus defining the boundary of the application for the clients. The services expose the operations the client can invoke and also take care of the nitty-gritties of those operations, such as data access, business logic, and workflow.

So far in this book you have learned GoF patterns and a selection of the P of EAA. The examples covered so far have applied the patterns to the server-side C# code. But patterns can also be implemented in JavaScript code. To that end, the next chapter will discuss just that. Moreover, you will also learn about code-organization techniques for your JavaScript code.

■ ■ ■

JavaScript Code-Organization Techniques and Patterns

So far you have learned the Gang of Four patterns and select patterns from *Patterns of Enterprise Application Architecture*. You applied your knowledge of patterns to the server-side C# code. However, patterns are not limited to server-side code. They are also applicable to the client-side JavaScript code. Modern ASP.NET applications rely heavily on the client-side script. Features such as Ajax are not at all uncommon these days. So, it is important for ASP.NET developers to understand how patterns apply to JavaScript code.

To that end, this chapter will introduce you to some of the JavaScript code-organizational patterns. These patterns will help you to structure and organize your JavaScript code so that it becomes more maintainable. This chapter will also illustrate how some of the GoF patterns can be utilized in JavaScript.

To be specific, this chapter will cover the following topics:

- What JavaScript code organizational patterns are
- How to organize your code in object literals and function objects
- How to create and use namespaces in JavaScript
- The module, revealing module, and sandbox patterns
- How to implement some of the GoF patterns in JavaScript

Although this chapter will cover a broad range of topics, in no way it is meant to give extensive coverage of these areas. The idea is to make you aware of various patterns used in the JavaScript world so that you can explore further.

■ **Note**　This chapter assumes that you are familiar with the basics of JavaScript programming. It also assumes that you are aware of some of the popular JavaScript libraries and frameworks, such as jQuery and AngularJS.

Organizing JavaScript Code Using Objects

As an ASP.NET developer using C# you are already familiar with object-oriented programming. Concepts such as encapsulation, namespaces, classes, objects, inheritance, interfaces, and polymorphism are quite common in server-side code. As a C# developer you might expect JavaScript to support all these features as a part of the language. If so, you might be surprised by how JavaScript deals with these features and object-oriented programming in general.

© Bipin Joshi 2016
B. Joshi, *Beginning SOLID Principles and Design Patterns for ASP.NET Developers*,
DOI 10.1007/978-1-4842-1848-8_11

This book is not intended to give you a sound understanding of object-oriented JavaScript. It aims to familiarize you with various features and concepts that are commonly used by professional JavaScript developers. This section and the sub-sections that follow limits themselves to illustrating how code can be organized in JavaScript objects.

In C# the basic unit of programming is a class. You create one or more classes and then you create objects of those classes as and when required. When it comes to JavaScript, many beginners organize their code using only functions. However, there is better way–JavaScript objects.

JavaScript doesn't have any formal way to create classes. There is no keyword such as class that specifically defines a class. Instead, you define an object. This object contains properties and methods. There are two ways to create objects in JavaScript:

- Object literals

- Function objects

The following sections will discuss each type of object creation, including examples.

■ **Note**   ECMAScript 6 (ES6) introduces many improvements to the JavaScript language, including a way to create classes. However, as of this writing ES6 is not fully supported in most of the leading browsers. One needs to use a transpiler to convert the ES6 code to JavaScript that can be understood by the current versions of the browsers.

Object Literals

A JavaScript object literal is like a dictionary in that it contains key-value pairs. A key represents a property or method name, and its value represents a property value or method body. You can add key-value pairs to an object at the time it is defined, or you can create an empty object first and then add key-value pairs to it. Consider the following JavaScript code:

```
var employee = {
    "employeeID": 1,
    "firstName": "Nancy",
    "lastName": "Davolio",
    "display": function () {
        alert("#" + this.employeeID +
            " - " + this.firstName +
            " " + this.lastName);
    }
};
```

The preceding code creates an object literal and stores it in the employee variable. Notice the following things about the object literal syntax:

- The object begins with { and ends with }

- It consists of four key-value pairs. Each pair is separated by a comma (,). A key and its value are separated by a colon (:).

- The employeeID, firstName, and lastName keys act like a property or field of a class. The display key is a method that simply displays the values of other keys using an alert.

- Inside the display method body, "this" points to the object being created.

You could have created the employee object using an alternate (and more C#-like) syntax, as shown here:

```
var employee = {};
employee.employeeID = 1;
employee.firstName = "Nancy";
employee.lastName = "Davolio";
employee.display = function () {
    alert("#" + this.employeeID +
        " - " + this.firstName +
        " " + this.lastName);
};
```

The preceding code creates an empty object using {} syntax. It then adds employeeID, firstName, and lastName key-value pairs using object-property syntax. Finally, a display key is also added, pointing to an anonymous function.

Once created, you can change the values of the existing members of the object literal using the familiar syntax:

```
employee.firstName = "Janet";
```

You can also invoke the display() method using the familiar syntax:

```
employee.display();
```

You can even add more members to the object at a later point in time.

■ **Note**   Most of the code fragments illustrated in this chapter can be tested in any HTML page. You can also create and configure an ASP.NET application as before and test these code snippets in MVC views.

Function Objects

In the preceding section you created an object using the object literal syntax. Many times when you need to create multiple objects they are based on a template. In C# you do that using the new keyword. If you wish to accomplish something similar in JavaScript, you need to define a Function Object.

Every JavaScript function is an object with properties and methods. You can create a function that houses the properties and methods required for an object. You can then create an object using the new keyword. This is best understood with an example:

```
var employee = function () {
    this.employeeID = 0;
    this.firstName = "";
    this.lastName = "";
    this.display = function () {
        alert("#" + this.employeeID +
            " - " + this.firstName +
            " " + this.lastName);
    }
}
```

The preceding code creates an anonymous function and stores it in the employee variable. Inside, the employee function declares three properties, namely employeeID, firstName, and lastName. It also defines the display() method, which shows the values of these properties using an alert.

To create an object based on the template you just created, the new keyword is used as shown here:

```
var emp = new employee();
emp.employeeID = 1;
emp.firstName = "Nancy";
emp.lastName = "Davolio";
emp.display();
```

The preceding code creates a new employee object and stores it in an emp variable. Note that the employee function (from an earlier snippet) acts like a constructor while instantiating an object using the new keyword. After the object creation, employeeID is 0 and the firstName and lastName properties are empty strings. You could have also designed the employee function to accept parameters if required. If so, it would have been a parameterized constructor.

The code then sets the employeeID, firstName, and lastName properties of the employee object. Finally, it calls the display() method to show these values.

Function Prototype

The employee object created in the preceding section works as expected. But there are a couple of issues that you should be aware of:

- All the properties of the employee object are public.

- All the properties and methods are contained in the employee object.

Since all the properties of the employee object are public, there can't be any check or validation of the property values. This is because the calling code is directly setting the property values. There are no getter and setter methods to access the actual value.

Secondly, every new employee object is going to have an exact replica of the template. This is quite alright with the properties, because different instances usually maintain their own values for the properties. But this behavior is not suitable for methods. Since each object also gets its own methods, there is duplication (and wastage).

The remedy is to create methods (getter or setter as well as methods such as display) using the function prototype.

▪ **Note**   This section is not intended to give you a thorough understanding of JavaScript prototypes. This section will discuss only the bare minimum amount of information on this topic that is sufficient to carry on the pattern-related discussed in later sections.

It was mentioned earlier that every JavaScript function is actually an object and gets a few pre-built properties and methods. One of these properties is the prototype property. The prototype property–often referred to as a function prototype–allows you to add properties and methods to the function under consideration. Let's review this by adding the display() method to the employee object's prototype rather than to the employee object (Listing 11-1).

Listing 11-1. Adding Display() to the Prototype

```
var employee = function (id,firstname,lastname) {
    this._employeeID = 0;
    this._firstName = "";
    this._lastName = "";

    if (arguments.length == 3) {
        this._employeeID = id;
        this._firstName = firstname;
        this._lastName = lastname;
    }
}

employee.prototype.display = function () {
    alert("#" + this._employeeID +
        " - " + this._firstName +
        " " + this._lastName);
}
```

The code creates the employee function. This time, however, the function accepts three constructor parameters: id, firstname, and lastname. Inside, the code declares three private variables, namely _employeeID, _firstName, and _lastName. Notice the JavaScript convention of prefixing a member with an underscore (_) to make it private. This way these members won't be directly accessible to the external world.

The constructor assigns some default values to these private members. It then checks whether parameters are passed to the constructor. This is done using the arguments.length property. If so, the parameter values are assigned to the private members. The employee function ends here.

The latter part of the code uses the prototype object of the employee function to add the display() method. The display() method has access to the private members since it's the part of the employee's prototype.

You can now create one or more employee objects as shown here:

```
var emp = new employee(1,"Nancy","Davolio");
emp.display();
```

As you can see, the first line of the code creates a new employee object by passing three constructor parameters. The display() method is then called on it to display the private member values.

This way you can add as many methods as you want to the prototype object. And now the methods won't be duplicated with each employee object, since they are part of the prototype. Listing 11-2 shows how getter and setter methods can be added to the prototype to access the respective private members.

Listing 11-2. Getter and Setter Methods Added to the Prototype

```
employee.prototype.getEmployeeID = function () {
    return this._employeeID;
}
employee.prototype.setEmployeeID = function (id) {
    this._employeeID = id;
}
employee.prototype.getFirstName = function () {
    return this._firstName;
}
```

```javascript
employee.prototype.setFirstName = function (firstname) {
    this._firstName = firstname;
}
employee.prototype.getLastName = function () {
    return this._lastName;
}
employee.prototype.setLastName = function (lastname) {
    this._lastName = lastname;
}
employee.prototype.display = function () {
    alert("#" + this._employeeID +
            " - " + this._firstName +
            " " + this._lastName);
}
```

Once the getter and setter methods are in place, you can access the private members through them as follows:

```javascript
var emp = new employee();
emp.setEmployeeID(1);
emp.setFirstName("Nancy");
emp.setLastName("Davolio");
emp.display();
```

This time the code doesn't supply any constructor parameters. The employeeID, firstName, and lastName members are set individually using the corresponding setter methods. Along the same lines, you could have used the getter methods to retrieve the values of the private members.

Immediately Invoked Function Expressions (IIFE)

Usually you create a function first and then somewhere in the code you call that function. For example, consider the following code:

```javascript
var HelloWorld = function () {
    alert("Hello World!");
}

HelloWorld();
```

Here, the function HelloWorld() is created first before being called on the next line.

An immediately invoked function expression (IIFE) is a JavaScript function that is executed immediately after it is created. Consider the following code:

```javascript
(function () {
    alert("Hello World!");
})();
```

As you can see, the preceding code creates an anonymous function. The whole function is enclosed in brackets and is immediately followed by (). This way function creation and execution are combined together. The IIFE can take parameters just like any other JavaScript function. An IIFE is useful in situations in which you wish to execute a piece of code immediately without formally creating a function.

■ **Note**   This term Immediately Invoked Function Expression (IIFE) was introduced by Ben Alman to accurately capture the essence of this technique. You may visit https://en.wikipedia.org/wiki/Immediately-invoked_function_expression for more details about IIFE.

Suppose you are developing an Ajax-driven web application. You want to display some advertisement or graphical announcement on the launching page of the application. The JavaScript code to do so is used only once, and hence there is no need to create a named function. Moreover, it would be a good idea not to pollute the global namespace with variables and functions that are needed only once. In this case an IIFE can do the trick. Listing 11-3 shows sample code that illustrates this:

Listing 11-3. IIFE for Displaying Advertisements

```
(function (elemID) {
    $.ajax({
        url: "/home/GetAdvert",
        success: function (advertData) {
            var markup = "<strong>" + advertData.Title + "</strong>";
            markup += "<div>" + advertData.Description + "</div>";
            markup += "<a href='" + advertData.Url + "'>" +
                            advertData.Url + "</a>";
            $("#" + elemID).html(markup);
        },
        dataType: "json"
    });
})("advert");
```

The code consists of an immediate function that makes an Ajax call to the GetAdvert() action method from the Home controller. The immediate function receives ID of an HTML element that contains the advertisement. The success function receives a JavaScript object with properties such as Title, Description, and Url. An HTML markup is then formed based on these details and is added to the element.

We won't go into the details of jQuery Ajax here. What is important is to understand how the immediate function is a good fit here. Notice that while invoking the function the element ID, advert, is passed to it. The GetAdvert() action used in this code is shown in Listing 11-4.

Listing 11-4. GetAdvert() returns JSON data

```
public IActionResult GetAdvert()
{
    return Json(new
    {
        Title = "Buy ONE Get one FREE!",
        Description = "Buy one large size Pizza and get one small size Pizza
        absolutely FREE!!!",
        Url = "http://localhost"
    });
}
```

The GetAdvert() action simply returns an object consisting of Title, Description, and Url properties. Of course, you can make it database driven if you so wish.

If you have ever developed a jQuery plugin, you might find this concept familiar. It is a common practice to wrap the plugin code inside an IIFE. Although a discussion of jQuery plugins is beyond the scope of this book, a skeleton of a sample plugin named decorate is shown in Listing 11-5.

Listing 11-5. jQuery Plugin and IIFE

```
(function ($) {
    $.fn.decorate = function (settings) {
        //plugin code here
    }
})(jQuery);
```

As you can see, the plugin template consists of an immediate function that accepts a jQuery parameter. The jQuery library uses $ as an alias to the jQuery object. What if some other JavaScript library being used in the application also uses $ for its own use? If so, it is possible that $ no longer points to the jQuery object. Obviously, the plugin code won't work as expected, as it depends on $. The immediate function can avoid this problem. By wrapping the plugin code inside an immediate function and passing a jQeury object to it, the meaning of $ is preserved inside the plugin code.

■ **Note** The JavaScript features discussed so far—object literal, function object, prototype, and IIFE—are useful while organizing the code. Moreover, these features are also used along with the patterns discussed in the following sections.

Namespace Pattern

As a C# developer you are already familiar with the concept of namespaces. Namespaces allow you avoid ambiguity between class names. A similar need arises in JavaScript also, especially when your JavaScript code consists of a lot of functions and objects.

When you create a JavaScript function or a variable inside a <script> block, it belongs to a global namespace. Suppose you are building a web application that heavily uses JavaScript for its functioning. Imagine that there are two JavaScript files, each containing a set of functions. It is quite possible that there could be name collisions between the two files. For example, say both of the files contain a HelloWorld() function.

It's not a good idea to place too many functions, objects, and variables inside the global namespace. It is best to house functions, objects, and variables needed by one library in its own namespace. Unfortunately, JavaScript doesn't have any inbuilt language construct for creating namespaces. That's where the namespace pattern comes to the rescue. The namespace pattern can help you devise a scheme that avoids naming collisions and organizes the related functions, objects, and variables in a better way.

■ **Note** In complex JavaScript-driven applications you may need to check whether a namespace has already been defined by some other part of the code. To keep things simple, we won't go into implementing such checks in our code. You may read Stoyan Stefanov's book *JavaScript Patterns* for more details about the namespace pattern and other related concepts.

To understand how the namespace pattern can be used, you will create an application as shown in Figure 11-1.

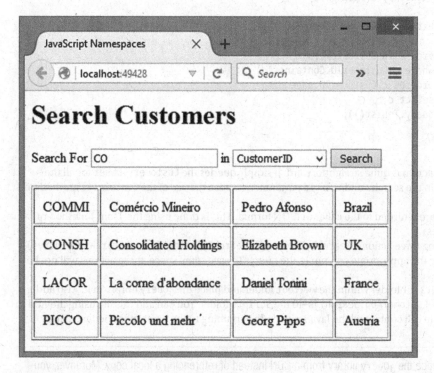

Figure 11-1. *Application using JavaScript namespaces*

The application allows you to search the Customers table of the Northwind database. You can enter a search condition in the textbox, select the search field (possible search fields are CustomerID, CompanyName, ContactName, and Country), and then click on the Search button. An Ajax call is then made to an action method using jQuery Ajax. The action does the searching and returns the results to the browser. The results are displayed in an HTML table.

To develop this application, begin by creating a new ASP.NET web application project using Visual Studio and configure it to use MVC and Entity Framework (see Chapter 1 for more details). Also store the database connection string of the Northwind database in the appsettings.json file.

Then add the AppSettings class to the Core folder and add the ConnectionString static property to it. Open the Startup class and write the code to set the ConnectionString property to the one stored in the appsettings.json file. Also create the Customer model class and the AppDbContext class required for the data access. You are already familiar with these steps, and hence they are not discussed here.

Next, add HomeController to the Controllers folder. In addition to the default Index() action, you need to create four actions that do the searching on the basis of CustomerID, CompanyName, ContactName, and Country columns. The SearchByID() action that searches the Customers table on the basis of the CustomerID column is shown in Listing 11-6.

Listing 11-6. SearchByID() Action Searches for CustomerID

```
public IActionResult SearchByID(string id)
{
    using (AppDbContext db = new AppDbContext())
    {
        var query = from c in db.Customers
                    where c.CustomerID.Contains(id)
                    orderby c.CustomerID ascending
                    select c;
        return Json(query.ToList());
    }
}
```

The SearchByID() action is quite straightforward. It simply queries the Customers DbSet for all the CustomerIDs that contain the search condition (id parameter). Notice the use of the Contains() method to accomplish this.

The search results are returned to the caller in JSON format. This is done using the Json() method of the Controller base class.

Create the remaining three actions–SearchByCompany(), SearchByContact(), and SearchByCountry()– in a similar way by using the appropriate column in the query. To save some space, these actions will not be discussed here.

Now create a Scripts subfolder within the wwwroot folder and place the jQuery library in it. Also add an empty JavaScript file–CustomerApp.Search.js–to the Scripts folder. You can add this file using the Add New Item dialog. This file will contain all the JavaScript code pertaining to the namespace being created.

■ **Note**   You can reference the jQuery library from a CDN instead of referencing a local copy. Moreover, you can use the Bower package manager integrated into the Visual Studio IDE to deal with the client script libraries. To keep things simple, we won't use those features in our examples.

Open the CustomerApp.Search.js file in the Visual Studio editor and write the skeleton of the namespace, as shown in Listing 11-7.

Listing 11-7. Skeleton of the CustomerApp.Search Namespace

```
var CustomerApp = {};

CustomerApp.Search = {};

CustomerApp.Search.SearchByID = function (id, target) {
  // code here
}

CustomerApp.Search.SearchByCompany = function (companyname,target) {
  // code here
}
```

```
CustomerApp.Search.SearchByContact = function (contactname,target) {
  // code here
}

CustomerApp.Search.SearchByCountry = function (country,target) {
  // code here
}
```

Observe the skeleton code carefully. The code begins by creating the CustomerApp empty object. This object acts as the top namespace (or container) for your searching library. Further, the code adds the Search empty object to the CustomerApp object. Thus, Search becomes the nested namespace of CustomerApp.

The code then proceeds to add four search functions–SearchByID, SearchByCompany, SearchByContact, and SearchByCountry–to the Search namespace. Each of these functions accepts two parameters–the search condition and the ID of the target element where search results are to be loaded.

These search functions are not part of the global namespace. Rather, they are part of the CustomerApp. Search namespace. Along the same lines you could have created other namespaces inside the CustomerApp object (say, CustomerApp.Utils).

Now it's time to add some code to these methods. Listing 11-8 shows the completed SearchByID() function.

Listing 11-8. SearchByID() Makes Ajax Call

```
CustomerApp.Search.SearchByID = function (id, target) {
    $.ajax({
        url: "/home/SearchByID",
        data: { "id": id },
        success: function (results) {
            var table = "<table border='1' cellpadding='10'>";
            for (var i = 0; i < results.length; i++) {
                table += "<tr>";
                table += "<td>" + results[i].CustomerID + "</td>";
                table += "<td>" + results[i].CompanyName + "</td>";
                table += "<td>" + results[i].ContactName + "</td>";
                table += "<td>" + results[i].Country + "</td>";
                table += "</tr>";
            }
            $("#" + target).html(table);
        },
        dataType: "json"
    });
}
```

The SearchByID() function receives two parameters–CustomerID to look for and target HTML element that houses the search results. Inside, the code makes an Ajax call to the SearchByID() action method of the HomeController. This is done using the $.ajax() method of jQuery.

The $.ajax() method accepts an object containing the settings that are to be used while making the Ajax request. The settings are as follows:

- url: The url property points to the server-side resource that is to be invoked. In this case, /home/SearchByID.

- data: The property holds the data accompanying the Ajax request. The SearchByID() action method requires the search criteria as an id parameter. So, a JavaScript object with an id property is created.

- success: The success property points to a callback function that is invoked once the Ajax call completes successfully. The success function receives the search results in the form of an array (recollect that the SearchByID() action returns a List of Customer objects). The success function iterates through this array and forms an HTML table displaying CustomerID, CompanyName, ContactName, and Country properties. The HTML table is loaded into the target element using the html() jQuery method.

- dataType: The dataType property indicates the type of data returned from the server; JSON in this case.

Along the same lines, create the remaining search functions: SearchByCompany(), SearchByContact(), and SearchByCountry(). These functions are quite similar to the one just discussed and hence will not be discussed here. You may get them from this book's source code.

This completes the searching library. Now add the Index view to the Views/Home folder. Add a <script> reference to the jQuery and CustomerApp.Search.js in the head section of the Index view as shown here:

```
<script src="~/scripts/jquery-2.1.1.js"></script>
<script src="~/Scripts/CustomerApp.Search.js"></script>
```

Then add the HTML markup shown in Listing 11-9 in the <body> section of the view.

Listing 11-9. Markup of the Index View

```
<h1>Search Customers</h1>
<div>
    Search For
    <input id="criteria" type="text" />
    in
    <select id="searchfield">
        <option>CustomerID</option>
        <option>CompanyName</option>
        <option>ContactName</option>
        <option>Country</option>
    </select>
    <input type="button" value="Search" id="search" />
</div>
<br />
<div id="results"></div>
```

The HTML markup consists of a textbox (criteria), a dropdown list (searchfield), and the Search button (search). The searchfield dropdown list contains four option elements: CustomerID, CompanyName, ContactName, and Country. The results div element is used to display the search results.

Next, add a new <script> block in the head section and write the code shown in Listing 11-10 in it.

Listing 11-10. Using the Search Library

```
$(document).ready(function () {
    $("#search").click(function () {
        var criteria = $("#criteria").val();
        var searchField = $("#searchfield").val();
        switch (searchField) {
            case "CustomerID":
                CustomerApp.Search.SearchByID(criteria, 'results');
                break;
```

```
        case "CompanyName":
            CustomerApp.Search.SearchByCompany(criteria, 'results');
            break;
        case "ContactName":
            CustomerApp.Search.SearchByContact(criteria, 'results');
            break;
        case "Country":
            CustomerApp.Search.SearchByCountry(criteria, 'results');
            break;
    }
});
});
```

The code handles the click event of the Search button by using the `click()` method of jQuery. The function supplied to the `click()` method grabs the search criteria entered in the textbox and stores it in the `criteria` local variable. The code also stores the selected searchfield value in the `searchfield` variable.

A `switch` statement checks the value of the `searchfield` variable and invokes the appropriate searching methods from the search library. Notice how the search functions are invoked using namespace-like syntax:

```
CustomerApp.Search.SearchByID(criteria,'results');
```

Also notice that `results` is passed as the target parameter since search results are to be displayed in the results `<div>` element.

This completes the application. Run the application, enter a search condition, and test the functionality of all the search methods.

Module Pattern

If your ASP.NET application uses JavaScript heavily to function, chances are the amount of JavaScript you need to maintain is quite large. Moreover, as the application grows even the JavaScript code might increase to cope up with the added functionality.

Organizing the JavaScript code using the namespace pattern is a good starting point when it comes to organizing JavaScript code. However, if your JavaScript code base is quite large and you wish to make it modular for the sake of easy maintenance and extensions, you may consider using the module pattern.

As the name suggests, the module pattern allows you to create self-contained modules of JavaScript code. The module pattern helps you to develop modules that are decoupled and can be added as and when needed. The module pattern uses many of the concepts you learned earlier in this chapter, such as object literals, IIFE, and namespaces.

Just to give you an idea of how a typical module is developed using the module pattern, see Listing 11-11.

Listing 11-11. A Sample Module Using the Module Pattern

```
var JsApp = {};

JsApp.Module1 = (function () {

    return {
        HelloWorld: function () {
```

```
        alert("Hello World!");
    }
};

})();
```

The code creates an empty JsApp object. Then a module–Module1–is created using an immediate function and an object literal.

The immediate function can contain local variables and private functions that are required for the internal processing. They won't be exposed to the external world. In this case the immediate function doesn't contain any such private members.

The public API of the module is exposed using an object literal. In this case an object with a single method, HelloWorld(), is formed and is returned from the immediate function.

In effect, Module1 points to an object with the HelloWorld() method. To invoke the HelloWorld() method from Module1 you would write:

```
JsApp.Module1.HelloWorld();
```

You could have created any number of modules to the JsApp.

Now that you know the basics of the module pattern, let's develop a more realistic example that demonstrates how it works. In this example you will develop an application, as shown in Figure 11-2.

***Figure 11-2.** Customer manager application*

The application allows you add, modify, and delete customers from the Customers table of the Northwind database. You can select a CustomerID from the dropdown list, and its corresponding CompanyName, ContactName, and Country values are displayed in the respective textboxes. You can then modify the details and click on the Update button to save the changes. To add a new customer you need to specify a new CustomerID and all the other details and click on the Insert button. Selecting a CustomerID and clicking on the Delete button deletes a customer.

More important, the operations just explained are performed by calling a Web API through jQuery Ajax. The jQuery code involved in performing these CRUD operations is organized using the module pattern.

To develop this application, begin by creating a new ASP.NET web application project using Visual Studio and configure it to use MVC, Web API, and Entity Framework (see Chapter 1 for more details). Also store the database connection string of the Northwind database in the appsettings.json file.

Then add the AppSettings class to the Core folder and add the ConnectionString static property to it. Open the Startup class and write the code to set the ConnectionString property to be the one stored in the appsettings.json file. Also create the Customer model class and the AppDbContext class required for the data access. You are already familiar with these steps, and hence they will not be discussed here.

Next, add a Web API controller named CustomerService to the Controllers folder. The CustomerService Web API wraps all the Entity Framework code to perform the CRUD operations and is shown in Listing 11-12.

Listing 11-12. CustomerService Web API Performs CRUD Operations

```
[Route("api/[controller]")]
public class CustomerService : Controller
{
    [HttpGet]
    public List<Customer> Get()
    {
        using (AppDbContext db = new AppDbContext())
        {
            return db.Customers.ToList();
        }
    }

    [HttpGet("{id}")]
    public Customer Get(string id)
    {
        using (AppDbContext db = new AppDbContext())
        {
            return db.Customers.Where(i => i.CustomerID == id).SingleOrDefault();
        }
    }

    [HttpPost]
    public void Post([FromBody]Customer obj)
    {
        using (AppDbContext db = new AppDbContext())
        {
            db.Entry(obj).State = EntityState.Added;
            db.SaveChanges();
        }
    }
}
```

```
[HttpPut("{id}")]
public void Put(string id, [FromBody]Customer obj)
{
    using (AppDbContext db = new AppDbContext())
    {
        db.Entry(obj).State = EntityState.Modified;
        db.SaveChanges();
    }
}

[HttpDelete("{id}")]
public void Delete(string id)
{
    using (AppDbContext db = new AppDbContext())
    {
        Customer obj = db.Customers.Where(i => i.CustomerID == id).SingleOrDefault();
        db.Entry(obj).State = EntityState.Deleted;
        db.SaveChanges();
    }
}
}
```

The CustomerService controller consists of five actions, namely Get(), Get(id), Post(), Put(), and Delete(). We won't go into the details of these operations here, because you created a similar Web API in earlier chapters. Here it is sufficient to say that Get() returns a list of Customer entities and Get(id) accepts a CustomerID and returns a single Customer entity matching that value. The Post(), Put(), and Delete() actions add, modify, and delete a Customer from the database, respectively.

This completes the CustomerService controller. It's now time to create the CustomerManager module that invokes this Web API through jQuery Ajax. Add a Scripts folder to the wwwroot folder and place the jQuery library into it. Also add a new JavaScript file–CustomerApp.CustomerManager.js–to the Scripts folder. Listing 11-13 shows the skeleton of the CustomerManager module that you will develop shortly.

Listing 11-13. Skeleton of the CustomerManager Module

```
var CustomerApp = {};

CustomerApp.CustomerManager = (function () {
    return {
        SelectAll: function (callback) {
          // code here
        },
        SelectByID: function (id, callback) {
          // code here
        },
        Insert: function (obj, callback) {
          // code here
        },
        Update: function (obj, callback) {
          // code here
        },
```

```
        Delete: function (id, callback) {
            // code here
        }
    };
}());
```

As you can see, the CustomerManager module is being added to CustomerApp. The immediate function returns an object with five methods:

- SelectAll: To fetch all the customers from the database

- SelectByID: To fetch a customer matching a specific CustomerID

- Insert: To add a new customer to the database

- Update: To modify an existing customer from the database

- Delete: To delete an existing customer from the database

Notice that all these methods accept a callback parameter. The callback parameter is a callback function that gets invoked upon a successful Ajax call. The SelectByID() and Delete() methods accept a CustomerID as the id parameter. The Insert() and Update() methods accept a Customer object to be added or modified, respectively.

These methods form the public API of the CustomerManager module. They are used to invoke the respective Web API methods. Listing 11-14 shows the code that goes inside the SelectAll() method.

Listing 11-14. SelectAll() Calls the Get() Action of CustomerService

```
CustomerApp.CustomerManager = (function () {
    return {
        SelectAll: function (callback) {
            $.ajax({
                url: "/api/customerservice",
                type: "GET",
                dataType: "json",
                success: function (data) {
                    callback(data);
                }
            });
        },
        ...
        ...
}());
```

The SelectAll() method accepts a callback function as its parameter. Inside, the code makes a GET request to the CustomerService Web API. This is done using the $.ajax() method of jQuery. Since the Ajax request is being made using the GET verb, it is mapped with the Get() action of CustomerService.

The success function receives the data returned by CustomerService (a list of Customer objects, in this case). The callback function is then invoked by passing this data to it. The other Ajax calls look similar, with a few changes. For example, the Ajax call that invokes the Put() action looks like this:

```
$.ajax({
    url: "/api/customerservice/" + obj.CustomerID,
    type: "PUT",
    data: JSON.stringify(obj),
```

```
        contentType: "application/json",
        dataType: "json",
        success: function (msg) {
            callback(msg);
        }
});
```

As you can see, the CustomerID is appended to the url, and the type property is set to PUT. Moreover, the data property holds a Customer object containing the modified details.

The remaining Ajax calls and methods will not be discussed here as they are quite similar to the calls just discussed. You can pick up the complete code of these methods from the code download of this book.

This completes the CustomerManager module. Now it's time to put it to use inside a view. Add HomeController to the Controllers folder and also add the Index view to the Views/Home folder.

Add <script> references to the jQuery library and also to the CustomerApp.CustomerManager.js file in the head section of the Index view:

```
<script src="~/scripts/jquery-2.1.1.js"></script>
<script src="~/Scripts/CustomerApp.CustomerManager.js"></script>
```

Next, add the HTML markup shown in Listing 11-15 to the body section of the Index view.

Listing 11-15. Markup of the Index View

```
<h1>Manage Customers</h1>
<table border="1" cellpadding="11">
    <tr>
        <td>Customer ID :</td>
        <td>
            <select id="customerid"></select>
            OR
            <input id="newcustomerid" type="text" />
        </td>
    </tr>
    <tr>
        <td>Company Name :</td>
        <td><input id="companyname" type="text" /></td>
    </tr>
    <tr>
        <td>Contact Name :</td>
        <td><input id="contactname" type="text" /></td>
    </tr>
    <tr>
        <td>Country :</td>
        <td><input id="country" type="text" /></td>
    </tr>
    <tr>
        <td colspan="2">
            <input id="insert" type="button" value="Insert" />
            <input id="update" type="button" value="Update" />
            <input id="delete" type="button" value="Delete" />
        </td>
    </tr>
</table>
```

The markup is quite straightforward. It consists of a table that houses four textboxes, a dropdown list, and three buttons. The four textboxes–newcustomerid, companyname, contactname, and country–are used to accept CustomerID, CompanyName, ContactName, and Country values, respectively.

The customerid dropdown list displays a list of existing customer IDs. The three buttons–Insert, Update, and Delete–are used to trigger the corresponding operations.

Now add a new <script> block in the head section, just below the script references added earlier, and write the code shown in Listing 11-16 into it.

Listing 11-16. Calling the CustomerModule's Public API

```
$(document).ready(function () {
    CustomerApp.CustomerManager.SelectAll(function (data) {
        for (var i = 0; i < data.length; i++) {
            $("#customerid").append("<option>" + data[i].CustomerID + "</option>");
        }
    });
});
```

This code calls the SelectAll() method of the CustomerManager module as soon as the view loads in the browser. The callback passed to the SelectAll() method iterates through the list of customers (data) and adds the CustomerIDs to the customerid dropdown list. This is done using the append() method of jQuery.

Upon selecting a CustomerID from the dropdown list, its details need to be displayed in the other textboxes. This is done by handling the change-event handler of the dropdown list (Listing 11-17).

Listing 11-17. Fetching and Displaying Customer Details

```
$("#customerid").change(function () {
    CustomerApp.CustomerManager.SelectByID($("#customerid").val(), function (data) {
        $("#companyname").val(data.CompanyName);
        $("#contactname").val(data.ContactName);
        $("#country").val(data.Country);
    });
});
```

The code uses the SelectByID() method of the CustomerManager to fetch the details of a single customer. The CustomerID selected in the dropdown list and a callback function are passed to the SelectByID() method as its parameters. The callback function fills the textboxes with the CompanyName, ContactName, and Country properties.

To add a new customer, you need to handle the click event of the Insert button, as shown in Listing 11-18.

Listing 11-18. Adding a New Customer

```
$("#insert").click(function () {
    var obj = {};
    obj.CustomerID = $("#newcustomerid").val();
    obj.CompanyName = $("#companyname").val();
    obj.ContactName = $("#contactname").val();
    obj.Country = $("#country").val();
    CustomerApp.CustomerManager.Insert(obj, function (msg) {
        alert(msg);
    });
});
```

The code creates an empty object—obj—and adds CustomerID, CompanyName, ContactName, and Country properties to it. These properties get their values from the respective textboxes. Then the code invokes the Insert() method of the CustomerManager module by passing obj and a callback to it. The callback simply displays the message returned from the Web API in an alert.

The click-event handlers of the Update and Delete buttons are quite similar and hence will not be discussed here. You can get the complete code of this script block from this book's code download.

This completes the application. Run the application and check whether you can add, modify, and delete the customer records as expected.

Revealing Module Pattern

The module pattern puts all the functionality of the module directly into an object literal and then returns it from the immediate function. While developing a larger and more complex module you may not be aware of the exact methods that are to be exposed as the public API. For example, there might be several private methods, helper functions, and variables that are used internally by the module but are not to be exposed to the external world.

In such cases the revealing module pattern comes in handy. With the revealing module pattern, you create functions and variables as you develop the module. At this stage you don't return anything. Once all the functionality of the module is in place, you decide what should be included in the public interface of the module. You return an object containing only those methods. Consider the code fragment shown in Listing 11-19.

Listing 11-19. Using the Revealing Module Pattern

```
var JsApp = {};

JsApp.Module1 = (function () {
    var msg = "Hello World!";
    var SayHello = function () {
        alert(msg);
    }

    return {
        HelloWorld:SayHello
    };
})();
```

The immediate function declares a private variable—msg—that holds a string value—Hello World! The SayHello() function is a private function and it simply displays the value of msg in an alert. At this point, the public API of the module is not yet decided.

Then the code creates an object literal with a HelloWorld property that points to the SayHello() function. This object is returned from the immediate function. This is where, after the completion of the module, you decide the public interface of the module. Here you decide to expose the SayHello method as HelloWorld.

If you wish to use the revealing module pattern instead of the module pattern, the CustomerManager module developed in the preceding example would have looked as shown in Listing 11-20.

Listing 11-20. CustomerManager Module Uses Revealing Module Pattern

```javascript
var CustomerApp = {};

CustomerApp.CustomerManager = (function () {

    var Get = function (callback) {
        //code here
    }

    var GetByID = function (id, callback) {
        //code here
    }

    var Post = function (obj, callback) {
        //code here
    }

    var Put = function (obj, callback) {
        //code here
    }

    var Delete = function (id, callback) {
        //code here
    }

    return {
        SelectAll: Get,
        SelectByID: GetByID,
        Insert: Post,
        Update: Put,
        Delete: Delete
    };
}());
```

As you can see, the immediate function now defines five private functions, namely Get(), GetByID(), Post(), Put(), and Delete(). These private functions make the Ajax call to the appropriate Web API actions (not shown in the listing for the sake of simplicity) and perform the respective operations.

Then an object literal is created with five properties, namely SelectAll, SelectByID, Insert, Update, and Delete. These five properties point to the Get(), GetByID(), Post(), Put(), and Delete() private functions, respectively. These five properties form the public API of the module. The object is then returned from the immediate function.

Sandbox Pattern

In the preceding sections you used the namespace pattern. Although it worked as expected there, is a drawback–more typing due to long namespace names. You can imagine a situation in which such long namespaces are used in dozens of places in your code.

The sandbox pattern can be used to avoid this issue. **A sandbox is a self-contained object that includes APIs from only those modules that your code needs at a given point in time.** Suppose your library has three modules, namely Module1, Module2, and Module3. At a given point in time, you want to work with the API exposed by Module1 and Module2. So, you construct a "sandbox" that contains the API from those two modules. Your code deals with this sandbox and not with the modules directly. Thus, your code reduces to:

```
sandbox.<some_method>();
```

■ **Note** There is one more issue with the namespace pattern. Since it depends on one, and only one, global instance of your library, you can't use two versions of the library on a page. When you use the sandbox pattern, your code gets its own sandbox and is not dependent on the application's global object as such. You may read Stoyan Stefanov's book *JavaScript Patterns* for more details about the sandbox pattern and its benefits.

To understand how the sandbox pattern works, let's modify the example you developed for the namespace pattern. Copy the same project and perform the modifications that follow.

Add the CustomerApp.Sandbox.js file to the Scripts folder using the Add New Item dialog and write the code shown in Listing 11-21 in it.

Listing 11-21. Creating a Sandbox Object

```
(function (global) {
    var CustomerApp = function (modules, callback) {
        if (!(this instanceof CustomerApp)) {
            return new CustomerApp(modules, callback);
        }
        for (var i = 0; i < modules.length; i++) {
            CustomerApp.modules[modules[i]](this);
        }
        callback(this);
    };
    CustomerApp.modules = {};
    global.CustomerApp = CustomerApp;
})(this);
```

This code is the heart of the sandbox pattern. It consists of an immediate function that receives a parameter—global. The object referenced by this is passed to the global parameter during the invocation. In JavaScript this points to the global object (window object, for web browsers) when used outside of any function. So, here the immediate function receives a reference to the global window object.

Inside, the CustomerApp object gets created. The CustomerApp function receives two parameters, namely modules and callback. The modules parameter is a string array that contains a list of modules required by your code. The callback parameter is a function that uses the sandbox being generated.

Inside the CustomerApp function, the first if statement checks whether this points to the CustomerApp object. If not, a new instance of CustomerApp is created by passing the modules array and the callback to it.

A for loop iterates through the modules array and generates a sandbox object containing the API of all the requested modules. Then the callback function is invoked by passing this sandbox object to it.

After the function definition, the code sets the modules property on the CustomerApp to an empty object and also sets the CustomerApp property on the global (window) object to point to the CustomerApp object.

Next, define the search module as per the skeleton shown in Listing 11-22.

Listing 11-22. Skeleton of the Search Module

```
CustomerApp.modules.search = function (sandbox) {

    sandbox.SearchByID = function (id, target) {
    }

    sandbox.SearchByCompany = function (companyname, target) {
    }

    sandbox.SearchByContact = function (contactname, target) {
    }

    sandbox.SearchByCountry = function (country, target) {
    }
};
```

As you can see, the search function receives a sandbox object. Methods such as SearchByID(), SearchByCompany(), SearchByContact(), and SearchByCountry() are added to this sandbox object.

■ **Note**   The code inside these four methods is exactly same as discussed in the namespace pattern example. You can simply copy and paste those Ajax calls here to complete the module. To save some space, that code will not be discussed again.

Just for the testing, add another module—hello—to the file as shown in Listing 11-23.

Listing 11-23. Hello Module

```
CustomerApp.modules.hello = function (sandbox) {
    sandbox.HelloWorld = function () { alert("Hello World!"); };
    sandbox.HelloUniverse = function () { alert("Hello Universe!"); };
}
```

The Hello module is quite straightforward and adds two methods to the sandbox: HelloWorld() and HelloUniverse().

This completes CustomerApp.Sandbox.js. Now open the Index view and adjust the <script> reference to point to the CustomerApp.Sandbox.js file. Then modify the <script> block from the Index view as shown in Listing 11-24.

Listing 11-24. Using the Sandbox

```
$(document).ready(function () {
    $("#search").click(function () {
        var criteria = $("#criteria").val();
        var searchField = $("#searchfield").val();
        switch (searchField) {
            case "CustomerID":
                CustomerApp(['search', 'hello'], function (sandbox) {
                    sandbox.SearchByID(criteria, 'results');
                    sandbox.HelloWorld();
                });
```

```
                break;
        case "CompanyName":
            CustomerApp(['search'], function (sandbox) {
                sandbox.SearchByCompany(criteria, 'results');
            });
            break;
        case "ContactName":
            CustomerApp(['search'], function (sandbox) {
                sandbox.SearchByContact(criteria, 'results');
            });
            break;
        case "Country":
            CustomerApp(['search'], function (sandbox) {
                sandbox.SearchByCountry(criteria, 'results');
            });
            break;
        }
    });
});
```

Notice the code shown in bold letters. This code calls the CustomerApp function (remember CustomerApp is a global property) by passing the modules array and a callback function. The modules array contains two elements—search and hello—that indicate the modules your code wants to use.

The callback function receives the sandbox object as its parameter. Your code within the callback function invokes the SearchByID() and HelloWorld() methods on the sandbox object.

Notice the other instance of the switch statement. There, you specify only the search module in the modules array. Hence, the sandbox object received by those calls won't have the API of the hello module. Your callback function won't be able to call HelloWorld() on the sandbox object.

This completes the application. Run the application and test it as discussed. If you log the sandbox object to the browser's console (console.log()) then Firefox will display it as shown in Figure 11-3.

Figure 11-3. *Sandbox object in Firefox*

Notice how the sandbox object includes six methods—two from hello module and four from the search module.

Using Design Patterns in JavaScript

You have learned all the GoF design patterns in earlier chapters. As mentioned earlier, these patterns are not tied to a particular programming language. The concepts and ideas suggested by these patterns can be implemented in any object-oriented programming language, including the JavaScript. Of course, the code-level implementation details will vary from one language to another.

In this section and the subsections that follow, you will see how some of the GoF patterns can be put to use in JavaScript. Specifically, you will learn to implement the following patterns:

- Singleton pattern (creational)

- Façade pattern (structural)

- Observer pattern (behavioral)

Since you already know the intent of these patterns, details such as the purpose and the UML diagram will not be discussed here.

Singleton Pattern

The singleton pattern ensures that only one instance of a class gets created. While implementing the singleton pattern in JavaScript, you need to keep the following things in mind:

- In JavaScript there are no classes as such. All are objects. Each object is unique in itself (even if its properties bear the same values as another object).

- Object literals are actually singletons. You don't need to do anything special to implement the singleton pattern in this case.

- While creating objects using the new keyword, you may wish to return the same object no matter how often new is called. Here you will need to implement the singleton pattern yourself.

Suppose you want to store various page-specific themes in an object. Also assume that the same settings are accessed at several places in your code, and hence you decide to make that object a singleton. Listing 11-25 shows a simple implementation of the singleton pattern that fulfills this requirement.

Listing 11-25. Singleton in JavaScript

```
var ThemeSettings = function () {
    var instance = this;

    this.colorTheme = "Office";
    this.fontTheme = "Modern";
    this.layoutTheme = "SideBySide";

    ThemeSettings = function () {
        return instance;
    }
}
```

The code creates a function—ThemeSettings—that has a private instance variable. The instance variable points to this. Then the code sets three properties of the object, namely colorTheme, fontTheme, and layoutTheme. In a more realistic case, these settings might be fetched from the server using an Ajax call.

The code cleverly rewrites the constructor of ThemeSettings. The new constructor simply returns the instance variable to the caller. So, when new is called on ThemeSettings for the first time, the original constructor is invoked. The original constructor sets the three properties and returns as usual. The next time new is called on ThemeSettings, the new constructor takes this into effect and simply returns the existing instance. Thus, each call to new returns the same object—the essence of the singleton pattern.

To test the working of the ThemeSettings object, write the code shown in Listing 11-26.

Listing 11-26. ThemeSettings Is a Singleton

```
var settings1 = new ThemeSettings();
var settings2 = new ThemeSettings();
alert("Is ThemeSettings instance same? " + (settings1 === settings2));
settings2.colorTheme = "Nature";
alert("settings1.colorTheme is " + settings1.colorTheme);
```

The code creates two variables—settings1 and settings2—using the new keyword on ThemeSettings. It seems that two independent objects of ThemeSettings are being created. The alert then checks settings1 and settings2 using the strict equality operator of JavaScript (===). The strict equality operator returns true if the operands are equal and are of the same type.

If you run this code, you will find that the alert confirms that settings1 and settings2 indeed point to the same object (true is returned). The code then changes the colorTheme property of settings2. Finally, the value of settings1.colorTheme is displayed using an alert. As you might have guessed, the alert displays Nature, confirming that both variables are pointing to the same object.

You can implement the singleton pattern with one more variation. Consider the code shown in Listing 11-27.

Listing 11-27. Alternate Implementation of the Singleton Pattern

```
var ThemeSettings = (function () {
    var instance;

    function createInstance() {
        var settings = new Object();
        settings.colorTheme = "Office";
        settings.fontTheme = "Modern";
        settings.layoutTheme = "SideBySide";
        return settings;
    }

    return {
        getInstance: function () {
            if (!instance) {
                instance = createInstance();
            }
            return instance;
        }
    };
})();
```

Here, the code creates an immediate function. The immediate function declares the private instance variable. The private createInstance() function creates a settings object using the new Object() syntax. Then three properties, namely colorTheme, fontTheme, and layoutTheme, are set on the settings object, which is then returned to the caller.

The function returns an object literal with a getInstance property. The getInstance() code checks whether the instance variable is null or not. If it is null, the createInstance() private function is called. The object instance returned by createInstance() is assigned to the instance variable. When getInstance() is called for the first time, the instance gets created. The next time and thereafter, the existing instance will be returned to the caller.

Listing 11-28 shows a code fragment that can be used to test the working of this alternate implementation.

Listing 11-28. Testing ThemeSettings

```
var settings1 = ThemeSettings.getInstance();
var settings2 = ThemeSettings.getInstance();
alert("Is ThemeSettings instance same? " + (settings1 === settings2));
settings2.colorTheme = "Nature";
alert("settings1.colorTheme is " + settings1.colorTheme);
```

This code is quite similar to what you wrote earlier. The only difference is that instead of using the new keyword it calls the getInstance() method on the ThemeSettings object. If you were to run this code, the first alert would confirm that settings1 and settings2 are pointing to the same object. The second alert would display Nature, proving that a change to a property on the second variable gets reflected on the first variable too.

Façade Pattern

The façade pattern provides a high-level, easy-to-use interface to the client by shielding the different interfaces of the subsystems. The primary goal of the façade is to simplify the client interaction with the other objects involved in an operation.

Suppose that you are developing an Ajax-driven application that processes orders submitted by the users. The application needs to perform three checks before approving or rejecting the application:

- Verify the address details.

- Ensure that the bank details are correct.

- Confirm the employment details furnished by the user.

Considering these requirements, you may come up with the JavaScript objects illustrated in Listing 11-29.

Listing 11-29. JavaScript Objects Required to Process the Load Application

```
var AddressDetails = function () {
    this.validate = function () {
        //complex code here
        return true;
    }
}

var BankDetails = function () {
    this.validate = function () {
        //complex code here
        return true;
    }
}
```

```
var EmploymentDetails = function () {
    this.validate = function () {
        //complex code here
        return true;
    }
}
```

As shown in the code, three objects, namely AddressDetails, BankDetails, and EmploymentDetails are involved in the processing of a loan application. How these objects perform the processing is not our primary concern here. Let's assume that the validation process is complex and involves several server-side calls as well as client-side processing. So, for the sake of testing, the validate() method of each of these object simply returns true.

The OrderProcessor object (you will create it shortly) needs to use all three objects to proceed with the order. The AddressDetails object can implement the façade pattern, as shown in Listing 11-30.

Listing 11-30. AddressDetails Implements Façade

```
var OrderProcessor = function () {
  //constructor code here
}


OrderProcessor.prototype.validateDetails = function () {
    var addresss = new AddressDetails();
    var bank = new BankDetails();
    var employment = new EmploymentDetails();

    var result = true;

    if (!addresss.validate()) {
        result = false;
    } else if (!bank.validate()) {
        result = false;
    } else if (!employment.validate()) {
        result = false;
    }
    return result;
}
```

The code adds the validateDetails() method to the OrderProcessor class. The validateDetails() method implements the façade pattern by simplifying the validation process for the client code. It makes use of the AddressDetails, BankDetails, and EmploymentDetails objects and invokes their validate() methods. The final outcome is returned to the caller as true (all validations succeed) or false (at least one validation failed).

The client code can then use the validateData() façade like this:

```
var app = new OrderProcessor();
var status = app.validateDetails();
alert("Are details valid? " + status);
```

The preceding code creates an OrderProcessor object and then calls the validateDetails() method. The outcome of the validation is displayed in an alert.

Observer Pattern

The observer pattern defines a one-to-many dependency between objects so that when one object changes its state all the others are notified about the change. It follows the publisher-subscriber model where one or more subscribers subscribe to an event, and the publisher notifies all the subscribers when that event takes place in the system.

The observer pattern is commonly used in JavaScript code for event-handling purposes. The parts of the application that are interested in certain events (subscribers), such as click or keypress, wire event handlers to the events. The controls such as button or textbox (publishers) raise the respective events and the handlers are invoked.

Let's understand this with a more specific example. Suppose you are building a blogging engine. Each post displayed by the blog allows users to post comments. The comment box needs to have the following features:

- As a user types in the comment, you need to show the preview of the comment.

- A character counter informing the user about the number of characters entered so far is to be displayed.

Figure 11-4 shows a simplified version of such a comment box.

Figure 11-4. Comment box with preview and character counter

Let's assume that a blog comment is represented by a `BlogComment` object. The `BlogComment` object is the publisher and implements the observer pattern as shown in Listing 11-31.

Listing 11-31. BlogComment Object

```
function BlogComment() {
    this.observers = [];
}

BlogComment.prototype = {

    subscribe: function (fn) {
        this.observers.push(fn);
    },

    unsubscribe: function (fn) {
        this.observers = this.handlers.filter(
            function (item) {
                if (item !== fn) {
                    return item;
                }
            }
        );
    },

    broadcast: function (data) {
        this.observers.forEach(function (item) {
            item.call(null, data);
        });
    }
}
```

The `BlogComment` object maintains an array of subscribers—observers. Initially the observers array is empty. To add and remove the subscribers and to broadcast notifications, three methods are added to the prototype of the `BlogComment` object—subscribe, unsubscribe, and broadcast.

The subscribe method adds a subscriber to the observers array using the push() method. The unsubscribe method removes a subscriber from the observers array. It does so using the filter() method on the handlers array. The filter() method regenerates the observers array by filtering out the subscriber that equals the one passed to the unsubscribe() method.

The broadcast() method notifies all the subscribers with some data. In this case, the data is the comment text. Notice how the broadcasting of data is done. The code iterates through the observers array using the forEach() method. Inside, the code invokes the call() method on an observer and passes the data to it. The call() method calls a function (item is a function in this case). The first parameter of the call() method is null, indicating that no specific value for this is to be used. The second parameter is the parameter(s) to be passed to the function being called.

This completes the BlogComment object. The HTML markup that renders the comment box is quite straightforward:

```
<h2>Comments:</h2>
<textarea cols="40" rows="4" id="text1"></textarea>
<br />
<div id="div1"></div>
<div id="div2"></div>
```

It consists of a text1 text area and two <div> elements. The div1 element is used to display the comment's preview, whereas the div2 element is used to display the character counter.

The jQuery code that attaches the subscribers is shown in Listing 11-32.

Listing 11-32. Creating and Attaching the Subscribers

```
$(document).ready(function () {
    var Subscriber1 = function (data) {
        $("#div1").html(data);
    };
    var Subscriber2 = function (data) {
        $("#div2").html("<h4>Count : " + data.length + "</h4>");
    };
    var comment = new BlogComment();
    comment.subscribe(Subscriber1);
    comment.subscribe(Subscriber2);
});
```

The code creates two subscriber objects—Subscriber1 and Subscriber2. The first subscriber simply displays the comment's preview by setting the HTML content of div1 to the data received from the broadcast method. This is done using the html() method.

Along the same lines, the second subscriber displays a character counter inside div2 using the length property of the data.

Then the code creates a new BlogComment object and calls its subscribe() method to add the two subscribers to the observers array.

Whenever you key in text within the text area, the BlogComment object needs to broadcast the comment data to the subscribers. This is accomplished by handling the keyup event of text1, like this:

```
$("#text1").keyup(function () {
    comment.broadcast($("#text1").val());
});
```

As you can see, the keyup callback invokes the broadcast() method on the comment object and passes the value of text1 to it.

This completes the example. You can run the application and try entering some text in the text area. You should see the preview as well as the character counter.

MVC, MVVM, and MVW Patterns

As an ASP.NET MVC developer, you are already familiar with the Model-View-Controller (MVC) pattern. The MVC pattern separates the application concerns into three distinct parts—Model, View, and Controller. Simply put, the Model represents the application data, a View represents the application's user interface, and a Controller acts like a middleman between the other two parts and also manages the overall application flow.

■ **Note**   This section doesn't attempt to teach you any specific JavaScript frameworks as such. The idea is just to make you aware about the patterns used by modern JavaScript frameworks.

ASP.NET MVC applies the MVC pattern to the server-side framework. In the context of client-side JavaScript frameworks, you will find these patterns mentioned frequently:

- Model-View-Controller (MVC)
- Model-View-View Model (MVVM)
- Model-View-Whatever (MVW)

In the context of JavaScript applications, a Model is usually a JavaScript object or a collection of objects. A View consists of HTML markup from the document object model (DOM) tree. A Controller acts as a layer that connects the Model and the View. The Controller might do tasks such as handling events, validating data, performing some business-specific processing, and changing the model data.

A View Model used by the MVVM pattern is an object that takes care of the presentation logic. The presentation logic might include things such as data binding and event handling. JavaScript libraries such as Knockout are based on the MVVM pattern.

The "Whatever" used by the pattern can be a View Model or a Controller or whatever suits the application requirements. JavaScript frameworks such as AngularJS are based on the MVW pattern.

Although this book doesn't go into any detailed discussion of using these frameworks, just to give you some idea a simple example built using AngularJS is shown in Figure 11-5.

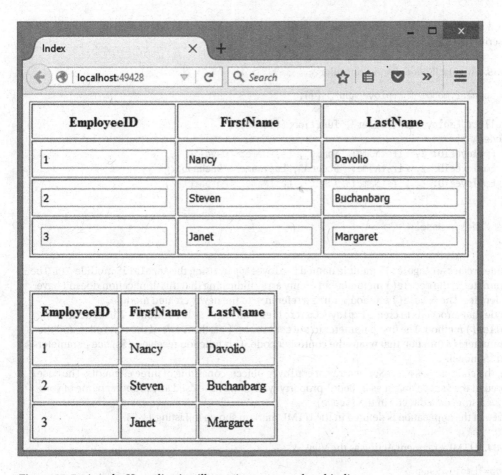

Figure 11-5. AngularJS application illustrating two-way data binding

The application displays a list of employees in two tables. The table shown at the top allows you to edit the employee details, such as EmployeeID, FirstName, and LastName. The table towards the bottom of the page is read-only. It is solely used to illustrate the two-way data binding.

To develop this application, begin by creating a new ASP.NET web application project using Visual Studio and configure it to use MVC (see Chapter 1 for more details). Also, place the AngularJS framework files in the Script folder under wwwroot.

■ **Note** I used AngularJS 1.2 to develop this example. You can download the AngularJS framework files from https://angularjs.org. You may even use a CDN to reference these files.

Then add HomeController to the Controllers folder and an Index view to the Views/Home folder. You need to add a script reference to the AngularJS as shown below:

```
<script src="~/Scripts/angular-1.2.js"></script>
```

Also add an empty `<script>` block below this script reference. Write the code shown in Listing 11-33 inside the script block.

Listing 11-33. AngularJS Model and Controller

```
var app = angular.module("EmployeeApp", []);

app.controller("EmployeeController", function ($scope) {
    var Model = [
        { EmployeeID: 1, FirstName: "Nancy", LastName: "Davolio"},
        { EmployeeID: 2, FirstName: "Steven", LastName: "Buchanbarg" },
        { EmployeeID: 3, FirstName: "Janet", LastName: "Margaret" }
    ];

    $scope.Model = Model;
});
```

The code creates an AngularJS module named `EmployeeApp` by using the AngularJS module API. The second parameter to the `module()` method is an empty array indicating that this application doesn't have any dependencies. The `module()` method returns a reference to the newly created module.

The code then proceeds to create `EmployeeController`—an AngularJS controller. This is done using the `controller()` method. The first parameter to the `controller()` is the name of the controller, and the second parameter is a function that wraps the controller code. This function receives a `$scope` parameter—the AngularJS model.

Inside, the code creates a JavaScript array of employee objects consisting of three elements. The `Model` array is stored in the `$scope` object as its `Model` property (you could have used any property name of your choice, or even store data directly in the `$scope`).

The View of the application is defined in the HTML markup shown in Listing 11-34.

Listing 11-34. HTML Fragment Acting as the View

```
<div ng-app="EmployeeApp">
    <div ng-controller="EmployeeController">

        <table border="1" cellpadding="10">
            <tr>
                <th>EmployeeID</th>
                <th>FirstName</th>
                <th>LastName</th>
            </tr>
            <tr ng-repeat="item in Model">
                <td><input ng-model="item.EmployeeID" /></td>
                <td><input ng-model="item.FirstName" /></td>
                <td><input ng-model="item.LastName" /></td>
            </tr>
        </table>

        <br /><br />
```

```
        <table border="1" cellpadding="10">
            <tr>
                <th>EmployeeID</th>
                <th>FirstName</th>
                <th>LastName</th>
            </tr>
            <tr ng-repeat="item in Model">
                <td>{{item.EmployeeID}}</td>
                <td>{{item.FirstName}}</td>
                <td>{{item.LastName}}</td>
            </tr>
        </table>
    </div>
</div>
```

The Angular view consists of a container <div> element that houses another <div> element. The ng-app attribute of the outermost <div> is set to EmployeeApp—the name of the AngularJS module you created earlier. The ng-controller attribute of the inner <div> is set to EmployeeController—the AngularJS controller. Attributes such as ng-app and ng-controller are defined and processed by AngularJS. They are called *directives* in AngularJS. Thus the outer <div> marks the application's boundary, whereas the inner <div> marks the EmployeeController's boundary.

The inner <div> houses two tables. The first table displays EmployeeID, FirstName, and LastName in an editable fashion. The table is rendered by iterating through the $scope.Model array using the ng-repeat directive. Notice how employee object properties are bound to the textboxes using the ng-model attribute. The second table is rendered using the ng-repeat directive. This time, however, the employee details are displayed in a read-only fashion. Notice the use of {{ and }} to display the data. As you might have guessed, ng-model performs two-way data binding (model to view and from view back to the model), whereas {{ and }} are used to perform one-way data binding (from model to view).

This completes the application. You can run it and try modifying some employee details. You will observe that as soon as you change the values in the textboxes the second table also reflects the changes. This happens automatically due to the two-way data binding feature of AngularJS.

Summary

This chapter covered a broad range of JavaScript patterns. Modern ASP.NET applications rely heavily on JavaScript and JavaScript libraries. That's why it is important for you to understand the code-organization techniques possible in JavaScript.

Although JavaScript doesn't support classes along the lines of C#, you can create objects. Two common ways to create objects include object literals and function objects.

This chapter covered several code-organization patterns, such as the namespace pattern, the module pattern, the revealing module pattern, and the sandbox pattern.

The namespaces pattern helps you to organize JavaScript code in namespaces. Although JavaScript doesn't natively support namespaces, you can still achieve a similar effect.

The module pattern is quite popular among JavaScript developers because it allows you to create modular libraries. Using the module pattern, you expose the public interface of a module to the client code. The revealing module pattern is a variation of the module pattern that organizes the code in private members and functions and then decides the public interface of the module.

The sandbox pattern helps you write sandbox code. It eliminates using long namespaces by creating a sandbox—- an object containing the API of specified modules.

Finally, the chapter gave you a quick introduction to MVC, MVVM, and MVW patterns as applicable to JavaScript libraries and frameworks.

Learning design patterns involves understanding their intent and usage guidelines and also the practical experience of using them. This book discussed SOLID principles, Gang of Four design patterns, select Patterns of Enterprise Application Architecture, and select JavaScript patterns in an attempt to give you a good understanding of the subject matter. It also presented many real-world examples to make the topic being discussed more relevant and practical. With this knowledge under your belt, you can leverage the full power and flexibility of these principles and patterns in your applications.

Bibliography

Martin, Robert C., and Micah Martin. *Agile Principles, Patterns, and Practices in C#*. Upper Saddle River, NJ: Prentice Hall, 2007.

Gamma, Erich, Richard Helm, Ralph Johnson, and John Vlissides. *Design Patterns: Elements of Reusable Object-Oriented Software*. New York: Pearson, 2003.

Fowler, Martin. *Patterns of Enterprise Application Architecture*. New York: Pearson, 2013.

Stefanov, Stoyan. *JavaScript Patterns*. Boston, MA: O'Reilly Media, 2010.

© Bipin Joshi 2016
B. Joshi, *Beginning SOLID Principles and Design Patterns for ASP.NET Developers*,
DOI 10.1007/978-1-4842-1848-8

Index

A

Abstract factory pattern
  DatabaseHelper class, 114, 117
  design requirements, 112
  ExecuteAction() method, 118, 120
  ExecuteQuery() method, 120
  ExecuteSelect() method, 118, 120
  GetCommand() method, 118
  GetConnection() method, 118
  HomeController class, 119
  IDatabaseFactory interface, 113, 116
  Index view, 121
  @model directive, 122
  OleDbFactory class, 116
  Read() method, 122
  ShowResult view, 122
  ShowTable view, 121
  SqlClientFactory class, 113, 116
  storage settings, 122
    Activator.CreateInstance() method, 124
    AppSettings section, key-factory, 123
    CreateInstance() method, 125
    ExecuteQuery() method, 123
    GetExecutingAssembly() method, 125
    NET reflection and
      Activator class, 124
    Unwrap() method, 125
  UML diagram, 111
Angular view, 389
ASP.NET application, 22
ASP.NET 5 application
  AddContact views, 36, 38–39
  AddMvc() method, 32
  commands section, 28
  Configure() method, 32
  ContactDb, 40
  contact management, 23
  DbContext and model, 33
  HomeController, 34
  Index views, 36
  new contact page, 24
  project dependencies, 28
  Project.json, 27
  references, 27
  settings, 29
  Solution Explorer, 27
  Startup class, 27, 30
  template selection, 25
  wwwroot folder, 27

B

Behavioral patterns, 239, 275
  chain of responsibility, 201–202
    AppDbContext class, 210
    AppendAllText() method, 208
    DataImportHandler class, 208
    data-import operation, 203
    FileStorageHandler class, 207
    FileStoreEntry class, 209
    GetString() method, 211
    HandleRequest() method, 203
    Index view, 211
    MapPath() method, 205
    NextHandler property, 207
    Process() method, 204, 206
    Split() method, 207
    UML diagram, 202
    Upload() method, 210
  command, 201, 212
    AppDbContext class, 215
    CommandQueueItem class, 215
    CreateEmailAccount() method, 217
    EmployeeManager class, 216
    Execute() method, 213, 218
    ICommand interface, 213, 218
    Index view, 220
    Invoker class, 219
    ProcessEmployee()
      method, 220
    UML diagram, 212
    UndoCreateEmailAccount()
      method, 217–218

© Bipin Joshi 2016

B. Joshi, *Beginning SOLID Principles and Design Patterns for ASP.NET Developers*,
DOI 10.1007/978-1-4842-1848-8

Behavioral patterns (*cont.*)
  interpreter, 201, 221
    ApiCall class, 225
    CreateInstance() method, 225
    DeserializeObject() method, 226
    ExecuteJSON() method, 225
    FileManager class, 227
    IApiCall interface, 224
    IExpression interface, 222
    Index view, 226
    Interpret() method, 223
    InterpreterContext class, 224
    JSON file approach, 222
    UML diagram, 221
  iterator, 202, 229
    Dispose() method, 235
    IAggregate interface, 230
    IEnumerator interface, 231
    Index view, 236
    MoveNext() method, 235
    Order class, 232
    OrderEnumerator class, 234
    OrderHistory class, 233
    Reset() method, 235
    UML diagram, 230
  mediator, 202, 239
    AppDbContext class, 243
    ChatMessage class, 242
    ChatRoom class, 246
    click-event handler, 250–251
    GetChatHistory() method, 245
    GetHistory() function, 251
    GetHistory() method, 248
    GetParticipant() method, 247
    IChatRoom interface, 241, 243
    Index view, 249
    IParticipant interface, 243
    Login() method, 246–247
    Logout() method, 246–247
    MediatorDb database, 253
    participant class, 244
    receive() method, 245
    send() method, 245–246, 253
    UML diagram, 240
    url property, 251
  memento, 202, 253
    Answer class, 260
    AppDbContext class, 260
    AppSettings class, 256
    Caretaker class, 261
    CreateSnapshot()
      method, 255, 259, 262
    GetAnswers() method, 259, 262
    Index() method, 261
    Index view, 262

    ProcessForm() method, 261
    Question class, 259
    Restore() method, 258
    RestoreSnapshot() method, 259
    Save() method, 258
    StoragePath property, 257
    Submit() method, 255, 259, 262
    Survey class, 258
    survey module, 254
    SurveySnapshot class, 257
    SurveyState class, 257
    UML diagram, 254
  observer, 202, 263
    ActivityLog class, 268
    ActivityObserver class, 269
    AddPost() method, 270
    AdminObserver class, 269
    AppDbContext class, 268
    Attach() method, 264
    Detach() method, 264
    ForumNotifier class, 265, 269
    ForumPost class, 267
    IForumNotifier interface, 269
    IForumObserver interface, 268
    Index() method, 270
    Index view, 272
    Notification class, 265, 267
    Notify() method, 270
    ShowActivityLog() method, 271
    ShowActivityLog view, 273
    ShowNotifications() method, 271
    ShowNotifications view, 273
    Subscribe() method, 270
    UML diagram, 264
    Update() method, 264
  state, 202, 275
    AddCaching() method, 281
    AppDbContext class, 279
    Approve() action, 283
    Approve view, 284
    AppSettings class, 279
    CampaignContext class, 277, 279
    campaign wizard, 278
    ConfigureServices() method, 281
    Context class, 276
    Create() method, 282
    CreateState class, 280
    ICampaignState
      interface, 277, 280
    Index() method, 282
    Index view, 283
    IState interface, 276
    Process() method, 277
    RunState class, 281
    UML diagram, 276

strategy, 202, 284
    AppSettings class, 287
    CompressFile() method, 290
    CompressionContext class, 286, 289
    DeflateAlgorithm class, 288 •
    File() method, 291
    GZipAlgorithm class, 288
    ICompressionAlgorithm
        interface, 286–287
    Index() method, 290
    Index view, 291
    IStrategy interface, 285
    switch statement, 291
    UML diagram, 285
    ZipAlgorithm class, 289
template method, 202, 292
    AppDbContext class, 296
    AppSettings class, 296
    Index view, 299
    in-person order, 294
    mode of purchase, 293
    online order, 294
    OnlineOrderProcessor class, 295, 298
    OrderLog class, 296
    OrderProcessor class, 295–296
    ProcessOrder() method, 297–298
    StoreOrderProcessor class, 295, 297
    Success view, 300
    UML diagram, 292
    ValidateOrder() method, 298
visitor, 202, 300
    Accept() method, 301
    Calculate() method, 303, 306
    Calculate view, 307
    Enclosure class, 304
    Index view, 307
    ISwitchboardItem interface, 303–304
    ISwitchboardVisitor interface, 302, 304
    NormalVisitor class, 305
    Switchboard class, 302, 305
    UML diagram, 301
Builder pattern, 125
    AddCPU() method, 131
    AssembleComputer() method, 127, 132–133
    ComputerAssembler class, 131
    ComputerPart class, 129
    Construct() method, 126
    DbContext application, 129
    GetComputer() method, 131
    HomeComputerBuilder class, 130
    IComputerBuilder interface, 130
    Index() action, 133
    Index view, 133
    OnConfiguring() method, 129
    requirements, 126

Success view, 133
    UML diagram, 125
Buy() method, 342

■ C

Cloning operation, 104
Create-Read-Update-Delete (CRUD)
        operations, 311
Creational patterns
    abstract factory, 88
    builder, 88
    DoWork() method, 88
    factory method, 88, 94
        BarChart class, 98
        ChartProviderFree class, 101
        ChartProviderPaid class, 101
        design, 95
        display charts, 97
        GetChart() factory method, 96
        GetImageFree() method, 101
        IChart interface, 97
        IChartProvider interface, 100
        Index view, 102
        PieChart class, 99
    overview, 87
    prototype, 88, 103
        AbstractPrototype, 104
        clone() method, 106
        cloning operation, 104
        deep copy technique, 108
        design, 103
        foreach loop, 107
        Index() method, 106
        Index view, 107
        IUploadedFile interface, 105
        MemberwiseClone() method, 104
        UploadedFile class, 106–107
        Upload() method, 106
    singleton, 88–89
        AppDbContext class, 93
        application metadata, 90
        design, 89
        GetInstance() method, 89
        Index view, 93
        SingleOrDefault() method, 92
        WebsiteMetadata class, 90
CustomerManager module, 372

■ D

Deep copy technique, 108
Dependency injection (DI)
    AddDbContext() method, 351
    AddScoped() method, 351

Dependency injection (DI) (*cont.*)
    ConfigureServices() method, 351
    HomeController, 352
    Index() method, 352
    lifetime modes, 351
Dependency inversion principle (DIP), 80
    abstraction, 81
    ChangePassword() method, 81, 84
    high-level class, 80
    INotifier interface, 82–83
    UserManager class, 82, 84
Design patterns
    GOF patterns, 17–18
    in JavaScript, 20
    principles, 21
Document object model (DOM), 386

■ **E**

Enterprise application architecture (EAA)
    business-logic layer, 310
    data-access layer, 310
    grouping patterns, 311
    lazy load pattern, 330
        data property, 332
        Employee class, 334
        employee data, 332
        GetDetails() method, 336
        ghost, 331
        if statement, 337
        Index view, 336
        lazy initalization, 331
        .NET framework, 337
        Northwind database, 333
        Order class, 333
        Orders property, 335
        Read() method, 336
        SqlCommand object, 335
        value holder, 331
        virtual proxy, 331
    overview, 309
    respository pattern, 312
        AppDbContext class, 316
        AppSettings class, 315
        CustomerRepository class, 314, 316
        design, 313
        Entity Framework, 312
        generic interface, 321
        ICustomerRepository interface, 316
        Index() method, 318
        Index view, 320
        IRepository interface, 321
        SelectAll() method, 316
        SelectByID() method, 318
        Update() method, 319

    service layer pattern, 340
        AppDbContext class, 343
        AppSettings class, 343
        Buy() method, 347
        callback function, 349
        dataType property, 350
        design, 340
        desktop application, 341
        GetAllTradingLog()
            method, 342, 345, 347, 349
        GetTradingLogForUser()
            method, 345, 349
        Id property, 343
        Index view, 347
        ITradingRepository interface, 344
        ITradingService interface, 345–346
        mobile application, 341
        Sell() method, 347
        StockTradingEntry class, 343
        StockTradingEntry entity, 345
        StockTradingService
            Controller class, 346
        TradingRepository class, 344
        TradingService class, 342, 346
        type property, 349, 350
        web application, 341
    unit of work pattern, 322
        AppDbContext class, 326
        AppSettings class, 325
        CreateProject() method, 329
        foreach loop, 329
        Index view, 329
        NewGuid() method, 329
        ProjectRepository, 327
        ProjectUnit class, 324, 328
        SaveChanges() method, 323
        TeamMember class, 326
    user–interface/presentation layer, 310
Enterprise application architecture (EAA), 19
Entity Framework7. *See* ASP.NET 5 application

■ **F**

Façade pattern, 381
Function object, 357
    getter and setter methods, 359
    prototype, 358

■ **G**

Gang of Four (GOF) patterns, 17–18

■ **H**

Hyper Text Markup Language (HTML), 388

■ I, J, K

Immediately invoked function
  expression (IIFE), 360
Interface segregation principle (ISP)
  CashOnDeliveryOrderProcessor class, 78
  Index view, 79
  IOnlineOrderProcessor interface, 75–77
  IOrderProcessor interface, 74, 75–77
  OnlineOrderProcessor class, 75, 77
  payment mode, 76
  place order button, 76
  ProcessOrder() method, 75, 78
  Success view, 80
  ValidateCardInfo() method, 74–75
  ValidateShippingAddress() method, 74

■ L

Liskov substitution principle (LSP)
  default settings, 65
  GetAllSettings() method, 68
  GetSettings() method, 62, 66
  GlobalSettings class, 66, 72
  GuestSettings class, 64, 66, 72
  HomeController, 68, 73
  Index.cshtml, 69
  Index() method, 73
  IReadableSettings interface, 64, 71
  ISettings interface, 62, 66
  IWritableSettings interface, 64, 71
  polymorphic behavior, 62
  portal application, 62
  SaveAllSettings() method, 71
  Save() method, 69, 73
  Save view, 70
  SetAllSettings() method, 68
  SetSettings() method, 62
  SettingsHelper class, 63–64, 67, 72

■ M

Martin Fowler's patterns, 19
Model-View-Controller (MVC) pattern, 386
Model-View-View Model (MVVM), 386
Model-View-Whatever (MVW), 386
Module pattern, 367
  AppSettings class, 369
  callback function, 371
  click-event handlers, 374
  CRUD operations, 369
  CustomerManager module, 370
  CustomerService controller, 370
  HelloWorld() method, 368
  immediate function, 368

  Index view, 372
  object literal, 368
  SelectAll() method, 371, 373
  SelectByID() method, 373
  success function, 371
MVC6. See ASP.NET 5 application

■ N

Namespace pattern, 362
  ajax() method, 365
  Json() method, 364
  SearchByID() action, 363
  SearchByID() function, 365

■ O, P, Q

Object literals, 356
Object-oriented programming (OOPS)
  abstract class, 7
  abstraction, 2
  polymorphism Calculate
    TaxAmount() method, 13
  class, 2
  Contact class, 5
  encapsulation, 3
  inheritance, 6
  interfaces, 8
  object, 2
  polymorphism, 9
    GetDetails() method, 10
    inheritance, 9
    interfaces, 12
    ShowDetails() method, 11
Observer pattern, 383
Open-closed principle (OCP)
  Calculate() method, 55
  CalculateTaxAmount() method, 58
  class design, 56
  HomeController class, 59
  ICountryTaxCalculator
    interface, 56–57
  IncomeDetails class, 59
  Index.cshtml, 60
  TaxCalculator class, 55, 59
  TaxCalculatorForIN class, 58
  TaxCalculatorForUK class, 58
  TaxCalculatorForUS class, 58

■ R

Revealing module pattern
  immediate function, 374
  object literal, 375
  SayHello() function, 374

■ S

Sandbox pattern
    callback function, 378
    definition, 375
    hello module, 377
    Index view, 377
    search module, 376
Search library, 366
Single responsibility principle (SRP)
    AppDbContext class, 49
    class design, 47
    CustomerDataExporter class, 50
    CustomerSearch class, 45, 49
    design flaw, 46
    design issue, 47
    Export() method, 52
    ExportToCSV() method, 46
    GetData() method, 52
    HomeController, 51
    Index view, 52
    main view, 48
    model class, 49
    OnConfiguring() method, 49
    root issue, 47
    Search.cshtml, 53
    Search() method, 52
    search results, 48
    Search view, 54
Singleton pattern, 379
SOLID principles, 14
    DIP, 16
    ISP, 16
    LSP, 15
    OCP, 15
    SRP, 15
Structural patterns, 135, 167
    adapter, 135–136
        IChart interface, 139
        Index view, 143
        MyChartAdapter class, 141–142
        MyChartGenerator class, 138, 140–141
        object *vs.* class, 143
        Operation() method, 137
        ThirdPartyChartGenerator Class, 140
        UML diagram, 137
    bridge, 135, 144
        AppDbContext class, 148
        AppendAllText() method, 149
        AppSettings class, 147
        DataImporterAdvanced class, 150
        DataImporterBasic class, 146
        IDataImporter interface, 148
        IErrorLogger interface, 146, 148
        Import() method, 146

        Index view, 152
        LogFileFolder property, 148
        MapPath() method, 148
        OpenReadStream() method, 151
        OpImpl() method, 145
        ReadLine() method, 151
        SaveChanges() method, 150
        TextFileErrorLogger class, 146, 149
        UML diagram, 145
        Upload() action, 152
        XmlErrorLogger class, 149
    composite, 135, 152
        component class, 153
        foreach loop, 158
        IComponent interface, 153
        IMenuComponent interface, 155, 157
        Index view, 158
        load menu and menu items, 157
        Menu class, 157
        MenuComponent class, 157
        MenuFilePath property, 156
        UML diagram, 153
        wwwroot folder, 156
        XML markup, 153
    decorator, 136, 159
        DecoratorBase class, 161, 163
        DrawString() method, 164
        GetImageOriginal() method, 164
        GetImageWatermarked() class, 165
        GetPhoto() method, 164
        IHostingEnvironment object, 164
        Index view, 165
        IPhoto interface, 161–162
        UML diagram, 160
        watermark, 161
        WatermarkDecorator class, 163
    façade, 136, 167
        AppDbContext class, 171
        AppSettings class, 171
        Book class, 171
        Compare() method, 176
        GetAsync() method, 174
        Get() method, 173
        HttpClient component, 173
        Index view, 176
        ISBN number, 170
        Operation() method, 168
        PriceComparer class, 169, 175
        requirements, 169
        Results view, 177
        Search() action, 176
        SearchBooks() method, 174
        ServiceAClient class, 174
        ServiceAController, 172
        ServiceBClient class, 174

ServiceBController class, 173
UML diagram, 168
Web API controller, 172
flyweight, 136, 178
administrative module, 179
analytics component, 179
AppDbContext class, 182
GetActiveUsers() method, 182
GetFlyweight() method, 178
GetWebsiteStats() method, 180
Index view, 184
IWebsiteStats interface, 180–181
ShowStats() action, 183
ShowStats view, 184
SingleOrDefault() method, 183
UML diagram, 178
WebsiteStats class, 182
WebsiteStatsFactory class, 180, 182
proxy, 136, 185
AppDbContext class, 191
AppendAllText() method, 195
AppSettings class, 190
AppSettings values, 190
ASP.NET application, 188
ConfigureServices() method, 191
customer class, 191
customer modifications, 188
Delete() method, 197
enable session, 190
HomeController, 195
HttpClient component, 186
HttpClient object, 195
ICustomerApi interface, 187, 192
Index() action, 196
Index view, 197
Insert() method, 197
Insert view, 199
ITarget interface, 186
MapPath() method, 190
ServiceController class, 192
ServiceProxy class, 194

UML diagram, 186
Update() method, 196
Update view, 198
Web API end point, 189

■ T

TaxCalculator class, 55, 59
TeamMember class, 326
ThirdPartyChartGenerator class, 140
TradingRepository class, 344
TradingService class, 342, 346

■ U

UndoCreateEmailAccount()
method, 217–218
Unwrap() method, 125
Update() method, 196, 264, 319

■ V

ValidateCardInfo() method, 75–76
ValidateOrder() method, 298
ValidateShippingAddress() method, 75
View model, 386

■ W

WatermarkDecorator class, 163
WebsiteMetadata class, 90
WebsiteStats class, 182
WebsiteStatsFactory class, 180, 182

■ X, Y

XML markup, 153

■ Z

ZipAlgorithm class, 289

Get the eBook for only $5!

Why limit yourself?

Now you can take the weightless companion with you wherever you go and access your content on your PC, phone, tablet, or reader.

Since you've purchased this print book, we're happy to offer you the eBook in all 3 formats for just $5.

Convenient and fully searchable, the PDF version enables you to easily find and copy code—or perform examples by quickly toggling between instructions and applications. The MOBI format is ideal for your Kindle, while the ePUB can be utilized on a variety of mobile devices.

To learn more, go to www.apress.com/companion or contact support@apress.com.